LIVING WITH THE DEAD

LIVING WITH THE DEAD

TWENTY YEARS

ON THE BUS WITH GARCIA

AND

THE GRATEFUL DEAD

Rock Scully with David Dalton

LITTLE, BROWN AND COMPANY
Boston   New York   Toronto   London

FIRST EDITION

Library of Congress Cataloging-In-Publication Data

Scully, Rock
    Living with the Dead : twenty years on the bus with Garcia and the Grateful Dead / Rock Scully and David Dalton.—1st ed.
        p.   cm.
    Includes index.
        ISBN 0-316-77712-9
        1. Grateful Dead (Musical group)   2. Rock musicians—United States—Biography.
1. Dalton, David.   II. Title.
ML421.G72s38   1996
782.42166'092'2—dc20
[B]   95-40235

10 9 8 7 6 5 4 3 2 1

RRD-VA

Published simultaneously in Canada by Little, Brown & Company (Canada) Limited
PRINTED IN THE UNITED STATES OF AMERICA

This book is dedicated to those who fell in the line of duty:

Ron "Pigpen" McKernan & Jerry Garcia
and
Milton Mayer, Keith Godchaux, Brent Mydland, Rex Jackson, Lowell George, Keith Moon, Tony Secunda, Sonny Hurd, Peter "Craze" Sheridan, Badger, "Loose" Bruce Baxter, Zohn Artman, Bill Graham, Janis Joplin, John Cipollina, Paul Roehlk, Zane Kesey, Bobby Petersen, Page Browning, Erik Alexander, John Belushi, Steve McKinney, Jake Smith, Ken "Goldfinger" Connell, Rick Griffin, and Thomas Jefferson Kaye.
God bless you all.

And to our children:

Lucas and Sage Scully, Spirit Connell,
and Toby Dalton.

Contents

Acknowledgments

No way could we have done this book ourselves. So here's to the people who made us look good: the hardworking people, the salt of the earth, our wives, ex-wives, friends, and people we talked into stuff.

May the sublime tintinnabulation of temple bells and the ululations of a thousand Tuareg tribeswomen ring in your mind's eye while you read your names, elevated ones! You, Tony Secunda, out of whose fitful head — like Athena from the head of Zeus — this book first sprang. May flights of angels sing thee to thy rest; Hannah Williams who tirelessly transcribed our interviews; Blair Jackson who read and annotated the manuscript (and saved us from innumerable embarrassments); and, *editrice divina,* Coco Dalton, whose celestial ear made us sing where previously we only mumbled.

Several drumrolls and the blowing of rams' horns, please! For Sam Cutler, Dan Healy, Betty Matthews Cantor Jackson, Gary Jackson, Bob Matthews, Mountain Girl, Ron Rakow, Danny Rifkin, Nicki Scully, Tangerine Steinbrecker, Sue Swanson, and Bob Weir, who gave freely of their knowledge (and opinions!).

Sleighbells and tin whistles begin your tumult! For David Gans, Dan Levy, Mike Mattil, Jeffrey Norwalk, Richard Sassin, John Scott, Frankie Secunda, Alan Trist, Brian Williams, and Ken Zeiger who skillfully led us through the labyrinths of arcana and the deserts of solecism.

And last but not least, greetings to you, O great pharaoh, our editor, Michael Pietsch, who had the wisdom and foresight to sign us up and must many times thereafter have asked himself, What hath I wrought? but continued politely to ask "When do you think I might see something?"

LIVING WITH THE DEAD

1

The World's Biggest Crystal

BRRRING! BRRRING! BRRRING!

"Rock, please! Just a little taste, I'm desperate."

Brrring! Brrring! Brrring!

"I think I'm too shaky to play, man. I'm not kidding."

Brrring! Brrring!

"Rock, ol' buddy, you know your phone's been busy for the last forty minutes? Say, you gonna be there awhile?"

It's been just two days since the Great London Dope Reformation in which we all burned our stashes in a gigantic bonfire. Funny thing is, now everyone is real *down* on themselves for having done it. My hotel room is fast becoming the set for a bad stage play — a farce in which one character appears at the front door while another disappears out the back. It is going to be a very long afternoon if this keeps up. Not even noon and there's not a damn thing to do until sound check at 4:30.

I have to think of something to get everybody's mind off my stash. I know . . . REDIRECT! Perhaps a little field trip — nothing too stimulating or time consuming (this eliminates whorehouses, barcrawling, and a search for needle park).

I flip through my chamber of commerce package: "Welcome to Munich, the carefree Bavarian world-city. The motto of our fair city, translated from the medieval Latin, is 'Live and let live.'" Aw*right!*

Let's see now . . . there's the German Museum of Hunting and Fishing with the world's largest collection of fishhooks, a scenic cruise down the River Isar, a guided tour of Dachau (I don't think so). Or there's Europe's oldest marionette theater, the porcelain museum, clog dancing, or a tour of the world-renowned Bavarian film industry ("Hollywood of the North"). Not exactly what I had in mind. "An invigorating climb into the colossal head of the statue of Bavaria." Now that *is* tempting but. . . . Aha! This is it! Definitely. The Museum of Everything Ever Invented! Bridges, guns, spirogyros, an actual operating sausage-making machine, tiny scaled replicas of the Reichstag and Köln Cathedral made out of matchsticks and . . . *"the world's most comprehensive display of pharmaceutical miracles."* This entry is quite innocently followed by a list of the favorite drugs of Garcia and company.

As a group, the Grateful Dead have a very finely developed appreciation for industrial surrealism, and this place sounds like a monument to insane contraptions. It promises to be an afternoon of pure Dada. Garcia is up for it. Lesh wants to rent a Mercedes and tour the local vineyards, but I talk him out of it by reading off a list of vintage cars and antiquated musical instruments in the museum's collection. Kreutzmann and Hart are game for anything and Weir is like your kid brother — he always wants to tag along.

The Deutsches Museum is about twenty minutes away on a little island in the middle of the River Isar. It's a cavernous place and it really does contain Everything a German Ever Made (excluding the two World Wars). Steam cars, banko engines, U-boats, the bridge project in Egypt, the canal in Morocco, dams, atomic watches, electric guns, peach pitters, rubber-band-making machines. Just all this *stuff.* It's their Smithsonian.

There's something spooky about the place, vast and oppressive like Xanadu in *Citizen Kane.* We seem to be the only people there, and our footsteps echo as we cross the main hall. "We all meet back here at the moon rock at four o'clock sharp. Okay?"

Lesh is dragging Weir off to see the three-wheel Messerschmitt cockpit car and in no time everyone has scattered. I yell "SOUND CHECK at four thirty!" and my voice echo-oo-oo-ooes through the marble halls.

I wander around looking at this and that. The world's largest collection of (empty) beer bottles, a working brewery. There's a section where you press a button and a miniature coal mine springs to life futilely hauling up wobbly little wagons filled with coal. Or a canning factory that shudders into action, shaking and rumbling. Any jerk with a job on an assembly line can see this any day of the week, but it's cheap thrills, and in the end I try them all out. It's almost four before I get back to the moon rock. Nobody there. Actually there's nobody in the whole joint except for a straggling group of schoolchildren, and when they leave, a sinister silence falls.

In a huge canvas sack like the Olympia Halle the sound check is crucial. Balancing the instruments, checking power surges and so on, not to mention greasing the usual officials. We're twenty minutes from the hotel, the hotel is twenty minutes from the Olympia Halle, and the band doesn't even know what city they're in.

Four fifteen. Still no sign of anyone. I find Phil Lesh buying post-cards and go to look for the others. When I get back with Mickey Hart and Bill Kreutzmann, Lesh has disappeared. I position Hart and Kreutzmann next to the moon rock and tell them not to move until I get back. Guards follow us everywhere. I finally locate Phil Lesh and Bobby Weir checking out the antique cars. Back at the moon rock, Mickey Hart is tapping out a samba with a couple of ball-point pens, but Kreutzmann has gone walkabout. He finally turns up outside, very pleased with himself for having pulled off a bunco scam in the gift shop.

It's closing time. Everyone's found except Garcia. Turns out nobody had seen him all afternoon. The others suggest we spread out through the museum. This, I know, is a terrible idea. The only thing to do is to get the four I have and put them in a cab (which I do).

The museum is closing, the lights are going out. I am crying *GAR-CI-A!* over and over throughout this desperate-looking place. He could be anywhere. And after a while, I realize *I'm* lost. Where the hell am I? I read the sign *Halle des Dampfmaschine.* Except for the guards (and, hopefully, the missing Garcia) I'm the only one left in the place.

The *Herr Wachtmeister* bars my way. Cold, chlorine blue eyes that look like two holes drilled through his head. I explain that Jerry Garcia — you never *heard* of the Grateful Dead? — well anyway, JERRY GARCIA is missing and I've got to find him in order to avoid rioting and a national crisis. See, we're late for our sound check, man, and . . . oh, never mind.

"Zer ist no vun left in museum. Absolutely. All guards are starting from back of museum and progressing exactly to front, starting at die Kriegesbaukunst Halle and —"

"Yeah, yeah, yeah. But listen, he's in here *somewhere* and no offense, man, but I'M NOT LEAVING UNTIL I FIND HIM!"

"You have ten minutes precisely then you leave, with Señor Barcia or no, *verstanden?*"

I begin running down the corridors. Past the Hall of the Sea Spiders. Good Lord! What *is* that? Endless warrens, corridors, alcoves, courtyards leading into other wings. There are ten miles of corridors in the place. Halls filled with atrocity machines specifically designed to obliterate you totally. A wall plaque reads: "With its unparalleled firepower it can cut a man in half at 200 meters."

Poor Garcia's been swallowed up in this vast, Gothic place. . . . He could be anywhere. Perhaps the guards mistook him for an exhibit. Nothing really about this in the roadie manual. Perhaps he's in the serious machinery department or . . . musical instruments! The pianos, the Klienhoffers, the Bössendorfers, the Steinways. No, my God, he's not in musical instruments. Ah, the gun collection! He *loves* Walther pistols. I find rows on rows of every conceivable issue of Walthers, Schmeisers, Lugars. Then on through the aeronautics — Stukas, Fokkers, V-1s. Machines, bridges, boats, cars. Then I remember *the world's most comprehensive display of pharmaceutical miracles.*

The Hall of Wonder Drugs is huge, a mind-boggling exhibition of German pharmacology. Morphine, methamphetamine, adolphine (a synthetic heroin named for Hitler), etc. Each drug exhibit has a complete mini-history next to it. The label next to methamphetamine tells how it was given to Stuka pilots during World War Two, how the soldiers on the Russian front took it to stay up. How it was a favorite drug of the Führer. We are informed of its various nicknames: ersatz café, blitz powder, etc.

And there, at last, is the Great Barcia himself, standing in front of a glass display case with a beatific look on his face. Inside this case rests a huge stalactite-like rock with little forests of crystal clinging to its surface, at least fifteen inches across. Garcia is enraptured, mesmerized.

"Hey, ma-aan, would you check out the size of this sucker? With a thing like that you could start a new religion!"

"But what *is* it?"

"What this is, man, is *pure cocaine hydrochloride.* We have before us the world's largest coke crystal! These professors grew it in a huge concave petri dish, and they've kept it since *1897!* Get the rest of the guys, man, get 'em in here, they've got to see this!"

"Jerry, they all left hours ago. We looked for you everywhere. C'mon, man, let's get out of here. Maybe we can still make sound check."

◎

In the dressing room backstage I lie down on the beat-up Naugahyde couch patched with gaffer's tape. I need a moment to collect my thoughts. I hear the soothing strains of "Tennessee Jed" over the PA. A thousand random thoughts float through my poor fevered brain, weaving in and out of the lyrics. God, I must've heard this song a couple of hundred times at least but suddenly they seem oracular: "You know you bound to end up dead / If you don't head back to Tennessee, Jed. . . ."

The fiends! Why are you singing these words to me? You know I have no Tennessee to go back to; I have no life outside the band and, er, drugs. The Dead *are* my Tennessee. Shit, I've got to get off this train of thought at the next station.

I haven't slept in days, I'm blitzed, I'm jonesing and running on fumes and beginning to understand how the Flying Dutchman felt after a couple of hundred years on deck. After some eight hundred or nine hundred Dead gigs, it's all blending together in one long endless tour. I'm a doomed sailor, O Lord, on the Ship of the Dead! As I drift off, my mind strays back to how I first came aboard. . . .

2

The Octagon Is in Place

IT'S THE BEGINNING of December 1965, the night I first see the Grateful Dead. I'm promoting a Family Dog concert at San Francisco's lovely old California Hall. The original Family Dog consists of Ellen Harmon, Luria Castell, George Hunter, amplified autoharpist from the Charlatans, and myself. We all live in a big house in the Haight at 1334 Waller Street. We hold parties there on the weekend and when they begin overflowing onto the sidewalk we move them to the old union halls. In our hapless way we have graduated to promoting concerts. If this works out we figure we can start booking groups like the Lovin' Spoonful and Frank Zappa. Then maybe the Beatles, the Stones, Dylan! Well, it *could* happen.

But, on this particular night we've neglected to find out what else is going on. This is the first rule of promoting concerts, but how were we to know? Turns out there's a Mime Troupe Benefit at the Fillmore Auditorium. There have already been two Mime Troupe benefits and they were wildly successful. I know that nobody in their right mind — given the choice between a Mime Troupe Benefit at the Fillmore and coming to see the Charlatans and a couple of other scraggly bands at California Hall — is going to choose our gig. It's too late for us to cancel. We've put a down payment on the hall and the bands are coming down. So I make an arrangement with the Mime Troupe whereby if you buy a ticket to their thing you can get into our show as well — and vice versa. There will be buses running back and forth every twenty minutes between the Fillmore and California Hall. Hippie tour buses!

Around eleven o'clock the inscrutable Owsley Stanley, the acid king, shows up at California Hall. I know him from various scenes in the Haight where he would turn up, a mysterious presence in cloaks and operatic hats, *lurking* and dispensing samples of his latest batch of acid to those he deems worthy. Apparently I am now one of the elect because here he is handing me a tiny misshapen orange barrel of LSD. Up to this point I've weathered only the minor chakras of drugs. The one psychedelic I've taken is a small dose of synthetic mescaline, mescaline sulfate, in my last year at the Jung Kress, my high school in Switzerland. We'd managed to score it from Sandoz on the grounds that we were doing a science experiment.

"Rock, come on over to the Fillmore later, there's something I want you to see," he says. Everything is enigmatic with Owsley. He's not going to tell the whole story right away. He wants to zap a little of the *mysterioso amigo* on me first. I tell him I'll try and make it. "Just be there," he says darkly.

I'm in no hurry to get over there. But by midnight I can't curb my curiosity any longer so I jump on one of the shuttle buses.

At the Fillmore, a scruffy group of musicians amble about the stage involved in what will become a trademark of their concerts: the interminable setting up and tuning of instruments.

"*Formerly* the Warlocks of Palo Alto," the emcee announces in his Don Pardo voice. "Ladies and gentlemen, I give you the . . . Grateful Dead!"

The *what?* A raking light plays over their name. G-R-A-T-E-F-U-L D-E-A-D. Hieroglyphic reeds swaying in a tomb painting. Brain-slicing words that spin endlessly across your mind like a demented skater.

They are a *bad*-looking bunch — not your average hippy-dippy Haight band noodling away into the noosphere. The most conspicuous member of the group is a greasy, overweight biker type in a headband playing a Vox electric piano standing up and wailing an old Howlin' Wolf song.

"*Ah-eetz-mo-chickenz-beh-beh-than-youz-ev-ahzeen,*" he growls. The voice is full of whiskey and unfiltered cigarettes and bad company. Little hippie chicks in their tie-dyed saris shrink back from the stage. There is something vaguely unnerving about the lot of them, but it's hard to say what. Apart from the Hell's Angel dude they really aren't all that mean looking, but man are they weird. Your eye darts from one to the other. Just how have such oddities gotten together in the first place?

The blues-bellowing biker appears to be the lead singer, although you wouldn't go so far as to call him the leader. No one is in charge. Most of the songs they do are covers and most of the covers are blues. They do "Little Red Rooster" and a lot of numbers that the early Stones used to do. The Brit blues/rock canon: Chicago blues, Chuck Berry, Elmore James. Plus some folk blues and plain old coffeehouse folk chestnuts like "I Know You Rider." But these are not covers in the usual sense of the word. "In the Midnight Hour," the Wicked Pickett's two-minute 40-second Stax Volt blast, is stretched out for a quarter of an hour or more before modulating into "Early Morning Rain" (complete with out-of-phase harmonies from the two guitar players). "Early Morning Rain" peters out midway in the second verse. No one can remember the words, and they're all too far gone to fake it.

Deep, mellow blues . . . I have never before heard such strange, sublime music. What *is* that sound? More mournful than the Double E rolling down the tracks on a moonlit night. The Arkansas Traveler is complaining that his cabin doesn't leak when it doesn't rain, the whippoorwill's too blue to fly, and the song we're in is leaking like an old boat.

An hour or so into the set and something very odd starts to happen. It's the room, doctor. The room is *breathing*. Breathing deeply, like a great sonic lung from which all sounds originate and which demands all the oxygen in the world. We inhale and exhale with it as if to the great collective heartbeat of an invisible whale. We are all under the hypnotic spell of this ghostly pulse. Whoever these guys are, they are uncannily tuned into the wavelength of the room. They hover over the vibe like dragonflies.

The words — *are* they words? — are sweating, liquefying back into the images whence they came. Little Mississippi Delta dioramas — shotgun shacks, live oaks, gris-gris conjure women with yellow teeth, rotting porches, bo weevils, demon-haunted crossroads, rootless, horse-mad heroes — popping up *between* the words.

I . . . I . . . I . . . think, I think the . . . the . . . the . . . acid, acid is starting, is definitely starting, to come on, come on, come on. . . .

It is the highest I've ever been. The roof is beginning to lift off of the place. Admittedly, on a couple of hundred mikes of Owsley acid even "This Old Man" played on a pennywhistle is going to sound pretty cataclysmic. I'm taking all that into account, but *still*.

As I'm leaving the Fillmore, Owsley grabs me by the arm. He wants to know what I think of the group. Who's kidding whom? I can't even speak! I settle for something a little more, uh, telepathic. When you're in this deep, semaphore will have to do.

"Groovy," I say, beaming the rest of the information directly through his third eye. I figure that should cover it.

Owsley seems to have received the transmission. "The octagon is in place," he replies. "I'll pick you up tomorrow night, ten sharp."

The next night I climb into Owsley's Morris Minor, headed on God-knows-what cosmic errand. The guy can be as inscrutable as the Silver Surfer. He hands me another of those orange barrels of Sunshine, but this time I use my head. Since this is a business trip, I only take half!

"So you like having your mind blown?" he asks like a sergeant sizing up a recruit for a bomb-dismantling unit.

"Uh, blown?" I mumble, trying to think. "May I ask where we're headed?"

"As if you didn't know. . . ."

"Uh, let's see. . . ."

"I'm sorry, our pilot has requested that at this time you please return to your seats. We will soon be approaching beautiful downtown Palo Alto."

"You mean that Prankster deal at the Big Beat Club?"

"No further information is available."

So, we're on our way to an Acid Test! From what I hear these are hair-raising all-night LSD parties where anything can happen. They are not for the fainthearted. And going to an Acid Test with a guy who *makes* acid is a little daunting, to say the least. Also, the Big Beat is some sort of Merry Prankster clubhouse, and I'm already in awe of Ken Kesey and his mob. "Never trust a Prankster" is their *motto*, for God's sake.

The Pranksters — Ken Babbs, Page Browning, Mike Hagen, Mountain Girl, et alia — are existential practical jokers formed around the novelist Ken Kesey. Their anarchic philosophy is based on the ingestion of LSD and freaking freely. I've got this quirky feeling that tonight's going to be psychic *mano a mano,* and Owsley is not making me feel any better. He warns me that Kesey has got the place wired.

"Wired? As in, wired into a sound system?"

"No, no! Wired into *him,* into his brain. Rock," he says in his Movietone voice. "He's *in* the wires — and when you walk into the Big Beat you are going to get wired too. He's figured out how to control people, through electricity. That's how he does it. I've seen it. He's already done it to me once. So for God's sake, don't let your mind *wander.*"

Poor man, I think, he's lost it! I am trapped on the highway with a raging paranoid schizophrenic. Then again, maybe he knows something I don't. After all, he has already been to a few of these acid maelstroms. How exactly do you protect yourself against this sort of thing? On two hundred mikes of Owsley acid there is no way your mind *isn't* going to wander, now is there?

"Owsley, I dunno about this, I feel like I'm walking into a Doctor Strange comic book, and I'm not really, you know, *equipped.*"

"Not to worry," he assures me. "You're not being *tested,* tonight, Rock. You're coming to hear a band."

"A band?" That sounds *safe,* at least.

"The Dead. The Grateful Dead." That name again! "You know, the guys you saw at the Fillmore last night."

"Oh, *those* guys," I say. "They're the world's ugliest band!" That's the first thing that comes into my head.

"Forget about how they look —"

"But, man, that really is a big part of rock 'n' roll. I mean, look at the Beatles or —"

"Forget the Beatles. Listen to me, all you have to know is the Grateful Dead are going to be *the greatest band in the history of the world.*"

Poor, deluded man! How can I tell him? From my brief acquaintance with Owsley I know better than to argue with him, even if I had enough brain function left to do so. He's a genuine monomaniac. I try my best to appease him.

"I see. . . . Yes, well, maybe I'll hire them for one of our Family Dog shows." I am trying to sound sincere.

"No, no, no! You don't want to do that. You don't want to become a *promoter.* Promoters all end up ripping people off."

"So . . . ?"

"So, you *manage* them! Find some gigs for them."

He's decided that I am just the person to manage this band. In three weeks I've escalated from grad school dropout to make-believe promoter to . . . rock manager!

We pull up to the Big Beat Club. The sight of it is oddly reassuring. Pure American ski-lodge kitsch. A big lumbering A-frame with neon beer signs in the window. Hardly the sinister *Schloss Frankenstein* filled with life-siphoning generators that I had begun to conjure up. It's a bar on the weekends and a pizza parlor the rest of the week. The owners, having not a clue what an Acid Test is, are planning to sell a lot of drinks. They don't.

There are screens and white stuff hung around the place with nonstop mirages being flashed on them. At one end of the big open space there is a raised stage for live music. Down at the other end there is yet another stage, low to the ground, that Kesey and his Pranksters have built out of what look like giant Lincoln Logs. In the middle of the room is a tower made of scaffolding from which radiate lights, color wheels, movie projectors, speakers, cameras, tape recorders, slide projectors, and fans to keep the equipment from overheating. This is the Pranksters center-of-the-galaxy command center. And up there in the tower of technology, Captain Kesey is at the controls.

Set in front of the stage is a tepee onto which slides are being projected from the *inside,* using the skin of the tepee as a screen. Geronimo, Sitting Bull, buffalo herds, Custer, ghost dance ceremonies, kachina dolls, war bonnets, peyote rituals. All flashing by in rapid succession on all sides of the tepee. It is killer looking, like a big camp fire with images swirling out of the flames. The America Needs Indians Sensorium, created by Prankster theorist Stewart Brand. Simultaneously — in the obligatory sensory overload mode — Kesey is up in his tower projecting his own nutty images on top of these: slides of the Prankster bus at every gas station between Stanford and Roncomcomo, parties with the Hell's Angels, the installation of a pay phone out in his front yard (daylight *and* evening — with the little light on), the Pranksters hanging speakers in the trees at La Honda, the last Acid Test at Big Nig's (with a seriously freaked out Owsley). The tribal history, in other words.

Every so often out of the vortex of images leap messages of great cosmic import: WHY HAVE WE NEVER SEEN A PICTURE OF THE WHOLE EARTH? Stuff that on a whole bunch of acid you probably don't want to dwell on too long!

Brand is the serious intellectual of the trip, but the intellectuals are all by themselves with this message stuff, let me tell you. The Prankster trip is too freewheeling for moralizing.

They have about six slide projectors, and a couple of 16mm projectors, opaque projectors oozing out the liquid light stuff. And then these incredible state-of-the-art 400-watt strobe lights that tick once a second or a thousand times a second depending on where you set the dial. A mind-boggling machine! With every flash, a million suns whirl through your brain and burst. Mountain Girl, Kesey's girlfriend, is running around pulling everything together. Plugging and unplugging tape recorders and slide projectors, repairing the microphone and cablemaking. Getting all the stuff that is constantly breaking down fixed.

Meanwhile down at the other end — Prankster corner — the Lincoln Log stage is available for anything that anyone wants to do. And they're doing it, believe me. Gourd shaking, Stockhausen tape loops, ululating Iglut shaman chants, mime, Dada word rebuses. . . .

Unreasonable advice is being barked out through a megaphone: "GET NEKKID! FREAK FREELY! KISS YOUR BRAINS GOODBYE! FUCK SANITY, GO CRAZY!"

Occasionally Kesey whispers cryptic axioms over the sound system: *"Stay in your own movie!"*

As a new arrival opens the door and hesitantly looks around, he is assaulted over the loudspeakers by a stream of running commentary on his every move by a demented sports announcer: "He's crossing the floor! Is he in the right place? Oh, man, don't look at your watch; ain't no clocks in the Ready Room. . . . *Wait a darn minute!* He sees the Day-Glo garbage can. Hmmmm. . . . Now what could that possibly be? Oh, come on, you *know* what it is — it's *Kool-Aid!* Well, that's what you're here for, aren't you? It's all right, Ma, we're all freaks on the midway here. . . ." The taunting voice rants on in deep echo as the poor guy catches sight of himself on a TV monitor.

The Grateful Dead begin setting up. They are the house band at the Big Beat. You can see at once why the Dead and Kesey get on so well, given the mix of overweening cosmic stuff and laid-back daze favored by both. But what Kesey is trying to do conceptually, through mental calisthenics, the Dead achieve almost by default.

From the sound and light tower Kesey is directing operations. It hardly comes across as someone issuing instructions. He has put echo on it so it sounds more like found poetry:

"Move move move that that that monitor monitor to to to to face face face the the the the stage stage stage. . . ."

Kesey paces his words so only Mountain Girl can hear them. If you are listening to music and stoned you'd never notice him. He *is* fucking with the mix. Owsley is right about that, but that is what the Acid Test is. And Kesey does it in the friendliest way possible.

For Kesey everybody is in a movie whether they know it or not. It's his central metaphor. By spotlighting people he's just letting them in on it.

Owsley is late setting up. He scurries around connecting wires and plugging in amps. Five minutes into the Dead set there is a big flash of light and sparks begin flying. A few people, thinking this is part of the show, cheer. Owsley patches things together but there's another blow-out. After the equipment fails a couple more times Pigpen starts yelling at him:

"What the fuck is going *on?* We want to *play,* man, just jam the fucking thing together."

Owsley is standing wide-eyed and frozen in the posture of inner debate. He's just too stoned and paranoid about Kesey to concentrate on making electricity run through the wires. You can see him looking at one wire, and then the other, saying to himself: "If I connect this wire to this wire, the whole *world* may go up."

☉

When the Dead start playing, none of the Prankster lunacy or tape loop sagas stops for one second. Of course not, it isn't as if Elvis had come on stage and everybody has to *hush.* No such thought — were there room for it! — would have entered anyone's head.

I try making a cold, professional assessment of the group while I still can. I begin taking inventory of the band members. Okay, there's the lead singer, a paunchy Hell's Angel type with dirty hair down to his tits and greasy leather vest covered with mojo pins. There's a

Mexican-looking guitar player with pyramid hair, a receding chin, and a missing finger. The bass player has a full Prince Valiant pageboy do. There's the second guitarist, a startled long-haired child who could be a girl. And then there's a surly, juvenile delinquent on drums. A sorrier-looking bunch you never saw. Just frightening, actually. You know they're never going to amount to anything. Just another local band getting gigs on Friday and Saturday nights, playing dances in high school gymnasiums.

They just don't fit into any known concept of a rock 'n' roll band. We are still in the era when there are only two acceptable ways for rock bands to look — the Brit-invasion flash or the matching-outfit bit. You can get yourself up like a Revolutionary war footsoldier, you can even look like Nehru's bodyguard, but you can't look like this. Even an unbuttoned mock jug band like the Lovin' Spoonful has a *look*. But no one is ever going to get these guys into coordinated casuals or collarless jackets. Clearly they don't give a damn what they look like.

And even putting the thorny dilemma of the look aside, where is the *connection* — is there one? — between these guys? They seem to be from entirely different movies. It is such a freaky mix. The kind of random sample of unregenerate human types you'd find in a police lineup, say, or a Greyhound bus terminal. No matter how I squint my mind's eye, they are simply a collection of oddities who refuse to fit in the same frame.

I am meant to have the vision of far-seeing managers — Brian Epstein at the Cavern seeing the Beatles for the first time, Albert Grossman at Gerdes Folk City catching his first glimpse of Bob Dylan. I am meant to see auras humming around each of them, to believe this is the band that will conquer the world, but, let's face it, I'm having a crisis of faith, despite last night's epiphany. I actually feel *sorry* for them.

For one fleeting moment I think I see a precedent. That other band of misfits, the Rolling Stones. Those first publicity shots of the Stones, especially. Man, did they look ugly! Pimply, sullen, arrogant, and weird. There is a mystique about that. Ugly guys making great music. And the Dead are even *uglier* than the Rolling Stones. But there is a serious flaw in this line of reasoning. The Brits, you see, can always get away with this sort of *faux sauvage* posturing. However scruffy your yobby group appears, you can always get some pricey shutterbug like David Bailey to come in with his eye-of-the-needle strobe lights and belly-of-the-whale blue backdrop to make the whole thing look *deliberate.* And however slovenly and adenoidal they appeared to be, the Stones thing was very studied. The Eton collars and Anello & David boots — the Stones were veritable fashion plates compared to the Dead. Plus they were seriously hip. The Dead are not hip and they're never going to be; they are just too goofy.

They're good musicians, even if what they do is somewhat unclassifiable. These aren't songs in any conventional sense, they are catchpenny epics of noodling, circling riffs. Holding patterns of songs. Garcia carries on these long, looping musical, telepathic conversations with his guitar, adjusting the flow from beat to beat, drifting from mood to mood. The idea seems to be to play everything *but* the tunes. Noodling it may be, but it is not your Haight garden variety of noodling born of ineptitude. This is the inspired, *consecrated* noodling of the gods. I am mesmerized. This band will never get anywhere, but, man, are they good.

As the acid comes on I begin to wonder if I haven't perhaps judged them a bit harshly. All these objections, what are they really? Just baroque worries. I see now that my approach has been all wrong. While earlier it had bothered me that the Dead were such oddballs, I now see this as a distinct advantage. Why in the world would anyone want a band that looked like something that already existed? It would be pointless. It would be redundant. Just another folk-rock band looking for bookings. An anachronism.

The Dead are a great band, I decide. What other band do you know of that can make chickens materialize on telephone wires right in the middle of the Fillmore? By now we're an hour, an hour and a half into the set. The piano player stabbing away at his Vox piano is in a groove not occupied by too many other people, you have to grant him that. He chugs into "I'm a Hog for You, Baby," which is, given the visual before us, perfect. R&B novelty song as Saturday morning cartoon. And just as you are wondering how many verses does this song *have,* it almost imperceptibly drifts into a bouncy version of "Good Day Sunshine" with dodgy harmonies and then into some frantic foggy-mornin'-breakdown Flatt and Scruggs type picking that with nary an introduction or a pause s-l-o-w-s *way* down and, uh, we're in some folk grotto on Grant Street and it's a nuclear holocaust protest song, disguised as an Appalachian ballad (that good old standby, "Early Morning Rain"), which melts into some sort of Sun Ra jazzy extra-terrestrial number and swing low sweet chariot. . . .

Okay, so they do bluegrass, blues, Beatles, folk, and jazz all in the same song. Well, that's *original,* isn't it? And you know, the more I think about it, there really *is* no such thing as a song. No. All songs are the same song. Top ten hits, singles, jukebox selections — it's all, you know, arbitrary, music biz categories, ways of packaging the stuff. Shipping units.

The individual, alienated tune does not exist, O my brothers! There is only this thing called *song,* an all-embracing Whitmanesque entity into which all songs empty themselves as if into the Mississippi. And like the Mississippi it's all one long uninterrupted tune that includes — in Child ballad form — the folktale history of America. The entire story of our groaning continent contained in a twelve-bar song. Big American panorama, like Kerouac. How had I missed this?

A moment of lucidity flashes by during which I try to remind myself that this is just a garage band on acid, but it's futile because in the core of my being I know I'm on to something big. The big picture, babe. Who says the bodhisattva has to come from Tibet? Why couldn't Soupy Sales be the Buddha? You have to leave an open mind about stuff like this. The idea is beginning to dawn on me, for instance, that the bodhisattva could easily be concealed in the person of, say, a ballad-singing country crooner. And from there it's only a small step to: Why couldn't the Grateful Dead become the greatest rock band in the world? Stranger things have happened.

Something makes me turn around, and when I do a truly alarming sight catches my eye. A man alone, in the center of the floor, is performing a very peculiar dance. A spastic Jackson Pollock alphabet dance with mystic hand signals. He is either mad or in the thrall of a demon. My God, it's *him!* Poor Owsley! After so painstakingly warning me about the dangers of Kesey mind control, he has fallen victim to it himself. The fiendish Kesey has him in his clutches!

Later on, I'm told I was mistaken. It was *interpretive* dancing, Rock. Haven't you ever heard of interpretive dancing? He was, uh, getting in touch with the house. Stupid me, I was present at the creation of the *ur* Dead dance and missed the whole point. When I saw this overdressed daddy longlegs doing a slow-motion version of Martha Graham free-form modern ballet I simply thought I'd lost my mind.

Finally the band wanders offstage. Owsley introduces me around.

"Boys, I want you to meet the late, great Rock Scully. This is the guy from the Family Dog I was telling you about." Owsley presents me as if I were Brian Epstein or Albert Grossman. And for that split second I am.

Close up, the bizarre nature of this tatterdemalion group is more glaring than ever. Bob Weir looks like a sixteen-year-old kid who has no business being in a place that's serving drinks, much less acid. And with the exception of Pigpen, they are all totally zonked. Their pupils are the size of saucers.

Owsley announces: "Rock's going to be your manager." Like a papal fiat. The group responds to this declaration with impressive casualness.

"Hey, good luck, dude," says Weir.

"Yeah, great. Got some skins?" Jerry asks.

"Did you say your name was *Rock?*" Pigpen wants to know. "Cool handle, man."

"Whaddya think of the set?" Lesh asks.

"You guys sure played pretty," I say lamely.

"Nah," says Jerry, "we played shitty. You should have heard us at Big Nig's. Tonight was just the usual mess, there we *really* fucked up!"

I am only partly tuned into the conversations going on around me because over Garcia's shoulder I see Neal Cassady, mythic hero of Jack Kerouac's *On the Road*. Dean Moriarty.

Flinty redneck cubist face. Sharp features all obtuse-angled and jammed together. Hinged, lantern jaw like a puppet's, constantly in motion. Camel dangling from the side of his mouth. Everything animated, zigzaggedy, tilted.

Neal is getting warmed up. He's juggling a ball peen hammer, winging it. *Zhwooom-zhwooom-zhwooom-zhwooom-zhwooom-zhwooom-zhwooom.* Up it goes like a throbbing heartbeat into the peak of the ceiling. He seems to be enthralled with the fact that this is an A-frame. He's doing the hammer thing and carrying on a multiphrenic conversation with no one in particular while people walk around completely oblivious to this deadly object whizzing inches over their heads. I am about to shout *Heads up!* when — in midsentence — Neal casually snatches it out of thin air.

Garcia shakes his head in awe, "Fucking Neal, man, he's amazing, ya know. Taught us how to play god and drive around blind corners."

It's four o'clock in the morning, London Bridge is falling down, all the clocks are striking thirteen and the one-eyed midget is shouting the word "Now!" This is no concert, no weekend two-bucks-at-the-door dance party scene. This is a meltdown, designed to induce a state of heart-clutching clinical schizophrenia.

Perhaps Owsley is right, after all. Maybe Kesey *is* in the wires. I think Owsley may actually know something about this stuff. He should — he spends more time examining his paranoia than most people. Maybe you can affect things just by thinking about them. It's possible things are a little more, uh, *porous* than I'd imagined.

It's time to leave, but the acid-making ballet dancer I came with is nowhere to be seen. I crawl into the back of Bill Kreutzmann's station wagon among drum kits, mike stands, and amplifiers, and pass out. I figure it's okay, I'm the manager.

3

Plaid Iguanas

ONLY A FEW days ago I was a hapless graduate student throwing the *I Ching,* casting about aimlessly for something to do with my life. Now, suddenly out of the blue, I'm a manager. But of what? Not exactly a rock band. Remnants, really, of a jug band. Coffeehouse folkies and music students. Just a ragtag, rooty, down-home bunch of people who have never been out of Northern California. Crazy-looking guys, high on acid, who had come together higgledy-piggledy and (like much else to do with the Dead, I would learn) pretty much by default.

Which is part of the enigma of the Dead. It wasn't all that thought out, to say the least, and it still isn't to this day. They are as amazed by the phenomenon as you and I.

San Francisco is a genuinely radical place in 1965. We are on a planet where the inhabitants frequent coffeehouses and clubs as places of worship. The hungry i, Vesuvio's Coffee House, and the City Lights Book Shop are our shrines. Kerouac, Kesey, Corso, Burroughs, and Ginsberg are our holy madmen. We idolize the Beats and Charlie Mingus and the crazy wisdom jazz angels. We zealously listen to smuggled tapes of Lenny Bruce at the Purple Onion.

You can still run into these guys — hipsters, jazz demons, and Beats — and talk to them. Lenny Bruce lives in a funky hotel over City Lights. He is in trouble all the time. People are constantly running around with petitions, saving his ass.

When the Grateful Dead began, San Francisco was still in that transitional period from Beat to Hip. We aspired to the bohemian, outlaw code of the Beats. They smoked grass, ate magic mushrooms, grew beards, and wore Levi's and plaid flannel shirts. They were into jazz, Zen, and existentialism. So what if they talked to themselves or took speed and drank Hearty Mountain Burgundy! We don't care, they are on the beam.

But it is not exactly a mutual admiration society. The Beats from North Beach look askance at us hippies. We are on a different wavelength. This has to do with musical tempo and electronics and the changing of an era. Of course, there is one other little factor: the mind-bending drugs.

And as engrossing as the coffeehouses and taking meth and sitting up all night discussing Sartre are, it is a worn groove. We have to find our own scene. We have discussed Sartre to death. It is all too cerebral and talky and dialectical, and with the advent of acid the rational thing is dissolving (fast). You can't read a book when you're on acid.

⑥

Jerry was born in San Francisco, as was Pigpen. Phil Lesh was born in Berkeley. Bob Weir in Palo Alto. We were Bay Area kids proud of the city's long line of hairy poets and eccentrics.

Garcia had come up through the coffeehouse scene in Palo Alto, a bohemian enclave if ever there was one. His beard is a coffeehouse beard. Bushy, nihilistic, Beat. Occasionally he ventured off to North Beach. That's where we all hung sooner or later, because that's where the music was. If you were going to hear jazz, or blues, or folk music, that's where you went. That's where we heard Jorma Kaukonen play guitar. Where we caught "this far-out chick from Texas" at the Coffee Gallery down on Grant Street, Lenny Bruce at the hungry i, Charlie Mingus at the Jazz Workshop.

The folk scene wasn't all music. It primarily revolved around books and ideas. It was a literate scene. Lots of scribbling on napkins and the backs of envelopes and precious little bound books, Mao and Kafka. Jerry's buddy Bob Hunter was writing poetry and Garcia was learning all the stringed instruments he could get his hands on. Playing the banjo and learning to play the guitar in the coffeehouses of Palo Alto.

The first time I saw Jerry Garcia he was sitting in the Coffee Confusion in the midst of a very agitated discussion about Cuba.

Garcia was appalled about the Bay of Pigs. Such things counted in those days. And then the conversation would move on to war *per se* and what the Greeks thought about it and what the women of Troy *did* about it. On and on it would go far into the night. In the background there'd be some chick with incredibly long hair leaning over her dulcimer droning "Down in the mine where the sun never shines. . . ."

None of the band members has moved into San Francisco yet. Bill Kreutzmann is living at his dad's house, Jerry and Bob Hunter are hanging together in a crash pad in Palo Alto, Phil Lesh is living in Berkeley, and Bobby Weir is living at home in Hillsborough in his parents' fancy digs. They get together in the coffeehouses of Palo Alto. Magoo's mainly and down at Kepler's Bookstore (he's Joan Baez's friend) and Dana Morgan's Music, where Pigpen works and Jerry is giving guitar lessons.

As early as '63, Jerry was a demon banjo picker, and by the time he and Pig and Weir put the Warlocks together Jerry was an accomplished musician. He is also very knowledgeable about traditional American music: folk, bluegrass, gospel. His dad had been a clarinet player and band leader who died young.

His mother ran a sailor's bar, south of Market down in the Mission District right next to the Sailors Union of the Pacific. This is their favorite bar. So not only does he come from a musical background, but from an early age he has been exposed to a lot of different scenes, meeting people from around the world. He is well read. The Beats are his guys: Jack Kerouac, Gregory Corso, William Burroughs, and Lawrence Ferlinghetti. Jerry was fifteen when *On the Road* came out, and it became his bible, one long be-bop wail to hedonism and transcendence.

At eighteen he enlisted in the army but it would be hard to imagine anyone less suited to military life than Garcia and within six months he was dishonorably discharged. Way to go, Jerry! At this point he considered himself primarily a painter and studied for a while at the Art Institute in San Francisco. But ever since he'd got that Danelectro guitar on his fifteenth birthday he'd been attracted to the folk music scene in the coffeehouses of Palo Alto. Following a car crash in February 1961, Jerry quit art school and began hanging out with the Beats, folk musicians, and proto-hippies at Kepler's Bookstore in Palo Alto.

And then there is Pigpen (né Ron McKernan). He is a veritable encyclopedia of bluesology. Anybody who has ever picked up a guitar by this time knows yer basic Brit-invasion Chicago blues bag — "Dust My Broom," "Rollin' and Tumblin'" — but Pig knows the arcana. He'd been introduced to esoteric stuff by his father who was one of the first white R&B disc jockeys on a black station. Only in California could you have a white Irish guy named McKernan doing a major shift on KDIA radio over in Oakland and commuting back to the South Bay over the San Mateo Bridge. Pigpen is not only a decent keyboard player — he plays a Vox electric organ standing up — he also has a lot of experience packed into his twenty years. He was an alcoholic by age thirteen.

This is the nucleus: Pig and Jerry. Then there is Bobby Weir, the wide-eyed kid. Jerry is like his big brother. Bobby had a band in high school named the Uncalled Four and spent his last year in school skipping class and teaching himself to play guitar, and now is taking acoustic rhythm guitar lessons from Jerry. He'd got to know Garcia on New Year's Eve of 1963. Wandering around the streets of Palo Alto with a friend — too young to get into any of the clubs — he heard ferocious banjo-picking coming from the back of Dana Morgan's Music. It was Jerry who, not realizing it was New Year's Eve, was still waiting for his students to show up. Weir and his buddy persuaded Jerry to unlock the store. They broke out some guitars, and after playing a couple of hours decided to form a jug band, Mother McCree's Uptown Jug Champions, with Pigpen and any number of other people dropping in and out. Bobby, who still couldn't really play guitar, was on washtub bass.

Mother McCree's Uptown Jug Champions became very popular on the peninsula folk circuit, but after about six months Pig began urging them to do more blues stuff. When Dana Morgan, the owner of the music store, offered to front them the electric instruments — his son, Dana Morgan Jr., played bass — they became the Warlocks.

Phil Lesh was studying electronic music with Luciano Berio at Mills College, an all-girls school in Berkeley. He was into horns and composing and *musique concrète*. He played trumpet in the Berkeley High School jazz band, but he came to look at music more in terms of charts and scores and cadenzas and adagios. Phil was the engineer for "The Midnight Special," a folk music program on Berkeley's KPFA on which Jerry became a regular guest. They became friends. They had many things in common, not the least of which was an enthusiasm for Kerouac and the Beats. Lesh loved Allen Ginsberg's *Howl* so much he was in the process of setting it to music. When he joined the Warlocks he took over on bass from Dana Morgan Jr., who was too busy to make the gigs. The thought of lifting up a bass had never crossed his mind. Jerry told him, "You can play the bass." (That was the only slot left.) He practiced on the bass a week — that's all it took to get in.

Billy Kreutzmann was not part of the coffeehouse scene. Unlike the other members of the band, he wasn't somebody Jerry knew socially. They needed a drummer and Jerry found him through the music store. He'd been in a few rock 'n' roll bands so he had more of a feel for it than the others. His heroes were jazz drummers like Joe Morello and Elvin Jones.

Rock groups are something new on the scene, a Brit concept, basically, and in 1965 people are just getting used to the idea. Previously considered commercial and crass by the coffeehouse set, rock 'n' roll is on its way in. It was only last summer that Dylan had brought the fire down from the mountain when he went electric at the Newport Folk Festival.

The only thing the Warlocks know how to play electric is the blues. Pigpen stands at that wobbly Vox electric organ on its shaky tubular aluminum legs and bumps his belly up against it and bangs out the blues. That makes Pig the front man. It is all very basic. Every band that doesn't start out trying to sound like the Beatles is playing Chicago blues: "I woke up the smornin' dum-de-dum-de-dum-de-dum."

But generic as it is, the Dead have a better shot at it than, say, Big Brother. Most Haight bands — like the Charlatans — began with the Look. Like "Does anybody here *play?*" The music is an afterthought. These guys, on the other hand, are already accomplished musicians. Jerry is *teaching* guitar, Phil is a music major in college, Bobby is learning guitar from Jerry and teaching it to grade school kids. Kreutzmann has been playing drums since sixth grade. They have also been through a more rigorous apprenticeship than other hippie bands. They've played in more demanding places — pizza pubs! Noisy, rowdy, smelly, filthy joints. Far from the hushed, reverential atmosphere of the coffeehouse.

The folky Mother McCree tunes are not going to go down in a tumultuous atmosphere like that. Most of them get thrown out except for the Pigpen stuff, the traditional blues like "Down So Long." Pig also brings the needed momentum of R&B to the repertoire. In the earliest incarnation of the band (as the Warlocks), Pigpen played a large role because he was the one with the most musical knowledge. He *was* the Grateful Dead, according to Garcia, according to me. I mean, four sets a night in bars! Who else in the band was going to do it? Pigpen had all that stuff *down*. In a pizza bar they don't want to hear a whole set of bluegrass and folk ballads. They want something that's *jumping*.

The Dead have to get tight fast. They play four to six sets a night for virtually no money; doing Pigpen blues songs in front of peninsula audiences. Pigpen is turning them on to records as fast as he can, old Kent, Chess Records 78s, teaching them songs like "Parchman Farm" — ancient moss-encrusted Delta blues. The Fillmore Mime Troupe benefit is their first gig as the Grateful Dead. Bill Graham is so appalled by the name that at first he refuses to put it on the poster. He relents, but only after adding "formerly the Warlocks."

Until 1965, change — when it did come — arrived with glacial slowness. The "sixties" hadn't begun. People still had black-and-white TVs and AC was hard to get. Your toaster looked like a space ship and your oven was an Oldsmobile. This was the slow time.

We are all young and ready to go crazy, and there never has been a better time for it than the mid-sixties San Francisco. By comparison, the late sixties happen at the speed of light. And when we start taking acid, the fantasies really begin to bloom! Everything erupting all at once. In a matter of six months — with the coming of acid and electric music — our lives are transformed utterly.

◎

The Grateful Dead at this point are barely a group, more a collection of people from different musical backgrounds and with varying levels of competence. Phil Lesh, for instance, is too precise, too well trained in the classical manner and consequently very stiff for a rock 'n' roll bass player. He has all this savvy about the music, he can talk circles around Garcia or anybody. He'll say, "No, no, no, no, wait. If we're going from a C to a B-flat minor you have to have the correct modulation." Lesh can chart it all, but he can't swing. It is probably our biggest problem with the groove.

The bass has to work closely with the drummer's foot, but Lesh and

Kreutzmann are plainly opposite kind of guys. Kreutzmann is this wild, woolly, uneducated, crazy drumming guy — almost like Animal in the Muppets — and Phil has this very filigreed bass-playing style. He's a highfalutin intellectual kind of a guy who's liable to turn his *back* on the audience. But there's Kreutzmann right in his face going, "Don't you hear that downbeat, man?" And Phil won't even *look* at him (he won't look at Jerry either). Phil has perfect pitch, but that perfect pitch just doesn't work with Garcia's voice. Or with Pigpen's, for that matter. Sometimes it works with Bobby's voice, but generally it doesn't blend in comfortably with the rest of the band.

Meanwhile Bobby Weir can't come up with a B-minor to save his life, not to mention a B-flat minor. He's contorting his fingers on the guitar, holding down the E-string while he's still holding down this other one back up there somewhere — torture!

The members of the Dead are far from being ideally suited to each other. They have to play to each other's weaknesses. But somehow what comes out is the inimitable sound of Grateful Dead.

◎

My role as manager of the Grateful Dead is at first minimal. Most of our early shows are Acid Tests. We are Kesey's house band and Kesey gets us the gigs. Now suffice it to say that the Acid Tests are not a demanding atmosphere in which to play. There are so many other things going on at an Acid Test that there is next to no focus on the band. The sets are casual in the extreme. Whenever enough people get up on stage, that's when they play. Sometimes for five minutes. Sometimes not at all.

At the Acid Tests Pigpen generally starts playing the melody line and everybody joins in. Real simple blues like "Good Morning Little School Girl," "Viola Lee Blues," "Caution," "Beat It on Down the Line." They put a bunch of songs together in a quick little set and then do an extended jam on something like "Sitting on Top of the World" or "Cold Rain and Snow." They are already wicked improvisers. A very short song can easily get stretched out interminably. Sometimes they ramble on not knowing how to end it. Soon everybody is off on their own: Weir's right behind Jerry, following this railway spur off into the wilds of Montana.

When they start to drift off, Pig pulls them back with a few sharp, jabbing chords. But it is unlikely that anyone else ever notices. A dozen other astonishing things are happening at once. Overload is the normal mode of the Acid Tests, and mad scenes are taking place everywhere. It's an intensely social scene with everyone partying furiously. People wander about and get involved in the phantasmagoria. They aren't there to hear the band. And then there's the *other* band, the Prankster cacophony band, blowing whistles and pipes and clanging away on pots and pans and tin drums. The Acid Tests are a great training ground — after learning to play against all that insanity the Grateful Dead can play anywhere. Nothing will ever faze them again.

We are running on pure high octane optimism and Owsley acid. We are doing *a lot* of acid. The band (except for Pigpen) usually plays on acid, too. What would be the point of being straight at an Acid Test? Halfway through the evening we usually put out a new trash bucket full of Kool-Aid and acid. The audience drinks it and after a while they feel like we do.

Like everybody else involved with the Acid Tests, we believe LSD is a cosmic truth serum, but after a couple of dozen trips we soon learn that acid is not infallible (especially about stuff like gravity). Flying, although tempting, is not a good idea. If we see someone trying to stand up on the balcony railings or climbing up on a window ledge, we lure them over to the black light corner. "Hey, man, look: space dogs!"

And as interesting as playing music on acid is, there are some serious drawbacks. Sets can go on interminably or end abruptly after a few minutes. It doesn't take me long to learn the signs. In Garcia's face I see a sudden, silent intercortical scream building at the back of the eyes and through the telekenetic mind-link I can hear its alien cry: *Aaaaaaaaaagh!!!* I know *they've* arrived: tiny monkeys, gibbering guitar picks, Barbies with the faces of Mexican *santos*.

The music takes a sudden lurch. It gets all loose and wobbly. The drummer may be banging away furiously, sweating, trying to keep time, Pig may be hitting the chords — but it's hopeless. They've become a phantom band. The beats are there, but Jerry isn't. You can see his hands *melting* before his eyes, his fingers dribbling down his guitar into waxy puddles. At a certain point Jerry stops playing altogether. He holds his hands out in front of him as if folding an invisible newspaper, awestruck by the fact that he has fingers.

Right then I call for a break. I give them Scully Lecture No. 3.

"This is not a rehearsal, guys. You cannot wander offstage in search of a plumed serpent. You cannot just quit after five minutes and lie down on the godforsaken stage. *Must* finish the set. *Must* do the songs."

"Fuck, Rock, lighten up, it's only an Acid Test, man."

"It's not just an Acid Test, it's a gig. We're selling tickets, you guys! Must remember: These people paid *money* to hear you."

"We're at a *gig?*" Smart-ass Weir.

"And just how do you explain the plaid iguanas?" Kreutzmann chimes in.

For years Pig used to tell them: "You guys can get as fucked up as you want, but you just can't look surprised when something weird starts happening. If they see that, the audience freaks."

Onstage, Pigpen is the anchor. When things get truly bizarre, they can always look at Pig and know he is straight. Might have had a few drinks, but he is ground base. He is seeing things as they really are. (More or less.)

The quickest way to short-circuit a bummer is to remind yourself you're just tripping. That lumpy purple barrel you put in your Coke, remember? But sometimes you take so much you can't remember you took any. So Pigpen will remind you. Just with a look he says: "Those Day-Glo spiders crawling all over your ax are something you *took*. You're *high,* fool."

The one thing that keeps us from full-blown chaos is that we think of ourselves as "professionals." Despite everything — through rain, snow, sleet, dark of night, broken fan belts, multi-microgram acid storms, and ongoing insanity — we never miss a show. We are always there on time and never (totally) blow a gig.

And these aren't wham-bang-thank-you-ma'am sets. These are four-hour shows. *Nobody* else plays all night. We'll take a half-hour break, come back and do another hour and a half. Right on till dawn. People come stumbling out of the Avalon or the Fillmore, ready to go out and party some more, planning to hit another club before they go home . . . and it's *daylight* outside.

Most of our gigs are *very* local. Our route includes Palo Alto, Berkeley, Marin County, the Haight. While we're still doing the Acid Tests, I function more as a road manager (and even that is very undemanding). All our gear pretty much fits into Kreutzmann's Dodge station wagon. The whole thing. Sometimes we have to make a separate trip for his drums. Take them down first, have one of us sit on them while we go back for the rest of the equipment.

The Dead don't have a pot to piss in, but they have the best amps, guitars, and drums money can buy. Owsley is always laying equipment on the band. He's our patron. He's making so much money from making LSD he can afford to bankroll the Dead. He is willing to do it as long as we do it on his terms.

We're playing music and making mistakes and not being all that graceful about our bungling. A recurring theme of these early shows is the fucking up. But everybody reacts differently. Jerry's attitude is always "Hey, we messed up, but these things happen. We'll get it together."

Just remembering the lyrics is good enough for Bobby. Phil is very touchy about his playing. You can't praise him, he's so self-critical. He's a classically trained musician and holds himself to a higher standard. What would Prokofiev have done if *he* played bass? At first I say things like "Man, you were *so* hot tonight!" and he snaps back: "Scully, you're so full of shit, you don't know what you're talking about." Finally I wise up and keep my big mouth shut.

Everything is going along smoothly as we approach the first Trips Festival, a kind of public, larger-scale Acid Test at Longshoremen's Hall, early 1966. The Dead, Big Brother and the Holding Company, the Pranksters and God knows who else in performance. It is the night before the Trips Festival, the Pranksters have been setting up all day, and Stewart Brand suggests they take a break and go up on the roof and smoke a joint. Kesey, typically, has a better idea: to cross over to the roof of the house next door. Unfortunately there are people living under that roof who don't know them or what they're doing and the air soon reeks of pot. There is a commotion in the alley. They look down and what do they see but some cops in a squad car pulling up. The cops get out and go in the building next door — which is actually the building they are *now on the roof of.* But they don't yet realize this. They're stoned, after all. They casually discuss the situation.

"Gee, I wonder what they're doing down there."

"They can't be after us. They're in the wrong building."

A minute later they turn around to find a dozen cops right behind them on the roof. Kesey freaks big time. He has a prior. He's out on bail. One of the cops finds the weed. Kesey snatches it out of the cop's hand and tries to swallow it, almost choking himself to death in the process. When this doesn't work, he tries to throw it off the roof but the cops grab it. Kesey is wrestling with them and they're hitting him with their flashlights. Then one of the cops pulls out his gun and says: "Okay, stand clear! I'm going to blow his head off."

Mountain Girl, Kesey's girlfriend, is grabbing at the cop's arm, screaming: "No, no! Don't shoot him! Peace!" The cops eventually quell him with a couple of good clobbers, but it isn't easy. They handcuff Kesey and Mountain Girl and take them off to the San Francisco County Jail.

The following day, the day of the Trips Festival, they let him out. This is the Pranksters' big show. Not only do they have to show up at Longshoremen's Hall and act like everything is normal, they also have to perform. Great! They drive straight to the Trips Festival from jail, putting their costumes on in the car because by now it's five o'clock and they're late setting up. People are beginning to show up. Hundreds of people. Kesey's bust has got a lot of coverage. It's made the Trips Festival even hotter.

Kesey, in a gold lamé space suit with helmet, jumps out of the car and runs up the stairs. But here's this guy at the door with a clipboard and a list who bars his way. He won't let Kesey in. He's not on the list!

Where did this deranged control freak come from? He's shrieking orders and throwing people against the wall. He's *hitting* people and uttering dire threats for the tiniest infraction.

It's *Bill Graham!* I know him from the Mime Troupe benefits, but most of us have never seen him before. Everybody is going: "Who *is* this guy?"

Kesey is already tightly wired from spending the night in jail and he's threatening Graham with mayhem and dismemberment.

"I'll tear your fucking head off if you put your hand on me again!"

"Go ahead. You're still not getting in."

"It's my *show*, asshole."

"Says fucking who? The line forms over there on Geary Street."

Kesey's face lights up. He turns to the crowd and shouts, cupping his hands around his mouth:

"My God, it's Big Nurse!"

Everybody laughs. That terrible, unstoppable cosmic chortle that comes from the other side of the looking glass and says: "It's all a big fucking joke, man, and it's unraveling all the time and you are never going to pick up every stitch so just — *let go!*"

The little fleck of terror at the center of Graham's eye starts to expand until it's threatening to engulf the whole scene. A Japanese dwarf in the core of his brain is shouting: *CONTROL! CONTROL!* But whatever is going on here is so out of control that it's ludicrous to try to contain it.

The man in the space suit is the prince of disorder. His mood is so infectious even those in the crowd who aren't high are catching it. It's powerful stuff and so unstable it's pulling everyone in its wake like a black hole. It's scary stuff for a control freak like Bill Graham. He's met his match in Kesey, a control freak of cosmic proportions. Neither one of them can let go of their bossdom for one second.

It's a stalemate. Finally Stewart Brand comes out and says:

"They're okay. That's Ken Kesey."

"Kesey," an exasperated Graham asks, "would you mind telling me what the hell you are doing *here?*"

Without saying a word Kesey flips the visor of his space helmet down. The audience with the alien is at an end.

Mountain Girl is still livid. "Stewart," she asks through clenched teeth, "how could you let that moron handle the door?"

And Stewart very meekly says, "Well at least he's efficient." He's right about that!

The irony of the whole thing is that Graham is *donating* his time. As usual, everything has been left to the last minute. Kesey's bust has only compounded the situation, and Graham has agreed to help out. What drives Bill Graham crazy is Kesey's laissez-faire approach to everything. Kesey sets great plans in motion and then disappears, running around being social, making appearances, signing books, attending parties. Meanwhile nothing's been done. *No* attention to detail whatsoever. Ken Babbs, the veteran Vietnam chopper pilot and Prankster majordomo, is the one who keeps it together, such as it is. Considerations such as where the electricity is going to come from and how big is the back door and can the Thunder Machine *fit* through it never cross anybody's mind until the very moment they're actually confronted with it. It is so early in everyone's experience of running these shows that the idea of leaving parking room so that the truck with the band's equipment can back up to the loading dock is like higher mathematics. And, on this particular occasion, when the truck pulls up to the back entrance of Longshoremen's Hall it can't unload. Some stupid jerk has parked his car right in front of the loading dock. It's my car, actually, and I can't find the keys.

By the time we get into the hall the Trips Festival is in full swing. We are immediately bombarded from all sides by the familiar Prankster maelstrom of slides, 16mm film, liquid lights, tape recorders all whirring away, all spewing out a phantasmagoric brew of flashing lights, gibbering voices, and roiling chaotic feedback. Kesey has video cameras and video monitors strategically set up around the room so as you walk around you constantly have jarring confrontations with yourself on the screen.

In the middle of the floor is the Thunder Machine, an amorphous metallic sculpture made by Ron Boise. Big metal figures fucking in different positions. The Thunder Machine is huge, like something you'd put in a children's playground. It's also a musical instrument. You can get inside it and bang on the different panels with wooden mallets and hammers. It's like a huge steel drum, so big that six people can play it at once. Like being in the belly of an iron whale.

Everything is designed to envelop and overwhelm. There's a Moog synthesizer with sound coming out of sixteen phased speakers so the sound rushes 360 degrees around the hall like a sonic demon. There are ices spiked with LSD. A gigantic speaker painted in spectacular Day-Glo colors is set up on the edge of the stage. It is so big that you can get inside it. At the top of the speaker box is a working tweeter and on the bottom is a couch. You climb in, lean back into it, and go, *"Whoa!"* Terrible speaker, but the effect is fantastic.

Neal Cassady is rapping, doing his cool world bit. Kesey orchestrates these things so that everybody has a chance to get on the mikes. Several delirious hippies have curled up at the base of the microphones like huge molluscs.

Ken Babbs, being master of ceremonies, is issuing orders to the hall on one mike and Kesey is on another mike mixing in the odd random noises while running novel fragments on the overhead projector. Big Brother is on.

After one song Babbs's voice booms over the PA: "A big hand of applause, ladies and gentlemen, freaks and friends, for Big Brother and the Holding Company. And now a little something from the great Tony Bennett. . . ." Babbs has been babbling all evening about "jungle bunny music" and such. Like a lot of the Pranksters he's from another generation entirely — Babbs was a *marine,* for chrissakes — and the thing about acid is that whatever is there is going to bleed through. He's so out of it that whatever he *thinks,* he says. Totally unedited mind-gibber.

Chet Helms, who manages Big Brother, leaps up onstage in his afghan coat like a skinny myopic Genghis Khan and grabs one of the microphones:

"*Goddammit!* Big Brother was brought here to play four songs and they're going to play four songs. What do you say, audience?"

And everybody, of course, yells "*Yeah!*"

I know Janis from the Grant Street coffeehouse scene. She was already astonishing back then. She blew the folk madonnas *away.* In combination with Jim Gurley's John-Coltrane-on-Mars guitar playing and the buzzy, lysergic sawmill of Big Brother, the effect is operatic. Janis so identifies with the girl in the song that she becomes her: Daisy Mae as Big Mamma Thornton comes to full-blown, Technicolor life, rips a hole in the song and jumps out. When Big Brother finishes their set, Garcia shakes his head in awe.

As we're talking we look up and see words curling out of the overhead projector. Words writing themselves. Well, how else would they get there? Huge uncial lettering with serifs and loops. But it is not writing the usual Dada utterances:

"JERRY GARCIA, PLUG IN."

And then, in a flash, it's gone. The moving finger writes and having writ moves on.

"Fuck, did you just see that?" Jerry asks.

"Unless we're both receiving the same subliminal telegrams, I'd say it's time."

But when Jerry gets up onstage he finds the neck of his guitar has snapped. The bridge has broken off, it's completely sprung, with strings sticking out everywhere. He cradles it in his arms like a wounded animal. The Dead play about five numbers that ramble on way past midnight.

Around two o'clock, the fire chief — like a character from light opera — shows up. The place is just going nuts, and he marches in with these four fire guys in full regalia — hatchets, firehoses, the whole bit. They look around. A beat as they take in the swelling scene and then it's "Ooooookay, let's turn it off now. EVERYBODY OUT! The party's over, folks." Permits, warrants, writs, and other fancy legalisms are being bandied about. In the midst of this a voice booms through the auditorium. Some guy has got hold of the microphone, he's standing up on the balcony going, "I AM LOBAR SPEAKING TO YOU FROM THE FUTURE. . . ."

4

Acid Rain

OWSLEY HAS A new theory, a theory of sound. He is forever generating theories, he's a veritable production line of theories, and being high all the time and staying up all the time these theories become more and more convoluted. He's a perfect monomaniac on any conceivable subject. And an expert on everything. There isn't anything you can name that he doesn't have an opinion about. Vegetables, transistors, ballet, cosmic drift. Talking to him is not an easy business. There is no conversation as such. He gets something in his head and that is that. Right now it's sound.

Owsley lives in a small house behind an apartment building that he has semi-soundproofed. The lair of the mad scientist. It is a hideout and a sound lab filled with the most fantastic gear. All these amazing toys. He has synthesizers that can make music out of any sound you can come up with. And this is in 1966.

Jerry and Phil love playing with these gadgets. Especially Phil. Phil is a *musique concrète* freak. It is in that lab that Professor Owsley Stanley expounds his theory of sound to us.

"What we're trying to achieve, guys, is a system sensitive enough to let the audience hear *everything* — exactly as played. Every instrument separately miked. This is not only a technical question, you understand, it has to do with the whole feeling of this band. We let the audience in on an ongoing process."

There's dead silence in the room — hey, who can argue with that? Even an egomaniac like Owsley can sense when he's losing his audience, so he takes another tack:

"Why aren't *all* bands heard in stereo?"

A long pause. Hands, anyone? For a moment the thought flickers across my mind: Could it be a trick question? Or is this the germ of a conspiracy theory?

"As we know, in real life sound moves. Like Einstein's train. From right to left, left to right," Owsley continues talking as he demonstrates this, playing "Three Blind Mice" on a Moog synthesizer. It's so trippy, like a mini doppler effect, that we all involuntarily go "Aaaaah!" when we hear it.

"*This* is the way we want to sound. This is what we're aiming for, and we can do it. Three-dimensional sound. In the future all bands will be heard in stereo, but I want the Dead to be heard in stereo *now*. From the get-go. Every instrument in stereo; every guitar and every drum set with a right and left channel. My friends, there are one or two little wrinkles to be worked out, but for all intents and purposes I believe we now have a stereo system."

Quod erat demonstrandum. After the briefing concludes we all get to play the instruments and try it out. It's stunning. Why hadn't anybody thought of this before? The concept of a stereo PA system is so ahead of its time it will be almost ten years before they start using it in movie theaters.

Owsley's axiom is basic, but farseeing — and so complicated and laborious and expensive to implement that it will be years before he gets it right. At first he uses Voice of the Theatre speaker boxes. Great big Altec speakers in huge cabinetry with subwoofers and horns on the top. The kind of things they use in movie theaters. He buys up a bunch of them, and for years we cart these plywood monstrosities around like the Ark of the Covenant.

He has figured out the best way of powering the speakers is with Macintosh tubes that put out a thousand watts of pure clean power. But they weigh a hundred pounds each and are alarmingly delicate. You have to treat them nicer than eggs. You practically have to talk to them. They can't stand extreme temperatures, you can't turn them on and off too often because they flare up and if you do it too often they wear out. We are constantly blowing fuses and burning out tubes. Because of their high rate of attrition, we have to haul piles of spares around with us, which gets harder as we go farther afield.

Okay, we now have the world's greatest equipment, but who *are* we? The very excellence of the sound system only compounds problems we are going to have to face sooner or later. Proving the old Tibetan adage: Even the dead can have an identity crisis.

Out of the context of the Acid Test, stripped naked of LSD, strobes, talking TV monitors, and frenzied monologues, we see all too clearly that we're just an old blues jalopy running on swamp gas. The Dead have gone straight from a club scene where we play the same set every night right into the Fillmore and the larger halls. We are a garage band on acid, playing *very* basic, hard-driving blues and covers. Great songs, but they aren't ours. We are getting away with it, but we need new material. Bad. Everybody in San Francisco and Palo Alto has heard every song the Dead ever learned at least a dozen times.

And just at that moment — O meaningful coincidence! — Owsley decides he has to get out of town for a while. Things are getting a bit too hot for him and he decides to book to L.A. There he can expand his LSD business while letting things blow over in San Francisco.

We follow. We need a place to woodshed, to go hide out for a couple of months and get ourselves together. Not to mention write some new songs, get a new set together.

Owsley rents a big pink house on the outskirts of Watts and moves us all in there. It's in the upper-middle-class area of Watts, originally a white area into which some wealthy black families have begun to move.

There isn't a stick of furniture in the house. Not a chair, not a table, not a lamp. Just the bare bulb in the ceiling. Instead of couches we sit on packing blankets. For beds we have foam mattresses with some army blankets, Indian covers, and a bunch of pillows. And that is it. No plates, either, and very basic cutlery. No spoons. Just a bunch of sharp steak knives and some forks. Spoons aren't needed. There is nothing in the refrigerator that you need a spoon for. Our diet is strictly regulated by Doctor Stanley.

Owsley runs everything. Where we sleep, what we eat. "Listen!" is the way he starts his sentences.

"The way you gotta eat now that I'm sponsoring you is as follows: We are going to eat nothing but *red meat*. And eggs. And we're going to drink only milk. No vegetables. No fruit. We, as humans, don't need them. We are born to eat meat. We're *car-ni-vores.* It's genetically built into us; what's called for in our race as humankind is to hunt animals and eat them. Steal their eggs and eat them, and drink their milk."

Owsley goes to the best butcher in town and buys huge slabs of meat. Giant filets. You open the icebox and there is a carcass. A great, bloody hunk of meat so huge he has to take out one of the wire shelves to fit it in. It sits in there. It is never taken out. You just cut a slice off and fry it up. It's very tender, cuts like butter. All the remaining shelves and the doors are filled with eggs and huge containers of milk.

We eat standing up in the kitchen. We fry it up — thankfully Owsley hasn't gotten to the *raw* meat stage yet. Take the frying pan over to the tile counter, slice it up, eat it right out of the pan, clean up the pan, and hang it up. We don't even bother with dishes.

Breakfast is steak and eggs, eaten standing there. Lunch, a steak sandwich (we have to sneak the bread). No orange juice. It is prohibited. After a while we come to consider this normal behavior. It isn't until we get back up to San Francisco and have a kitchen table with chairs around it and some easy chairs that we realize how nutty this all is.

Owsley has picked our location very carefully. A nice big house with a black gambling den next door to us. Lots of traffic. Cadillacs pulling up all night long. It distracts attention from what we're doing there. Our neighbors are up all night creeping in and out in their porkpie hats, running card games. In the morning we watch them leave as we're cooking our steaks.

The only bone of contention between us and the card sharps is the noise. We are very loud. The band rehearses during the day, which pisses off the neighbors because they are day sleepers. All those Voice of the Theatre speakers and piles of pre-amps. But since they are up to no good themselves, we maintain an uneasy truce.

The reason we rehearse during the day is that up in the attic Owsley is running a noisy old tabbing machine. It makes a terrible racket — *thump-atta-thump-atta-thump-atta-thump* — churning out barrels of Sunshine. The music covers our sins very nicely.

The LSD is in powder form. It feeds into an old German pill-making machine from drums. It's like a bakery. The dust rises out of the bins and wafts all over the house. Every time the machine punches out another pill, a little poof of purple haze sprays into the air and filters down from the attic, a fine layer of LSD dust settling everywhere. Heavy at the top of the stairs and then getting lighter and lighter as you go down.

I wake up in the morning and feel it gritting against my teeth. My skin is dry and itchy. We are all so high the whole time we are there it is hard to sleep. When we do sleep we sleep fitfully and have bizarre dreams. Awake or asleep, like figures from Dante's *Inferno,* we are perpetually gnashing our teeth. You can never relax under this acid rain, and I get up every morning with terrible backaches, as if I've been tormented on the rack all night. Plus we're getting sloppy about working with the stuff. Owsley gives us rubber gloves, but they're so uncomfortable we rarely use them. Eventually the dust seeps into your skin and you get high as a kite.

Everybody is having a hard time getting to sleep and we're all starving despite the overflowing refrigerator because when you're high on LSD bloody slabs of meat look grotesque. Carcasses!

Our form of parlor games takes place in Owsley's big old attic room with the neon dust flaking off the walls, smoking DMT just to come down.

Garcia puts out his hand and you can see fire streaming off the ends of his fingertips. We all watch the fire roll itself into a ball and fly across the room, smashing into a thousand opalescent fragments. We are insanely in synch from the acid and the DMT. We are beginning to see things happening simultaneously in nanosecond bursts of quanta. We play these psychic games for hours. Nobody moving, just zinging these phantom fusillades back and forth. Seven or eight of us sitting silently in the attic and then someone says: "Did you feel that ping?"

One day a week we are allowed a rest from red meat. On Friday nights we go to Kanter's delicatessen on Fairfax where we can order anything we want. The vegetable-of-the-week club. Asparagus! Cauliflower! Peas! But as far as Owsley is concerned, meat is still the food of record. He glowers at us if we order vegetables. A salad he takes as a personal affront.

But we aren't at Kanter's for the food. We are there to make money, to earn our keep, to sell our goods at the Casbah. Kanter's is a music-biz watering hole. It's a hangout for Captain Beefheart and Zappa's crowd and all of the crazies, open until four in the morning. The parking lot is a supermarket for drugs, an outdoor souk under the lamps. Everything under the sun, but no cops. It's a Jewish neighborhood and there's no crime to speak of. The cops have better things to do. Up on Sunset or down on Santa Monica Boulevard is where they cruise.

One of our jobs while we're down here is to meet people and let them know we have LSD. *Owsley* acid, babe. Brand-name LSD. Everybody hustles. Jerry, Bobby, Phil, Billy. Everybody. We meet people inside and walk them out to the parking lot. This is cash for per diems, rent, food, gas.

It isn't even that dangerous. We never feel any of that "jiggers, the cops!" vibe. If the cops come through, we just lean on the hood and kick the stuff under the car and look as if we're just standing there smoking a cigarette and talking. When we get home Owsley sits down and counts up all the money he's made.

We hand out samples, especially to guys in bands. Musicians are excellent at getting the word out. Soon we have a crowd around our car whenever we arrive.

"You the guys with the Owsley Sunshine? That was some wild shit, man!" Nobody can get enough of it. Emissaries begin arriving from Hollywood *illuminati*.

"Is this a good batch, man? We only want the dynamite stuff. It's for *Jim*."

"What I'm giving you is our *special stash*. Owsley makes this stuff himself. Only fifty hits a week. It's just for the inner circle, understand? There's just not enough of it to go around."

Well, we *are* salesmen, aren't we? And anyway, if Jim thinks this is the primo stuff, he's going to have a better trip, now isn't he? In L.A. you don't have to ask who Jim is. Lord Jim, the Lizard King. Wrote some of his best stuff on Owsley Sunshine.

Jerry loves this scam, but Phil isn't happy about it.

"What is this 'special reserve' shit?" Phil asks. "Everybody is asking me for the select batch. What am I supposed to tell them?"

"Just separate out a dozen hits, stash 'em in some tinfoil, and put 'em in your jacket. Everybody wants to be an insider. It's all in the head, anyway, man."

⊚

As the weather gets warmer, we spend more time hanging on the porch smoking doobies and laughing and talking. We are there long enough for seeds to start sprouting in the garden in front of the house.

One day we look down and there's a pot plant growing right there next to the front steps.

We begin taking the instruments out on the front porch and practicing. Unplugged, but still it can get pretty rowdy. Our neighbors on the other side of the street file a complaint and two cops show up. They knock on the door and I open it just a crack. The place reeks of pot, but cops don't really know what pot is yet. Soon they'll have little kits and seminars and smell-ins. Anyway, what with all the cigarette smoke and patchouli oil and joss sticks and burnt steak, even a hardened customs dog would find it hard to tell what it is.

"What can we do you for, officer?"

I'm standing in the entranceway. On one side there is Jerry looking that crazy way he can look and on the other side is an even scarier-looking Pigpen. And right behind us is this great big TV set. Owsley has set up a video camera above the door. When the cops come up to the door we step to the side so they can get a good look at themselves on the TV monitor. One of the cops puts his cap on, sees himself doing it on the monitor, and says:

"Oh, is that me?"

"That's you," I say, deadpan.

"Smile," says Jerry. "You're on candid camera!"

"I am?" They're a little slow, these guys. Still, this is L.A. and in L.A. even the police are in show business.

"But we are being filmed, right?"

"You sure are."

You can see that little flicker of doubt dart across their faces as they start worrying about procedural stuff. Maybe we're going to use this tape in some way. Maybe they're going to do something stupid and end up getting in trouble for it. They back off.

"We're just here to deliver a complaint, ma'am/sir."

"There was a complaint, officer?"

"About the noise, so keep it down!"

"Please."

"We sure will, officer."

L.A. is good for us. We do our bonding thing down there, take a lot of acid, and come up with glimmers of what ends up on the first album.

The band works up a few old songs and scouts around for new material. The revamping consists mainly of speeded-up tempos — a chronic Garcia habit, but it does have the advantage of catapulting a band that started out as folkies into new, danceable rhythms.

The mix is basically blues, R&B uptempoed folk and jug-band songs with a few current chart hits and Dylan numbers. Let's see . . . there's "Deep Elum Blues," an old Ida Mae Mack cowboy jug-band song that Jerry Lee Lewis rockabillied up; there's a new Pigpen favorite, Junior Parker's 1957 blues shuffle, "Next Time You See Me," that later became a hit for Elvis; there's a lost-in-the-mists-of-time, sexual-innuendo blues, "I Know You Rider," with it's great old drifter's complaint: "I'd rather drink muddy water, sleep in a hollow log, than stay down here in West Los Angeles [you know, supply name of town you're in], be treated like a dog." There's even a hybrid jug-band blues, "Viola Lee Blues," a classic prison blues written by Noah Lewis and recorded by Gus Cannon's Jug Stompers (the band Lewis played in). Jerry got it off an early sixties Jim Kweskin Jug Band LP, *See Reverse Side for Title.* But the band play "Viola Lee" like crazy and make it their own.

There's an old Blue Ridge Mountain white blues, "Cold Rain and Snow," played at a giddy pace. Equally uptempo is "Beat It on Down the Line," a recent blues by the ancient blues singer Jesse Fuller (born 1896!) who lives out in Oakland. Dude with a wry sense of humor — he also wrote "The Monkey and the Engineer."

Their choices are not that remarkable. Folk groups have long been enamored of the good-timey sound of jug-band music — groups like the Lovin' Spoonful have already amplified it — and blues is the very fuel of sixties rock. The interesting thing is the deformations the Dead's style of playing together has on these forms. Their approach (much too strong a word for what actually happens here) is different from most other groups in that they are navigating these genres in search of a hybrid of folk and rock that is not, however, folk-rock. Jerry's genius at this point is in finding a way to incorporate his past into the new configuration of the band by applying a psychedelic rock momentum to jug-band music and country blues.

Eventually they come up with a few sketches for new songs and one more or less finished song, Jerry's "Cream Puff War," a Brit-invasion-style rocker complete with worked-out three-part harmonies

(Phil and Bobby chiming with Jerry), swirling organ and screaming blues lead guitar. It reflects the sort of thing we're hearing on the radio, Manfred Mann, Stevie Winwood, the Yardbirds. Jerry and Pig love Brit-invasion blues groups. The words are a schizy blend of lover's song, psychedelic blues, and retort to radical bluster.

"Cream Puff War" is Jerry's song but almost everything the band does at this point is a group effort, everybody jamming, with Garcia supplying most of the words. Plenty of false starts and unfinished numbers. They go through Pigpen's material and weed out the chestnuts. Hone it down and develop new material that can be spread out among the other band members.

They'd written a song a year earlier, "Otis on a Shakedown Cruise," a $2\frac{1}{2}$-minute rock 'n' roller that was the B side of their first independently released single (as the Warlocks). There's a quarry of ideas buried there, I just know it! Something amazing's got to come of all the movies playing in these guys' heads. Pigpen thinks he is Howlin' Wolf live at the Sugar Shack. Jerry's pickin' banjo with the Flints and the McCords up in High Lonesome, Arkansas. Kreutzmann's Gene Krupa, Weir's Marty Robbins in El Paso, and when Phil Lesh looks in the mirror he sees Karlheinz Stockhausen.

With this mosaic they are going to come up with some crazy collage of American folk music. Freaked folk music. All those spooky ballads and crazy Appalachian songs that had got all the mojo smoothed out of them from being played at too many hootenannies — the Dead are going to put the rumples, wrinkles, and knots back in them.

When they begin writing songs, everybody comes to the process with their own sound, but only Jerry knows enough alternatives to be able to maneuver. Pigpen is too in love with the blues to consider changing them. The blues are Pig's Koran. Phil is too new to his instrument and Weir is still essentially playing acoustic guitar on a Guild solid body.

Jerry started out playing acoustic, too, but he has a much wider grasp of American folk music, of gospel, bluegrass, and country music. He has a very eclectic range. He's delved into obscure stuff and has more sources to pull from. His musical range is broad enough to allow him to be flexible when trying to put words to music. It was inevitable, once they started writing songs, that Jerry would take over the musical direction of the band. By default, of course. Default and digression being the principal *modus operandi* of the band.

Jerry can really tinker. Play a riff from his repertoire and see if it fits. He also has a vast hoard of chords to draw on. Playing configurations out of chord books is his principal offstage activity. Once Jerry finds a groove close enough to the drift of the lyrics he goes back again and tries to make them fit. Sands them down until they run smoothly with the melody.

Along with songwriting comes an inevitable shift in the band. Jerry in spite of himself becomes the leader. Not that this causes any great friction. The Dead have always been a band without a leader and without a plan. Jerry does everything humanly possible to live down this role, but come what may he is sooner or later thrust into that position. And he is a natural born leader. He grew up with it. His dad was the leader of a big jazz band who knew what it took to hold anywhere from ten to fifteen pieces together. And when the Grateful Dead turn into the Hippie Buffalo Bill Show, Jerry is the obvious focal point. He's the innovator. The symbol. There are no ice-cream flavors named after Phil Lesh.

The Grateful Dead manner of writing songs is a very haphazard, hit-or-miss business. Nothing is nailed down. First they try their songs out in front of an audience. For most groups the song gets written and arranged, then it comes out on record and gets played on the radio. Only then does the band go out on the road and back up the record, basically lip-synching their own songs. The Dead, however, like to go out onstage and play a totally new song — something that they've just written or are still writing — long before it ever appears on an album.

Their sets are four-hour exercises in "let's just see what happens." Never have a play list, never write it down. The only exception being a fifteen-minute New Year's Eve–type deal, or half-time at a football game, or Hugh Hefner's penthouse. There they do the standard thing, then mess up the rest of the time!

From the very beginning, Grateful Dead songs are constantly changing. There is no such thing as a finished Dead song. It will always be different. You never know what's going to pop up at a Dead concert, or what form it will take. The freedom to fuck up is something we took to heart from all those Acid Tests. Bobby Weir will often forget a new song in front of, oh, fifteen thousand people. The crowd loves it. What is that? It's a new song. And the Dead don't make announcements. They don't say, "This is from our new album, it's called 'New Potato Caboose.'" If they can't remember it, they just stumble through it, make a mistake, and get back to the groove. If they start out tentative because someone in the band can't remember the changes, then it just becomes a hiccup of a song and they slide into something else.

It takes sometimes two or three years of performing a song before it gets a personality. It's only through playing these tunes to a live audience that you'd ever get such a radical transformation of a song like "Good Lovin'," which began life as a funky Detroit boogaloo and then after years of playing it and leaning on it, turned into a reggae, Island hip-hop number.

At the same time the Dead are writing songs, we're organizing our own gigs in order to get out in front of people at least once every two weeks. But L.A. is so spread out, our little gigs are difficult to promote. We scout around, rent the hall on Monday, make up a poster, print up fliers, and put them up all over town. We go up to the Hollywood Bowl and hand out fliers. Staple them to phone poles, hand them out at high schools. At night we walk along Sunset and give them away and tell people to come. Danny Rifkin, a friend from San Francisco State, comes down to help organize booking the halls. We generally rent these fraternal order halls — Elks, Odd Fellows, Esteemed Order of Lithuanian Lensgrinders. We have no promotion budget — radio or even newspaper advertising is out of the question. Owsley is spending every penny on equipment so there's nothing left. This will become an endemic problem with the Grateful Dead. I can never get a budget out of them for anything like taking out an ad in *Billboard*. It all goes to RCA tubes and amplifiers, new computer stuff, and new guitars. It's still that way.

We cart the equipment around in a truck belonging to Laird Grant, the original roadie. He and Tim Sculley, our engineer, move the stuff on a couple of pieces of ceremonial plywood. And that's it! Owsley sits back there turning the dials like Baron Frankenstein.

The first gig only about 450 people come, but it gets better fast as word about us spreads. The fact that you can score LSD at the shows doesn't hurt. They become mini–psychedelic events. In the meantime Kesey's people are down organizing their Acid Tests and we play at a couple of those.

Love and the Doors are the two biggest draws in L.A. They rule the roost, totally. We are this upstart acid-taking bead-wearing, hippie band from San Francisco trying to do shows on their turf. But it is really no contest. They're working the Whiskey a Go-Go and La La Land and all the places up on the Strip. We're renting union halls and trying to advertise it all ourselves.

To most people who see us in L.A. in those early days we are just this crazy, raggedy band. The best the emcee can do is: "Direct from *San Francisco!*" We are not known personalities. We are just part of that crazy hippie thing up the coast. But nobody can ever accuse members of the Dead of not having confidence in their illustrious future.

Me and Bobby Weir go out one night to catch a show. We borrow Daddy's car and drive up to Sunset Strip to see the Paul Butterfield Group with Mike Bloomfield and Elvin Bishop. They've just come out with the *East Meets West* album and they are *cookin'*. I am seriously impressed.

We are sitting at the bar, both pretty high. Bobby turns to me — almost defiantly — and says:

"You think *those* guys are good?"

"Hell yeah, Bobby. They're hot. *Smokin',* man!"

And with the deadpan delivery of the hopelessly deluded, Bobby says, "Yeah? Well, we're gonna be more famous than those guys."

Here's this spaced-out kid who's overdosed on LSD. Long, long hair. Looks sixteen, running around on a phony I.D. A few drinks and he's pontificating.

"Sure, Bobby," I say, "that's why they're there and we're here."

After the show we go backstage and I introduce Bobby to Elvin Bishop.

"Not bad, not bad," Bobby says earnestly as if grading a paper.

Bishop laughs. "Heard a lot about you guys. Are you any damn good? I'll have to catch your set one of these nights. Where you playing?"

I tell him, "The Trouper's Hall, Friday night."

"Gotta stay out of those gymnasiums, man. They're too rackety. Kills the sound."

As we leave Bobby whispers in my ear, "I'm better than that guy." Wrong, but a great fucking attitude.

☺

The acid is so strong and we have taken so much that we now have to do super doses to get high. Still it's in *micrograms*. Minuscule amounts. Virtually undetectable. There is no way to this day that you can test a person for LSD. You can't even *see* 100 micrograms. It's pinhead stuff. They don't do that on the side of the road yet. Scanning the cerebral cortex. Let me tap your spinal column, sir, and we'll rush the sample up to the hospital and see if you're allowed to drive or not.

The persistence of the acid in our systems begins to cause weird warps in our little group. We go through periods where everybody is intensely afraid — all the time. Pure, heart-clutching fear. When you're that high, fear can take eerie shapes and provoke strange reactions. One person starts looking fearful and soon *everybody* looks fearful. The fear becomes contagious.

We have some interesting acid trips in L.A. The whole band, Owsley, the girls — everybody drops. We go up into the ravines around the Griffith Observatory. For a bunch of Northern California boys to be out in that desert scrubland in the summer is very spacey. The water barely trickling through the aqueducts, the otherworldly cactus. It's like being on Mars.

One day we are tripping up in a canyon and we find ourselves under some power lines. We begin to feel an insistent throbbing in our temples.

"It's the power lines, man. Obviously. We're picking up the radiation from the lines and it's pulsing at a different rate to our brain frequencies and it's, uh, you know. . . ." That's Lesh's theory, and it is so indisputable we at once become aware of the energy streaming down from the wires. We can actually *see* it. Virulent, oscillating lines of force, beaming right at us. Death rays!

But, wait a minute, there's something wrong here. It's just too obvious an explanation. Too rational. Old Nobodaddy Newton's Euclidean racket. And nobody knows this better than our resident professor of Quasi Cognitive Cosmology. Space *curves,* man, don't forget that.

"The power lines," as Owsley points out, setting us on the right track, "are just a *symptom.*"

"But of what, O maestro?" Jerry asks, knowing full well what such a question will elicit. We are about to hear another of Doctor Owsley's galactic Just So stories.

"It's because . . . we live in a universe that is going through immense changes. . . ."

"No shit!" says Phil. "If you're going to demolish my theory, you'd better come up with something better than that."

"Listen! Our solar system and all the surrounding galaxies are undergoing stress on a grand scale while the universe itself has to pass through the eye of a needle. That squeeze you feel is *real,* but it's not from power lines. We're in the intergalactic grip of the Cosmic Squeeze!"

This, mind you, is not some *ad hoc* theory, spun out during a trip. The scary thing is that this has actually been thought out.

Okay, so it isn't the power lines, but it's *something.* Something galactic and . . . *imminent.* Right now the solar wind is blowing, our hands are turning cerulean blue and an aureole of orange mist is forming around the dome of the observatory.

We are in an alien presence, we can feel it. It's the force field of a spacecraft, drawing us in, extracting our thoughts. Good luck!

"Fuck, you know I saw a flying saucer this morning," Phil's girlfriend says, as if reading our minds.

"Come on, Rosie. Quit messin' around."

"Yeah, hovering over Griffith Observatory."

We spend the whole afternoon on the lookout for alien spacecraft. We have now convinced ourselves that they have landed in our vicinity. Our combined energy has called them in. Definitely. They have come to see *us.*

At one point we're all sitting, huddled under a scraggly tree trying to get out of the sun and suddenly here comes Rosie running down the hill screaming hysterically.

"They're here!"

"It's about time," says Jerry. "Are they holding?"

"They're on that ridge up there and — God, it's so *horrible.* . . ."

"What, Rosie?" Phil asks, hugging her. "What is it?"

She bursts into tears. "They look just like our parents."

Warily we scramble up to the top of the hill and peer over. There they are — a bemused middle-aged couple walking their dog. He in madras bermudas and baseball cap, she in a print dress and cardigan sweater. A flawless snapshot of normality, yet to us it is a tableau of pure horror. We scan one another's faces for signs of alien life, transfixed with that roiling mixture of revulsion, curiosity, and terror with which Cortez and the Aztecs must have regarded each other. We have seen the aliens and they is us!

5

710 Ashbury

ONE MORNING AT the beginning of April '66 we throw the *I Ching.* We get "Crossing the Great Water," the gist of which is: "Time to get outta town, boys." What can we do, the hexagram has spoken! Admittedly, there are also more mundane considerations. . . . The visit from those two cops is still hanging in the air. They've seen strange and unaccountable things; it's only a matter of time before they come around again. And then there's the little matter of Captain Alfred W. Trembly, intrepid LAPD narcotics chief, who has discovered that Owsley recently bought five hundred grams of lysergic acid from the Cyclo Chemical Corporation in L.A. Enough — in the cops' typically inflated calculations — to make some ten million hits of LSD. LSD isn't even illegal yet, but once those statistics hit the press all hell breaks loose. Things are hotting up in Tinseltown; better hit the road before an incensed citizenry arrives outside our house with flaming torches and a hank of rope.

We load the instruments and the tabbing machine in Laird's van, leave everything else behind, and head back up to San Francisco. There, we plan to continue this experiment in communal living. For one thing, it's crucial to my blueprint for the Dead. Didn't the Beatles all live together in Hamburg? Didn't Keith, Mick, and Brian share a grungy flat together in Edith Grove? If it knit those pimply lads into rock's premier blitzkrieg units, think what it can do for a band that is already fused into the group mind through ritual ingestion of massive quantities of LSD.

Shortly before we left for L.A. I had found the ideal place for us and proceeded to move in there myself. 710 Ashbury is one of those high-ceilinged, crumbling old Victorian mansions the Haight is full of. Once homes to railroad magnates and robber barons, now crash pads for the hippie *Anschluss.* Big bay windows, billowing like sails into the street, and a stoop worthy of Henry James: gingerbreaded porch, stained glass in the entry, a front door the Bank of England would be proud of.

At this point 710 is a boardinghouse managed by Danny Rifkin. Shortly after I move in, Danny and I embark on an ill-fated LSD-making venture which almost immediately, uh, crumbles. But one good thing does come of this sugar cube madness. In the middle of our doomed enterprise, I have a revelation that this is the *place,* the cosmogonic point of origin from which the band will launch itself.

"Doesn't this place have Grateful Dead written all over it?" I ask Rifkin, who rolls his eyes in a there-he-goes-again way.

"We just move everybody in here, and then we can easily —"

"Hey now, wait a fucking minute, ol' buddy, before you embark on a grand unified theory of the universe. In case you didn't notice, there are seven other people living here. What about them?"

"What *about* them?" I say with the ruthlessness of the true visionary.

I can see he is a nonbeliever so I deputize him co-manager of the Grateful Dead, adding the obligatory tag: "Insofar as the little fuckers *can* be managed." In return, Danny makes me co-manager of 710 Ashbury. Titles are flying! We give the lodgers thirty days' notice, but the endemic inertia of the Haight weighs heavily against us. I know we are in for the long haul.

By the time we get back from L.A. only four boarders have been persuaded to leave. The remaining stragglers — the unreasonable three — will not be budged. There's the chemically deranged poet who will later jump off the Golden Gate Bridge (high on Valium and so loose he survives), the recluse whom no one ever sees, and, most bizarre of all, the normal person who gets up every morning and goes to work. How unreasonable! Moreover, she is demanding a rational explanation of why she should move out to make room for a bunch of shiftless, dope-smoking beatniks. She seems to have no clue about the overarching cosmic plan and the part the Grateful Dead will play in it.

Desperate measures are needed. We install Pigpen as our beach-head. Pig moves into the back room right behind the kitchen. He uses it as his living room, the lair of the beast. It is not a pretty sight. Early in the morning he's there frying up terrible stuff, and late at night he's *still* there, playing his harp and howling the blues. To come down first thing in the morning and be greeted by the sight of Pig in his godaw-ful bathrobe surrounded by greasy dishes, cigarette butts and crum-pled beer cans must be a bit daunting, at least we hope so.

The battle is a long one, but Pig manages to push everyone out except the recluse. The "kitchen campaign" doesn't work on the recluse for the simple reason that the guy never leaves his room. So Pig starts blaring his raunchy old blues records day in, day out. Mag-num force Chicago blues. And finally one day, with Howlin' Wolf rattling the windows and Little Willie John shuddering the steam pipes, the last remaining holdout wobbles down the steps and is gone. But not till around August.

In the meantime, I am scouting out other possibilities, somewhere outside the city where we can rehearse undisturbed: Big Sur, New Mexico, and, closer to home, Marin County just across the bridge from San Francisco. We need a place where we can all live together until 710 is free of boarders.

Out near Novato in northern Marin County, I find Rancho Olompali. A Spanish colonial ranch built on the site of an old Indian village. Perfect! Olompali is where the one and only war of the Bear Flag Republic was fought, a little Indian uprising that lasted about four days and was put down by the cavalry. Later on, a wealthy Span-iard had built a huge stucco house around the old Indian adobe, and put in a swimming pool and a big bunkhouse for the ranch hands, which looks perfect for a set of apartments. By the time I get back from a trip to New Mexico, the band and girlfriends, Rifkin, and the Dead extended family have already moved in.

⊚

My first day at Olompali is instant immersion in the communal lunacy. In New Mexico you drive seventy-five miles just to do your laundry, you're lucky if you see two people all day, and suddenly *this!*

Sue Swanson and Connie, the original teenybopper Deadheads, are lying on the grass screaming at the top of their lungs at invisible aircraft flying inches above their heads. These girls are only about fifteen years old and they've taken acid every day for a year. Their favorite thing to do is to go out to the San Francisco airport and lie down at the end of the runway and let the planes fly over them.

Half the people lolling on the lawn in front of the big house are naked and everybody is stoned or tripping. They're watching the afternoon show — Neal Cassady dancing in circles all over the lawn, juggling his hammer, talking that talk and making no sense at all. With his short hair, khaki pants, and Boy Scout belt he is such a bizarre sight that it's only natural Gus, my friend from Taos, gets the wrong impression: "Fucking hell, Rock, I think they dosed the neighbor!"

It's dusk and people start drifting into the house. The day is turning strange. Odd scenes start appearing. Up in Weir's room there's a woman sitting transfixed on the floor, holding her newborn baby who is beet red and whimpering. Whatever it is she's going through, she's too spaced out to deal with it and we're too stoned to help.

Outside, people are yelling. We run downstairs. A kid has fallen in the pool and almost drowned. Someone gives him CPR and he's all right but it's a terrifying few minutes.

Back in the house I peek in the living room. Jerry is sitting on the floor with his back to the door moving his fingers very slowly over the old adobe wall. The house had been built around the original Indian adobe and in the new walls there is a glass door that you can open up and see the foundations of the house. You can put your hand in and feel the original adobe walls and that's what Jerry is doing (*veeery* slowly). Total immersion.

I hear Owsley's voice. He's up in the big round room with the fireplace. It looks toward the pool. You can see all the way to the East Bay from this room. Owsley's expounding. It's twilight, people drift in from outside, sit on the floor, and roll joints.

After an hour or so — and Owsley still droning on — people start leaving and there's just the core group left. Out of the blue Weir begins sobbing uncontrollably, I don't know why. *He* doesn't know why. He's just touched in some way. He's just a kid, barely eighteen. I am finding it hard to be there. All this interior mental stuff. I go outside again and walk up the hill and play with Lady, the family dog. Her big sparkling eyes.

Down below I see Jerry sitting cross-legged in the same position as he had been in his room, but now facing the old oak tree that stands between the big house and the dormitories.

I met the Dead on acid, and on acid I made an immediate connection with Garcia. Jerry was always great on acid. Very mellow, profound, funny. I'd never seen him freaked behind acid at an Acid Test or anywhere else, but today he is agitated. At first I think he's just more loaded than he has ever been — which may be true — but it is also the place.

It is a wonderful old tree that the Tamal Indians had obviously cooked in. It is hollow. There are remnants of adobe bricks in there and a kiln. The tree had died and they had built a clay oven inside it. Baked their bread in it. And the smoke filtered up through the hollowed-out branches.

All the color has gone out of Jerry's face, his eyes are fearful and anxious. He looks like a ghost himself. People are wondering what's with Jerry, going over to him and saying "Uh, hello? Everything okay in there, man?" But he isn't answering. He just sits there in front of the tree, mesmerized.

Eventually a terrified Jerry comes inside and, without speaking to any of us, proceeds to crawl under the dining room table. Not the best place to hide, especially from ghosts! We talk him into coming out and after a while he tells us the story. Seems that down in that lower living room, the room where he spends most of his time playing guitar, he made contact with . . . a Tamal Indian medicine man. And this Shaman was accusing him of ancient outrages perpetrated by the Spaniards against his tribe.

"You, Garcia, descendant of conquistadors, murderer of my brothers, usurper of our sacred land! Yes, you. Our blood is on your hands, our bones will rise up and pursue you to the ends of the earth. There is nowhere you can hide from us, no one who will give you sanctuary for the crimes committed by your forefathers!"

The adobe was the longhouse of the Tamal Indians, and circled around it were the tepees and lean-tos of the tribe. There are Indian artifacts all around us. The place is saturated with their vibes, and LSD does make one extremely, um, *porous*. So at some point Garcia must have gotten a whiff of these Native American ghosts. And when it's no longer that easy to distinguish yourself from the chair you're sitting on, *everything* becomes animated. The living and the dead mingle, and it's hard to tell which is which.

◎

Summer of 1966 is when the sixties start rolling. Up until now it was all Pop, but suddenly up and down the coast it is one big endless party. Something is happening, something is growing out there. There are people living in tepees up in Shasta and down in Big Sur. The Psychedelic Rangers, the first hybrid pot growers in California, have a commune down in Carmel and all these little high school girls like Tangerine and Girl Freiberg and Martha Wax are dropping out of high school and running away to move down there and hang with them. They hold big harvest parties with congas and bongos and red mountain wine and all-night pot-smoking and dancing around bonfires after the first rains. The seeds of things to come, dress rehearsal for the Summer of Love. The *un*dressed rehearsal.

Even we had no idea people were gonna get that loose. None of us had been in this situation before. The sun's hot, there's a swimming pool, there's trees to cover us, and everybody's high on mescaline and grass and LSD. There are tepees pitched on the hill, tribal drums are beating through the woods, live music playing on the lawn . . . and greased watermelons in the pool!

At Olompali all our gear is set up on a flat stage on the grass in front of the big house and anybody can play at any time. Big Brother and the Charlatans and the Grateful Dead and the Quicksilver Messenger Service are all hanging out and playing together. Totally disorganized because everybody is so high, wandering off and tripping. Phil Lesh and Bill Kreutzmann are riding horseback up into the hills, Bobby Weir's hooking up with the peyote ceremony that's going on in the back of the property (which is huge, it backs onto state land). People get lost for days. Whoever is around plays. David Freiberg gets up and plays with Garcia, Janis Joplin sashays up and sings with Pigpen.

And soon news of these parties and the scene around San Francisco reaches the ears of the Europeans, whose heads are always close to the ground for the sound of anything new and outrageous coming out of the U.S.A. So they start getting on planes and trains and coming to see what it is all about. These guys have an almost anthropological interest in us! They count on the U.S.A. for periodic eruptions of uncouth and bizarre behavior, unthinkable acts and savage teen rites. Unremitting surrealism is what we're renowned for over there.

We hear that a crew from the BBC is coming to visit us. "We'd like to film one of your psychedelic parties. We've heard they're quite wild," the man says. "Do you think we might be lucky enough to catch one?" Sure thing, squire, I'll just round up some local savages and get them into war paint. The BBC's idea of a hippie party is outlandish dress, a bit of weirdness, a talk with the Grateful Dead or Big Brother, and what's it all about, Alfie?

They are greeted by a bunch of Hell's Angels insolently lounging at the entrance. The Angels are watching the gate and, given their peculiarly inverted sense of decorum, they don't like the cut of these guys' jibs. The guys from the BBC talk funny, and they're wearing funny-looking clothes. They're clearly full-blown squares of the first rank, a species closely related to lawyers and bankers. Foolishly they pull out their credentials, but the Angels aren't interested in any stinking badges. They make them get out of their clean little Hertz rent-a-van and walk the quarter mile or so in the blazing sun, carting all their shit.

When they get down to the house they're already twisted and twitchy, huddled down in the driveway in their Carnaby Street outfits — bell-bottoms, desert boots and dueling shirts — sweating and exasperated. They're taking in the local color, hippies dressed like light-opera pirates and hussars, pantomime outlaws and cowboys and Indians and galoots — jolly nice! — but wherever they point their cameras there are a few extras who aren't quite fitting in. Like the stark-naked hippie chicks. Everywhere they turn there are people in the nude jumping in the swimming pool, naked couples making love on the grass and kissing in the trees. Kissing the *trees,* actually.

The BBC crew makes a strategic retreat to the house. They've stopped shooting. They're signaling to me with comical urgency.

"You know, Mr. Scully, this really won't do," they intone in their best colonial manner. I'm fucking with them, saying, "What is it, exactly, that won't do?"

"Well . . . there's all these, uh . . . naked people. They don't have halter tops and some of them aren't even wearing bathing suits! You're going to have to tell everybody to put their clothes on, that's all there is to it."

I tell them, okay, I'll make an announcement.

"I don't know if any of you have noticed but the British Broadcasting Company is here," I say over the PA system. "They're here to make a documentary about us but they have one request. They want you all to put your clothes back on."

"Screw the BBC!"

"Fuck the documentary!"

"Did he say to put our clothes *on?*"

"Nah man, you must be high or something!"

The BBC throw up their hands.

"But they're *hippies,*" I explain. "Isn't this what you guys came to see?"

"Yes, of course, but perhaps we could make a compromise, Mr. Scully. What if the girls put on panties and halter tops. Do you think we could accomplish that?"

"I doubt it."

"Look here, I've got an idea. What if all the people without clothes on just got in the pool?"

"Now *that* we might be able to do."

Soon most of the offending pubes and boobs are underwater, but they still want this one to stand over here and that one to stand over there.

"Look, I don't want to be rude but this isn't a Navaho reservation and I'm not staging a rain dance for a package tour. They're hippies, they do what the hell they want. If you don't mind, I've got to get on with my day! I'm trying to get the band set up."

At this they perk right up.

"Oh really? There's going to be music?"

Well, of course. It's not *just* fornication. But as soon as the first strums out of Garcia's guitar come through the amplifiers, all the naked people get out of the pool and go over to the stage. There goes the shot!

This is clearly a case for a token adult. Perhaps our dauntless criminal attorney, Brian Rohan. "Let me get my lawyer," I tell them. I find Rohan, who is almost naked himself at this point. He's down to his shorts and he's ready to take them off at a moment's notice because he's a very horny Irishman (friend of Kesey's and all that) and he's been to all the Acid Tests and so on.

"Maybe you ought to put on a shirt or something, Brian, and go talk to the BBC."

"Talk to the BBC? Ooooooo, man!" His eyes light up. You can see the dollar signs click into place the way they do when some demented money-making scheme comes to Scrooge McDuck. He's into the action, the commissions, the *German rights* for chrissakes! He is also high as a frigging kite.

"Rock . . . remind me, Rock, of . . . what to . . ."

"They're about to pack up their equipment and walk away. Brian, see if you can convince them to do the shoot and just keep the tits out of the frame, if that's what they're worried about."

But I see at once as I peer into his dilated pupils that this is something too bizarre for him to comprehend.

"What?! Get rid of the *tits*? Get *rid* of the tits? Why would they want to do that?"

◎

On the weekends we go into town and play. The Grateful Dead are still very much a dance band. They are young and bouncy and playing basic pumping R&B numbers, along with some of the new tunes from L.A. And there are plenty of places to play. The Fillmore and Avalon ballrooms have been in full swing since the last Trips Festival in January. Bill Graham and Chet Helms have essentially taken over the Acid Test/Trips Festival concept and institutionalized it. Every Friday and Saturday night they've got a mini Trips Festival going on. Weekend dance parties with a bunch of different groups booked — a name band from out of town along with a bunch of local bands on the bill. We play for Chet one weekend and for Bill the next. The weekend dance concerts have everything the Acid Tests had: light shows, strobes, face painting.

A typical set might include "Viola Lee Blues," "Stealin'," "I Know You Rider," "Sittin' on Top of the World," "Big Boss Man," "Don't Ease Me In," "Next Time You See Me," and "It Hurts Me Too." Mostly traditional and blues and folk songs with an occasional contemporary hit like "In the Midnight Hour," or an original like "Cream Puff War."

Over the summer of 1966 the Haight, like some nursery of alien pods, grows and grows. Every day new people arrive to await the coming of the Age of Aquarius: peace, love, music, drugs, and obscure publications. To some extent the news is spread by word of mouth, but what really stokes the Haight is FM radio. Our parents watch TV, everybody else listens to top forty AM. FM radio is the kids' channel. FM comes in around '65 and by the spring of '66 it is going full swing. We are growing up (sort of) and the music is getting better all the time. Radio is no longer churning out musical wallpaper. FM is out there in the far reaches of the night beaming all these great sounds.

Without FM we wouldn't have heard the Yardbirds, Them, the Stones, Dylan, Stax-Volt, Buddy Guy and Junior Wells, along with the crypto stoned commentary. The Dead are a second-generation sixties band — they do covers of Stones covers — and this is their lifeline. We stay up late to tune in.

Without FM, there wouldn't be an audience large enough to sustain the Dead. Radio is our tribal drum, it's how we find out what is happening. Overnight, radio can spread the word over several hundred square miles. People pile into VW buses and head down the road to the latest tribal gathering.

The other source of news is Ralph J. Gleason. Everybody reads his columns in the *Chronicle* about upcoming events or some festival he's attended. Every day the *Chronicle* goes out all over Northern California, from Monterey to the Oregon border.

In July our first single comes out on a small local label, Scorpio Records: "Don't Ease Me In" with "Stealin'" on the B side, both recorded in John Estribow's attic. Estribow was a friend of the band who had a small label with almost zero distribution. Traditional blues songs that pre-date our L.A. sojourn. We do quite a few demos in '66 (the above plus "Otis on a Shakedown Cruise," an original rocker, and the old country traditional, "Silver Threads and Golden Needles"). We owe these demos to Dan Healy, a friend of ours who is a technology wizard and has done amazing things for Quicksilver.

Healy works at a place called Commercial Recorders, in a turn-of-the-century firehouse on Natoma Street. The studio is closed at night but Healy sneaks the band in to make tapes. In the beginning I assume Healy is managing the place and what a nice guy he is for not charging us. For a while even Healy thinks he is getting away with it, but it turns out that the owner knows about us all the time. He'd come in at nine o'clock in the morning and couldn't see across the room for the cigarette smoke. The place was still humming. But the owner — Lloyd Pratt, a jazz bass player — never said a word to us, not once, bless his heart.

It is at Commercial that the Dead make demos of many of the songs that will appear on our first album, *The Grateful Dead*. A few arrangements of traditional tunes, two or three of our own songs, and that's pretty much it. All the folky tunes left over from the Mother McCree's jug-band era are now replaced.

Dan Healy also has the midnight-to-six shift at KMPX, and often plays the single and the demos. KMPX does not have a very strong signal at the time — the police band probably has more listeners — but this is the onset of our music being played in the middle of the night.

Suddenly antennae begin twitching in glass and steel skyscrapers in L.A. Corporate dogs are sent out to sniff around. Talent scouts in sharkskin suits, getting on planes and showing up at the ballrooms. All of the major record labels virtually overnight establish branch offices in San Francisco. And we begin to attract serious attention from the L.A. pack. Tom Donahue — later *the* counterculture deejay at KMPX — talks Warner Brothers into checking us out. Tom is a successful Bay area promoter who put on the last Beatle concert in San Francisco at Candlestick Park in '64. He has his own label, Autumn Records, and manages a Beatle clone group, the Beau Brummels. Garcia has done session work for Autumn Records (including Bobby Freeman's single "Do You Wanna Dance?") so Tom already knows him. Tom is still very much part of the straight music scene, but this is all about to change . . . we've recently dosed him!

The band is eager to take the next step — an album! — and so we hustle up more demos. Coast Recording, on Bush Street, is a big, boomy place, a former church at which Bing Crosby once recorded. There we do a bunch of demos including "Early Morning Rain" (with Phil singing lead), "Silver Threads and Golden Needles," and a take of "Otis on a Shakedown Cruise."

Our sessions at Coast come to an abrupt end when the studio manager walks in one day and sees an American flag draped over Pig's organ. This is around the time when the Stars and Stripes ceases to be merely a flag and becomes both the sacred insignia of the right and the fashion statement of the left. He has an absolute fit, screaming, "Go back where you came from, you hippie scum!"

Tom Donahue is making trips down to Warner Brothers himself on behalf of Autumn Records, and mentions us to them. We are a little wary of getting involved with a major label, but over the next few months we warm up to the idea. Then Warner starts sending people to come and hear us.

Early summer of '66 some executives from Burbank make several trips to San Francisco to see us play. They are as straight as TV. After-shave and ties and jackets. It's like dealing with aliens. They all have the same uniform, the spooky Southern California leisure wear that is affected by most of the industry at the time: V-neck velour sweaters with high collars (and golf slacks, bright yellow and orange and black). Very slick, cheery, ultra-tanned faces, and all topped off with the *de rigueur* Jay Sebring haircut, a type of razor cut so immaculate it looks sprayed into place. These record execs look like golfers without the spikes on their shoes. The spikes are in their teeth! Out for us! Out for blood!

You can put your finger on them anywhere. Up in the balcony at the Avalon you certainly can't miss them. They are basically indistin-guishable from your average narc. They regard the scene unfold-ing below them with a mixture of horror and fascination. They've never seen anything like it. Tripping and crazy dancing, everybody high, openly smoking pot. They have anxious, *fearful* faces. They've been briefed through little interoffice memos. BE AWARE AT ALL TIMES WHILE ATTENDING CONCERTS. UNSCRUPU-LOUS PERSONS MAY ATTEMPT TO SPIKE YOUR DRINKS WITH MIND-ALTERING SUBSTANCES. DO NOT, UNDER ANY CONDITION, DRINK OUT OF AN OPENED CAN OF ANYTHING.

These guys are highly skeptical of the whole thing. Tom Donahue can talk their talk, but — once having introduced us — even *he* is having a hard time convincing these guys that what they're witnessing isn't just a temporary aberration. He's telling them "Outside of the Airplane, they're the biggest draw in the Haight. They're the band of the hour." At least they like that band-of-the-hour stuff (they can use it at board meetings).

Tom is foisting newspaper clippings on them, news service reports. There it is in black and white: polls, radio stats, box-office receipts, stuff they can understand. "Take my word for it, these guys are not going to go away," he is saying. And by now the number-crunchers up at Warner Brothers already know the demographics: the exploding

FM radio scene, the bell-bottom sales . . . and paisley's up 300 percent since the last quarter.

They hear it, but they can't quite grasp it. We don't look or sound like anything they've ever seen (or *want* to see). They are confused. Rockabilly, novelty, folk-rock, bubblegum, Hispanic Beatle groups, no problem. The British invasion was no exception to this formula. After all, Brit managers like Andrew Oldham and Kit Lambert are Denmark Street hustlers who had modeled themselves on the American formula.

But it seems that the Lord of Forms has decreed that a precedent must exist for everything that can possibly rear its pimply little head. For as long as anyone can remember — since Elvis at least — no act has shown up that doesn't in one way or another fit into the scheme. The second law states that you can only be successful in the music business by dealing with the record company supergiants who, long ago, have worked all this out. Say you are Sonny and Cher and you have a hit. It is the record company that arranges everything: does the publicity, sets up the appearances at the radio stations, books what shows you'll be on. You get a fifteen-minute set and then off — followed by other acts sponsored by the label, everybody using the same backup band. It is all geared to make money for the promoters and the record companies and very little for the musicians. We have no intention of fitting into any of these molds.

◎

Midsummer, we leave Olompali and move to Camp Lagunitas near Fairfax in West Marin. There've been too many people coming out on the weekends to use our swimming pool! We need a place we can all hide out together.

Lagunitas is an old summer camp with a little red main house, cookhouse, bunkhouse, and showers. Perfect for us. There is a whole wall lined with *bunk beds.* At night we walk with the ghosts of all those past campers. We are like giants in kiddieland. Pigpen lives in a one-room cabin that sits on stilts right behind the cookhouse, Rifkin lives underneath the cookhouse in a cave with parsley growing outside, and the rest of us live in the main house. We behave just like campers. We all eat together in the cookhouse and sleep in the bunkhouse. In the pool all day, a little bit of rehearsal at night. On nights we have gigs, we head for San Francisco and play the old Fillmore or the Avalon, trading off each weekend with Quicksilver or Big Brother. The competition is great for us. We go home thinking, God, we've never played so good.

Janis Joplin and Big Brother are living up the hill, and Janis comes down through the woods and sings with Pigpen on the upright in the cookhouse. They drink Southern Comfort and play "Walk Right In" through the night air.

Quicksilver lives nearby in Olema. We have this crazy rivalry going with Quicksilver. So one day we all get dressed up like Indians, Garcia too, and *raid* their house. Just a friendly game of cowboys and Indians. The first raid we make on their house we get a big surprise because their guitarist, John Cipollina, keeps a pet wolf. Wolves are very possessive about their turf and they *will* attack. They also like to wander off and kill sheep. In sheep herding country like this, that wolf caused a lot of trouble.

The raids go on back and forth all summer, and on one of our forays we get into Quicksilver's kitchen and take their pot. This is war! To get even they decide to get us during our encore at the Fillmore. Their plan is to come onstage with all their antique guns, tie up everybody in the group, corral them in the middle of the stage, take their instruments and play the old Hank Williams song "Kaw-liga."

There they are out in front of the Fillmore waiting for us to do our encore so they can put their plan into action when some old lady sees all these guns coming out of the trunk of David Freiberg's car and guys carrying rifles running down the alley and up the back stairs of the Fillmore. She thinks they're terrorists and calls the police. The police swoop down, there is a big melee in front of the Fillmore, and they all get arrested, which is not all that funny for David Freiberg, Quicksilver's guitar player, who has a prior from the Lovin' Spoonful pot bust a year earlier.

From the time we start talking to Warner Brothers until we finally sign takes about eight months. Joe Smith, the president of Warner Records, comes to see us himself — with bodyguards! Outside of the Jefferson Airplane we are the only Haight-Ashbury band being offered a contract by a major record company. But compared to the Dead, the Airplane are a commercial rock 'n' roll band (a category we don't exactly fit into). It's terra incognita. We are blazing a trail for those still to come! Commander Cody and the Lost Planet Airmen, Quicksilver, Big Brother and the Holding Company, Country Joe and the Fish.

It soon becomes apparent that no one has ever before questioned the system. Royalty rates since time immemorial have been carved in solid vinyl. The big boys are horrified by our demands.

"What? You wish to alter the sacred scrolls?"

Hell yeah, we wish to alter the world! They eventually give in, probably out of sheer fatigue. The key issue is artistic control. The labels don't want to hear about it. We get Stanley Mouse and Alton Kelley, two San Francisco poster artists, to do the cover. The big boys never allow anyone to do that. Plus we own the publishing, which the boys have never before given up, plus the mechanicals of the album. Revolutionary stuff for Burbank.

Even our lawyer, Brian Rohan, is telling us there is no way you are going to get this. This is their bread and butter. They don't give this stuff away, ever. We'll see. . . .

What the San Francisco bands achieve, they do by hanging together. In the end we raise the royalty rates for musicians probably ten points in those years. It eventually goes from 5 percent to 15 percent, and some go to 18 and up. Publishing for groups used to be twelve cents a side, and basically you had to have six songs to get the twelve cents. The Dead, however, are doing seven-minute songs, eighteen-minute songs, one whole side of the album. Nurse!

The standard song length in those days was three minutes. Most groups made three-minute songs so that there would be twelve songs on an album and the band would get royalties for each of those cuts. But what if you have only two tracks on the whole album? Or, in the case of Quicksilver Messenger Service, *one* track on the whole album? Side One of their first album consisted of one long, extended jam on Bo Diddley's "Who Do You Love." In order to get the royalties due they had to make up arbitrary divisions: Who Do You Love, and then, of course, Who *Did* You Love, Why Do You Love, When Do You Love, How Do You Love, *Should* You Love? (They get publishing for the phony divisions, as does Bo Diddley.) The most valuable information on how to deal with this quandary comes from jazz musicians like Thelonius Monk, Dizzy Gillespie, Charlie Mingus — because tracks on jazz records are traditionally much longer. So I go to see the jazz wizards and I ask them: "How do you do it? You guys are putting seven- to twelve-minute tracks on an album — how do you get paid behind that?" And they say, "Hey, brother, get hip to our trip. You rock 'n' rollers get paid by the cut. We get paid by the *minute.*"

☺

Okay, now that we have an album it is time to take our first official group photograph. The whole-group-leaping-in-the-air Beatlemania pose is out, and the chiaroscuro portraits of the Rolling Stones wouldn't work for us either. Bob Seidemann, a photographer from New York who lives in the Haight, comes up with a great idea for a picture. He wants to go out to the suburbs and shoot it in one of the new developments.

We drive out to Daly City. All you see for miles and miles are streets winding up in endless crescent moon terraces past row on row of ticky-tacky houses. Fifties and sixties pastel-colored tract houses marching up the hill in neat little rows. The whole place looks deserted, like houses built to test the impact of a bomb. There is no traffic whatsoever. Everybody has a garage, so you don't even see any *cars* on the street.

The band members in cowboy hats, headbands, Levi's and Beatle boots are posed ominously in a semicircle in the middle of the street like five gunslingers at high noon. Stark, sinisterly illuminated faces against dark clothing. In front of each of them is a hippie kneeling on the asphalt holding up a mirror to catch the sun rising in the east. The mirrors reflect a small eerie circle of light on the band's faces. It's straight out of a Roger Corman "aliens invade the suburbs" drive-in movie.

It is about ten o'clock in the morning when we get there. The husbands have gone to work, the housewives are watching soap operas and talking on the phone when . . . hey, what *was* that? Faces start appearing at windows. Crabbed, angry, confused faces in shower caps and rollers. Pointing.

"Officer, there is something very peculiar going on in the middle of our little street. Please get out here quick, *and bring all the firepower you can get!*"

At first, the police figure it's just some housewife on the wrong medication, but after a dozen very agitated tract-dwellers have called in about hairy degenerates doing it in the road, the cops are finally forced to check it out. They get out of their squad cars hoisting up their pants with that serioso cop look, prepared for the worst. When they see what it is — a photo shoot — they start laughing. As we begin to pack up we hear one officers explain that it is nothing to get upset about. Just a publicity shoot for *Star Trek,* ma'am.

By fall of 1966 we're back from Lagunitas and nearly the whole band has moved into 710. It is at this moment — take note, ye Deadbase scribes! — that the First Great Psychedelic Age begins. Not the Broadway Age of Aquarius with show tunes, but the Merry Prankster, rock 'n' roll, Haight-Ashbury version. If there ever is a Haight-Ashbury theme park — and I'm betting there will be — it'll have 710 as its epicenter. Deadland! It will always be 1967, the streets filled with Hell's Angels, hippie chicks, patchouli, communes, and antiwar demonstrations. Everywhere, like little Latin Santa Clauses, there'll be Jerry Garcia impersonators in black T-shirts and motorcycle boots, smoking joints and dispensing Cheech and Chong–like koans. And outside the gates of Deadland, the evil empire of the UnDead: the uncool, unhip, unhigh ones of the straight world.

At 710 we have the whole house to ourselves, but everybody is still piled on top of everybody else. There isn't a nook, cranny, or ratty armchair that someone hasn't claimed for a bed. The front room downstairs is an office during the day and a bedroom at night. Weir sleeps there in the bay window, stretched out in an easy chair. Bob Matthews, who is also helping with our sound, is in the other one. These chairs don't recline so you have to stretch out stiff as a dead gunslinger to get any sleep. Rifkin is still in 710A in the basement, someone is crashing in the bay window upstairs, Pigpen's room is right behind the kitchen. Garcia's is the room at the top of the stairs, mine is the closet next to it. Up in the attic is Neal Cassady. He has a hammock slung from the rafters and a couple of planks laid down so you can walk without falling between the floor joists. Plus there's the various people just crashing here and there. There'd be Sue Swanson and Connie sleeping on the floor and Gary Jackson, one of the early high-tech guitar guys, under the kitchen table.

"Uh, they're fumigating my house, man, okay if I just crash?" You wake up in the morning never knowing what is going to happen. Some freak shoving a bottle of water in your face more often than not dosed with LSD, and away you go, with no way to claim your day.

Even with the whole house finally to ourselves we can't fit everybody into 710 Ashbury, so Lesh and Kreutzmann live in another house up the street. And we have no sooner settled in than we are on the verge of losing the place. Because in the early days, before they begin to hassle us about dope, it is the sanitary conditions they nail us for. The tidy police are on their way and the place is a disaster area. The kitchen is a shambles. The freezer's been so permanently ice-bound that the latch that closes it no longer works. The old restaurant stove is so encased with grease and grime it looks like a rusty Balkan freighter in dry dock. The bathroom is a Sargasso Sea of moldy towels and dirty clothes, the bedroom's strewn with empty Spaghetti-O cans, wine bottles, and stale donuts. Old carpets and crumbling plaster, glass everywhere from broken windows (when someone forgot their key), and the ceiling is caving in from the attic. Nothing in the place has been upgraded for a hundred years. It still has working gas jets. It is so far off code finding infractions will be easy. We are sitting ducks.

I am yelling at Garcia and Pigpen to get the place cleaned up before the Health Department gets here. I'm pleading with them, cajoling them, threatening them with total doom (like our parents would). "If we get busted we're gonna lose the house, and if we lose the house we won't have any place to live and then . . ." Out of the corner of my eye I see Jerry, leaning on the bannister, eyeing me intently. It isn't that he has any intention of *doing* anything, he's just spellbound by my jeremiad. He's got an idea.

"Say, maaan," says Jerry, "why don't we just tell them the truth?"

"Which is?"

"We're time-traveling gunslingers from the planet Zircon and our transporter beam ran out of, you know, aludium fozdex, so we're *stuck* here. . . ."

Meanwhile out on the porch my girlfriend Tangerine is trying to tell the Health Department guys that the reason the place is such a mess is because we're, uh, renovating.

"And officer, have you ever had your kitchen redone? Well then, you know how it just takes forever to get the house back in order. . . ." She is practically in tears, caught without her house clean in front of such important people. Sheepishly they back down the stairs, mumbling apologies.

It's hard on women at 710 Ashbury and one after another they leave. At first Tangerine, bless her heart, tries to make 710 into a real home, cooking meals, putting flowers on the table. A heroic endeavor, but hopeless. Trying to cook beef Stroganoff for twelve guys who would be just as happy with ice cream straight from the container. Or *parmesan cheese* straight from the container, for that matter. Nobody's helping her with the dishes or the laundry or doing any cleaning whatsoever. She gets everything straightened up, then sometime after noon Pigpen comes down and makes his breakfast and there goes the kitchen.

And all this is compounded by spontaneous DMT-inspired re-configurations of the furniture. There's something about coming down on DMT that makes you want to arrange the view for the next hit. Entire afternoons are spent taking every stick of furniture in the room and piling it up against one wall in an effort to find a satisfactory geometric pattern, then take another hit, fall back on a pile of pillows, and critique our design, making little adjustments along the way.

The setting can be critical with DMT. Eric Jacobson from Buddah Records flips out badly one day at the Charlatans' house simply because of the way the place is *decorated*. Come to think of it, it does seem like a truly horrible place to freak out in. Filled with fun-house gewgaws, grotesque Victoriana, Mickey Mouse alarm clocks, and other demented trivia. It's heavily draped, like a big tent — that Victorian swamp look favored in the Haight. Jacobson thinks he's dying. Thinks he's died and gone to hell! First the stuffed owl is threatening him, then he is humiliated by a Shirley Temple figurine. We try to reassure him that although he *is* a scheming, no-good mother, we would never stoop to anything so diabolical as to enlist the *furnishings*.

Our threads mainly come from the Goodwill. But as we get a bit of a reputation, the boutique owners start laying stuff on us. Like Peggy Casserta, who also wrote the irreproachably trashy memoir *Going Down with Janis*. Which begins with the immortal words: "I was stark naked, stoned out of my mind on heroin and the girl lying between my legs giving me head was Janis Joplin." Peggy's store, Mnsidika, is our principal source of sharp clothing, and we in turn are her walking display. The more expensive stuff like leather jackets are on loan. For a week at a time they grace the backs of the Grateful Dead and then they go back in the window. The Dead have never been considered clothes horses even by their most ardent fans, but Weir is definitely into this trip and Lesh too, for that matter.

Bobby Bols has the shoe store next to Mnsidika and he lets us have shoes at cost plus 10 percent. Beatle boots with Italian heels and a little zipper on the side are the things to have. They have soles like glass, so slippery you could slide and slip from our front steps to the corner of Waller — it is all downhill — and then with a skip launch yourself over to the next block and all the way to Haight Street. Six or eight skips past Page and you're in the Panhandle.

☺

It's a struggle making the rent and paying the bills, but we're surviving (and nobody has a day job). We do the occasional oddball function like the North Face Ski Shop with Hell's Angels as the doormen, but most of our gigs are still at the Fillmore or the Avalon.

The room where Weir and Matthews sleep is also our office. They wake up to me on the phone booking gigs. Anyone who happens to be around joins in the decisions but, let's face it, they aren't all that difficult to make. We take almost any gig we're offered. With the money we're getting — three hundred to four hundred a night if we're lucky — we can't go much out of the Bay area. Out-of-town gigs are few and far between. Rifkin and I have worked out a good cop/bad cop routine for dealing with promoters. I soften them up and then Danny nails them.

A key gig is the long-planned Acid Test Graduation Ceremony. Kesey has been in Mexico much of the year, a fugitive from the FBI and the San Francisco police after faking his suicide. He obviously isn't going to be able to attend any kind of Acid Test in the flesh. The moment he walks onstage there are going to be a dozen guys in shiny black shoes and white socks just waiting to nab him. Still, it is a tempting scenario for a Prankster: to tweak their noses in plain view of a thousand freaks high on acid. How to pull it off? Kesey gets this wild idea. He will be there and he will *not* be there. A sort of lysergic transubstantiation. The perfect McLuhanesque fake-out. And where better to pull off his Houdini hoax than at San Francisco State College — Acid U. itself! Plans are laid. Word goes out, handbills get passed, posters go up. It's going to be the social event of the season!

Now he makes plans to get back into the States. A typical over-the-top Ken Kesey movie. Drunk cowboy singer (Jim Englund Jr., out of Las Vegas) has been boozing it up in Mexico all night, gets rolled outside the cantina (hence no I.D.) and comes across the border early in the morning. Kesey rents a horse, douses himself with gin, ingesting quite a bit of it along the way, and comes weaving across the Brownsville bridge, playing his souvenir guitar and singing old Gene Autry songs. Dressed up as foolish as a dude rancher — cowboy hat, buckskin jacket, shiny red dude boots — and stinking of booze. The customs guys don't even ask him to get off his horse, they just wave him on through. He is obviously American, and you don't need a driver's license to ride horseback. He just rolls off on the other side, gives a kid a few bucks to take the horse back, gets on a Greyhound to Salt Lake City, and then flies into San Francisco airport right under the noses of the carabinieri.

Meanwhile, we begin setting up the Trips Festival in the Commons at San Francisco State. A big cavernous cafeteria. We take all the tables and pile them up, fold the chairs and stack them in a corner, put up big screens, hang banners, and build a mini-tower in the middle of the floor. An industrial-strength Acid Test.

Everyone jamming, hammering, cabling, constant soldering going on. We get a bunch of big square boxes and pile them up and put TVs on top of them. Live cameras placed around the room. There's one on the band and one showing people dancing and another one right at the door so you can see who's coming in. Strobes, liquid lights, plus there are the slides playing all over the walls. The Dead set up in the corner right on the inside of the big glass doors as you walk in. No stage, we just set up on the floor.

Even the narcs have dressed up for the occasion in their Ironsides-goes-to-the-hippie-club outfits. But where's the Cat in the Hat? The instructions are: Bring a portable radio with you. You can't get in without one. The emcee then tells everybody to tune into KSFS, the San Francisco State station, and when you tune in — there's Kesey! He's broadcasting from some unknown location — only a couple of buildings away — but it's as if he's in the room. The Shadow knows! He is calling the shots like your favorite zonked-out sports broadcaster, walking around the Olympics and doing a running commentary on all the events. "If you'll just proceed to stage right you'll find Mr. Neal Cassady juggling his world-renowned hammer. . . . If you are wondering what all that equipment is in the center of the floor, so am I. The TVs were donated by Owsley Stanley."

Everything is going along magically. We finish our first set and are all hanging out backstage when I see Pigpen acting very strangely indeed. He moves jerkily across the room, dragging his feet along like a seaweed-encrusted crab, his face a mask of pure terror.

"*Qu'est-ce que c'est,* mon Pig?"

"Rock, I can't walk."

"Pig, my good man, you *are* walking." Albeit at sporadic intervals. "Get a grip, sir!"

"Fuck me, man, I no longer have legs, you know, in the usual sense of the word."

"Listen, Pig, I had a dog once had the same thing and y'know what it turned out to be? Eating too many nachos." I'm saying anything, whatever comes into my mind, trying to figure out what's going on, when I notice his face is all flushed and rosy and his eyes are huge. Big brown eyes — all pupil — that have expanded all the way out to the edges.

"I think the man's been dosed," Laird whispers to me. No kidding. That open can of beer that's always standing on top of Pig's Vox organ must have been too much of a temptation for someone. Just strolled by and added a wee bit of liquid acid to the beer, that's all. No harm meant! Pig makes it through the first set okay, but during the break he begins to fall apart. Pig's never taken acid before! Terrified of the stuff, actually. Won't even smoke grass, so he is absolutely freaked. Now he is convinced that something is desperately wrong with him; he thinks he needs medical attention. Amputation maybe.

He's telling me his legs are *loose,* about to fall off, but meanwhile he's standing there in front of me steady as can be.

He puts his arm on my shoulder and we walk out to the parking lot. I help him into Laird's truck and we drive back to 710 Ashbury. I keep talking to him.

But once in front of 710 he's perplexed as ever.

"Where are we?" he asks, pale as a ghost, "and who are *you?*"

"Pigpen, my friend, this is 710 Ashbury, famed in song and story and ancient lore. Don't you recognize the ancestral castle?"

He doesn't, and what's more he's very hesitant about those steps. Even to me they are beginning to look a little . . . sacrificial. Like the steps up to the Temple of the Jaguar.

"Where is everybody? And what the hell's that thing slithering down the wall?"

"Everybody is out at San Francisco State. Remember? The gig?"
And what *was* that thing, anyway?

In the kitchen he snaps to, realizes he's home. Momentarily. I start
turning on lights, which comes as a major revelation to him.

"*Damn* that's wicked stuff! How'd you do that?"

This must be what electricity would look like to someone from
the Stone Age. Industrial magic! I turn on the radio hanging in the
kitchen, and there's Kesey's voice coming over the speaker. From
the look on Pig's face I realize a disembodied Kesey coming through
the airwaves isn't helping. I put on an Otis Redding album and help
Pigpen into the bedroom and get him to lie down, put his legs up.
He's still pampering those pesky legs of his that won't work.

I leave Otis on and go and find his girlfriend's phone number.
Veronica is a big black nurse you'd think could handle anything, but
when I tell her that Pigpen has been dosed she becomes very alarmed.
Pigpen is a very predictable guy when straight, but Pig on acid is a
daunting image. What could he not turn into?

I put Pig on the phone but he's making no sense whatsoever.

"That boy talkin' nothin' but trash, Rock. What the hell you fellahs
up to over there anyhow?"

I am high myself and I have to do some fast talking to get her to
come over. She's still dubious.

"He's not gonna die on me or something?"

"Veronica, *please!* He walked out of San Francisco State, he walked
up the stairs at 710. I do not see any need for medical attention" (*not*
the kind of attention the band is looking for just now).

As soon as Veronica shows up he calms down. By the time I leave
they're fucking, so I know he's going to be all right.

I have to get back to San Francisco State. I have Laird's equipment
truck, which the band needs to bring the equipment home in. I get
out there in time for the last song, "Alice D. Millionaire," based on
that wonderful headline in the *San Francisco Chronicle* when Owsley
got busted the first time. The headline read: "LSD Millionaire Arrested."

Owsley is in his element, dancing to a song *about* him by *his* band,
and everyone tripping on *his* acid. There's Mountain Girl right up
front, boogying her ass off. She's an R. Crumb hippie-chick vision,
swinging her bright orange bleached hair, her baby girl, Sunshine, her
kid with Kesey, bouncing in the basket on her back and just *beaming* at

Jerry. She'd been with Kesey but she saw Jerry play and she just fell hard!

(๑)

For a while there is a concerted effort to share the housekeeping chores at 710. Tangerine has a plan. On Saturday mornings I'll wake everyone up early and try to get them to clean the house. It's a good idea, but it'll never work. Everybody has a story.

"Any other day, man. I'd love to help out but . . ."

"C'mon, Rock, it's *Saturday!*"

But it's more than endemic shirking. 710 Ashbury has become the Haight's unofficial community center and Saturday is a heavy visiting day. By ten o'clock there are a dozen freaks hanging out on the steps. Just the nature of the neighborhood (which is fiercely social) works against any sort of order ever being maintained. Nonstop visiting goes on from eight in the morning until four the next morning. By the time twenty or thirty hippies have trudged through the front door looking to meet the Dead, the place is demolished. There is no normal home life whatsoever. Tangerine finally issues an ultimatum. "It's either me or them, Rock."

Kesey is getting back together with his wife, Faye. Mountain Girl picks up with Jerry and moves in. The day she shows up is the very day Tangerine is moving out. As soon as Mountain Girl walks in the front door, Tange says, "Oh, another woman. I'm so glad to see another lady around here. I'm going. Good luck!" Mountain Girl is thinking, "Oh, she's so nice. I wonder why she's leaving?" She puts out her hand to shake hands and Tangerine gives her a vacuum cleaner. "Here's the vacuum. Here's the dustpan. I've got to get going."

With Mountain Girl, a new order begins at 710. She's the only girl who could ever hang in here. She's strong willed and smart and very funny. You have to be on your toes around her. She has survived La Honda, the Prankster bus trip across the country, and having been Kesey's old lady. With her arrival, things at 710 straighten up immediately.

She's strong, like a crew boss, and what she says happens. She has a biting, scary wit that can just shrivel you up if you get on her wrong side. If Mountain Girl is angry with you, there is nothing worse — she just won't let up. She is energetic and hefty enough to embarrass us into vacuuming. She was a Prankster and used to everybody taking responsibility. If you see a mess, clean it up, doesn't matter if it's yours or not. The house runs on her rules, and she is big enough to back it up. A very scary lady!

With Mountain Girl, you don't repeat your mistakes. When she's pissed off you can hear her mule skinner's voice down the block. And when you hear it, you thank your lucky stars you are not the object of its wrath.

"What the *fuck* is this?" Oh God, it's that voice. Mama Bear is home and finds Goldilocks sleeping in her bed. No amount of fine foot-work will get Jerry out of this one, but that doesn't mean he's not going to try.

"This is, uh. . . . Hey, do you two guys know each other?"

"Cut the crap, Jerry. What the fuck is this chick doing in my bed?"

Jerry is stalling, trying to sound reasonable. "Mountain Girl, please, just let me explain. What're you going to believe, what you see or, uh, what I'm going to tell you? I mean. . . . You know, it all started . . ." But this is something not even the resourceful Garcia can talk his way out of. Bumbling sweet reasonableness will not save his ass this time. This is *the* unreasonable situation, par excellence.

"What is there to explain, motherfucker? You're a dead man."

6

The Gathering of the Tribes

WE NOTICE, OF COURSE, that the Haight is getting bigger, but nobody realizes just how *much* bigger. The Dead have barely started to tour so we really don't have that much comprehension of just what a potent thing is afoot or how many people are turning on. It's a thrill just thinking about how we can now play Oregon, or maybe Washington! It's the Human Be-In at the Polo Grounds that shows us. On that day the submerged kingdom of Metaluna materializes out of the blue: thirty thousand pot-smoking, headband-wearing acid-heads — an entire medium-sized town composed entirely of freaks! It's the gathering of the tribes, all right. All the cannabis farmers and Martian Incas come out of their paisley caves and into the light.

Let them come! Anybody and everybody, come all without, come all within! All we want to do is play music, but almost immediately there is polarization. Within days there are countless factions, all wanting to impose their version of the new age. The most vociferous of these groups are the politicos.

We have invited the Berkeley rads because we consider them outlaws like ourselves, but we make it a condition of their participating that there be absolutely no rabble-rousing. It is obvious from the get-go that this is a hopeless cause. Rabble-rousing is their very raison d'être. As soon as Jerry Rubin and those guys show up at our planning meetings down at the Psychedelic Shop on Haight Street it is clear they think of the Be-In as nothing more than a huge platform for their own political agenda. And it isn't only the politicos who see the Be-In as a bully pulpit. The neo-mystery religion guys, Leary and

Alpert and Ginsberg — the walking glasses of milk — can't wait to get up there in their nightgowns and deliver their Sermons on the Mount.

We're happy to have them join our parade, but over in Berkeley they're not so sure. They think we're not *serious* enough. To the radical crowd we're nothing but wastrels! Drug-taking, time-wasting, frivolous *entertainers* (that's the worst put-down they can think of). The Grateful Dead, who have fought at the barricades with Kesey, Owsley, Babbs and Cassady, are now considered the mere creators of frothy spectacles. Can't these snotty-nosed students see we're lysergic storm troopers (and serious artists, to boot)?

The Berkeley agit-prop people single us out because by now the Dead have become symbolic of the Haight. For over a year there have been buttons floating around the Haight saying "Good Ole Grateful Dead." That says it all, in a crypto-lysergic way. Which, for Garcia, is the only way *to* say it. He has no truck with the literal agenda of Berkeley's ideologues. The very mention of the B word sets him off.

"Aw, *maaaaan,* not that poo-poo again!" Garcia says with comic exasperation. You can gauge the intensity of his feelings on any particular subject just from the way Garcia twangs the word "man."

"We are now in the first psychedelic era, ma-an. What about LSD and music and love and the goddamn fuckin' new consciousness?"

We're on a roll now. Phil Lesh picks up the baton.

"*We're* the ones who live in a war zone. This is real life, here, in case you didn't notice." No doubt many of us haven't, but who cares — Garcia has got Lesh going now.

"Over in Berkeley all they've got is dorms and cafeterias. It's lame, man, all this getting up on your soapbox and declaiming stuff. Just *do* it!"

"Aaaaawright!" says Jerry. "Amen, brother Phil! And now a word from our sponsors."

Jerry had long ago registered his attitude to radical rhetoric in "Cream Puff War":

> *Your constant battles are getting to be a bore*
> *Go somewhere else and continue your cream puff war*

The rads see themselves as firebrands out to terrorize the military-industrial complex but — get it straight! — it's we who are the real outlaws and renegades. The Haight has social activists with strategies far more inventive (and witty) than the Berkeley crowd. Moreover, they're actually doing something. Peter Berg and the Mime Troupe guys, Peter Coyote, Emmett Grogan and the Diggers. The Diggers are the Haight's own revolutionary group, radical psychedelic activists. They run the Free Store (where everything is given away) and scrounge free food for the hippie hordes. They want to replace the money economy. Their slogan: "Free means free."

And with acid, dialectics just *melt*. It's the First Ten Seconds, you're this polymorphously perverse single-celled *thing* humming with the mad intentionality of DNA. Can't they see we're getting involved at the *molecular* level?

And who organizes the Be-In? Not the student body over in Berkeley. They couldn't organize a beer run. It's the so-called feckless hippies who actually pull it together, get the permits and sound trucks. By now we have the whole parks thing *down*. When we first started to apply for permits the Parks Department would take one look at us and say "Out!"

"But what about democracy and the free rights of citizens and stuff?"

"Out!"

So we get smart and instead we send kids like Terry Lane from the White Panthers down there.

"Please, sir, our high school fraternity band wants to have a meeting in the park."

"Sure thing, son, this is what the parks of our great land are for." They pat them on the head and hand them a permit on the spot.

One of the more farcical encounters connected with the Be-In involves the Musicians Union. Local 6 has forbidden our playing free in the park. This is so absurd it is (almost) funny. They're quoting Gertrude Stein to us: "A gig is a gig is a gig," they say. "If bands play, they must get paid. Or we pull the plug."

We switch to the lysergic defense: "Guys . . . I don't know if you know it or not but something new is happening in the music scene. Musicians are taking drugs and they aren't, uh, thinking like they used to."

"What are you talking about?" they say. "Musicians have been taking drugs since the beginning of time." Ha! Ha! Ha!

"Yeah," we say, "but not *these* kinds of drugs."

"And what kind of drugs would those be?" they naturally want to know.

We offer to demonstrate. We invite two union heavies over to Ron Polte's place on Market Street. Ron is Quicksilver's manager and very involved in communal hijinx. They arrive expectantly about six o'clock, but they have no intention of actually dropping acid. So we take them on an *imaginary* trip. Roll up, roll up, for the magical mystery tour! We keep them there for three hours, actually *talking* them through it.

"The acid is starting to come on, now, can you feel the vibrations?" And right on down to the talking wallpaper and the animated furniture.

"Okay, now you're into the second hour and you're an electron traveling at the speed of light through the moons of Jupiter. . . ."

They're incredulous, but the amazing thing is that they're relating to it at all. Of course, they *are* musicians. They have plenty of experience of altered states. . . . They've been on the road, taking speed, staying awake from town to town. It's not like trying to take your *parents* on an imaginary acid trip. And after three hours of LSD soap opera they do seem to have some glimmering of what we're talking about. They agree to go back to the union boss and tell him that he should consider letting us play free — one time! — in the park.

And that, as it turned out, was the Be-In. Nobody, least of all the musicians union, expected so many people to show up. Everybody high as a kite, bands playing, pills flying through the air. Handfuls! After that, we never had a problem with the Musicians Union. It would have been like trying to turn back the Red Sea.

When the day in question finally dawns, you see the Polish Soccer League playing the Yugoslav Soccer League at one end of the Polo Grounds and down at the other end . . . thirty thousand hippies zonked on acid. Funny thing is, nobody minds.

There is much blowing of conch shells, lighting of incense, altars of feathers, mirrors, fur, bells, and wax. More macrocosmic consecrations, divine invocations, blessings in extinct languages, and mantras to hashish-smoking gods take place that day than have probably graced any secular spot on earth before or since. The ground is fairly *humming* with karma.

And when you get that many people together it has to *mean* something — in the eyes of the media, at least. You can't print "Yesterday

30,000 people gathered in the Polo Field to groove on the vibe." The vibe is too ineffable a quantity to be news, so the stated purpose of the Be-In according to the *San Francisco Chronicle* and even the *Berkeley Barb* and the *Oracle* is the coming together of the radical and hippie factions. It turns out to be a lot more casual than that: stoned people wandering about blowing bubbles and checking out the bands. The politicos are shunted to one corner up on a platform the way they like it, with a crummy PA. Few people pay them any mind. Even the unstoppable Jerry Rubin is speechless, coming from a night in jail. And Leary telling the crowd to "Turn on, tune in, and drop out" is a little like preaching to the choir.

People have come here to groove. They want to hear the music, and there are a lot of great sounds. Besides the Grateful Dead there are Big Brother, the Airplane, Quicksilver, Sir Douglas Quintet, the Loading Zone, the Charlatans, and some members of Country Joe and the Fish. The Dead play three longish numbers: "Morning Dew," "Viola Lee Blues," and "Good Morning Little School Girl" on which the jazz demon Charles Lloyd joins in.

Owsley has donated a bunch of turkeys (white meat!) to use for making sandwiches, along with samples of his new batch of acid in the form of little white pills called White Lightning.

In the middle of the Dead set a parachutist lands at one end of the Polo Field. Not exactly the extraterrestrial craft bearing intergalactic tidings . . . still, on acid a man falling out of the sky is a pretty amazing sight.

The only speaker that goes over at all that afternoon is Allen "Howl" Ginsberg, whose only suggestion — after a chant to the Coming Buddha of Love — is "Let's all breathe together!" It works. At the end of the day Ginsberg, like a mystic Pied Piper, leads the crowd to the western edge of the park and across the highway to the Ocean Beach strand where people build fires or stare ecstatically as the sun sets like a giant ball of fire over the ocean.

710 has become a sort of hippie chamber of commerce for the Haight. People coming in and out of town always pass through with the latest news, and all calls come to that house. There is never a time when there aren't several extra people there for dinner.

Predominant personality traits begin to emerge at 710: Bobby's iron will, Pigpen's paleolithic habits and hipster lullabies, Kreutzmann's fiscal obsessions, Jerry's chronic equivocation. . . .

The Dead are a tribe and — as in a tribal powwow — everything is decided communally. Jerry may be the tribal elder, but he doesn't make the decisions. The most he'll do is back ideas to his liking. Still, it's Jerry's nod that is always needed to get the tribe moving in one direction.

The core being of Garcia is enthusiastic, big-hearted, incredibly outgoing, and, above all, curious. His is an astonishing, insatiable curiosity. He quizzes you about everything under the sun, and listens intently to the answers. His questions come in at an elliptical angle and have to do with some internal clock. Just information that he seems to need and depend on. Not knowing what the master plan is, you just try to answer as best you can.

Weir, on the other hand, has a magpie knowledge of the world. He knows a little about everything, and since he's dyslexic it's not because he's *read* about it. At this point he's still a very loose assemblage, suggestible and so dazed that he appears high even when he isn't. He's a space case, an LSD space case on his way to being a macrobiotic space case! Jerry is his anchor; Weir's always the kid and Jerry's this father figure. Everything he knows about guitar he's learned from Jerry.

At the core of the Dead, like some mangy totemic animal, is Pigpen in his lair. Pig has the TV in his room, but aside from the flickering screen no other light penetrates. I never see the curtains open. For the longest time I thought there was no window. He's got an upright piano in there and God knows what else. It's a strictly no-drug zone, just bottles of Wild Turkey and beer cans. . . .

As ferocious as he looks, Pig is a very tender guy. If someone falls asleep on the couch, it's Pig who covers them with a blanket. He even tells bedtime stories. Pigpen lulling Sue Swanson to sleep by reciting old Lord Buckley routines.

Lesh is a guy who *feels* he has had a European education, but actually has never been out of California. He's read enough and studied enough to have formed some pretty definitive opinions about the world that aren't really convincing! Because everything is based on his California experience. Actually, I don't think *any* of them have been out of California except for Jerry, who shipped out as crew for *one* cruise on the *Duncan Bay*. But he's been *around* people who have been around, plus he's been in the military (which we all find terribly impressive and strange). Pigpen, for instance, has practically never been off the peninsula, except to go over to his dad's radio station in the East Bay. I don't think Weir has even been to San Francisco much. A really rural bunch of guys. Even Bobby is just a suburban kid. Kreutzmann's just intensely curious and ambitious to become a hot musician, intensive at his drumming.

Every band has an internal manager, and before Danny and I came along it was Kreutzmann. He made the deals for the Warlocks, and dealt with club owners though he was under twenty-one. Even after Danny and I come into the picture Billy keeps his hand in on the business end. He always signs the checks, always has his eye on the lookout for what could be. Only later on does Kreutzmann develop a virulent strain of stinginess.

It first raises its head when we sign our record contract. As soon as we get our first advance, Kreutzmann wants a new car, feels he *deserves* a car, demands a new car.

"I sacrificed my station wagon to carry the band and all our gear all over creation. It was my car. My dad gave it to me. We beat the shit out of it. I never saw a penny for it. You guys owe me."

But he doesn't want a replacement Dodge station wagon. What he wants is a bright, brand-new, shiny red '67 Mustang. True, by now we have Laird's pickup truck to carry our equipment, but how is the *band* going to get to gigs? We're all arguing with him.

"C'mon, Billy, be reasonable. You know what the seats are like in the back of a Mustang. Christ, forget about instruments, try carrying people in it! You can't even fit a guitar in there. If we're gonna spend this kind of money, let's get something *practical.*"

But it is critical for Billy's ego to have a shiny sports car. Eventually his obstinacy (combined with general inertia) wins out. It always comes down to Jerry, and Jerry couldn't care less.

"Let him have it," he says. "Let's not get all hung up on this trivia. Let's get on with it. Make our record, get some songs together. So what're we going to put on it?" Jerry is not concerned about wheels.

And then God (and our contract with Warner Brothers) said, Go make a record. So we do.

In January we head down to RCA Studios in Hollywood. It's a

great fifties *faux moderne* building. It has fins! It looks like a '55 Chevy with a porthole in it. Stucco spaceship job.

Inside it is very straight and businesslike. The receptionist sits in a pink-glass booth. Her desk is liver-shaped bird's-eye maple, the thick carpeting is robin's egg blue. Indirect lighting, Muzak, Naugahyde banquettes, *Esquire* magazines liberally strewn about a kidney-shaped coffee table, plastic palms.

Dave Hassinger is the producer Warner Brothers has foisted on us. Putting their own producer on the sessions is the only way Warner Brothers can insure coming in under budget. This is their one loophole, their one condition to acceding to our outrageous demands. The company producer is really a time clock. Dave Hassinger functions in the old studio-genre style. The mad metronome mode of producing records.

"Come on, boys, take one. All right, that song's okay, take two! Next song!" For us this means instant freakout. We go into shock. Hassinger is very alien, very L.A. The archetypal West Coast Promotion Man. But he's worked with the Stones, so we figure we're lucky to have drawn him.

And Warner Brothers is very anxious about these sessions. They think we're going to take too long making the album (I wonder why) and Hassinger is meant to streamline things. It's the tail end of the era when A&R men (Artists & Repertoire) ruled the earth. Traditionally, when you went in to make an album you were turned over to a record company A&R man who "handled" you. Of course with the Grateful Dead there is no way in hell this is going to happen. It is the classic confrontation.

It can't be all that easy for him, either — being thrown in with the Furry Freak Brothers. He's from another planet, entirely. The Planet Clyde, perhaps. Looks like your typical androidal talk-show host circa 1967, Merv Griffin or Mike Douglas. Deep tan, velour pullover with the collar turned up, and a coif so hair-sprayed that it looks carved. Everything's a hustle with Dave.

"What's happenin', baby?" (accompanied by the reverse slap five with the hand stuck out behind his back like a vestigial flipper). He's married, lives out in the Valley, cool wheels, the customized Corvette with the bug bra. Locked in the studio with *that* for five days is like a long weekend in a wilderness cabin with your Uncle Jack.

Producers deal in categories, so right away Hassinger has to pinpoint us somewhere in the great Minoan laundry lists of musical types. *Ting!* Let's go to contestant number four. We're . . . *psych-e-delic!* His closest model for us is the Electric Prunes — whom he's just produced, so he *knows* whereof he speaks.

And "psychedelic" is just what he says — after every take. Now the Dead, despite anything you may have heard, have never been a psychedelic band. They may play while *on* psychedelic drugs, but what they play is not psychedelic music. Well, not usually, anyway. Seriously, Dave, do you hear any sitars on this track? A subtle difference, but you'll get the hang of it. (He never does.)

The Jefferson Airplane are at the studio, too, cutting *Surrealistic Pillow.* They're in Studio B — the big one — and we're in Studio A, looking around in awe and wondering how we got this far.

With a couple of exceptions, all the songs we record in L.A. have been in the Dead repertoire for a while. The songs the band have played longest — "Viola Lee Blues," "Cold Rain and Snow," and "Beat It on Down the Line" — all date from our sojourn in L.A. last spring. The band's frenetic version of the old Blue Ridge Mountain white blues "Cold Rain and Snow" doesn't bear too much resemblance to the folky versions favored by old-timey groups (like Mother McCree's Uptown Jug Champions). "Viola Lee Blues" is the only extended cut on the album (running ten minutes) and the closest thing to the way we play live.

A couple of songs on the album were added last summer: "Good Morning Little School Girl" and "Sittin' on Top of the World." The latter is a traditional blues first recorded in the thirties by the Mississippi Sheiks. But it's not this version or Howlin' Wolf's early sixties version (beloved of Brit-invasion blues bands), but rather Carl "don't-you-step-on-my-blue-suedes" Perkins's uptempo rockabilly version that inspires Garcia to start playing it. "Good Morning Little School Girl" (in the Sonny Boy Williamson version) is another Brit R&B favorite and Pigpen first latched on to it from the Yardbirds' *Crossroads* album. The way Pig sings "School Girl" is positively salacious. Very down and dirty, trying to talk her out of her lunch pail and out of her pants.

Then there's two songs that the band only started playing very recently, Bonnie Dobson's "Morning Dew," a folk lament about nuclear madness, and "New, New Minglewood Blues." Originally recorded by Gus Cannon's Jug Stompers as "Minglewood Blues" in

1928, it was written by the group's harmonica player, Noah Lewis, who revamped it when he went solo, calling it "New Minglewood Blues." Hence the Dead title, "*New,* New Minglewood Blues." Weir sings lead and he's the one who substantially rearranged it (twice actually — again on *Shakedown Street*).

The only original so far (the band members are still tinkering with their collective effort, "The Golden Road (To Unlimited Devotion)") is Jerry's "Cream Puff War," which the band has played only a couple of dozen times since Garcia wrote it at the pink house in L.A. last spring.

At this point in time the state of the art is four-track. We basically record live with the whole band, then bounce that over to another four-track, overdub a couple of instrumental tracks, and put on the vocals. There isn't much room to maneuver. Everything has to be combined, then ping-ponged to another track. Bass and drums on one track, guitars on two different tracks, and a track left open for ping-ponging. We're on the cusp of the Age of Stereo so we end up with two different masters: one in mono and one in stereo. From which you can see this is very early days, and the technology to actually *do* what the Dead can conceive of is always lagging behind. So we do whatever it takes. When the Hammond organ in the studio won't change from high speed to low speed, Bob "the human switch" Matthews sits behind the Leslie speaker flipping a lever at the given moment.

Work begins slowly and then speeds up madly. It happens fast, a four-night, five-day project. We get into town on Saturday afternoon. By Wednesday night we're back on the plane to San Francisco. Everything to do with this album is speeded up like a motherfucker. Fifteen tracks in five days. Three tracks a day on black beauties. You can hear the Dexamyl humming through the album.

One reason for our haste to finish the album is that we get to keep whatever's not spent after we finish. Warner Brothers gives us around $50,000 to do the album and we end up splitting about $20,000 after the sessions. That's one of the reasons we take all that amphetamine: we realize that otherwise there won't be anything left over. We're not going to see any more money from Warner Brothers until we come up with another record. Got to keep it going. We're talking five guys in the band, two managers, an equipment guy, and Owsley. Plus the band has this voracious appetite for gear. Garcia wants a new sound system, doesn't want to deal with these crummy house systems in the theaters anymore. And it's true that if we're going to play bigger places, we need more gear, *and* a more powerful PA, *and* bigger trucks to haul it.

Sleep is further eroded by the company we keep. You can't even catch forty winks at the *motel,* for crissakes! We are staying off Sunset at the Tropicana, where people think nothing of knocking on your door for rolling papers in the middle of the night. And the Airplane have this monster pad in Beverly Hills with an electric gate and a swimming pool. Any time of the day or night there's a nude swimming party going on. The Airplane play us a couple of demos, actually two songs still in a pretty rudimentary state — although they've been playing them for some time — that they think are going to be red-hot singles once they've buffed them up. To wit: "White Rabbit" and "Somebody to Love."

Everybody goes "wow!" of course. But in the long pause that ensues, Garcia says: "Ya know the middle part, there? Well, maybe you . . . nah, forget it!" And suddenly they *know.* There's a piece missing at the heart of the engine, and Jerry knows what it is. They start covering themselves, saying "Was this so-and-so's mix?" And "Yeah, we should have gone with the one with Jorma's solo."

Back in San Francisco we cut one last track for the album, "The Golden Road (To Unlimited Devotion)" at Coast Recorders with Hassinger producing. It's a group effort credited to an invented joint persona — McGannahan Skjellyfetti — thought up by Phil Lesh. "Golden Road" is basically the band getting in a Brit-invasion chunka-chunka-chunka-chunk groove behind Jerry's acoustic guitar with psychedelic lyrics and superblues lead guitar by Jerry. And dig those "hey-hey's!" "Golden Road" and "Cream Puff War" show Jerry has promise as a lyricist, but it's something he just chose not to pursue.

We've only been back at 710 a few days when I get a call from the Airplane. Jorma wants to know if Jerry can, you know, come down and help them out for a few days.

"Maybe Jerry could tweak this mix a bit, Rock, I dunno, there's something . . . something . . ."

"Something in the *middle* part, maybe?" I say, as deadpan as I can manage.

We hop on a flight to L.A. and head straight to the studio where the Airplane are still working on "White Rabbit" and "Somebody to Love." Garcia takes his little Princeton amplifier in there and tinkers with the guitar parts and essentially arranges those two songs, which eventually became Top Forty hits. His contribution is so crucial that the Airplane want to list him as producer on those two tracks. But Rick Jarrand won't permit it. Which is how the Airplane end up listing Jerry Garcia as "spiritual advisor" on the back of *Surrealistic Pillow*. Anyway, the *lurch* that really makes those songs is Jerry's. He actually lays down the rhythm guitar parts, then Jorma and Paul come in later and overdub them. I don't know if they just mixed Jerry way back or erased him altogether. Some future sonic archaeologist will no doubt come along and unearth the Garcia ur-track and make it the cornerstone for some theory of ancient rock.

After we return from L.A., Weir goes on a health kick. He's even — get this! — giving up drugs. You mean even *psy-cha-del-icks?* Yup. Nothing impure will from this day forth disturb the sacred equilibrium of Weir's constitution. Takes a stand and stops doing *everything*. Goes completely clean and macrobiotic . . . totally. Seaweed and rice cakes is all he'll eat.

"My system is now so clean I don't need to use toilet paper," he announces. That kills us. Everybody falls down laughing but he doesn't budge. He's like that, easygoing with people, but not with himself. Sticks to his guns and does it (at least through the end of the sixties).

But not all of us are quite ready to renounce drugs. One morning Owsley's chemists show up at 710. Tim Sculley and Melissa Cargill are the ones who actually make the Owsley acid. Owsley himself is not that great a chemist to begin with, and once he's embarked on his quest for the ultimate sound he wants to simplify his operation — stick with making LSD and leave the day-to-day lab stuff to them. He certainly has no interest in developing new drugs. Tim and Melissa want to push on into the psychedelic future. What if we stopped at LSD, man, and the next one turned out to be the *real* breakthrough.

They want us to guinea-pig a new drug they've just formulated. A new synthetic straight from the lab. One of the alphabet psychedelics: MDA, MDMA, MMDA, the speed-based psychedelics. All these new concoctions get tried out on the Dead first. This time Bill Kreutzmann and I volunteer, along with an old roommate of mine, Eddie.

With any of these new drugs there's always the question about what constitutes a dose. On this particular occasion, we take it and after about forty minutes . . . nothing happens. Then we remember that Tim said we might need to do a little speed, just to potentiate it.

"Let's see what we've got here . . . how about some crystal meth? That should do it, don't you think?"

"Yeah, we'll just do a few lines until it feels right."

And sure enough, after a few *big* lines of nostril-lacerating powdered methedrine, we do feel something coming on. Definitely!

Once the alphabet soup starts hitting us, our foremost urge is to head for the woods primeval. But first we have to get there. We get into Kreutzmann's car, his brand-new shiny red Mustang with the smallest backseat in the world. Eddie is huge, but manages to squeeze himself in. We start driving down Haight Street, but after ten minutes we have only gone two blocks. We are moving very slowly, *disturbingly* slowly. I glance at the speedometer. The needle is barely hitting five miles an hour. It's like being in the clown car at the circus. But even at this speed Billy's knuckles are white on the steering wheel, just trying to keep the willful thing steady as she goes. After a few minutes — hours to us — even he can see it's a hopeless struggle. He pulls over to the curb and we sit in the car under the shade of a huge tree for several centuries trying to figure out what to do next. Shadows of pigeons pass over us. Hieroglyphics of some kind, obviously, but without our rune glossary we're lost. We are mesmerized as the fleeting characters of an inscrutable leaf language scroll by when all of a sudden the tree bursts into flame, showering the car with chunks of burning tar. We leap out of the car and run down the street.

"Christ what was that?"

"Fuck, it's napalm!" Eddie barks.

"We're Americans," Kreutzmann shouts urgently to an invisible marine helicopter. "Am-er-i-cans. . . . For God's sake!"

At a safe distance we look back expecting to see a wreck of smoldering, twisted metal, but there sits the beauteous Mustang with nary a scratch.

"You . . . know . . . man . . . ," Kreutzmann confides to me, each word taking an eternity to emerge (I am listening to a dolphin who has recently been taught to speak phonetic English). "I think we . . . might . . . need a little . . . you know . . . help. . . ."

"No shit, Chester!"

Somehow I manage to get Tangerine on the phone and she agrees to come along as designated straight man. She's going to be the control, someone to tell us what's real and what isn't (but only when absolutely necessary).

We drive up into the mountains — Lake Tahoe — and suddenly the thing starts to come on real, real strong. We have forgotten to tell our friendly neighborhood chemists that we are going to a higher altitude (the higher up the stronger the effect).

We get out among the redwood groves and Eddie starts stripping. The first thing he always does on psychedelics is take all his clothes off. Today I somehow understand that he's had the right idea all along. Clothes are superfluous, absurd trappings. We *all* take our clothes off, stripping away the accumulated dross of five thousand years of civilization.

We are scudding down the evolutionary ladder, each of us assuming the form of our totem animals — creeping, prowling, skulking about the antediluvian glen stark naked. I am lion and with feline satisfaction I regard my animal brethren. Brother leopard Eddie, brother coyote Kreutzmann, sister fox Tangerine. We move stealthily through the brush, alert, listening, trying not to make the slightest sound.

We are tripping around in the woods and just about the time we're getting really into this scenario . . . cars. Whooshing, grinding, alien machine entities. We are still quite close to that damn highway, and each time a car goes by we look at each other as if to say, "What *was* that, man?" Tangerine, I'm afraid, is by now happily sacked out somewhere. So much for reality.

Must get away from man machines, must go up mountain. We keep climbing up, up, up. Eight thousand feet, maybe closer to ten, way up in the Desolation Wilderness. It's a beautiful day, and we come upon a clear stream. We wade into the cool water and get down on all fours and drink. Across the stream about ten feet up is a fallen tree, and Eddie climbs up on it and goes to sleep. I climb up a cliff with an agility that astonishes me.

We haven't seen anybody all day when out of the primeval wilderness we hear voices, *human* voices. Two-legged ones, and they're *singing*.

"Hu-mans coming," I whisper to Kreutzmann. "Might see us. . . . Must hide. . . ."

We stay still as can be. Down the path come four drunken fishermen clanking their poles, wearing vests full of lures, their hats full of pins and flies, drinking beers, laughing and splashing along the creek, singing "The Happy Wanderer." And then, abruptly, the singing stops.

The log is right over the stream and there is Eddie lying on it in the sun, happy as a sandboy and naked as the day he was born. Here is this big black man, stark naked, six foot four, 250 pounds of cold black muscle. They spot Eddie and they freeze.

Eddie rouses himself. Now he sees them. He doesn't know who these people are, he doesn't know whether to eat them or run away. He's a leopard. I watch this unfold with animal curiosity. They start looking around to see if there are any more of us. Now they see me perched up on the cliff. I am naked too. And there is blood pouring down my face. The combination of the altitude and the speed we took to activate the MDA has caused nosebleeds. The humans are rooted to the ground, their mouths gaping open. They get real quiet, clutching their gear to their chests, not saying a word, barely daring to turn their heads. Now they see Kreutzmann down in the creek and he's frozen solid too, like a statue. We are all just standing there like a diorama in the Museum of Natural History. I guess we're actually scary, because they tiptoe away downstream. We feel lucky they didn't *eat* us.

We give them about an hour to get out of there, which I'm sure it doesn't take them. The remainder of the afternoon we spend making our way downstream. The incident with the fishermen is forgotten; nobody has thought it necessary to put any clothes on. Why would we need clothes, we're animals! By late afternoon we're almost down the mountain; we can see the shore. We're breaking quietly through the jungle on our way to the lake. We come to a little river. Eddie smells water and the big cat is ready to get in it. We sniff the air. Hu-mans! But on the other side of the river where we expect to find spear-waving cavemen we see not a Stone Age encampment but — a bird sanctuary. A dozen old gents and dames are peering through binoculars at the rarely glimpsed yellow-tufted *Marmelukus obfuscatus* when they catch an even rarer sight: the buck-naked Eddie. *Rara avis,* indeed! The whole place rises as one being. People are scattering, binoculars dropping from birders' hands like hot potatoes, as they knock over tables and chairs in their panic.

We quickly leave the habitat of the quaking *Homo sapiens* and make our way down to a less-populated part of the lake. As long as the sun is up we frolic in the sand. But night must fall. *Dusk.* The coming of night to the savannah. Things start getting creepy. Spirits are abroad, shadows of our forgotten ancestors foraging for their bowl of blood.

We are, needless to say, fully freaked by this time. Hey, it's been a long day. Several eons, in fact. But no, we are men again. Man wears clothes. Man makes things to buy from other man. Kreutzmann is quite manic normally and right now he is an absolute demon. I can tell by his eyes he is having some difficulty. His face is undergoing critical fluctuations. On an overdose of this magnitude you can't hide anything.

But to hell with Billy's problems. Some immense, leathery-winged *thing* has lurched its fiendish way out of the primeval forest. It has been following us, obviously, tracking us all day and now it has set its sights on *me*. The others seem curiously unaware of their imminent annihilation. How can they not see it? It's huge, it's fiendish, it's *hungry*.

There's not much hope for *me* now, but I must warn them. I am trapped all by myself on a sand spit and the pterodactyl has got me in its sights. I haven't got time to explain it to anybody, it's all happening too fast.

"Billy, Eddie, Tange, run! There's a . . . a . . . pterodactyl tearing up the beach!" My mind is shouting, but my lips aren't moving.

In my panic I plunge into the lake, which up here in Northern California is freezing. It is an instant bring-down. All of a sudden I am standing in the surf shivering in my wet clothes (the pterodactyl has split). We build a fire and it alters our mood entirely. You can always see a thousand things in a fire, but when you're this high it becomes a roiling volcano spewing ghosts and demons.

Just getting into the car we go through major changes. Major adjustments every few seconds. Geological timespans frozen in a series of historical tableaux. *Click* Pleistocene . . . *click* Stone Age . . . *click* Industrial Revolution . . . We have just emerged from the prehistory and suddenly — cars! Metallic presences anthropomorphizing into sullen grillwork mouths, accusing headlight eyeballs. What does it want from me? You want me to get *inside* this thing? A feeling of stifling claustrophobia. Trying to look out the window, bumping my face against it, forgetting there's glass there. Golden Gate Bridge. Traffic. Faces flashing by. Tangerine trying to reassure Kreutzmann that his new car is not going to get wrecked.

Back at 710 we put on dry clothes. We begin to think we're normal again. Thank God *that's* over! We decide to go to the movies. Wrong. We get out in front of the movie theater and all of a sudden the trip comes on again, full blast. Lights exploding, pouring all over the car like molten lava. Ensor faces, melting wax marquee. We can't get out of the car.

"We are not going in there."

"All right, guys," Tange says brightly, and drives us back to 710 Ashbury. I lie awake all night with my eyes wide open hallucinating, pullulating, completely ragged and wondering when this is going to end.

"Dear God, dear Thing-Out-There, I will never *ever* again, etc. Just bring me down, O Lord, have mercy on Thy servant, a sinner, and if you get me through this one, I'll become a Buddhist, or a Unitarian, as Thou wishest. . . ."

Our first album and second single ("Cream Puff War"/"The Golden Road (To Unlimited Devotion)") comes out in March '67, and we've been getting a little airplay on the underground FM stations. As a result we start getting offers to play outside the Bay area. One of our early out-of-town gigs is with the Doors at Earl Warren Showgrounds in Santa Barbara on April 29. It's good for us, but it isn't exactly a great meeting of musical minds. By the time Morrison gets there he is already jazzed, but I make sure he knows who we are. I go into his dressing room and hand him a baggie filled with Owsley acid.

The Inca examines it as if it were a bag of baubles from a conquistador.

"Wow, purple barrels!"

"You recognize them?"

"Yeah, this is the stuff, uh, Wendell scored for me last week. Dynamite acid, man. How much are they?"

"They're yours, man. Compliments of the Grateful Dead."

"Thanks, man. *Owsley*, right? Where'd you get 'em?"

"We *make* them. See that guy over there? That's him."

"Is that right? Okay, okay. Great meeting you guys. Hey, I wanna meet Garcia, seriously, man. After the show. Okay?"

But after the show he is *so* wigged out, plus wading through his entourage is pretty daunting. He has this retinue of crazy bitches and roadies and courtiers. He breezes out of there in his leathers, which is okay too. Jerry doesn't care to meet him anyway. Doesn't care for the music that much, isn't that impressed with Morrison's histrionics. Then again, Jerry's never been all that impressed with *himself* either.

At the beginning of June 1967 we go to New York to do a week of gigs (6th through the 11th) at the Café Au Go-Go with Luke & the Apostles. This is the Dead's first time off the West Coast. These guys are like kids in candyland. Real innocent babes and darlings at the same time. They're in the big bad city for the first time and look it. Wide open smiles, glowing faces, big eyes astonished at everything they see.

We check into One Fifth Avenue, which at that time is like the Chelsea Hotel — musicians and writers and layabouts. I think I am keeping my eyes peeled but apparently not, because we have hardly been in the hotel five minutes when I get ripped off. I put the briefcase down on the front desk right next to me — it had all our expense money in it — and the next thing I know somebody comes up and asks a question. I turn around and when I turn back, *bang!* the money's gone. So we are all walking around New York with no money; we can't even buy a hot dog!

But it is a warm day and everybody decides to investigate the Village. The musicians are out in Washington Square Park, circles of drummers and fife players and guys playing the Emperor concerto on metal drums.

When we get back to the hotel there's a delegation in the lobby waiting to see us. Thomas Hoving, the head of the Parks Department, and the police captain from the local precinct are there. Like we're visiting dignitaries. Hoving welcomes us to the city and asks us if we would do the City of New York the honor of putting on a concert in the bandshell in Central Park. Hey, now! That's more like it! Then the other shoe drops.

"I wonder if you'd also give us a hand with this little problem we've been having in Tompkins Square Park."

Apparently there's been a turf war going on in the Lower East Side for the past few weeks over who gets to play their music in the

Tompkins Square Park bandshell. All the cats get together and play the congas and the bongos. The Puerto Ricans want the stage to themselves. They're in the majority and they're going to play their music, which does not sit too well with blacks, who want to do their thing. Meanwhile, the hippies are saying, When do we get to play some of *our* music, man? Fighting in the park has escalated over the last few weekends. Hoving shows us newspaper clippings with photos of pitched battles in front of the bandshell. He's come to ask us to help out! The band is dubious about having anything to do with it. We've been warned to stay clear of Tompkins Square Park. It isn't even such a great place for hippies to *hang out,* never mind intervening in a turf war.

We can't even hang on to our per diems and they want us to sort out a gang war in Alphabet City? They must be desperate. They don't want to bring in any heavy police action that might incite race riots. And we're from California, considered at the time to have something to do with the future of the planet.

Aren't you the people who organized that Human Happening or whatever it was called, you know, that thing last January?

Yeah, maybe.

And aren't you guys who play *outdoors?* (This is a big thing at the time, equivalent to the arrival of the two-piece bathing suit.) At this point Hoving turns to Captain Whatsisname and says, "See, I told you these guys would help us out."

Phil is saying, "Now, wait on a minute. We'd like to accommodate you, however due to previous —"

Despite his better judgment, Jerry decides this is the perfect situation for us.

"Hey, guys! Come on. They don't want us to represent just the hippies, they want us to bring everyone together. We'll get bands from the different factions, give everybody a chance to play. Don't you see, we can do it because we're outsiders." Also, we have by now figured out that what Hoving is basically saying is if you want to play in Central Park you must do this for us.

Even before we get up onstage there are major skirmishes out there. It's a miracle that the cops don't shut it down entirely, but they are up against the wall. They need us. There's a lot of skepticism and vociferous mumbling from the crowd when they see a hippie band get up there. But we are so loud that at first our sheer sound overpowers them. Pig is howling down-home Delta drippings — *Aaaaaahm a kingbee, behbeh, buzzzzzin' aroun' yo' hive* — the drummers are drumming, Jerry's guitar is wailing, and pretty soon people are just listening to the music. Then other musicians come up with their congas and marimbas and bongos and cowbells, and they see this isn't a turf thing at all. Music is music as far as the Dead go. African music or Puerto Rican salsa, it don't make no difference to Garcia.

Soon the politicos are lining up to make speeches. Every ten or fifteen minutes while the band was playing, someone comes up to me with their notes: When do we get our chance to speak? I say we have this hard-and-fast rule. The microphones and the sound system are ours and they are for playing music only. There are going to be *no words spoken* while we're in charge! No more talk. It's all been in the papers, anyway. We've seen enough of it.

A lot of different groups get to play that afternoon and for the rest of the summer things go pretty smoothly. Hoving is thrilled and the cops are almost grateful. Hoving says to them: "Look at this, there was no trouble here. These guys would be good for Central Park." So the Grateful Dead go on the radio the night before and we have about seven, ten thousand people out there in Central Park the next day.

While in New York we play the Café Au Go-Go. Zappa's group is there too, they have this glorious room upstairs and we are down in the basement in a long narrow room with a brick wall right in front of us. There's nothing worse than a full electric band blaring up against a brick wall. At the sound check we despair, but when the place begins to fill up, the audience soaks up the sound and it became bearable. However, the racket from that wall is so loud that it bounces all the way up the stairs. Frank Zappa complains! Turn it down! But our audience wants it turned up. We are forced to stagger our sets.

Zappa is a jerk about the whole thing. Instead of coming down himself, he gets the manager and *demands* we turn our amps down. He has top billing! Later on I come to dig his music, but at the time I think this guy is a phony and no good to boot (not that we're much better).

The Dead set at the Café Au Go-Go is pretty characteristic for the band at the time: blues ("I'm a King Bee," "It Hurts Me Too," "The Same Thing"), R&B ("Beat It on Down the Line," "Big Boss Man"), folk (John Phillips's "Me & My Uncle," "Cold Rain and Snow"), a couple of jug-band numbers ("Don't Ease Me In," "New, New Minglewood Blues"), an occasional song from our album ("Alligator"), and a couple of covers of current songs ("In the Midnight Hour" and Dylan's "It's All Over Now, Baby Blue").

People think Zappa is so hip he must be high on acid (he contributed to this illusion by calling his first album *The Mothers of Invention Freak Out*), but he's actually vehemently antidrug, not only in regard to himself but toward everybody else in his band as well.

Zappa warns them not to hang out with the Grateful Dead. He sniffs their clothes like a customs' dog. And these are Latinos from East L.A., very funny guys who talk like Cheech Marin. We're in the same hotel and we're up all night smoking, half of them have passed out, and when the phone rings they hide under the bed.

"Don' answer it, maaan, if he finds us here we got to rehearse extra!"

At least that's *one* problem we don't have!

7

High Noon in the Haight

<<<<<<<<<<<<<<<<<<<<<<<<<<<<<<<<<<<<<<<<<<<<<<

BLAZERED SIX O'CLOCK news anchors and quizzical foreign corre-
spondents have invaded the Haight. Every major newspaper in the
United States is beating a path to our door with the burning questions
of the day: "Why are you smiling so much?" "What do the beads
mean?" "Where did you get your headband?"

"Hey, Jerry, guess who's interviewing outside right now? Harry
Reasoner! I wouldn't shit you on this one. He's already been over and
talked to the antiwar people and everything and now he's talking to
the prodrug people, and he wants you on his show."

Jerry goes to the window and peeks outside. He sees the setup and
shrinks back like Dracula before a clump of garlic.

"Nah, man, it's gonna be stupid. No way am I going out there. I
gotta go to the bathroom."

"But, Jerry, it's Harry fucking Reasoner. It's showtime! Prime time,
the seven o'clock news."

"I don't give a fuck if it's Ho Chi Minh, okay? And anyway, isn't this
what *managers* do, Rock?"

Turns out Jerry's smart to cop out, cause this guy's not asking
mildly off-center questions like the Northern California TV guys
(how long have I been growing my hair). Harry the merciless is
getting to the hard-core stuff right off the bat.

"Do you (or did you ever) do drugs?"

"Uh. . . ."

"And how long have you been taking drugs?"

I'm caught off guard. Everyone including my mom and second-grade teacher are going to see this. Fuck, I'm being interrogated. They've got one of those key lights pointed right at me and they're rolling down a sheet of black no-seam paper behind me. It looks like I'm in a cop shop getting grilled.

"I can explain, officer! I'll admit anything, just stop torturing me!"

Harry's a relentless, severe-eyed little fucker:

"How long?"

"I dunno, sir, I guess I've been using it for a couple of years."

"And where do you get your drugs?"

"Uh, let me see now. I don't recall. Actually, I . . . find them around! Yeah, somebody leaves them on my doorstep in the morning."

The crew laughs, but Herr Harry is not amused. He pushes on.

"*Why* do you use drugs?"

Dear God, is he going to chew through every interrogative known to man? It's like that Quicksilver album: *who* do you love?, *when* do you love?, *how* do you love?

"Well let's see, they make my hair grow long and my eyes get real big and I get laid. And, obviously, I get *high.*" Never omit the obvious! I try saying this all in a diplomatic way, being the Dead's manager and all, putting it across in some way that he might understand as a show-business guy himself. But, no, he doesn't understand a word I'm saying. He's on the other side of the glass. The finished piece makes me look like a doper. Very honest reporting, when you got right down to it! We didn't really care at the time, drugs are still a big joke.

Gene Anthony comes by and takes those pictures on the front porch of 710 Ashbury that end up in *Time* magazine, the Summer of Love issue. There we are featured in a big old magazine with Garcia in his Captain Trips hat, and Lesh in his Student Prince cap with the feather in it, and Pig in his chauffeur-on-acid outfit with the paisley waistcoat, and there's me at the bottom with Rifkin and the dog! And who's the star of this shoot? Why Curly-Headed Jim of course! Just a pot smuggler from Texas, but he's got the longest hair.

"Where are the girls?" is what Nicholas von Hoffman wants to know. He's with the *Washington Post.* And, you know, he sees all these chicks with see-through blouses and big goo-goo eyes and he's obviously starting to get kinda heated up. He's nudging me and he says, "Can you maybe introduce me to some of these girls? Maybe I'll do a piece for the *Washington Post* on the girls in the Haight." Yeah, right. Well, I can see where this is headed so I start thinking who am I going to introduce him to? And then, along comes this gal who used to be the girlfriend of a much-loved Hell's Angel, Chocolate George, and George being still in the clink, I figure what the hell. Von Hoffman can take her out to dinner, he's probably got a big hotel room down at the Jack Tarr. The lonely writer from Washington, D.C., doing his research on the Haight-Ashbury. But now the guy doesn't want to leave, so when he finishes his series of articles he starts writing a book about the Haight. He's going to call it *We Are the People Our Parents Warned Us Against.*

Tour buses are driving by 710 every day like it was the hippie White House or some damned thing. The route is called the Hippie Hop and is billed as "the only foreign tour within the continental limits of the United States." Even the bus drivers have become sociologists, tonelessly listing the pastimes of Hippie City: "Marijuana is a household staple. Their recreational activities — besides drug-taking — are parading and demonstrating, soul-searching, and malingering." And then there's that great kid running along beside the buses holding up a mirror to the tourists.

Poor old Haight-Ashbury. Being exploited like crazy by the media *and* the bus companies! Everybody jumped on it like a big piece of free cheesecake. But of all the shifty schemes and scaly exploitations of the hour, the Monterey Pop Festival is the most nefarious. We know from the outset it's going to be a rip-off, but it's galling to get ripped off by guys who are making millions of dollars doing "California Dreamin'." We're the ones doing the dreaming, they're the ones making the bread!

We already knew from friends in the Airplane and others that the principals of the festival, Lou Adler and Papa John Phillips of the Mamas and Papas, have something up their sleeves. Nobody knows quite what, but we know from experience that somebody somewhere will be making money from all this free music and free love. . . .

It starts with John and Michelle Phillips of the Mamas and Papas coming to see us, representing themselves as fellow musicians who have also taken acid or *maybe* taken acid. But whatever they've taken, they aren't anywhere near as crazy as we are. Or as naïve. Phillips is a musician whose group we respect, but why, we wonder, is he talking like that? The hip malapropisms, the music-biz clichés, the fake sincerity. We are soon to discover that once you get beyond the fur hat and the beads he is just like a goddamn L.A. slicko. We all get the same vibe from him: he's here to exploit the San Francisco hippie/love phenomenon by building a festival around us and Janis and Country Joe and Big Brother and Quicksilver and the Airplane.

The meeting is over on Fulton at the Airplane's palace. In spite of our misgivings we are led on because we aren't big yet, we don't have a hit record and the Mamas and the Papas are huge. We never even hope to achieve the kind of success that the Mamas and the Papas have on AM radio.

Phillips has no idea what we're about, and he doesn't much want to find out. For one thing, we're asking too many embarrassing questions.

"Hey, brother," he's saying, "what are you guys so paranoid about? You've got us all wrong. You're gonna dig this trip if you give it half a chance. You're really going to flip when you hear who we're bringing in: Jimi Hendrix, Otis Redding, and the Who, for starters. And we're working on getting the Stones. Isn't that right, Andrew?" They've brought the Stones' manager with them, the infamous Andrew Loog Oldham. Sir Fucking Andrew himself! We're impressed, all right.

"Out the door and around the back, man, innit?" Oldham remarks dryly and proceeds to embark on an extravagant automotive metaphor.

"It's a bit like a car, a festival. D'y'know what I mean? Well, unless or even *if* your engine is frozen up like a Swanson's TV dinner, if you got the right ingredients it will still roll over. See what I mean, love? Only problem with a gig like this, that's got its own momentum, is will it *overheat?* Y'know?"

As beguiling as it is being shined on by John and Michelle Phillips, cajoled by superpromoter Lou Adler, and, uh, *talked* to by the redoubtable Andrew Loog Oldham, Danny and I have to blow them off, which we do by saying we'll think about it.

Time for Andrew and Lou Adler to drive back up the coast. They drove down together and Andrew is *still* going on about it.

"Lovely drive," offers Sir Andrew. "Although the fuckin' waves were a bit overdone, didn't you think?" So just to make their trip back even *more* scenic . . . we dose 'em.

At this point nobody in Berkeley or the Haight wants anything to do with the Monterey Pop Festival. Big Brother, Steve Miller, Country Joe and the Fish, Quicksilver. They all turn them down flat. The

Airplane are down in L.A. finishing up their second album and there-fore more susceptible to the importunings of Adler & Co.

More righteous people get involved. Paul Simon commits and tries to get us to do the same. He comes out to San Francisco. Jerry and I give him a tour of the Haight and Golden Gate Park, up to hippie hill, over to the Airplane mansion and Big Brother's house. We take him for a walk all the way down Haight Street from one end to the other and not a soul recognizes him. We tell him what bothers us about the setup, the cast of rogues running the thing, etc. All of which he grants, but then adds:

"Guys, we don't have to get so hung up on the legalities; let the lawyers take care of that stuff. That's not what's going to be remem-bered about this festival — who got the Japanese rights. Without the Dead and the other San Francisco bands, Monterey will just be an-other Dick Clark production. And besides, I only got involved be-cause they told me *you* guys were doing it."

In the next few weeks other heroes of ours start getting involved with the festival. Derek Taylor, who'd been the Beatles publicist, be-comes the press agent. The Airplane sign on, and then some bands from San Francisco start committing. The Byrds get involved. We hear the Who and Hendrix are definitely coming, and how could we miss out on that? And now Otis! Gotta-gotta-gotta-gotta! The damn thing is a steamroller.

By now we're also getting heat from Joe Smith at Warner Brothers and Mo Ostin at Reprise because they're bringing in Hendrix. They don't want San Francisco to walk out as a block. They claim the San Francisco scene is the only reason Otis wants to do it.

A few days before the festival there's a big last-minute meeting in the Fairmont Hotel. Lou Adler comes up with his buddies. They're racking their brains thinking of ways to talk us into this thing. They're willing to swear on their grandmothers' graves (or the *Hollywood Reporter*, if we prefer) that they aren't going to burn us.

Phil Lesh is saying, "Why do we get the impression you guys are going to film this thing and make umpteen double albums and sell it from here to Singapore?"

This is greeted with great rolling of eyes. As if Lesh is being crass to even think about such things! Bass players are supposed to think about music, not money. But Phil just keeps on coming.

"Let's say, just for argument's sake, that you *do* film it. How many times is it going to be shown on TV? Why don't you just be honest about it and tell us about it now and we'll settle the whole thing up front."

And Adler, looking as guileless as he's capable of, gets this really hurt tone of voice.

"No, no, no, baby, you've got us all wrong. Where'd you ever get these crazy ideas?" He looks around perplexed, looking for confirmation.

"Look, guys, this is going to be great for everyone. The L.A./San Francisco/London axis strutting its stuff and the whole fucking world watching us. Can you dig it? It's going to be *magical,* baby. Something you're going to want to tell your grandchildren about. Hey, it doesn't *get* much better than this."

All that L.A. jive talk. And right in the middle of this Fourth-of-July oratory, Lesh gets up and says, "Oh, shit! Now I *know* we're gonna get screwed!" He just walks out. Somehow, until they started talking that talk, Lesh had been hoping he was wrong.

It's a Mexican standoff, typical of the yawning gulf between L.A. and San Francisco. We are putting all our stuff out front, saying: Here are our concerns, tell us what can be done about them, and they're saying: Which shell is it under?

Paul Simon is the spiritual leader of the festival and most of us get involved because of him. He rises above all the scaly maneuvering and makes us see it from the audience's point of view.

"Who cares what these guys are up to? Let's show them who we are." He got behind it initially because the festival was supposed to be a benefit for music lessons in inner-city schools and to buy instruments for kids who can't afford them. But beneath the surface, all is scaly politics and conniving.

The combination of Paul Simon's vision and Derek Taylor's acidic poise convinces us in the end. We do it for the fans and fuck the rest of it. Derek's beauty is that he keeps the two camps apart and looks after the musicians. He's our guru and a true believer in the children's crusade.

The festival rolls for June 15–16–17. I get to the fairgrounds early to help take care of all the stuff the promoters forgot about. We know from the Be-In that people will be coming in from all the communities up and down the coast: Big Sur, Shasta, the communes in Oregon.

Two days before the festival opens, the buses begin arriving filled with people who want to know where they can pitch their tents and tepees. We realize that we'll have to look after them because the L.A. contingent certainly isn't going to. The kind of people who come to see the Grateful Dead will most likely want to camp out. We get the Monterey Peninsula College to provide free camping on the football field and open up the showers and turn on hot water and all that good stuff. We make arrangements with the people who run the floral show to use their pavilion to accommodate the overflow of people who have nowhere to stay and no tents either. All of which is right next door to the fairgrounds. Just walk under the highway and you are there.

When you walk through the fairgrounds at twilight with the tepees painted with Sioux symbols, people playing guitars, and children and dogs running around the tents, it's worth all the hassles in the world. We've infiltrated the enemy camp, turned it into our own event. A Digger underground action. The promoters are busy catering to Brian Jones and the Monkees and all the people who aren't even playing. We have our peyote-ceremony tents set up just as you walk in the gate. The Laws are there, they started the New Buffalo commune in New Mexico. Also Steve Gaskin, who started a commune down in Tennessee and wrote a great book, and whose self-styled messianism is satirized in "St. Stephen." There are bonfires going, and smoke coming out of tepees.

Meanwhile, backstage the sharks are busy scheming and maneuvering. All those L.A. record company types. Man, are they scary. Bill Graham is a Boy Scout compared to them. Holy cow, here comes Albert Grossman — the Band's manager, Dylan's manager. Grossman's trying to snag Janis and is doing it in the most ruthless, shabby way. Dangling Bob Dylan, whom Janis worships, right in front of her eyes.

Very soon we dream up a new piece of folly. It starts, like so many great ideas, with a simple desideratum. Jerry says, "A jam or something might be nice. Yeah, a jam might be *real* nice. . . ." Stop the presses! The great Barcia has spoken (I think).

"Well," say I, "what about the floral pavilion? Or even the football field? It's full of all those people who couldn't get into the shows."

Garcia is up for it, so is Pig. The plot hatches at the Jokers Club (where the musicians hang out behind the main stage). And as soon as it's been conjured up, Hendrix says, "Hey, now *that* sounds like serious fun!" Pigpen, Jimi Hendrix, Jerry Garcia, Pete Townshend, David Crosby. They're all into it. And as soon as the other musicians hear about it they're going yes, yes, yes — count us in too.

At one end of the floral pavilion we set up the PA system on a little platform that is already there. The quippies skank the electricity and get juice into the hall, and we borrow some amplifiers off the stage and move them in. All this is done furtively, as people are going to sleep, so nobody will twig. The lights are off, so the whole setting-up process is done with flashlights. We get everything ready and then Jorma Kaukonen, Jack Casady, Garcia, and Jimi Hendrix (all of them high on acid) come tripping out onstage.

With the first chord the lights go on and the projectors start flashing their amoeba-like images. People wake up to bubbles moving across the ceiling (one of the light companies installs a liquid light projector) and here's the Airplane, the Grateful Dead, and Jimi Hendrix cranking through "Walkin the Dog." The Dead are like grease. Here take another tab, and everybody knows "Good Morning Little School Girl," right?

The best part of it is seeing people's faces when the lights come on. Some of these people have never been to San Francisco. Most of them have never seen a Haight show with the lights and the bubbles.

We do the same thing over at the football field, except there we don't have any screen for the lighting, so we have lights on the stage, actually the bed of a flatbed truck.

Eric Burdon, the Byrds, the Who. You can imagine people sitting straight up in their sleeping bags! People who never got in to the show because it was too crowded, waking up in the cold and seeing Eric Burdon on a flatbed truck croaking out "House of the Rising Sun" with Pete Townshend on lead guitar. Whoa! I know I went to bed high, but this is ridiculous!

There are a few fancy hotels up at the other end of Monterey where Scott McKenzie and the Mamas and the Papas are staying, but that isn't where the action was. There is a whole strip of awful motels right behind the fairgrounds, where we're staying, and they are popping! An awful lot of commingling is going on. Everybody back and forth and in and out of rooms. Irate girlfriends knocking on doors in the middle of the night.

I look out my window and there's Hendrix walking around the parking lot, talking to the moon. You take acid together, go down to the roots, come back up again, and then move on from there! Unexpected friendships are springing up all over the place. Brian Jones and Ravi Shankar, Jimi Hendrix and Pigpen. Friendships evolving, some that will last for years.

There is a ferocious mutual-admiration society going on among the musicians. Garcia has all the Who records, Townshend gets turned on to acid. The guys in Hendrix's band, Mitch Mitchell and Noel Redding, love Pigpen. Pig's introducing them to Janis and all the hippie chicks who follow him around, and everybody is on this purple acid that Owsley had seen fit to break out for this event in massive quantities. Purple rain dissolving all the usual categories: musician, roadie, fan . . . manager!

Unexpectedly at the center of this swirl is Jerry. To all these international celebrities Jerry *is* Haight-Ashbury. And at this moment in the history of the cosmos, the Haight is the axis of all the emerging strands.

That Jerry is such a magnetic figure among this stellar cast is due in part to his boundless curiosity and his outgoing nature. People naturally gravitate around him. He's affable, inquisitive, approachable, and infinitely benign. On acid, Jerry is the Buddha. Also, he's caught a touch of the cosmic bug himself. Dealing with the babbling tribes of the Lower East Side has enabled him to develop a global vision of hippietopia. He believes — we all fervently believe! — in the prevalent hippie prophecies, to wit: The straight world will turn on and see the error of their ways; this is the beginning of a new era; in forty years marijuana will be growing in Times Square.

My biggest mistake is booking the Dead into a club in L.A. the night before they are to play at Monterey. And to make things (much) worse, Jerry's *guitar* gets stolen, so I end up with a demoralized Garcia and an exhausted band. Plus we are all ragged since we just got back from New York. But we're hungry, and we're not even sure we're going to *do* Monterey, so we book another date just to be sure to make some money that weekend.

Unfortunately, by waiting until the last minute to decide whether we'll play, we've gotten screwed as to position: we have to go on Saturday night, between the Who and Jimi Hendrix. We know we don't stand a chance. A leisurely Saturday or Sunday afternoon spot would be more our speed! Squashed in the middle of the bright lights and flaming guitars, we are utterly lost.

The Who go on in their mod regalia. Whirling mikes, crashing drums, scything power chords. It's a careening amphetamine cartoon of rock 'n' rage at the end of which Townshend smashes his guitar with apocalyptic glee, and Keith Moon demolishes his drum kit. Their final "My Generation" is rock armageddon. That's all, folks! And the poor old Dead are up next.

On our way up the stairs to the stage John Phillips waylays us with, I'm not kidding, a piece of paper to sign! Giving our permission to let our set be filmed. Which is exactly what we said was going to happen back at the hotel meeting. Here is Papa John right on cue and bold as brass. We refuse to sign. Just plain refuse.

"Look," I say, trying to maintain some composure lest I inadvertently bite the fucker's head off, "this is way, *way* out of line. It's got nothing to do with anything we discussed."

"What's the hang-up now, brother?" Phillips whines. "The Airplane signed, Country Joe and the Fish signed, Big Brother just signed. You're gonna be the only ones left out." We don't sign, and consequently don't appear in the movie *Monterey Pop* or on any of the subsequent albums.

But to hell with all that. It is a great crowd, and the day is foggy, dark and cold, so everyone is concentrating on the stage. And when the Dead amble on, there is a great headlong rush for seats. The Dead are underground heroes and as soon as they start tuning up all the people out on the fairgrounds want in. Someone had left the door open in the back and they all come rushing in. The promoters freak! They get Mickey Dolenz from the Monkees to run out onstage in an Indian chief's war bonnet to make an announcement. He grabs Lesh's microphone (while he's singing) and tells the crowd not to panic.

"The Beatles, despite all the rumors you may have heard, are not here. There are no Beatles, folks! So will all those without tickets please leave the arena, now." Naturally it stops the song right there, and Lesh is so pissed off he boots Dolenz off the stage. The band do a couple of our old standbys: "Viola Lee Blues" and "Cold Rain and Snow" from our album.

It's a bummer, but it isn't as if it ruins one of the Dead's greatest moments. The set is indifferent. The Dead never do well in the spotlight. Those critical events where we're supposed to shine, we invariably fuck up. It's part of our charter. Jimi Hendrix goes on after us and just kills everybody. It's our first eyeful of Jimi and it's scary. His show is so outrageous, playing his Stratocaster with his teeth, pouring lighter fluid on it, kneeling over it like a voodoo shaman and setting it on fire. It's a million light-years away from what the Dead are doing. Sandwiched between the Who and Jimi Hendrix is like doing a set in the middle of a firestorm. We just evaporate. People have a hard time remembering the Dead played at all.

Jimi Hendrix and the Who are our personal favorites among the bands, but when Otis Redding shows up he puts Townshend and Hendrix in the shade. Forget about flaming guitars and exploding drum kits! Otis is a force of nature. He is handsome and dynamic and onstage he is a total flash. When he comes out in his electric lime green suit with the killer backup band he is a living blur of energy. And Otis Redding from li'l ol' Macon, Georgia, is agog at the hairy-hippie-drugs-free-love lifestyle!

Otis carries a big entourage around with him: the band, the horn players, and everybody's girlfriends. Pigpen's got his eyes on the girls that are following Otis. Pig is skankin' around Otis's motel, picking up on the black girls, whereas Janis is in love with Otis Redding and is hitting on *him*. Pig loves Otis too, of course, but Janis's recent "Otis-is-God" business is driving him a little nuts. Confronting Janis as she returns to her room in the early-morning hours, Pig asks: "So, does God have a big dick?"

"Only if you believe in him!" she drawls, not missing a beat.

☉

The last day of the festival comes and — surprise! — all the money has mysteriously disappeared. Adler & Co. claim that their accountant ran off with it to Mexico. The amount of the embezzlement is estimated at $50,000, but it's a lot more than that since $35,000 of it is later recovered. In the end the Los Angeles free medical clinics get $5,000 each and $25,000 goes to the Sam Cooke scholarship fund. But Adler is in no hurry to dispense these funds. He is collecting interest on the money. And then there is the money from the film and the TV rights and the double albums (which are still coming out).

The forces of darkness have ripped us off. They've stolen our music, stolen the San Francisco *vibe* for crissakes! So we figure the best way to respond is to show how little we care about all this stuff by *giving* it away. We plan a little prank. A big prank, actually.

Fender has lent all this equipment to the festival in return for advertising — "Used exclusively at the world-famous Monterey Pop Festival." It is the most beautiful gear we have ever seen. Fender bassmans and twin reverbs. The bands are just salivating over this stuff. We are used to playing on banged-up, cigarette-burned stuff cobbled together by Owsley.

Why don't we just take this gear back up to San Francisco? Maybe set it up in the park and put on some free shows. Yeah, but how? Sunday night, during the last show, Danny and I take Lou Adler's two security guys backstage and dose them. They're initially a little suspicious, so Danny and I each take a big swig from the bottles.

"See? Now do you believe us?" I know that by the end of the show they're going to be helpless; hopefully they'll run off to a motel in search of groupies.

After the show there's a million and a half dollars' worth of amplifiers sitting on the stage with nobody there to guard it but two (dosed) guards. Oh yes, *and* the back door is open. And everybody's gone. Who can blame us? We commandeer a T-shirt van belonging to Mouse and Kelley, our friends the poster artists. We just move the T-shirts and stuff out of the way, back the van right up to the stage, and load it with what we need. We figure, okay, three guitar players, let's get the rhythm covered, let's get *two* sets of Fender twin reverbs and the speaker boxes and stuff just in case Jerry and Jimi want to play together. We've still got some room, so why don't we grab some power amps? We're putting together these imaginary bands in our heads, Jimi on lead, Casady and Lesh on bass (which actually happens).

We leave a note on the stage saying: "P.S. Hope you dudes don't mind, but we've borrowed your gear for a few days. Reason is, the musicians that played on this equipment loved it so much that they wanted a chance to use it again. You'll get it back!"

All the way to San Francisco and we're still high. *Now* what are we going to do? Jerry, Phil, and Pig come out. Their eyes are as big as saucers. "Will you look at this shit?"

"Let the wild rumpus start!"

It isn't until Monday afternoon that Fender, who has just been bought by CBS, discovers several big discrepancies in their inventory list. A million-plus dollars' worth of gear gone! We send telegrams to CBS and to Fender, with copies to Ralph Gleason at the *Chronicle,* which Gleason prints in full:

> We have liberated the following amplifiers and speaker boxes, in order to provide free music to the people of San Francisco and Northern California. They will be used three or four times for free events and returned to you at the conclusion of this week.

We have to find a generator and some flatbed trucks. We know lots of these bands will be showing up: Otis Redding, Jimi Hendrix, Eric Burdon and the Animals. They're all coming to San Francisco to play the Fillmore and the Avalon after the festival. Bill Graham is a budding promoter — he will rule the city yet! — but for now he has the smarts to consult Jerry on whom to book.

"Who would you like to hear play the Fillmore if you could choose any lineup from Monterey that you wanted?"

Jerry peruses the list. "Well I'd have the Who and the Animals. Otis Redding, natch. And Jimi Hendrix definitely has to come. What more could anyone ask for?"

After the last show everybody from Monterey comes to San Francisco, where the focus of energy is. Nobody goes to L.A. We have this funny feeling that more people are going to show up than anybody ever imagined. We know all the people who came to Monterey aren't going to just turn around and go back to Colorado or Idaho. They are going to come to San Francisco, and we had better have something ready for them. And when the migratory hordes of hippies finally descend on San Francisco, the Haight bursts its seams.

Even the ever-resourceful Diggers are hard pressed to keep on top of it. They have set up huge soup kitchens and every day there is a hot meal for all those kids who have not given one thought as to how they are going to get by. They think they are going to live on air. They have no money; what money they had they spent in Monterey. They are going to come to San Francisco with nothing but a sleeping bag. Some of them stay in communes in the Haight-Ashbury, but even those big Victorians can't accommodate all of them. Many of them camp out in Golden Gate Park. No fires are allowed in the park but they camp under the trees and stars, knowing they can come down to the Panhandle and get a hot meal. There are all-night bongo parties up on hippie hill. Some of them will still be going in 1995.

The Diggers are running all over town hitting on every supermarket for bad heads of lettuce. They take the outer leaves off, boil the heads, and make lettuce soup. The Wonder Bread Company kicks in some loaves and more are scavenged from the day-old-bread stores — the Dumpsters outside the supermarkets. One slice of Velveeta and two slices of Wonder Bread with lettuce soup or bean soup on the side, and, presto, Haight cuisine!

The Diggers provide food, we provide the entertainment. Naturally we aren't about to disclose where we are going to play because we're afraid they'll interrupt our shows (and take the equipment away). We set the thing up in Panhandle Park in the middle of the week and put our usual tactics into effect: find someone who lives on the street opposite the park and skank the electric, stringing any old extension cord (a brown lamp cord if necessary) down through the trees and across the street. We use a circuit breaker so we don't blow out the gear. It's camouflaged, the cops can't find the generator, can't find anybody in charge, and we get away with it all afternoon. Eric Burdon and Jimi Hendrix come down and play with the Dead to seven or eight thousand people.

Then we set up out in Linley Meadows. Again, we bootleg the electricity. Unfortunately, at the big show out in Golden Gate Park we have to use a generator, which is always a dead giveaway because somebody has to rent it. If the police show up and ask, "Who's in charge here?" they'll eventually find out, because all they have to do is call U-Haul or Abbey Rents and find out who rented the damn thing.

The cops are not all that aggressive, however. For one thing, they're on triple overtime! We park the Hell's Angels on the amps. Although we tell the Angels not to resist, just the look of them sitting up there in their colors, scowling, is enough to keep the cops at bay. The game of looking-for-the-ones-in-charge begins. The cops would happily do this rather than tussle with the Hell's Angels. You can play this game for hours; meanwhile, everyone gets to play their set.

We use the gear and then give it back. In perfect order, too. We even replace tubes. We set up a drop: "Be at the Ferry Building, Market and Embarcadero, at 12 noon. Don't expect to find any of us hanging around, either. So long, folks, and thanks for the loan!"

We get a bit of a tongue-lashing from the papers. "GRATEFUL DEAD MANAGERS MASTERMIND MILLION-DOLLAR EQUIPMENT HEIST," the usual over-the-top sort of thing! Gleason rags on us in the *Chronicle* but at the end of the piece makes us out to be Robin Hoods, stealing from the rich to give our music away to the milling throngs. We get more press for stealing equipment that we actually return than the promoters do for stealing our money.

The party goes on all week in San Francisco, everybody still tripping except Pigpen, who is holding open court in the kitchen. He makes friends with everybody in Otis's band and finds a couple of girlfriends. Eric Burdon and Chas Chandler from the Animals treat him with a reverence that the Brits usually reserve for Delta bluesmen.

Then Otto Preminger comes by to talk to us about being in a Jackie Gleason movie. Hollywood calling! A huge limo pulls up in front of the house and a big fat guy with a bald head struggles out. Flanked by secretaries and flunkies, he hobbles toward our front steps. Otto Preminger has come shopping in the Ashbury.

It just so happens that we are in the thick of water-balloon frenzy that day. It is summer, and it's hot. The day Otto arrives, Weir and Mountain Girl just happen to have a whole box of water balloons ready to go. And a couple dozen bottle rockets. And they're going, "No! I tell you, no! You can't have my life story." He is looking up at our house, a bit befuddled by all the Scarlett O'Hara dialogue, when *kapow!* They lob a couple of balloons onto the emerging Otto and he gets his feet wet big time. Water balloons are splattering on the sidewalk, bottle rockets are shooting off. The man is terrified! He turns around and the great shiny dome goes right back into the car. In ducks his head and the door slams. Then the chauffeur jumps in and away they go. I am pissed off because I really want a break, but everybody else in the house is chanting "L.A. no way."

And some of us have moved a little beyond pranks. A few days later some high school buddies of ours move across the street. One of them has brought all this weaponry back with him from Vietnam. He has taken the powder out of the warhead of a mortar and made a dud out of it. Just another version of a bottle rocket.

To impress us, our new neighbors launch this mortar from the roof.

They aim it at the police department all the way over by Kezar Stadium, and it lands right on the front steps of the Park Precinct. The telemetry is perfect. Now admittedly even without its warhead it could have hit someone and obliterated them, but happily it didn't. It just goes *ka-thud!* plunk, plunk, and rolls right up against the front door of the police station, that's all! Then some cop on his way to the donut shop steps on it. They cordon off the whole area. It's a major scare. Mayday! Mayday! There's a live bomb on the front steps! They all have to go out the back door, put up crime scene tape, and do all that other fun police stuff. Time to get out of Dodge.

8

Anthem of the Sun

WE'RE ON THE road, babe! It's heady stuff. New blood, new places, new faces. Direct from San Francisco, ladies and gentlemen, the one and only Grateful Dead! Our audience is growing daily. After the Monterey Pop Festival and the Summer of Love, the word goes out and all of a sudden the Grateful Dead are — rock stars! Sort of.

We're getting our first taste of what the future holds in store: a steady diet of greasy burgers and cardboard in-flight dinners, burrowing from one backstage cinderblock bunker to another through interchangeable airport lounges and indistinguishable hotel rooms — that terrifying painting of windmills that follows us from town to town! And just think, if we're lucky we may be doing this shit for a very long time to come.

Bill Graham indulges us by setting up our first international tour. Okay, Canada isn't exactly an exotic foreign land (and we've been there once before, for a phony Trips Festival in Vancouver). Still, it's our first big, official (as we can get) road trip.

July 31 to August 5, 1967. A week in Toronto's O'Keefe Center with the Jefferson Airplane as headliners. It's Graham's first out-of-town promotion, the beginning of his true world-class megalomania.

The O'Keefe Center is a newly constructed concert hall, plush and huge, just like Radio City Music Hall. We aren't all that well attended in Toronto. The first couple of nights are sold out, but after that the hall is barely half full. Bill Graham has been perhaps a wee bit optimistic.

There is a hippie area in Toronto called Old Town that's similar to the Haight-Ashbury, filled with American kids escaping the draft. They tell us the real action is in Montreal and we all want to go so Graham reluctantly books us for an afternoon gig at the Youth Pavilion at the Montreal Expo. We've already got a head of steam going about doing a free concert. Word has spread, and we are constantly asked about it, especially by the underground press.

"We hear you play for free in the park in San Francisco — are you planning on doing anything like that in Canada?"

And Lesh goes, "Hell, yeah, we'll play some free concerts. You guys get it together and we'll do it." Thanks, Phil!

On Sunday, the morning after the last gig at the O'Keefe, both bands pile on a bus and head for Montreal. We get off at the Place Ste. Marie, a square downtown between two featureless skyscrapers. There is a fountain and iron railings and brickwork everywhere. It's clearly going to sound horrible. In the middle of the square is a tiny stage about the size of a Frisbee with thirty or forty thousand kids milling around it. I guess word got out!

It's so crowded it's scary. We have to carry in the gear by passing it over the heads of the crowd. There is no place to get on and off the stage. Each band manages to play for about an hour and then we pack the equipment up and wrestle it all the way out again, and put it on the bus to the Expo.

After the Expo Show (on a rotating stage!) the Airplane, stars that they are, head down to do a Canadian Broadcasting System show. We are cordially not invited along, and they unceremoniously dump us on a sidewalk.

"Fuck it," says Jerry, "this calls for Millbrook."

Millbrook is LSD East, an estate in upstate New York where Timothy Leary is living. We've been talking about going to see the Reverend Tim, on our way down to New York. Ron Rakow, our confidant, and his girlfriend, Peggy Hitchcock, are on tour with us, and it's at the Hitchcock family estate that Leary is holding court. Peggy comes from one of the richest families in America and Ron is a banker who's taken acid and dropped out.

Our next date is in Detroit, Michigan, several days off. We have some free time and it is still easy to talk ourselves into doing some really off-the-wall thing. It's an amazing lark and I don't think we're ever quite like that again. Everything from here on in will be a little more plotted, and as a group only once will we ever put ourselves in such jeopardy again.

Peggy Hitchcock knows some people in downtown Montreal, so we schlep all the gear over there in taxis and pile up our suitcases and equipment in front of their house. Fortunately Peggy has credit cards, and she and Ron run around town picking up enough rent-a-cars so that we can load all this stuff up and get out of town. In the meantime we are basically camping out on the sidewalk in front of a fancy town house.

I take the last car to drive down with Peggy, Ron Rakow, Garcia, and Bobby Weir. We're getting ready to go and suddenly discover Weir is *not* on the bus. He's wandered off somewhere in the jungle of downtown Montreal. It is his nature to get lost. We find him sitting cross-legged in a comic book store.

"Hey, man, dig this, the Incredible Hulk, ish number three!"

We don't get out of Montreal until nightfall, and then drive all night in a convoy of rented cars down the New York Thruway. With me in front are Pig, driving, and Veronica riding shotgun. In the back are Peggy, Jerry, Mountain Girl and Sunshine, and the other car has everyone else. We all go in tandem down to the fabled acid palace of Millbrook.

We call Billy Hitchcock on the way to ask if we can stay in the bungalow and he says no. So we go there anyway! It's a five-hour drive to Millbrook, and we arrive around six in the morning, seriously frazzled and dingy from smoking STP. STP is the new drug this summer and it's what keeps us rolling. Like DMT, it's an instant trip. It has about a two-hour life, but it doesn't reek like DMT. DMT has this terrible smell when it burns. The band forbids its use onstage because if you smell it you can have a flashback right on the spot. STP comes like a big stick of chalk from which you whittle powder and roll it in a joint and smoke it. We are doing it on airplanes because it doesn't have a telltale smell. You can roll it with tobacco. And it keeps you up, which we definitely need.

Our initial reception is very cool indeed. Egad! the Hirsute Simian Horrors have descended on us! Peggy takes us to her brother's big old stone mansion on the grounds, which are huge. The back of the house looks on to rolling hills, with patios and decks and stone terraces cascading down to the swimming pool. Beyond that there are lawns stretching out for miles. Those of us who want to sleep stumble into bedrooms and pass out. Garcia crashes as soon as we get in.

Out of karma or whatever reason, Jerry and Mountain Girl happen to get Billy Hitchcock's room, the big bedroom in the bungalow. The next day Jerry goes poking around in Billy's closet, and what does he find but a big fat bag of Acapulco Gold from which Mountain Girl rolls us a couple of bombers and we get really fucking loose and spend a very nice day in the country!

Pigpen is asleep within minutes of arrival. He always looks after himself that way, has to have his critter comforts as he calls them. Raids the liquor closet to get whatever he can find and then repairs to his own bedroom with lots of pillows. Only after he has his crib totally together will he scope out the wenches, see if maybe the maid is amorously inclined.

The rest of us stay up. Lesh and I walk all over the grounds, which are so huge you *drive* between one residence and the next. We go over to see Tim Leary, who's ensconced in the main house. It's a giant wooden structure, three or four stories high, with a huge painting of the Buddha stretching the entire height of one wall. Inside it's a huge rambling sixty-eight-room mansion where Leary and his flock hang out. He's all dressed in white and bare feet. Delighted to see us and wants us to set up and play, but we're all *sooo* ragged. Nobody wants to haul all the gear out of the cars and put it all back again. Especially me.

On the walls of the Learyites' abode are little life-affirming aphorisms: a copy of the Desiderata, the latest bulletin from the League of Spiritual Discovery ("You have to be out of your mind to pray"), posters of hairy swamis. There are Hindu ragas playing on the turntable, and Buddhas and Shivas all over the damn place. And then — what's this? — there's a large candlelit room off the kitchen with mattresses on the floor.

"Jesus," Lesh says, "take a look in here. They've got a fucking orgy room, man."

One of Leary's acolytes corrects us: "That's the Psychodrama Room, actually."

"Yeah, well like I said . . ."

Did we see Tim's poem, "Homage to the Awe-full See-er" in *The Psychedelic Review*? Why, no, we must have missed that one.

"How does it go, man?" Like I really gotta know.

Tim sits cross-legged on a beanbag while somewhere in the back-

The Ur Dead at the center of the cosmos. Jerry Garcia, Ron "Pigpen" McKernan, Phil Lesh, Bob Weir, and Bill Kreutzmann at the corner of Haight and Ashbury, San Francisco, 1966.

Trying to find a lost chord at one of our early gigs, 1966.

Getting the *un*coordinated look together outside 710A Ashbury Street (the basement apartment), 1966. Lesh, Garcia, Weir, and behind them, Kreutzmann and Pigpen.

Jerry pickin' at 710 Ashbury, 1966, when the flag still belonged to all of us.

Family portrait outside 710A. Back row: Pigpen, Garcia, Lesh, Rosie McGee, Laird, Kreutzmann. Front row: Scully, Tangerine, Danny Rifkin, Weir.

Herb Greene

Cowboy Neal Cassady.

Mickey Hart during his
Russian émigré period.

Above: Pigpen in his lair at 710 Ashbury.

Right: Mountain Girl and Jerry at Olompali, 1967.

Herb Greene

Opposite, bottom: Post-bust press conference. Left to right, Kreutzmann, a disgruntled Pigpen (also on front page of the *San Francisco Chronicle* above his head), Lesh, Scully, Rifkin, Weir, Garcia, our lawyer, Michael Stepanion, and Bob Matthews.

Lesh, Kreutzmann, and Weir get their pictures taken at Herb Greene's studio, 1967.

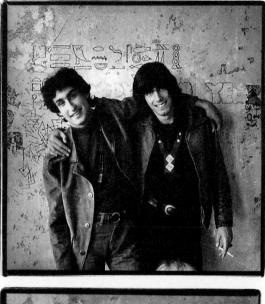

Rifkin and Scully, 1967.

Our leader, signifying.

Mickey on Papa Jerry's lap. Back row, from left to right:
Tom Constanten, Weir, Kreutzmann, Pigpen, and Lesh, 1969.

Pigpen, the newly bewhiskered Garcia, Kreutzmann, Lesh, and Weir on stage, 1968.

Woodstock, 1969.

ground a sitar drones. Dear God, he's actually going to recite the damn thing!

> At each beat
> in the earth's rotating dance
> there is born. . . .
> " . . ."

Here he pauses for the entity, the thing in the space between the quotation marks, to enter the room. A heady moment! With breathy articulation, he continues:

> . . . a momentary cluster of molecules
> possessing the transient ability to know-see-experience
> its own place in the evolutionary spiral.
> Such an organism, such an event,
> senses exactly where he is
> in the billion-year-old ballet. . . .

Just as it's getting truly insufferable, in walks Pigpen. "Hey, where are all the chicks, man?"

Millbrook has become more a small village than an estate. Not only is Leary incapable of turning anybody away, he is by now more famous than the pope. He's the pope of dope, actually, and we have revised his catchphrase "tune in, turn on, drop out" to read: "plug in, freak out, and fall down."

Millbrook is just jammed with people and it's not exactly a fastidious crowd. I'm amazed the place hasn't burnt to the ground. There are candles and joss sticks burning all over the house not to mention sloppily rolled joints spilling out of ashtrays and balanced on window ledges.

The weather is warm and a lot of Leary's tribe have lit out for the woods. A mile hike through the forest and we're in a small Indian village. Hippie Indians. Eight or nine tepees, plus makeshift tents and ramshackle lean-tos. Everybody is into living the tribal life. Babies, dudes, chicks, and dogs. Sitting around smoking pipes and beating on tom-toms. Everybody getting high on *Cannabis americanus.* Hippies from New York and San Francisco and Mount Shasta and Sweden, all living stark naked in the woods. Loincloths, buckskins, and moccasins are the only acceptable outfits. Here authenticity is everything, but not *every* aspect of Indian life is faithfully duplicated. These are supermarket hunter-gatherers.

Despite the fact that he hadn't wanted us here in the first place, the following evening Billy Hitchcock calls everyone he knows in New York and tells them "The Grateful Dead's at my house in Millbrook and they're gonna play for us!" provoking a great exodus of affluent acid-eaters and the curious rich from New York City.

The band sets up in a corner of the living room of the bungalow. "Living room" being another colossal understatement. It's actually a great hall large enough for Beowulf and his soldiers to carouse in. All Billy Hitchcock's rich friends and all the Learyites file in to see us play. There must have been seventy-five people, plus the seventy-five that were already living on the property. So, that night we sing for our supper. It's that or wash dishes. I am standing on the terrace smoking a joint when Weir straggles in: "Shit," he says, "this is like a fucking gig!"

The next day we head on down to New York City, to the Chelsea Hotel. Everybody stays at the Chelsea, everyone who has been touched by wings of madness. Painters, perverts, dopers, dealers, poets, poseurs and transvestites (and the odd Belgian traveling salesman who's misread his guidebook).

On the Chelsea roof there is a penthouse with awnings and a view of the Hudson River. We're going to play, heaven help us, a free concert on the roof. It is our intention to hit up the hipoisie for contributions to the Diggers' travel fund (Trip Without a Ticket). The invitees have all been instructed to bring their checkbooks.

It's amazing out there on the roof. A tent has been set up and champagne is flowing. The crowd is principally stockbrokers and bankers and wealthy heads come to see and hear the Dead. All these dressed-up society folks, and here we are literally at the end of our rope, having come from the wilds of Millbrook half drunk and totally stoned on the STP. And we're trying to make *small talk* with these people.

"Is it true, Mr. Garcia, that people stoned on acid are immune to radiation?"

"Oh, definitely. Want some?"

"Is it true, Mr. Garcia, that Grace Slick put LSD in the punchbowl at Tricia Nixon's wedding?"

"That's a damn lie! *I* put it in. . . ."

These guys have seats on the Stock Exchange, their great-great-grandparents' great-great grandparents came over on the *Mayflower,* they own pet-shop chains, or even whole *cities* out on Long Island. But we seem to have a wicked effect on these people; they never should have come.

"Jerry, I'd like you to meet Roger Lewis. . . ." The aforesaid Roger subsequently sells his seat on the Stock Exchange and gives away all of his money (well, *almost* all of it). Later he gets busted in England for selling LSD and moves to Nevada.

"Phil, this is Huntington Hartford's daughter. You know, the A&P heir? She's a big fan of yours. . . ."

"Rock, do you know Thayer Craw? You two should really hit it off. . . ." And that, my friends, is the end of *that* famous old name. She ends up marrying one of the Pranksters.

MEMO TO JOE SMITH, WARNER BROS. RECORDS
FOR OUR NEXT ALBUM WE RE PLANNING SOMETHING VERY SPECIAL: A MUSICAL INTERPRETATION OF AN LSD TRIP. COME ON, GUYS! YOU'RE ALWAYS PROMOTING US AS A PSYCHEDELIC BAND, SO NOW WE'RE GIVING YOU A PSYCHEDELIC RECORD. IT'LL BE THE HAIGHT'S ANSWER TO SGT. PEPPER. ONLY WE'RE GOING TO DO IT IN REAL TIME. A TEN-RECORD SET. AT LEAST!
  JUST KIDDING (I THINK).
  YOURS, GRATEFUL DEAD

As soon as we're back home from the tour the pressure is on for new material for the second album. We have an idea, we just don't have any *songs.* The contract calls for an album a year for five years. There are men, serious men in white shoes, waiting for *product.* And I, most recklessly, have told these impatient souls they shall have their vinyl calf before the first full moon in December. Jerry, man, what *are* we going to do next?

For rock groups the second album is always the crunch. Or maybe it's the third (I hope). Anyway, by hook or by crook we have to come up with another album. We used up all our old chestnuts on the first album. *Plus* we are going to wear this material out. By the time the record's out and in the stores, the band is *way* tired of it. They've already been doing "Silver Threads and Golden Needles" for a year and a half, at least.

Most of the songs the band comes up with are developed in rehearsal and are taken to the stage almost immediately. From the start the Dead have an incredible ability to just be balls out, playing stuff at gigs they've only dicked with during practice. I'll hear a riff at rehearsal and two days later they're doing it at the Avalon or at the Fillmore. Pretty risky, especially because none of them will ever cop to not knowing the words. They'll just make up what they can't remember, and then in the dressing room afterward everybody's talking at once, going, "Jeez, that was interesting. What *was* that you were singing out there?"

What the hey, it came out better on Friday than it did on Wednesday, didn't it? So they try it again Saturday, and on Saturday it's different (again), but the goddamn thing is actually evolving, just wending its gnarly way toward becoming a Deadsong.

But now, my friends, we must to have *many* Deadsongs, so epic of Grateful Dead can continue. We must to have — dare I say it? — *new* material. Never-before-heard, *minty* stuff. And where is it going to come from? We can't just count on members of the band periodically *forgetting* songs and having to make up new stuff onstage, now can we?

Coming up with the *words* is the hardest part for the Dead, so they start bringing in outside lyricists like Robert Hunter. Hunter's an old friend of Jerry's from the Palo Alto days when they used to live in their cars and bum around the folk clubs. A couple of months ago Hunter mailed Jerry a bunch of lyrics from New Mexico, among them some of the verses that will become "Alligator."

In August 1967 we go up to the architect John Woerneke's ranch on the Russian River to do a bit of woodshedding. He's an old friend of the band and he foolishly turns his whole place over to us. Oh well, I rationalize, he'll have this colorful past to remember after he gets reeled back in by his family's wealth.

It's a wonderful place, right down on the river. It is a very hot summer and the river is really cold and as Hemingway used to say it was good. There's a fleet of canoes and a little pagoda sundeck thing right at the edge of the river. That's where the equipment is set up, in that little gazebo place, and that's where the boys rehearse and try to come up with songs. *Everybody* is crazy on this one. They try out "Alligator" and all these silly tunes that they pull out of their sleeves.

They finish up "Alligator" right out of the scene in the river, all these boaters and punters and inner-tubers floating downstream.

Pigpen lies around like an alligator in the shallows and waits for an inner-tubing party of girls to come floating down the Russian. There are a lot of naked ladies floating down that river. He waits patiently, under the water up to his eyeballs. They can't see his long hair or his tubbiness or any of that. He lays in wait and finally they come around the bend drinking beers and smoking joints and he goes "*AAAAAAAAAAAAGGH!!!*" and scares them half to death.

Mountain Girl and all the chicks make huge meals and we eat outside on the grass and it is very bucolic and scenic and a wonderful place for tripping, but it is also a rough time. We are not getting along all that well up here. It's too claustrophobic, and there's nothing else to do. There's no place for us to *go*. No way out!

So it's back to the city. One day we're playing at the Straight Theater — now known as the Grateful Dead School of the Dance in one of our more strained attempts to circumvent the limitations that the city of San Francisco keeps placing on live music — and a young drummer shows up and asks if he can sit in. Everyone is high on acid and it's the usual befuddlement. All very casual. *Too* casual; the band's sound has begun meandering wildly. We're a bunch of beatniks who started out drinking red mountain burgundy and smoking pot, and moved on to acid and MDA and DMT and other brain-numbing psychedelics, and by this point we're *dangerously* laid back. We're taking it easy, as usual, when suddenly in roars a B-52 in the person of Mickey Hart. And Mickey turns out to be the shot in the arm we so desperately need. He has that New York energy, a driving force that lights a fuse under us. He's a "different drummer," all right. It is strange, given the drive differential, that he gets along so swimmingly with the band. Soon Mickey and Billy Kreutzmann are the tightest of buddies. Their styles of playing are way different — Kreutzmann's more fluid — but Kreutzmann loves that.

Mickey's very disciplined. He counts it off, *one-two-one-two*, whereas Kreutzmann is a downtown swing drummer, a trap drummer essentially, whose heroes are jazz drummers. Mickey, on the other hand, is a stone percussionist. He's used to playing military marching music and he's right on the count. He's a black belt karate guy to boot. He drops the martial arts and loosens up a bit when he joins the Grateful Dead, needless to say.

There aren't many bands that have two drummers, much less two very different drummers playing in different styles. Trust the Dead to go for such a nutty setup! But the Dead desperately need the punch Mickey brings to their sound, in part because of the "Bobby Problem."

Like Jerry, Bobby Weir started out playing acoustic instruments, but for Jerry the transition from acoustic to electric is an easy one. He has more years of experience than Bobby, plus his playing is more intricate. He is a picker and thus a natural lead guitarist. And from his exposure as a banjo player in jug bands and bluegrass bands he knows how to pick and comp the rhythm at the same time.

But Weir is an acoustic guitar player who has yet to master the electric. He is still trying to play the electric guitar as if it were a Guild hollow body. Garcia is tearing his hair out. His constant refrain after practice is: "Uh, Weir, s'cuse me, but you gotta understand the nature of the beast. It's an *electric* guitar." He keeps saying it, as if maybe Weir just didn't hear him last time, or hasn't noticed.

As the rhythm guitar player, Bobby Weir should be the one holding down the groove, but Bobby's too spaced and unfamiliar with the electric guitar to play straight-ahead attack rhythm. Nobody else in the band is nailing that beat either. Certainly not Pigpen. His Hammond organ is more fill than pulse, and Phil Lesh is playing complicated bass right from the get-go. Rather than keeping the bottom end together, he plays the bass more like a lead instrument!

There's no bottom anywhere to rely on, no solid rhythm to lean on because Weir is playing late on the beat. More fill than rhythm. Fill is midrange sound, it comes after the attack of the beat, so it translates to the audience as filler. Between Bobby and Pig we are getting mostly midrange fill, which leaves the rest up to Jerry. Which means he can't play all the leads he wants to play. Instead of being able to fly, he is constantly having to bring the rhythm back to earth. This seriously undermines the Dead sound, because it's Jerry's soaring that is the heart of it.

Jerry is overjoyed at Mickey's arrival. With that extra drummer, the sound gets a lot sharper, and holding down the rhythm is no longer up to Kreutzmann and Garcia. We later find out that Mickey Hart was national drum champion. And his dad was a drum teacher. He knows the most complicated rhythm patterns imaginable and he is always on the money.

Mickey's drive has the additional side effect of straightening Phil Lesh out. Lesh has been under the illusion that he is "leader of the rhythm section," but he isn't funky enough to tack down the beat. Phil wants to wax symphonic on four strings! But he's got this very basic instrument. (That's why they call it a bass. . . .) Also, Phil has been taking more lead vocals, which doesn't exactly help him hold the bottom. Mickey and his energy galvanize the rhythm section and get the bass and the drums together.

Mickey Hart is the first musician that the Grateful Dead ever even considered for the band who doesn't come from their own backyard. He has a sunny disposition, which makes it easy for him to blend into the group. But laid back, he's not. He's intense as hell. Here's a guy from New York that has been in the military, a drummer in the Air Force Band, middle-class upbringing, middle-class values, impressed with all the wrong things. After he joins the Dead, he hires a limo whenever he visits his grandparents — so when he goes to his old neighborhood everybody will see him getting out of a limousine. He also brings his grandparents, the Tessels, backstage. Grandma Tessel bakes us chocolate chip cookies — they are *dynamite* cookies and we all gobble them up even though our mouths are dry and our noses are caked.

Almost immediately Mickey becomes part of the group and moves in with Phil Lesh and Billy Kreutzmann, just up the street from 710 Ashbury. One day Kreutzmann comes by 710 and I finally ask him something that's been on my mind.

"Listen, Billy," I say, "there's something I've got to know. How in the hell do you guys play so perfectly in synch?"

"Hypnotism," says Billy.

"You're kidding."

"No, man, I swear it. Mickey's been hypnotizing me, that's how it works."

"*Real* hypnosis?" I mean this is a bit unusual even for the Haight. We all wonder about it. A *lot*. Whether or not this is how Mickey Hart got to be the other drummer. "YOU WILL HIRE ME AS THE EXTRA DRUMMER! YOU WILL MAKE ME THE NEXT DRUMMER OF THE GRATEFUL DEAD!"

Once we have a few songs ready we make our first false start on *Anthem* in a little studio in L.A., doing some of the basic tracks for the first side. We're living in a fake Moorish castle in the Hollywood Hills.

Thirty-foot living rooms, huge ceilings and white carpets everywhere. Ever so slightly crumbling, another one of those places where we are strictly without furniture. It's Halloween and we're right up the street from Bela Lugosi's house. Jerry loves that — his favorite movie is *Abbott and Costello Meet Frankenstein*. Lugosi's house looks like the pyramids, with very imposing walls like those of a mausoleum with hieroglyphics on it. Designed by Frank Lloyd Wright.

While we're in L.A. we go check out the Maharishi. I think the Airplane got us tickets. As Jerry, Mountain Girl, Weir, and I go in, there are dozens of devotees swarming around, wearing little knee pads so they can crawl around in a perpetual devotional mode.

"Oh yes," they say, "his holiness will be with you shortly." He's a sweet old guy, a bearded swami straight out of an R. Crumb cartoon. And then he says, "I must tell you something, children. . . ." We are all breathless, awaiting the sacred wisdom, and he says: "You must not be calling yourselves 'Grateful Dead.' You must call yourselves 'Eternal Living'! And you must wear silken pajamas." I'm serious! He gives us each our mantra — mine sounds like a phone ringing.

We try. Mountain Girl's really into it: "You guys got your mantras together?" she asks us every morning. She even gets Jerry to go back for a second session. He hates it, but Mountain Girl is tenacious. For the next couple of weeks you can hear Mountain Girl saying to Jerry, "I got my little mantra, and it works. C'mon, if Ringo can do it, you can do it. *Anybody* can."

And Jerry's going, "But what would Madame Blavatsky say?"

After a few weeks we decide to call it quits with L.A. We have at least enough control to say we want to do our album in New York. We want New York because we're playing at the something-a-go-go that later becomes the Cheetah, and we're also looking for a studio with more than four tracks. The record company allows us to go because they want to get the record out, but they make the proviso that Dave Hassinger has to be the producer again.

We camp out in some falsetto group's mansion in suburban New Jersey, Jay and the Americans, I think, not too far from the tunnels and the bridges. It's on a tree-lined street and set back — and empty. Another one of those houses with no furniture where I have to rent beds for everyone. We commute into the city every day to record.

Relations with Dave deteriorate fast. He didn't want to go to New

York in the first place. We're about two-thirds of the way through the material that comprises Side One — all that studio stuff — but the studio cuts aren't making it. Hassinger is becoming more and more anxious because we are spending huge amounts of time doing things like stuffing quarters and feathers into the sound box of the grand piano to get those seldom-achieved sound effects.

Naturally much of this psychosonic experimentation looks to Hassinger like a big waste of time. We're at Century Sound less than a week when things start to fall apart. Ironically, it is Hassinger's little buddy, Bobby Weir, who provokes the violent reaction. As the band becomes less and less reasonable, Hassinger has come to see Bobby as the only one in his corner. Bobby is trying his best to be polite and isn't (currently) smoking dope. Still, even reformed acid-eaters have strange thoughts.

"Born Cross-Eyed" is Weir's first original song and he has some very specific ideas. But he doesn't quite have the vocabulary to convey the ineffable idea he has in his head and while listening to the playback says to Hassinger, "I don't like the sound of that."

Hassinger's jaw drops open. "What are you talking about? There's nothing going on there! It's just air. Dead air or something."

To which Weir answers: "Well, that's what I want. I want the sound of, uh, heavy air, only more of it."

"What the hell does 'heavy air' mean, anyway?"

"It doesn't *mean* anything, Dave. It means whatever you want it to mean. Uh, y'know, summer air with linnets' wings. Like, a lot of bugs and the light filtering through."

This sound-of-heavy-air business is the straw that breaks the camel's back. Hassinger goes berserk. Mentally and physically falls apart before our eyes and becomes a mass of twitching enraged protoplasm. The guy loses it. He becomes speechless, literally unable to speak. The Dead can do that to people. He's ahead of his time, one of the early casualties of culture shock. The guys running the record companies are a generation older than us and from an earlier school of making records. It isn't just Dave Hassinger, it is us trying to mesh with that straighter, earlier generation world of how things are done.

The heavy-air effect is achieved by splicing a three-second strip of paper — called an "island" — in the tape, which in one enveloping "ooooooooosh" inhales the sound of a sultry August night.

After Hassinger goes belly up the whole thing is dumped in our lap, which is the way we want it anyway. We tell Warner Brothers: "Don't send us any more guys in golf shoes." It is time to move the Neanderthal recording industry into the next era. Dan Healy's been taking care of our equipment, and he is an electronic wizard who speaks our language and the studio's language, so he is the natural choice to take over. The only person really who might be able to deal with our overwhelming dilemmas. He's not simply replacing somebody who went ballistic, he's also replacing the way people go about making records.

Of course, who's going to do what on the album is always a bit tricky when you're dealing with a group of independent-minded people. Especially so with the Dead who have, at this point, four potential lead singers: Garcia, Weir, Lesh, and Pigpen. Juggling all this is a delicate operation. And don't forget the drummers who don't sing but want their piece of the pie, too.

It's like a family anywhere. Someone is always feeling left out: "Hey, I got ideas, too!" Someone else is saying in a whiny voice: "How many songs does Weir have on this album?" And I'm like Mother Goose ladling out tracks in a singsong voice: the first track is Jerry's, the next is Weir's, the next is Phil's, the next is Jerry's, the next is Weir's, the next . . .

It's during the making of *Anthem* that Tom Constanten gets involved with the band. He's a music school friend of Phil's and in November, Tom starts playing piano on some of the tracks. In those days you ferreted out freaks in whatever area you could find them. But Tom is an oddity even for the Grateful Dead.

He has a ridiculous Napoleon Bonaparte haircut — with kiss-curl pulled down and trimmed ever so carefully across, wearing a four-button jacket buttoned all the way up with a new immaculate white collar. The rest of us are all shaggy, growing beards, wearing ripped T-shirts — clearly the man has no sense of appropriate studio attire.

He has an erudite wit, which doesn't always chime with the prevailing acidic sense of humor of the Dead family. He perhaps takes things more seriously than we do, especially his new "religion," Scientology. Probably a reformed speed freak like Monsieur *con brio* Lesh.

Anthem of the Sun evolves into a picture book of images that meanders all the way through a trip and comes out the other side. In other words, you can't make head or tail of it, and that's sort of the point.

And what would a trip be without sound effects? In the section after Jerry's song "That's It for the Other One," we use UFO landing sounds and other strange noises. It's a forerunner of the space jam. And a lot of this stuff — just plain guitar weirdness — the Dead do *live*. We have this box called the Insect Fear Device, that you can plug the guitars or microphones into and play or sing through it and it makes all kinds of unearthly sounds.

The prepared piano is pretty much Tom Constanten. The term "prepared piano" means doing things to the piano, but it is used in its widest sense here. Stuffing things in it, partially damping strings, causing strings to rattle against things. Tom puts quarters and half dollars and shit in between the strings or weaves cellophane through the strings and it makes really eerie cracking sounds. A grand piano is an amazing contraption. You can use a grand piano to actually *launch* stuff. There's also a little prepared *comb* on this record. Pigpen is wicked on cellophane-and-comb combo. He plays a bit of jaw harp and all those little sort of trinkets that you horse around with.

And then there's the sounds of destruction. Abusing and misusing equipment to come up with those strange and obscure noises. The Dead go through a whole period of demolishing microphones and seeing what sounds you can get 'em to make as they die. Dropping them, closing them in a door, that type of thing. Random destruction of the sacred cows of our parents' generation. Our parents came out of the Depression and their motto was: "Take very good care of this stuff, you may never get another one."

We were all raised with those pieties, so trashing your shoes or a piece of equipment or trashing your instrument is something that we all have to get out of our system. It's the same as getting away with saying "fuck" on the radio, which we are doing a lot. Garcia gets sixteen "fucks" into one interview in Philadelphia.

It is a fragmented process because we're jumping from studio to studio. Jerry doesn't feel that we can do a good mix at Century Sound and prevails on me to call Paul Simon and find out if we could use one of the CBS studios. So that's what we do, but all these scenes are unionized to the max and in the middle of mixing down "Cryptical Envelopment" Jerry just forgets and reaches over and touches a knob and bang! we're outta there. We get thrown out of a couple of other studios for smoking grass — in quest of that elusive sound we hear all the time onstage. But we aren't getting it on tape. The band are looking for that live sound in the studio, but the technology just isn't up to it. Neither is the band. They're used to playing together. We can't isolate the drums so they don't bleed into the microphones on the other instruments. To the Dead this business of listening to a drum track on headphones while playing guitar is downright creepy. And it's at this point that it occurs to us, why don't we use live tapes that already have that spontaneous feel?

The idea of pressing on with a studio album is not that appealing because the Dead are and always will be a live performance band and don't flourish in a studio environment. The gigs are so much more fun and yield so much more interesting music. Trying to duplicate our sound in the studio seems futile.

The stigma against live recordings is entirely a record company thing, and needless to say it comes down to the scaly business of money. Since the songs in live concerts are usually rerecordings of material for the most part already on studio albums, there isn't a new set of songs to scoop the publishing gravy off of. And because it doesn't go through the normal channels, the producers and A&R guys don't get a cut either.

Anthem in the end is part live/part studio, but we tell Warner Brothers it's a studio album. This is possible because everything is so far out of whack that by the time it gets down to the fine point of what is actually on the album, it is ten light-years beyond the question itself. In the meantime we resolve to take recording equipment with us on our next tour and begin packing stuff up to head back to the West Coast.

☺

Back home we find we can't take the Haight anymore. There are tour groups passing by all the time. The Gray Line buses stop *right in front of the house.* And everybody who comes to the Haight has the idea that they can go and talk to Jerry or Janis anytime they like. Casual intimacy was one of the great things about the Haight, but once the population multiplies it is lost. You can't be intimate with fifty thousand people. Most visitors to 710 are polite, sincere, and stoned, but eventually it does get to us. Even us hippies can't be nice to everyone!

The strain is so great that things are actually becoming tense in our very laid-back household.

Being Hippie Central does have its perks. People like Neil Young and David Crosby come up and visit us. Even Sir George Harrison comes and spends the weekend, and I end up showing him around the town. We are smoking as we go. Smoking, smoking, smoking. He can't believe people openly rolling joints on Haight Street, people *throwing* joints at him. English visitors are always boggled by the whole pot scene. And he loves the fact that he can walk down Haight Street more or less without hassle. People just hand him joints and maybe walk along and chat for a minute and then let him go his own way.

On Divisadero we run into a couple of Hell's Angels, Tumbleweed and Pete. Wow! Real sweaty, savage Hell's Angels. The terror of the West. He's impressed, all right. *They're* impressed, too.

"Fuckin' George Harrison, man!" Somehow in the heat of the moment George invites them to come and stay with him "whenever you're in London, man." You know, at *George's* house! Now in England, this sort of invitation is taken for what it is: perfunctory politeness. Besides, he must have thought, when are two Hell's Angels ever going to show up at Savile Row? But this is California, baby! The West — where a man's word is a man's word. . . .

"Well, Jesus, George, that's real decent of you. Real decent. We've been planning a trip to check out swingin' London, haven't we, Pete?"

"Yeah, take the tour of the Triumph motorcycle factory and all. Hell, we'll bring the Harleys, it'll be a hell of a time." Whereupon George proceeds to hand them . . . his *card*. A bit formal, I think, but the boys fall on it as if it were a fresh kilo of dope. They hand it to me — to sniff, I presume — and I notice it's an Apple Records card. Oh well, I guess he's not actually going to give them his home number, now is he? I mean, what if these guys actually show up?

We continue on down Haight Street. Kids are lying on the sidewalk, dogs in kerchiefs are running up and down the street, people are panhandling. It's so crowded in spots it's hard to walk. George suddenly seems alarmed.

"How do the Dead *deal* with this?" I tell him we're planning to bail out sometime soon, maybe move out to Marin.

The bus tours and crowds aren't the only drawback to our becoming Big Stars in the Haight. It's October 2, 1967, and Jerry and Mountain Girl have scored a big block of Acapulco Gold wrapped in beautiful blue cellophane. It's the happiest weed imaginable. Hallucinatory pot where you see little halos around everything. We also have some really second-rate *Cannabis americanus* out on the table in the house. Real stringy with lots of stems and seeds. Jerry and Mountain Girl are sitting in the pantry with the colander out on the counter and the shoe boxes, cleaning this Mt. Shasta weed and rolling some doobies when there's a knock on the door and, hey, it's Hermit from the Pranksters.

"Listen, I'm out of grass and I thought maybe you guys . . ." Now, this is a little odd because Hermit hasn't come by 710 before now, even to visit. But M.G. thinks, what the hell. "Hey, Hermit, sure. Help yourself to a couple of joints out of the shitweed on the kitchen table." Which he does and then she gives him a baggie full of grass. But instead of going off whence he came and getting high, he starts asking what Mountain Girl is going to do during the day, like he's going to hang out, which she definitely doesn't want to encourage and anyway she's going over to a store in Sausalito to look at fabric and buy some ribbons. She's making a stage shirt for Jerry.

Right after Jerry and Mountain Girl leave, Hermit skips down to the corner and gives the bag to the cops and they bust 710. When Jerry and M.G. get back a couple of hours later they are about to set foot on the steps of 710 when Brian Rohan's girlfriend, Marilyn, from across the street comes to her window and begins hollering to them, "Hey, you guys! Come on up! We're waiting for you up here." She lives right above the offices of HALO, the Haight-Ashbury Legal Organization. As M.G. and Jerry look out Marilyn's window they see the heat, a lot of guys in suits pouring out the front door of 710. They used Hermit to come in and set up Mountain Girl and the rest of us.

Shortly afterward I show up. I've been out of town and when I get back to the house everything is strangely quiet. It's already a bit weird that there's nobody hanging out on the front steps and when I see all the news vans I get a little pissed off: "Hey, who's havin' a press conference without telling me?"

I come storming up the steps and the door is locked. That is also a little strange because we never even shut that door unless it's freezing out, on account of people forgetting their keys. When I look into the office through the window and I can't see anybody, I immediately know there's trouble. I begin banging on the door: "Come on, you guys, open up!" The door flies open and a cop reaches out, grabs me by the shoulder, and yanks me inside the vestibule and says, "You live here?" and I go, "Uh, sort of."

"You're under arrest," and he reads me my Miranda rights. They've got Florence, Pigpen, Bobby, and Sue Swanson. Danny and Bob Matthews and I are already in cuffs and they take us all downtown.

Nobody really thinks we're going to be sent to San Quentin. We know we aren't even going to spend the night in jail. They put us in a holding cell for a few hours and ask us lots of questions. There's nobody in the slammer but us and we just sit there until Brian Rohan bails us out.

When we get back to the house we see to our amazement that the fuzz haven't found the kilo of dope in the pantry. How is this possible? The last view I had of it, it was sitting open on the shelf right there among the plates and dishes with the weed falling out of it, and the blue wrapping all ripped and hanging down. At eye level. It's inconceivable they could have missed it. We are very suspicious, and immediately think they're planning to come back and bust us again. Somebody takes it out of the house and hides it, and we never find any of it again. It's like they say: They'll never legalize marijuana because no one can find the petition!

Since the Dead have no intention of forsaking the demon weed or anything else for that matter, they decide they're just gonna have to think outlaw, and they keep that outlaw thing going forever. Especially Garcia. It's very important to him. For him it's a god-given American value. He says, "We're a nation of outlaws. A good outlaw makes a new law, makes it okay to do what he's doing."

As we're getting to the end of our rope in the Haight-Ashbury, there is a definite shift from the psychedelics and experimental drugs to the hard-drive drugs. Coke is becoming common, and recently speed has been making quite a spectacular comeback in Hippie City. A lot of the momentum of the Haight had to do with methamphetamine; it's something that we all experienced. Phil has been on speed for years, and Garcia and Bob Hunter could definitely have been called speed freaks during their coffeehouse days in Palo Alto. They lived on meth, grass, and cheap red wine.

When hard drugs come to town rumors fly around that some of us are doing smack. When Mountain Girl hears of this she has everybody on inspection. Weir, Lesh, Hart. At Winterland she catches up with me and nails me up against one of those vomitory ramps, slams me up against the wall, and rolls up my sleeve to see if I've been using a needle. Doesn't ask, just does it. I'm not pissed off that she's doing it, but I'm pissed off that she could believe that I'm using. I am proud to show her my arms. "Look, Mom, no tracks!" She scrutinizes me thoroughly, her eyes an inch from my skin. When the examination is over, there's no apology or embarrassment about the search. But then this *is* Mountain Girl. All you get is a clean bill of health: "Okay, you're clean. Good, I was worried." And you walk away very pleased with yourself.

But Mountain Girl has definitely picked up the right vibes. Hard drugs are humming through the scene. None of us are yet enough aware of their effects to be able to tell who is on what, and anyway everybody is tolerant of unforeseen mood swings even if we can't put a finger on what's causing them.

One afternoon I'm kibitzing with Peter Coyote and Emmett Grogan of the Diggers in the office at 710. There's nothing going on, the phone ain't ringing, and Peter and Emmett are getting antsy. Let's go upstairs, they say. I think we're going to smoke a joint. So we go upstairs and Emmett immediately starts cooking heroin in a spoon and I think, Ooohhhh, man, he's going to shoot up, which just makes me queasy, but he's enthusiastic about the stuff. He's raving about it. "Gotta try this shit, Rock! How do you know you don't want it if you never tried it?"

Emmett says it's really cool, so of course I decide to try it. Story of my life! He ties me off and shoots me up and when he takes the tie off I feel this incredible hot rush and the next thing I know Pigpen's in the room screaming and yelling at me. I guess I must've passed out. I am sweating all over, clammy and cold as a bitch, and Pigpen is just livid. He's screaming, "What the fuck did you do to him? I'm going to go call an ambulance."

Peter calms him down. "No, no, no, we don't want to *call* anybody, for chrissakes! He'll be okay, he'll be okay." I wake up with Grogan slapping my face and Pigpen's on top of him, ready to kick his kidneys in. And that's my first brush with smack. Scared me to death.

Drug-dealing had always been an easygoing, amateur affair in the Haight. You bought a few kilos of grass and sold ounces to your friends. But shortly after the Summer of Love a more sinister species of dealer moves in. It doesn't take long for the career criminal element to figure out that these hippie kids have money and want drugs. Most of these kids don't have a clue what pot is and by the end of that summer oregano is going for thirty-five dollars a bag, aspirins are being sold as LSD for five dollars a hit. Little hippie kids catching a buzz off Bayer. And in no time at all drug turfs spring up. When they find Super Spade's body out in Marin County thrown off a cliff, we know we're in trouble. Super Spade was a classic Haight-Ashbury dealer, pot and acid is what he dealt. It was a Mafia hit. Up until now there wasn't serious money being made — except by chemists like Owsley. Mobsters didn't know where to buy LSD and even if they could find it they didn't know how to distribute it, but they soon found a way.

Crime comes in with a vengeance. Of the old hippie dealers only Goldfinger is left, up against this enormous group of gangsters who are trying to muscle in on Haight-Ashbury.

By the end of '67 things are beginning to come apart very rapidly. It's become a runaway train. We march in the Death of Hippie parade. It's a Mime Troupe–inspired event designed to catch the attention of the news media and send a message that will hopefully say to kids thinking of coming to the Haight: "Stay where you are, it's getting worse here by the moment. We can't feed you, there's no housing, there's bad drugs." Staging symbolic events is a Mime Troupe specialty, and in this we support them wholeheartedly. Not that it does a lot of good. The scene in the Haight will go on for a while, but after the Summer of Love invasion we just want the party to end. Turn out the lights and everybody go home.

◎

Thanksgiving 1967 feels like a last hurrah. The Airplane come, and the Charlatans, and Stanley Mouse and Alton Kelley and Neal Cassady, our *genius loci,* presiding over all. We open all the big sliding doors that separate the different rooms — the front room from the dining room, the dining room from the back room, which is Pigpen's room. We finally get to see Pig's room. He has to clean up his room and make his bed and do all the things that he hates to do, because we are incorporating his room into the festivities.

We put together every table in the house, take doors off the hinges to make tables, and then cover the whole thing with motley table-cloths. We have tables winding through from the front of the house to the back, all on different levels. It goes up and down with the height of the different tables. People are sitting on easy chairs or towering over the tables on stools. Everybody brings something to this wonderful Thanksgiving dinner, their favorite thing or the best thing that they make.

The dinner is elegant: pies and soup, rice and all kinds of exotic side dishes, from American Indian recipes and Zen macrobiotic to traditional American turkey and stuffing and sweet potatoes and gravy. Everybody eats themselves silly except for Neal Cassady. Aside from sixteen diet pills, he doesn't eat a thing. For him those Desoxyn are the best brown meat, white meat, stuffing, mashed potatoes, sweet potatoes and pie and gravy and cranberry sauce imaginable.

Le tout rock 'n' roll of San Francisco comes. It's probably the first time a lot of us have a celebration like this that isn't with our families. It's one of those moments where we realize that we're making our own kind of family here.

Cassady never sits down. He's up on the table, doing a little dance from corner to corner, rapping out his own Dada digest of the news. A futurist collage of an article on Vietnam and then on to movie reviews or some book review and then back to how the folks at the White House are planning to celebrate Thanksgiving. This is our dinner music. Jerry loves it because you can talk over it or under it, relate to it or ignore it. Jerry and Phil, who are both well read, listen to it like instantaneous poetry and toss lines back to him and feed the frenzy. Cutup conversations pieced together out of the dross and everyday surrealism of American culture, a Mahabharata of gossip, mental mumbling, song lyrics, weather reports, and menus. You can see why Kerouac and Kesey loved him so much. The guy was a brilliant writer who never stopped long enough to write it down.

But under the camaraderie and high spirits runs a strain of melancholy. We know something we believed in with all our hearts has ended. The Haight is going all to hell and shortly the Dead family is going to be splitting up. We're never all going to live together again. We are being cast out of Eden. Time to roll another joint.

9

Whores, Wars, Weed and the Wild, Wild Northwest

<<<<<<<<<<<<<<<<<<<<<<<<<<<<<<<<<<<<<<<<<<<

WE WANT TO get out of town! Need to mix it up a bit, get our vibes out on the street, and we are hot on the trail of . . . something! Not to mention we need to record some live dates to complete *Anthem of the Sun*.

The Quick and the Dead Tour of the Great Pacific Northwest (January 20 to February 4, 1968) is the first really full-scale out-of-state Grateful Dead tour. It is the first tour we do that actually has the word *tour* in it. It's also the first traveling Haight-Ashbury hippies-on-the-road show. We are at last able to stand back and look at it and say, "Hey, yeah — we're the guys from San Francisco. Fuck you!"

The Northwest tour is the start of a long and endless road, and with it begins the whole homeboys-leave-home thing. We know we can make it at home, but can we put it all together and jam it into some vehicles and *take* it anywhere? For a bunch of guys with guitars from the Haight, the concept of the Dead spreading their vibe to the whole country is awesome. Being that it's the first time on the road, we all dust off our funniest jokes and our coolest look, the fringe jacket and fancy boots, and put it all together to see what happens. Everybody is incredibly colorful and everybody has a rap, everybody has a shtick, everybody has a routine. It's all happening simultaneously: the Grateful Dead poking its collective hoary head out in the world and each of us individually emerging from our cocoons and transforming and all the people out there on the road are doing the same thing, too. It's a carnival, a hippie Buffalo Bill show with young, freaked American rock 'n' roll music.

Bobby Weir is jumping out of his skin with excitement, anticipation, mischief. Girls and pranks! Before we even leave town he gets busted for water-bombing a cop (I think maybe he took the rap for Mountain Girl on that one). He's still a kid, a goofy, spaced-out kid, acid or no, and seriously into pranks.

"Raaaaa, squirt 'em in the face!" At the Seattle airport he pulls out a toy gun. It's just after the first Piedmont Airline hijacking and there are signs everywhere, "NO GUNS — NO FIREARMS — NO JOKES."

"What the hell is this?" Weir says scrutinizing a sign. "No jokes, are they kidding?"

He carries those stupid cap pistols around that look like real guns, and right in the middle of the airport he fires off this ammo. Next thing there are twenty cops encircling us with drawn guns yelling "FREEZE!" They bust him and I have to bail him out — we're playing Eagles Hall in downtown Seattle that night. He's the most bust-prone person in the group. He's the least focused so he's always getting in trouble, and he's just incredibly naïve.

The Quick and the Dead Tour poster looks like an old Wanted poster. George Hunter and Mike Ferguson do it. It features an old steam railroad train — landscape with galoots. John Cipollina and Bobby Weir take to the outlaw theme a little too realistically. They both have blank guns and they shoot each other on the street in carefully staged little *High Noon* scenarios. People watching go, "My God! He just shot him!" And then Cipollina and Freiberg pick Weir up and throw him in the car and drive around to the back of the motel.

The cops take this outlaw business seriously — hey, it's a *show,* dudes! After we play the Quonset Hut at the University of Oregon in Ashland, they pull the roadies off the highway, make them take everything out of the truck, and proceed to search it item by item. This is the very beginning of that kind of harassment. And there is a *lot* of shit to search through! Not only the sound equipment, which is growing almost daily, but all the recording gear.

We play Seattle, Eureka, Ashland, and Eugene, where Kesey lives. Also, Portland's Crystal Ballroom and Portland State right in the middle of downtown. It's immediately before the sort of straight, adult community realizes what's going on, so we can still get away with a lot of craziness. And naturally we don't waste any time. These are the days when, if the show is late, or if something happens, it isn't like it is now where there's millions of dollars hanging on the event and it's all real serious and businesslike and everything has to be backed up by a B Plan or a C Plan. It's pretty much by hook or by crook and it's frequently hanging by a hair. I don't think we make *any* money on this tour. By the time we pay for all the catapulted TVs and broken Magic Fingers and monstrous long-distance phone bills, there's not much left in the kitty.

It's way more than a musical camaraderie between the two bands — it's friendship. Hustling girls and stuff like that. There is always some diversion. On the road, music isn't the only or even the central thing. There's always some debacle in travel arrangements or in hotel reservations to complain about, or the food, and on and on. And, of course, there's the endless rapping. We spend *a lot* of time getting high and sitting around and talking about stuff we want to do. Always some pie-in-the-sky dreams.

"Wouldn't it be great if we could play on top of the Space Needle?"

"What about the Grand Canyon?"

"Shit, why not the Pyramids?"

@

After the tour Jerry and Healy hole up in the studio trying to mix down the live tracks for *Anthem*. Healy has to essentially invent the future in order to solve the problems that are coming up with this album.

Anthem is a very organic production; we take pieces here and there wherever we can find them. Some eight-track, some four-track, some quarter-inch combined with a lot of different tape configurations, mostly stuff Bob Matthews pulled off the PA on the Quick and the Dead Tour and from a show at King's Beach Bowl in Lake Tahoe.

The first album had been done on a four-track machine, and getting the sound we wanted involved a lot of ping-ponging. We went to New York at the beginning of the *Anthem* sessions because we wanted access to eight-track and there weren't any eight-track studios in San Francisco. But by the time we get around to the final mix, Apostolic has opened an eight-track studio called Pacific High on Brady Street just south of Market. We have the little studio in the basement and there we bring our tape hoard: the Hassinger tapes from the studio plus all the live tapes. Thousands of pieces of tape of all different configurations. They all have to be synchronized *by hand* — this is well before automated equipment. It's a long and monstrously tedious project. You start by picking a performance, say "New Potato Caboose" from Eagle Auditorium in Seattle. But halfway through the song it turns to shit because when the wind blows at outdoor gigs the sound goes all to hell. Then the painstaking process of looking for another "New Potato" begins (so we can cannibalize sections in order to, eventually, get one complete take).

But not all of these tapes are going to match. There's no way you can physically splice them because some of them are on half-inch tape and some of them on quarter-inch tape and so on. So Healy invents a system of complicated leaders and backtiming to synchronize the tapes as close as he can by hand. He starts up the tape machines and puts the sound from one performance in one ear of an earphone and the sound of the other performance in the other ear, climbs down underneath the tape machine and rubs his thumbs on the flywheels, listening until it gets together inside his head. When he has them synchronized he shouts to Jerry, who flicks the switch.

Healy's models are the Beatles recordings and Brit production in general: stacking vocals, the whole technical, philosophical approach to recording. British pressings are superior, and that's what the Dead aspire to. Each and every one of us is over his head in terms of experience and knowledge, but we manage to get up early enough and go to bed late enough that we stay one step ahead of the devil.

The mixing is done by Jerry and Healy on huge quantities of DMT and nitrous oxide. They lug monster tanks of nitrous into the studio and mix all night (just to make it doubly strange).

Finally Jerry and Healy fuse *Anthem of the Sun* into one long continuous work. It's a miracle of ingenuity, but I suddenly realize that unless we break it into tracks, we aren't going to get paid more than two cents for publishing rights for the whole record. And so, after they have achieved the near impossible by putting together these thousands of scraps of tape into a coherent seamless whole, I have to tell Healy and the rest of the group that we have to take the thing apart — band it. For the purposes of the publishing (and airplay) there's got to be moments of silence between "Cryptical Envelopment" and the electronic weirdness that comes next on the album.

There have to be bands to differentiate between cut one, cut two, and so on. Thus, a lot of the song titles are arbitrarily stuck on, and if you were to say to Phil, "What does this title mean?" he might even have trouble identifying the song. In a frenzied last-minute brainstorming session, we divvy up the number of minutes into songs, artificially cutting it up into tracks. In one mad swoop we come up with "Quad-libet for Tender Feet" (that would be Phil's) and "The Faster We Go the Rounder We Get" (Jerry).

When we lift our heads from recording *Anthem* we see that the kids the Summer of Love dumped on our doorstep have never left. And new ones are arriving daily, not knowing anybody, living in the rain, crashing on people's floors.

We continue to get inundated with kids and problems, and all our plans for this beautiful hippie community go to hell in a handbasket. Well, we tried. Free soup kitchens, music in the park, the Free Clinic, the Haight-Ashbury Legal Organization. But there's just too many kids for us to deal with, and when the hard core dope dealers move in, it's the beginning of the end.

As the weather gets warmer, the streets of the Haight are getting *fiercely* crowded. Kids are still coming from around the country, pouring into San Francisco, escaping miserable winters in New York, Boston, Kansas City, St. Louis. The street scene, moreover, is starting to get hairy. The Fillmore district is close at hand and roving bands of hoods are preying on the innocent babes and naïve guys from the Midwest, coming to town with their stakehold of eleven bucks or eleven hundred bucks or maybe some grams of speed to sell. It's all escalating ominously.

And to top it off, the streets in the Haight are filling up with tourists from the Bay Area itself, coming to see for themselves what they've been watching on the national media about one of their own neighborhoods. Every weekend it is bumper-to-bumper traffic. The cops can't even move down the street because they're stuck in the huge throng of tourists.

We make a deal with the city to close Haight Street to traffic on the weekends. From seven o'clock in the morning it is wall-to-wall people in the middle of the street from Divisadero all the way to Golden

Gate Park. Ten to twelve blocks of solid people, walking in both directions. This incredible flow back and forth, going to the Army Navy Store, looking into the head shops, going to the Psychedelic Store . . . eating peroushki.

It's a perfect opportunity for the band to play a gig in the street, but we can't get a permit from the Parks Department and the police aren't cooperating. Sometime in the middle of the week we decide to take the matter into our own hands. We start to plot. We target March 3. Pulling the wool over their eyes is one of our favorite pastimes from Prankster days.

"Oh, fuck, if we can figure out a way to do it before they figure out how we did it, we'll get away with it. . . ."

"Yeah, let's prank 'em!"

The whole thing takes about three days to set up. We rent two flatbed stake trucks that we can set the gear up in (and nail it down to). We lie to the traffic cops at the barricades on our way in: "We're just coming to get our equipment out, officer, we've got a concert to play tomorrow, da, da, dada, da." Laird does the same deal with his truck, which is backing down from the opposite street. "We're just loading, man!" "We're just unloading, officer!" Our stories don't mesh, but the cops can't leave their posts — they have to watch the barricades. We back the two trucks together — bang — lash them to one another. The Straight Theater gives us electricity right out of the office upstairs over the marquee. We plug in and we're on! We get away with it because we are better at this stuff than the cops. We'll be out of there before they can find the last extension cord.

At least twenty blocks of solid people, just coming to do the tour of the Haight-Ashbury, and here is the Grateful Dead *playing* to them. The Dead do four songs: "Viola Lee Blues," "Smokestack Lightning," "Lovelight" and "Hurts Me Too." By the time the cops figure it out, it's a done deal.

We're in the middle of Haight Street and can't hang the crowd up forever, so Phil Lesh invites everybody to the park:

"And now for a little *cosmic* entertainment. It's a beautiful day . . . the park is only four or five blocks away. Why don't we all walk through Golden Gate Park and watch the sun go down over the sea. . . ."

We pull the trucks apart, the crowd sweeps right through, and the street is empty in about an hour. And some ten thousand people walk through the park to the ocean and watch the sunset.

Everywhere in San Francisco, it's getting harder and harder to play. One of the Dead's aspirations lo these many years has been to find ways of functioning outside straight society. It doesn't immediately occur to us that this might involve changing social patterns that have been around since the Stone Age, and that going from the Stone Age to the Stoned Age ain't going to happen overnight.

Some of our early skirmishes with the old order are over the ballrooms. Those lovely old dance halls — the Fillmore, the Avalon — are, to us, as sacred ground. The old order sees them, quaintly, as real estate. As protégés of Kesey and the Pranksters, we look upon dance halls as communal spaces where people can come and freak freely. The Acid Tests began in the ballrooms, created the audience for the ballrooms in fact. And at the early concerts at California Hall, the Fillmore Auditorium, and Longshoremen's Hall, admission was minimal (just enough to cover the cost of putting the thing together and keeping the bands in groceries).

Only a year ago you could rent the old Fillmore for around two hundred bucks a night. We would bundle up the rent money, get together some bands, and go do a gig there. We would charge a buck or so at the door, whatever anybody was willing to give, and as soon as we got back the two hundred bucks, everybody else sort of got in free. It was very, very lenient. All that came to a screeching halt when Bill Graham had his fiscal epiphany and wanted the place all to himself.

Six months or so after the beginning of all of this, the Fillmore Corporation issued a decree that whoever first came up with five grand could have the year's lease on the place, and guess who had the five grand? Virtually overnight the place became Graham's.

So instead of the Fillmore belonging to all of us, it becomes a venue. Graham has absconded with it and you now have to pay him to play there. Chet Helms has the Avalon over on Sutter Street, which is another, albeit feckless (hippie) venue, but you can only play there so much because it doesn't hold that many people and by now the crowds are getting larger. We are on the lookout for other halls where we can create a cooperative scene.

I remind Jerry of the time he and Pig and I went to see James Brown in his electric green suit at an ice rink called Winterland.

"Why don't we check that out?"

"Yeah, it's humongous, man, you could get the whole state of Rhode Island in there."

Through the manager of the Ice Follies we get the place. The floor at Winterland has plywood over ice and it's *freezing.* It's so cold you can see your breath in there. Still, it's big and brassy and the sound is good. Our first gig is a Halloween '67 bash with Quicksilver and Big Brother for which the Dead do up a wonderful orange poster with a multiplied Frankenstein mask on it. For our finale we wire Billy's drum kit with the help of a crazy pyrotechnic named Mike Freeman. He puts a wee bit too much powder in the little pots and it blasts the drums about five feet in the air and just about blows Kreutzmann off the stage.

Another ballroom enters our lives. One day in the fall of 1967 Dan Healy comes over to 710 like a man possessed.

"Jesus Christ! Holy Fuck! You won't believe this ballroom! Matthews and I were over on Market Street and Van Ness to pick up an Ampex 3-Track tape machine from the Irish Rovers and we stumbled on this *amazing* place. You guys'll cream! It's even got a spring-loaded dance floor!"

The Carousel is everything he says it is. It's a thirties ballroom owned by the League of Irish Voters. They hold their own special events there, their wakes and potato feeds and stuff. It has a red velour ceiling draped around these incredible chandeliers that look like falling stars. It is very, very plush. The stage is low like an orchestra bandstand and in front of it is a sign that flashes "fox-trots" or "waltzes," whatever the band happens to be playing, just like a skating rink. We're all totally into it, but Garcia and Hart are the driving force.

We quickly put together some money and the Carousel Ballroom becomes a co-op of the Grateful Dead, Jefferson Airplane, Quicksilver Messenger Service, Big Brother and the Holding Company, and the Hell's Angels. It's perfection. The only dissenting voice is that of Janis, wailing like Cassandra above the general rejoicing:

"It's like turning over the Bank of America to a bunch of six-year-olds. I give you guys six months at best. A bunch of hippies high on acid running a business — my Lord!"

At the Carousel we have one of our worst psychedelic nightmares. The notorious smuggler Goldfinger shows up one night and empties a bunch of mescaline sulfate into an apple juice jug. Within half an hour of that, another distributor shows up and he's got a bunch of powdered purple LSD that crumbled and he wants to get rid of it. So it goes in there. And then Jonathan Riester, the road manager, throws something in there, too. Soon it's a pharmacopoeia of acid, mescaline, MDA, and whatever else anybody feels like putting in there. By the time I get to the jug it's about three-quarters full. I put it up to my lips and stop. I take the tiniest, tiniest sip I can possibly take, and hand it to the next guy. And man, do I get ripped. Everybody gets into it (a big mistake on a lot of people's part). People are taking huge swigs, going "glug, glug. . . ." I can't imagine what's coming. Luckily, I have a sensor on the tip of my tongue developed by long, careful programming. This is mutation at its finest!

We also start running out of beverages, and a lot of people don't know that the jug of apple juice has become a science experiment. It's a steaming cauldron that's starting to look very organic — it's *purple!* It's a mess because the Carousel is a family place and kids love purple beverages and consequently a lot of them get dosed and end up at the hospital.

Snooky Flowers, Janis's sax player, gets dosed and Janis blasts Owsley (whose fault it isn't, by the way): "You son of a bitch! You dosed my sax player and he's had to go to the hospital!" Mountain Girl, who also gets badly dosed, sees blood pouring out of Janis's mouth and pouring all over the room. She runs out of the Carousel screaming. Jerry takes M.G. home and spends the night playing guitar to calm her down.

Bob Hunter loves this punch and he just keeps drinking. It hits him all at once. He's disappeared into a wall of hallucinations. Everything looks like an X ray, the corners of the room are missing and even the ceiling has a face. He gets into a fight and punches Owsley. He's at the end of his rope, ready to kill himself, and he slinks down the back stairs and disappears. He's all rolled up, down at the bottom of the back stairs outside, in the street. He doesn't know who he is or what he's doing there. It's kind of depressing when you take acid in the middle of downtown, in an alley off Market Street, and find yourself melting away.

As we're taking the gear out we walk right past Hunter without noticing him, thinking he's a bum sleeping it off. People end up freaked all over Northern California that night.

Owsley finds Hunter in terrible shape outside the back of the Carousel and — the saint! — goes back inside and takes a big gulp of the punch himself to try to figure out what's in it. He drives Hunter over to Goldfinger's house and leaves him with Nicki, Goldfinger's girlfriend (and my future wife), and then keels over himself.

Hunter raves on through the night saying he's being eaten by tigers, being shot with Kennedy, assassinated with Lincoln — he died a thousand times that night — and in the morning Garcia and a recovered M.G. come over and sit with him and calm him down. It's a long and bumpy ride — a quarter-million micrograms will do that to you.

The big problem with the Carousel is that it is downtown, on the edge of the Tenderloin, right in the path of the California riot zone. After the assassination of Martin Luther King, in the spring of '68, the area around the Carousel becomes an armed camp. There are police all over the place, riot squads marching in formation up and down the street, and at night the National Guard patrolling the street with big army trucks filled with helmeted troops. Nobody wants to come downtown; the city is practically an occupied zone. We have this new ballroom and nobody shows up. After thirteen losing weekends in a row we're pretty much out of money. Bill Graham is in the middle of San Francisco's black ghetto and taking big losses himself, but he can afford to.

And then to top off our woes there are the inevitable tawdry scenes of mismanagement that leave the Carousel weak and vulnerable. And who should come along but Bill Graham. He has a couple of guys from the Board of Health on his payroll, and he gets them to come out and condemn the place. Something to do with regulations about the flushing mechanism on the urinals.

Janis, beneath all the Mae West bravado, is a hard-headed woman when it comes to business and has always been scornful of the hippy-dippy frivolity about everything, a sort of devil-may-care attitude that comes from psychedelics. When she has fun she likes to drink and get down, get raucous and rowdy, and here we are, tripping on acid and reading the Akashic Record on the ceiling.

At the meetings we have with all the other bands when things start to fall apart, Janis usually is saying, "I knew it, I knew it! See, when you boys were taking acid back in 'sixty-six, I knew this was going to happen. You can't run a business and take LSD! Get real! Get serious! Or go broke!"

And then comes the last straw. We are playing a benefit for the school food program and some joker changes the sign on the marquee from FREE CITY CONVENTION to FREE CUNT CONVENTION. The theater is on the corner of Market and Van Ness right in the path of all the trolleys and traffic from the suburbs, so the cops end up getting about eleven hundred calls from irate commuting Catholics. Forty TAC squad cops burst into the hall wearing flak vests and plastic visors. And by the next weekend, guess who is up and running it as the new "Fillmore West"? Bill Graham.

The decline and fall of the Carousel Ballroom is a depressing spectacle. It's another scene where, if we'd been more organized, we could have hung on to it. We are out on the road and gone (and stoned) so much of the time we let a lot of shit get away from us.

Maybe we just don't have the form of greed it takes to wind up with all that stuff. The specific losses are depressing enough, but what makes us all feel bad in the end is that it is back to the same old system with the same old people running the store. When the greedy person wins, it means it's all by their rules — that bums us out and never stops bumming us out.

◎

As our tours take us farther afield, independent promoters are popping up all over the place. They are a shady bunch at best but none can quite compare with the pair of hustlers who book us in Philadelphia in March '68. They own a string of skanky nightclubs, and the Electric Factory where we're playing — Three nights only! Direct from San Francisco! — is their flagship. And have they got a deal for us! Part of the package deal is that we get to stay in their hotel.

"It's right over a nightclub, boys, you'll love it. And, Rock, at no extra charge, there's a bar downstairs at your disposal with live music. A fuckin' blues club and everything your little hippie hearts could desire."

It's in Old Town Philadelphia, and when we get there the front of the place is boarded up. There's nothing but a buzzing neon sign saying the Maggott Arms or something. Eventually a gnomish character leads us around the back of the building. We walk upstairs to what's supposedly the lobby. It's half the size of your average living room and smack in the middle is an iron grate with a plastic bulletproof window behind it and underneath that a metal drawer that slides out for you to put your money in. Well, okay, so the security is tight.

"Hi, we're the Grateful Dead, we're checking in. Can we have our keys, please?" There are no keys.

"You're all on one floor — straight up. Enjoy!" the man in the booth chuckles. We get a towel, a very thin, white towel with a bar of soap on it. We're all looking at each other like "Is this what I think it is?"

"No one to take the bags up, I assume," Phil asks. The guy in the booth just laughs and chokes on his cigar smoke. As we look down the hallways we see girls in various stages of undress — garter belts, lace teddies, dental-floss bikini panties, dog collars, six-inch heels and not much else. We've been put up in a whorehouse! Pigpen's eyes light up like flashing neon signs, but Phil is not amused: "I'm not getting unpacked and I'm sure as hell not leaving my stuff in this room. You can't even lock the goddamn doors."

"Relax, man, I'll see what I can do." I run downstairs. The guy in the booth doesn't understand the concept: "So why do you need keys? Are you worried one of your friends is going to steal something? It's guaranteed safe. Larry says so. You got the whole floor."

Pigpen's the only one who wants to stay there. Bobby is kind of amused by the whole thing but not enough to actually move in. Phil flat refuses to spend one more minute in the joint so his bags have to go back out on the equipment truck. Jerry doesn't want to stay, either, but he's typically laid back. "Actually, I think we need something a little *more* funky, don't you?"

For once, everybody is early at the gig. No one wants to stay around the hotel, as is generally their wont — room service, big color TV blasting away. But we'll have no money for other hotel rooms until *after* the gigs. Everybody is sitting on equipment cases, trying to nap and drinking coffee. Jerry sends me over to the music school next to this little hall we're playing to meet girls who have pads where we can crash.

"Jesus, Jerry, I didn't think pimping was in my job description."

"Read the manual, bro."

That night Garcia and I sleep under a grand piano at a student's apartment, Phil finds a lady to put him up, and Bobby, needless to say, finds a girl. Everybody has a place to stay, but it's a nightmare trying to find everybody in the morning, and we're in Philly for three days.

Pig, meanwhile, is having the time of his life. He loves me for this scene. He ends up with this helluva hooker, wooo! He hangs out down in the blues club every waking minute, and he plays harmonica all night. They love him, and by the time we got back to that hotel to fetch him and to get what little we've left there (we have to turn in the soap and towel), Pig doesn't want to leave.

⌾

While we're in New York in June to do some shows at the Electric Circus, some of the students who've taken over the Columbia campus uptown come by the Chelsea to see us. This is before we have things like whales and the planet to save; we're just down and dirty and dealing with "us" and "them." They lay that radical rap on us: "The board of governors say we can't, but we're the students and we're payin' for this, so screw you!" Aw*right!*

We're heroes to these kids, but we're far from the flaming radicals they imagine us to be. The Dead have always been in this precarious place where people see them as wild radicals, which they aren't. And they're not going to go along with someone else's idea of what they should be, either.

We are against war, obviously, but we've never gotten involved with Vietnam war protests because we have friends over there. The Angels and many of the Merry Pranksters have been in Vietnam and Cambodia. We say till we're blue in the face: "We don't want to be connected with anti-anydamnthing. We're not anti-war, anti-this, anti-that, we're just pro–music, pro-party, and pro–getting *down*." But these distinctions are lost on the students. They want the Grateful Dead to come up to the campus and play. There's a big radical town meeting that night and they invite us to sit in on it.

But first there's a band meeting. "Do we want to support this?"

"Hell, ya!"

"Look, guys," I say, "I'm proposing [not unselfishly] that we go for it. It'll be good for us. It'll be a fuckin' gas, man, and it's just the kind of *desperado* effort an outlaw band like ours ought to get involved in." Purposely phrasing it in such a way that it'll appeal to Garcia. His stance may be apolitical but his disposition is decidedly piratical. He's into doing it just for the hell of it.

"Let's do it! Why not? We're lending our music to this cause because it feels right. We're not going to get out there and say anything other than what the songs say. Just as long as they don't make any damn speeches."

Phil, on the other hand, is very practical. And cautious:

"Well . . . I dunno. We've gotta remind ourselves what we are. We're musicians, man, not revolutionaries. What are we doing with these guys? We've no business getting into this kind of stuff."

Phil is far more restrained about clashes with authority than the rest of us. He's been to Berkeley and seen enough "student unrest" to last him a lifetime. He's a *graduate* student, not a hotheaded undergraduate — his parents have put him through school — and he's a little less sanguine about trashing university property and holding the dean hostage. He's chary of what the papers will say about us: "We're already *personae non grata* for the drugs and the hair, who knows what they're going to make of our supporting a student riot."

Bobby Weir is just up-and-at-'em. Let's stir it up! He's the guy that's ready to water-bomb the Park Precinct station. And Weir loves college girls.

Kreutzmann tries to be stand-offish and cynical, like, "Okay, whatever makes us rich, whatever makes us famous."

The big question is how are we going to get the Dead in? Because by now, the campus is surrounded by police — it's way uptown, bordering on Harlem.

At a planning meeting that night, somebody says: "Don't the Dead use an International van to cart their gear around in?"

Hmm, this is one observant kid. "Yeah," I say, "we do as a matter of fact."

And the student says: "Well, I was thinking. Wonder Bread uses International vans for their delivery trucks. We could fit all your gear in the back if we remove all the bread except for the last layer. Just put a bunch of bread right at the back to conceal it."

Everybody is very enthusiastic. These are like long-haired, early Deadheads who really had the spirit about them. But then Abbie Hoffman gets up and lurches into his rant: "Are the Dead coming to Chicago? Or are they going to fink out and stick flowers in their hair?"

I bring the students' proposal back to the band.

"Hey, guys," I tell them, "we found a student who works in the kitchen at Columbia and knows the whole setup. Every morning a bread truck arrives underneath the plaza. The bread is unloaded and goes up in elevators to the various cafeterias. That's how we bring our gear in. It's just like a fucking caper movie!"

Jerry loves it. He loves movies!

All goes according to plan, and we set up in the Low Library Plaza quadrangle. The politicos take one look at our sound system and go crazy. They want those microphones badly, because their raps go on for hours and they're hoarse from shouting into these battery-operated things, their knuckles are white from squeezing the triggers, and their voices are gone. Several radicals overcome with PA lust jump up onstage and try to speak but we firmly remove them. Mikes are for singing! That's our simple philosophy of life. The Dead do a quick (for us) forty-minute set including "Cold Rain and Snow" and "Sitting on Top of the World" from the first album. Then without further ado we hustle offstage — and make our getaway in a Wonder Bread van.

In May 1968, "Dark Star," our second single on Warner, is released — lyrics by Hunter, music by the band — with Bobby's song, "Born Cross-Eyed," from *Anthem* on the B side. *Anthem* itself is released in July, appropriately with images of the band as Hindu demons — the only truly recognizable portrait being Pigpen's (right center). I'm hardly surprised when our noodling single fails to make it onto AM Top Forty, but the underlying motive in putting out a single is to give the band (and Warner's!) a glimmer of hope that we can make it as a commercial entity. We buy a lot of cheap time on FM late at night and it's on the emerging hip FM stations that the Dead get their airplay. *Anthem* does about as well as our first, which is encouraging considering its experimental premise.

We have another album due at the end of the year, which we're already rehearsing, but rehearsals are not going all that well. For the Dead a new studio album is always fraught with trepidation because whatever we do in that antiseptic white box is *never* going to approximate what the band does best: play live on stage. You're never going to bottle the default Zen energy between band and audience.

But, even if we put this dilemma aside, there remains the tug-of-war between experimentation and just plain songs. Jerry and Phil are both by nature inclined to the experimental approach, but Jerry (the folkie) is also strongly drawn to storytelling songs whose structure is the very antithesis of the improvisational route.

Weir's the group's rock 'n' roller, the one who wants to do more Chuck Berry songs. He wants, in fact, to be a rock star. Pig steers away from the experimental stuff. For one thing, he doesn't have the chops for it.

With this third album, a creeping panic begins to set in. The band is over the elation of the first album ("Hey we got a record deal!") and the experimental charge of the second ("We can do anything we want!"). Now cometh the existential moment when all is called into question — especially the merit of other band members.

In July '68, the Dead are rehearsing out at Hamilton Air Force Base in Marin County, and Garcia's frustration is beginning to show. He's exasperated that Weir can never keep his guitar in tune or on time. Garcia is bitching that Weir is spaced out most of the time (the macrobiotic phase has been forsaken for the moment), which wouldn't be so bad except that his playing is also in outer space. Jerry is becoming increasingly impatient over Weir's difficulty in grasping the fundamentals of the electric guitar.

Yes, the Bobby Problem is still with us. He isn't chunking down the rhythm so much as noodling, and for Jerry to play his solos he needs a solid musical bedrock under him. Without that, it all goes *fffwooooshhhh!* into outer space. Which admittedly is part of the Dead's charm, but the sound is getting *way* too psychedelic. In the ballrooms you want to keep everyone dancing, and the band is sliding out of the groove that keeps people moving.

Onstage, Jerry brings Bobby back into focus through cues. Just an eyeball and some heavy-duty (loud) rhythm from Garcia and — just at the point where you think Bobby's totally lost — he drops right in on the button. But it's very frustrating in terms of trying to figure out where a song *starts* and where it ends, where the break is and when the lyrics come in.

Pigpen is getting on his nerves as well. Pig is not getting into the new songs, isn't practicing, is drinking more and paying attention less. He's just turning up at rehearsal in his desultory way with a short span of attention and doing the same stuff he's been playing for the last two years. The material Jerry and Phil are coming up with is, to put it in the kindest possible terms, way over Pig's head. Pig is lost on anything outside basic blues and straight-ahead rock.

Pig is sitting at his big new Hammond with two huge Leslie speakers. Compared to his Vox this is like flying a 747. Pig is very slowly getting himself acclimatized. The Hammond is a complicated instrument. He's used to playing a keyboard half the size of a kitchen table. It sits up on a set of aluminum legs and is so light he can carry it around himself. Whereas the Hammond is a gigantic motherfucker, the size of a church door, and it weighs a ton. You need the crew to move it. And it's so much more complicated than his rooty-tooty little box organ. There're multiple keyboards, dozens of stops to pull out, and a daunting array of wooden organ pedals. He's got to figure out how to play the bottom end with his feet while playing the keyboard with his hands. And he ain't the practicing fool that Garcia is.

Garcia's a perfect maniac about practicing. *That's* his primary addiction. He's got to be playing all the time. On the road, in his hotel room, he's constantly going through his chord books, shopping for new ones when he's in New York, haunting the old music stores, scouring Brill Building music shops in an endless quest for finger exercises and chord charts.

Jerry's guys are Wes Montgomery and Django Reinhardt, the jazzy guitar players. Also the Spanish guitar maestros, Segovia and Montoya. He loves Spanish music because it's so intricate, but since it's by nature acoustic it isn't always relevant to what the Dead are doing.

For the electric, Garcia raids the technical manuals that the Fender guitar company put out. Leo Fender understood better than anybody how to get the most out of your solid-body guitar. All the variations you can run on a theme, exercise books. Jerry practices all the time. Just chords upon chords upon chords, all the possible configurations for fingering and diagrams for picking.

One day, after Bobby Weir and Pigpen leave rehearsal, Jerry asks me to hang around. Garcia and Lesh, it seems, have an important assignment for me. They tell me it is a matter of the utmost delicacy that they want me to handle as tactfully as possible: the firing of Bobby Weir and Pigpen. Not in my wildest dreams could I imagine firing either of them.

"May I ask what infraction the worthless scum have perpetrated now?"

Jerry approaches the issue with characteristic crablike obliqueness: "Weir for never coming down from planet Zippy and Pig for never getting off this one. One of them does too fucking much acid and the other doesn't do any. I don't care how you do it but you go tell them, Rock. The band just isn't happening, my friend."

"Tell them *what?* To clear out their desks? Why don't you tell them, you're so much more convincing a talker than I am."

We are just all plain crazed, and Jerry talks me into holding a band meeting.

Somehow I lure Jerry into kicking it off, but after some initial, esoteric mumbling he gets right to the point: "Shit, maa-an, I can't *do* this. . . . You tell them, Rock, you know, what you told me?"

"Say *what?*"

"Well, the stuff about . . . you know . . ."

"Oh, *that!*" (May the lord have mercy on my soul.) "Well, Bobby, uh, I think what Jerry is *trying* to get at and, uh, now don't take this the wrong way, but . . . have you ever thought about how attack oriented an electric guitar is?"

"*Attack* oriented?" Bobby has an annoying habit of repeating what you say when he doesn't understand or want to understand. He's just fucking with me. How dare I, lowly worm of a nonmusician, address him with this techno shit!

I'm drowning, obviously, but I press on: "You know, man, the snap the, uh, bite?"

I feel like a complete idiot.

"Jerry, old buddy," I say, "help me out on this one. . . ."

"Bobby, have you ever seen one of those TV shows where they show you what sound looks like?"

"What sound looks like?"

"Yeah, you know, a bird is singing and, uh, they show the highs and the lows on an oscilloscope?"

"Oh, like little mountain ranges or something when the sound goes up and down?"

"Exactly, amigo! The shape of a note is like a mountain and how steep the first slope is depends on the attack. It has a little swell in the middle as it gains its full resonance through the electronics and then fades out. So the bite has got to be on the opening part of the chord. If you're not biting that first part, the swell comes in the midrange. The midrange gets lost in the bass and foot pedal of the drummers, it's kind of the lost area in rock 'n' roll. Fill is what it is."

"Phil who?"

"Come on, ma-an! You know how, on a solid-body electric, there's the *ch* part of the note, which is the attack, and the *unk* part, which is the fill. And Bobby, what we need from you is more *ch* and less *unk*."

"More *ch*."

"Right. Cause the *unk* is in the midrange of the sound spectrum and midrange doesn't move correctly through air; it's slower, like a bass. The bottom end is the hardest amount of air to move, which is why the bass has got to have so much power. The attack of a bass is hard to hear. It's a broad, rounded-sound shape. Those big bass speakers move so much air you can feel it in your solar plexus. With that amount of air you don't get the bite. With me so far?"

"I'm not playing so good, eh?"

"Okay, let's take it from the top. . . ."

Aoxomoxoa. . . . O, great and terrible word! As you peer into its hermetic syllables do you discern there the mysteries of the ages? A self-chanting "om"? Do you see a skull and crossbones in the "oxo"? The genetic code? The Eye of God itself?

Aoxomoxoa. One of many strange titles that came up during the frenetic album-naming sessions at 710.

"Hold everything, guys! How about something simple and straightforward . . . like 'Aoxomoxoa.'"

"Now, *that's* more like it!"

"It is?"

"Yeah, it was so obvious!"

Actually Rick Griffin, God rest his soul, comes up with the word *Aoxomoxoa* while designing the cover. It's graphic, it's freaky, it's pseudo-Egyptian and . . . it doesn't mean anything! Rick was fascinated by palindromes — words that read the same backward and forward — and this cool-sounding nonsense word not only reads backward *and* forward, but you can *stack* it as well!

A
OXO
MOXOA

Also, it has that all-important vaguely cabalistic ring, the inscrutable cry of Griffin's flaming eyeball surfer.

An added bonus to the title is the contortions the Warner's execs go through trying to pronounce the damn thing. You can hear them in the next room, talking on the phone in these strangled voices, just trying to spit out the damn word.

The model for *Anthem* had been the long jams with songs embedded in them, but on *Aoxomoxoa* the Grateful Dead go back to conventional song structure. This has everything to do with Robert Hunter becoming the Dead lyricist. Bob is a poet, and poems, you might say, are songs without music. The initial stages of the Hunter-Garcia collaborations happen by mail. Hunter mails the lyrics to "St. Stephen" and "China Cat Sunflower" from New Mexico (along with the packet that has "Alligator" in it). The rest comes out of brainstorm sessions at Garcia's house in Corda Madeira.

Jerry never writes a song until he absolutely *has* to, and then only at the last minute. He hates the whole business, and the only way he can get through it is to collaborate with someone. The songs evolve from snatches of verse and riffs, Jerry banging on the piano and singing scat for Hunter to write the lyrics to. Sometimes they're just old tunes that Garcia dusts off and revamps — like "Dupree's Diamond Blues" lifted from the old tune "Jelly Roll Blues."

One of the first songs they cut is "St. Stephen," and after the initial Bay Area drifting intro you can hear how everybody comes down ka-chunk on the beat like hammering in nails. Then you hear Bobby's wail of joy — his homage to Big Brother.

Pig is seriously out of his element; he's being pushed around musically by Garcia and Lesh as the band moves away from the blues. They yell at Pig a lot. Some of this has to do with the psychedelic club. Pig isn't into psychedelics, never mind psychedelic music. He isn't into drugs, period. And here's Garcia and Weir stretched out to the max, and Phil taking acid through his *eyes* with eyedroppers!

"What we need," says Phil, "is someone who can play more philosophically complicated stuff, who can handle a bunch of different sounds. Not just that Sugar Shack shit, no offense."

Phil succeeds during these sessions in bringing his good buddy, Tom Constanten, into the group. The guy who played pianos prepared and unprepared on *Anthem of the Sun* is a well-versed student of music with no soul whatsoever. Constanten can handle the cadenzas all right, but he has a hard time with the funky chicken. It'll take Phil a long time to get soul, too. (In fact, there will always be some question in that area.) He has a hard time getting into the righteous bottom of rock 'n' roll. Isn't particularly interested in finding it, either. He's a complicated bass player. He plays the bass like a lead guitar — like Jack Bruce in Cream. Which is all right if you're Jack Bruce. If not, not.

Constanten and Pigpen are the odd couple — the conservatory pianist and the pizza parlor blues thumper. It's kinda okay since they don't exactly play duets together. Tom only plays the stuff that Pig can't handle: piano and harpsichord stuff. Pig on harpsichord? Hmn. . . .

Tom introduces us to a new breed of instrument: pianos with pedigrees. While the Dead have burned-up Fenders with cigarettes crammed into the strings, Tom plays clavichords that are inlaid with ivory and come from ancient plants in Czechoslovakia trailing contracts from Sotheby's and vast insurance documents from Lloyd's of London. And I have to admit Tom's harpsichord accompaniment on "Mountains of the Moon" is exquisite.

The Dead are a solid old rock 'n' roll band that had come into being through Pig and suddenly Pig doesn't have the faintest idea what's going on. The sessions are going on their merry serpentine, esoteric way and Pig's listening and listening and listening and becoming more and more perplexed, and by the end of each session, Pig is utterly crushed. I feel so sorry for him. Bobby is equally out to sea. His eyes are glazed over. He has a habit of putting his hands on his head and uttering a piteous "*Aaaawww,* man!"

Eventually Pig starts secretly taking lessons from John Cipollina's mom to learn the fingerings on the Hammond organ.

Aoxomoxoa is a patchwork of musical styles — the Elizabethan "Mountains of the Moon," the Spanish guitar on "Rosemary." The album's most obvious shift is back to the Dead's old jug-band sound, which comes close to parody on "Doin' That Rag" with its cartoony, skating-rink sound. Pig making his Hammond sound like a calliope. And Jerry is playing a lot more acoustic and bottleneck guitar. The sound they're reaching for is Americana filtered through the British invasion. On *Aoxomoxoa* the band tries out different techniques ad nauseam, and as a result much of the album is overproduced. And learning-as-we-go in the studio turns out to be an expensive process.

The quintessential Dead sound is a live sound. So we again run into the problem of how to bottle that high lonesome, good-timey sound in the sterile environment of the studio. For the band, it's a painful experience at best. Somewhat akin to hearing your voice for the first time on tape. When the Dead play "Cosmic Charlie" in dance halls, everyone jumps up and does the Owsley hop, but once they haul it into the studio the zing evaporates. Starts out bouncy and then goes, well, *sideways.* It's apparent once again that what we're getting in the studio is never going to approximate the symphonic experience of a live Dead concert.

"God, we make shitty records" is Garcia's constant refrain.

Aoxomoxoa begins Jerry's search for different ways to record his voice, filtering it through a number of devices in order essentially to disguise it. When Jerry sings through the phaser, it's as if he were singing against himself. The one that Jerry uses on *Aoxomoxoa* is the very first real phaser used on a record. It is designed by the ever-resourceful Healy, who creates a phaser box that you can actually *play* in a musical sense. Previously, you had to take two tape machines and make a copy of the same tape and run them side by side to make the phasing noise as they went by each other.

Aoxomoxoa is one long quest by Garcia for a vocal style that will complement the Dead sound. Which accounts for the chameleon-like singing styles he adopts on the album. Let's see, there's Jerry doing Traffic-era Stevie Winwood on "Mountains of the Moon" and a Lovin' Spoonful's John Sebastian vocal on "Dupree's Diamond Blues." There's his Dylanesque "Rosemary" and Beatlish "China Cat" (that's Phil Lesh on the high part and Bobby Weir on backup vocals). In the list of Jerry's vocal impersonations, I'm not even counting the muezzin's-call-to-prayer and Gregorian chant on the utterly weird "What's Become of the Baby" (which I attribute to too many hours spent under tungsten lighting). It's around this time that Garcia and Weir start taking lessons with a vocal coach in the East Bay to learn how to flex their vocal muscles by doing scales.

☺

Things are still so fast and loose at this point that we don't even have our own accountant, we use a gal who's doing the Jefferson Airplane's books. We figure, hey, *they're* doing great, so it ought to be fine for us too, right? Okay, so we haven't paid our taxes yet. But Ms. Pencils has put money aside, I'm sure. We figure we'll just pay the taxes out of the *next* check from Warner Brothers. Mañana, baby!

But we have learned the joys of credit. Ron Rakow, bless his pointed little black heart, cooks up a wicked scheme: the great car scam. He creates a corporation, the *All Our Own Equipment Company*, and suddenly we have an outrageous line of credit. We could have bought America with that. Downstairs from the Carousel is a car dealership, ripe for plucking. Using the company as a front, Rakow gets everybody in the Dead extended family an English Ford Cortina.

Thirteen Cortinas! Jerry has a blue one, Pigpen has a really cool two-door, I end up with a black four-door, and even Healy gets a fire-engine red Ford van out of it. The thing is, it's like giving monkeys a bunch of diamond rings. Within a week or two, they are all gone! We lend one of them to Kesey and Hunter to go to L.A. and never see it again; another goes into the Bay; the van we give to Lydia, who loans it to the Black Panthers. And then there's my habit of totaling cars while trying to back out of gas stations.

Our financial problems really mount with *Aoxomoxoa*. It takes forever to record, so we rack up a formidable amount of studio time. Plus the band is buying more and more gear all the time. Not to mention our new band member, Tom Constanten, who can only play on a spinet that has once been fondled by Marie Antoinette.

Our ears prick up when Mickey Hart begins pitching us on his dad, Lenny, who is allegedly a financial wizard. He's amalgamated companies (whatever *that* means) and knows all about the stock market and why it goes up (or is it down?) when women's hems rise. Danny and I are impressed, Bill Kreutzmann's fascinated, Jerry Garcia and Phil Lesh are relieved, Mickey Hart is proud, and Bobby Weir (the true plutocrat in our midst) is making invisible snowballs. We welcome Lenny to the fold.

After a cursory perusal of the books, Lenny Hart announces: "Collapse! Ruination! Disaster!" He convinces Garcia that through our incompetence Danny and I have let the Dead get a million and a half dollars in debt. Wow! I'd known we were making more and spending more, but this strikes me as really impressive. Jerry (naturally) is totally freaked out.

Lenny Hart holds a financial meeting out at Mickey's barn in Novato, a revival meeting is more like it. He's a Jew who's converted to Christianity and he's more Pentecostal than a Baptist. He laces his "spread-sheet rap" with God and fear talk. Danny and I are beginning to look like a couple of bumbling idiots who have led the Dead to the brink of financial ruin. "But, despair not, O my brothers, Lenny Hart shall deliver you from the jaws of Chapter Eleven." Jerry isn't worried about hellfire and damnation (no way!), but it does scare him to death that imminent catastrophe threatens the House of the Dead in the here and now. So the band members in typical fashion say, "Okay, save us, Rev. Lenny!" Why the hell not? And they hand him the control of the whole damn thing. So great is his victory that he even has compassion for miserable sinners like Danny and me; we are allowed to continue on as band managers, but only under his strict supervision.

While we're making *Aoxomoxoa,* we get a taste of hippiedom's slow crawl into the straight world. Jerry and I have run into a humorous old hipster named Shel Silverstein at the No-Name Bar in Sausalito from time to time. He draws cartoons and writes for *Playboy,* and Jerry and I have always been impressed — like everyone else! — by the quality of the articles in that publication. Where else can you find pubic hair and Vladimir Nabokov face to face?

Shel is close to Hugh Hefner. One day he asks if the Grateful Dead want to be on *Playboy After Dark,* Hefner's TV show. We get the impression that Hef is trying to be part of the swinging sixties. Hippies! Free love! Mind-bending drugs! Even though he doesn't get out of the Playboy Mansion too much, he knows that something is going on out there and he wants to be "with it." And what could be more with it than a psychedelic hippie band from San Francisco. Now, *that's* swinging! Jerry's for it totally: "What a goof! And a great way to shock people. *So* difficult to do these days, no?"

It's shot at a sound stage in West Hollywood. This is our first encounter with any kind of network television (CBS) and Owsley, now affectionately known to one and all as "Bear," is really keyed up. This is his main chance to show the world the Great Owsley's contribution to modern audiophonics. Now they'll see! This show could be a milestone in broadcasting but — the ignorant fools! — they won't let him touch anything. They just want him to set it up and then *they'll* mike it and *they'll* do all that other, thank you. That's the way it is, by law, you know, union regulations.

He can't get his way with the sound and he's really pissed off. Owsley Stanley, relegated to the deep recesses of the studio! I'll show *them!* Bear has his way of dealing with petty functionaries. He hits this big old coffee urn with an industrial dose of liquid acid and waits.

It's a random sampling because you don't know who's going to have coffee out of that urn and who isn't. But apparently before dinner everybody has at least one cup, which is quite enough. The ones that have a good time behind it never leave; the ones that leave never come back.

The LSD effect is soon all too apparent because *Playboy After Dark* is a very stiff-looking show. Hef walking around in his velvet smoking jacket sucking on his pipe like some bad actor in a fustian Brit upper-class drawing-room comedy. It's all goofily phonied up. The cheesy set is meant to look like a Chicago lakefront penthouse full of suave rich guys and beautiful women of easy virtue. Everybody's desperately trying to make it look like there's a real fun cocktail party going on. Some swingers come by to check out the evening's entertainment at Hef's place. And who should drop by but the Grateful Dead (just like they do *every* Thursday).

The cast consists of stacked babes in evening dress. Upwardly mo-bile, secretarial-type women with the bouffant hair and big tits es-corted by smooth, soigné, model-type guys in tuxedos posing, smoking cigarettes, and fingering their cocktail glasses as if they are little glass zebras. A tacky American middle-class diorama with up-tight people in it! Everybody here is fully versed in the *Playboy* phi-losophy (which differs from Existentialism in important ways that, uh, I don't think I'll go into right here). Anyway, the show is all about achieving the ultimate after-shave attitude. Bunnies in their bunny outfits are running around with trays of hors d'oeuvres. The extras affect nonchalance, affluence, and sophistication. And in the middle of this robotic scenario one of the bunnies begins to strip (too many cups of coffee!). It is a perfectly acceptable response to several hun-dred mikes of Owsley LSD. Hefner is used to seeing naked women too, but only under clinically controlled conditions. He sees his suave-to-the-max trip beginning to crumble and he freaks.

"Shel! Shel!" Hefner is shouting. "What's going on? This isn't in the script!" Shel soon figures out what's happening (Shel is hip), and calms Hef down: "It's all just part of the effect the Grateful Dead have on people. This is that Hippie Thing I told you about."

Hef nods knowingly. "Oh well, if it's all part of the, uh, psychedelic *thing,* that's okay. Really neat."

One of Shel's jobs is to make sure that no one doses Hugh Hefner, which Owsley is trying like crazy to do. But Hefner only drinks

Coca-Colas, *sealed* Coca-Colas (it's in his contract). He does not want to take LSD — he's paranoid as hell about the stuff. The Coca-Cola bottle-opening ritual is as elaborate as any at the Sultan's court. Hefner's valet sits on the royal stash of Coca-Cola bottles like a hen on eggs. When Hef wants a Coke, Shel goes over to the valet, who opens one and gives it to Shel, who hands it to Hef.

People are falling apart and leaving, right and left, saying, "I don't feel well. I think I got a fever, I gotta go home." You can see acid beaming out of people's faces: the glow, the big, dilated pupils. Usually Hef's swinging soirée is a low hum rather than anything resembling an actual party, but by now people are seriously getting down.

Meanwhile, George, the cameraman on the boom, has stopped filming the show. He can't take his camera off the babe. She's un-hooked her bra and she's dancing loosely and seductively, and then starts to lift up her shirt. George's eyes are *wide* open, as big as saucers, and he's got a huge smile on his face. His boom has turned into a dinosaur's neck that he's riding across the set. He's shooting overhead shots, extreme close-ups down girls' blouses. It's too bizarre. He's stripped down to the waist and his headset's all askew and finally the director comes out of the control room and shouts at him: "Put your headset on!" But how absurd! Why should he? He's doing his own thing and who the hell is that hysterical little insect shouting at him?

George has better things to do. He's having the time of his life, oblivious to the chorus of voices yelling at him: "George, watch it! What are you doing? Come on down from there!"

"No I ain't coming down." He's right over the girl who's undress-ing. You can see on the tape where she is getting crazy and now she has all her clothes off and George up on the boom has positioned himself right above her and will not get his camera off her. You can see it start to happen on the tape where they can't edit her out completely. For a change, some really crazy stuff gets on the show.

They're now down to two cameramen. They have to string this show together out of bits and pieces. At this point they are so short-staffed (and the sound man is dosed beyond all recall) that they have to recruit Owsley — which is just what Owsley wants.

Then we come to the interview with Garcia. Garcia is by now high, too, because — that's right! — he drinks a lot of coffee. You can tell it is going to pieces and Hugh Hefner is watching Jerry like an entomologist who has just spied a new species of dragonfly. Jerry's sitting opposite him looking real weird in a Guatemalan poncho — brilliant, psychedelic colors that vibrate right off the screen — and he's just grown his beard, big muttonchops, and his hair is tied in ponytails. Hefner, sucking thoughtfully on his pipe, asks Jerry a perfectly ordinary question like "So where do you guys see yourselves going from here?" But instead of the usual pitch ("We're doing two weeks at the Rally Room in Lake Tahoe and then on to the EZ-Boy Convention in Omaha"), Jerry gives him a long convoluted psychedelic rap.

"See, man, I don't know where we're going any more than you do, man. It's like we're not *going* anywhere, so much as we're closing the circle . . . the *ourobouros,* dig? The snake that eats its own tail, y'know?"

Hef's going along with it, even though he doesn't understand a single word Garcia's saying. Not even a hippie could figure it out, and here's Mr. Leisure Wear trying to reconfigure his face into the "Hmmmmmmmmmm, how *interesting!*" expression but it just won't go. He manages to get out a panicked "Yes, oh, I see — why don't you play us a few songs?" The people are clapping, and Garcia ambles over to the rest of the band and picks up his guitar, straps it on.

The Dead do a beautiful "Mountains of the Moon" with Tom Constanten on the harpsichord. They play for almost an hour. We've got the crew and the cast so high that nobody stops us.

Shel pretends to be very mad at us: "Okay, who did this?" Privately, he's thrilled. *Playboy After Dark* is generally a stiff, weird-looking affair, like a cocktail party for the recently deceased. Tonight everybody's telling us this is the closest thing to a party Hugh Hefner ever had.

10

This Darkness Got to Give

‹‹‹

AFTER 1968 NONE of us wants to live in the Haight anymore, and so begins the long exodus of the Grateful Dead to Marin County. For a while we keep 710 Ashbury as an office and a place for Jerry to come in and practice his pedal-steel guitar.

In 1969 we move the office to Union Street. That lasts until the FBI begins bugging our phones, convinced that the Grateful Dead are a front for a sinister acid-making cartel bent on corrupting the world's feckless youth. A Deadhead phone technician tips us off and we move the office to its final location in San Rafael. It's around this time that we shift our rehearsal space from the air force base in Marin to 20 Front Street in San Rafael.

Meanwhile, band members start drifting off one by one to their own houses outside the city. After almost three years of communal living, it's going to be an interesting experience for all of us. For "the oldest juveniles in the state of California," as Bill Graham has taken to calling us, it's a bit like leaving home all over again.

In the summer of '69 Garcia and Mountain Girl move out to Larkspur. A crumbly two-story adobe house among towering redwoods where you hear the creek babbling below from the open windows. At some point early in the spring he has bought a porky little orange school bus that he's fitted out with funny-looking curtains on strings. Collages on the walls and a mattress in the back and everything is glued together with chewing gum.

The bus is parked right next to the house. It serves as an office and playroom for the kids, Sunshine and Annabelle, and sometimes as a guest house or a place for Garcia to nap in the afternoon.

After his parents die, Weir uses his inheritance money to buy a house in Mill Valley with his girlfriend, Frankie Hart. No relation to Mickey, except previously his girlfriend!

Weir's personality is beginning to come into focus. It will never entirely gel, due, I would say, to doing too much acid at an early age. Aside from his own appetite for psychedelics, Weir also gets dosed a lot. The crew is merciless. He gets onstage not knowing how much he's taken and starts fumbling with his guitar as the strings liquefy.

During the 710 period, Phil and Billy live in an apartment on Clayton. Phil is with Rosie McGee (née Florence Nathan) and Billy is married to his first wife, Brenda. They were high school sweethearts, had married in 1962 when Billy was just eighteen, and on July 3, 1964, had a daughter, Stacy — the little girl next to Pigpen in the Dead family photograph on the back cover of *Aoxomoxoa*.

Toward the end of 1967, Kreutzmann got divorced from Brenda and around the time of Woodstock moves to Mill Valley with his new girlfriend, Suzila, who has a T-shirt and beads store called Kumquat Mae in Mill Valley. He eventually marries her and on June 10, 1969, they have a son, Justin.

Kreutzmann at home is a very different quantity to the wild man we know from the road. He has an unexpected spiritual side to him that he gets from his father who is a Raike healer. Raike is a Japanese method of channeling energy for healing. Needless to say, the spiritual Kreutzmann is not someone the band sees too much of. Its a side of him he deliberately keeps secret for fear he'll be laughed at. When he gets home from a long tour he rids himself of his demons by going on wilderness survival expeditions. He comes out on the road healthy and goes home sick!

Phil Lesh moves out to Fairfax (just over the hill from Camp Lagunitas) with his girlfriend Maria, the first in a long succession of women.

Mickey Hart moves in with me. It's a horse ranch in Novato, and when I leave it becomes his place. This is where he builds the recording studio where some of the Dead spin-off records like Robert Hunter's *Tales of the Great Rum Runners* will be made. Garcia and David Grissim's *Old and In The Way* is mixed there. It has a tin roof, which means you can't record when it rains (and it rains a lot in Northern California). Mickey also starts a little label called X-rated 45s featuring material so blue he can't get a distributor for them, but they sell like crazy around Marin County.

Mickey's ranch is *very* rural. Goats in the kitchen, chickens laying eggs in the beds, couches made out of hay bales. Mickey loves to ride, and as various acid-eating stockbrokers and L.A. rockers leave Marin County and go back home, he collects quite a herd. You'd wake up in the morning with a horse chewing away at your bed.

After Frankie Hart left him for Weir, he takes up with Cookie Eisenberg, who'd been involved with Leary in early LSD experiments, and then with Jerilyn Brandelius.

Despite all the house-moving and mate-changing, we manage to play some 143 dates in 1969. We've got a substantial repertoire by now, almost a hundred songs, way up from the fourteen-odd numbers we had under our belts when we went to L.A. a couple of years ago. The venues are getting bigger, and since Monterey, promoters have got festival fever. We're booked into a big one in upstate New York on August 15. It's called the Woodstock Music and Arts Fair. Woodstock in honor of the Bard (Bob Dylan) who resides there, but the site is actually on a farm in nearby Bethel, New York.

It's Saturday, August 16 and, Jesus, we're almost to Max Yasgur's farm. Cue Crosby, Stills and Nash soundtrack!

I'm late getting to Woodstock — something I'll try never to do in the future! I've been tying down loose ends in New York, along with the rest of the managers. We've been negotiating right up until the last minute because none of the bands is going to play until we have our deals settled. We aren't going to allow our groups to play without everything being established up front. We are determined this is not going to be another Monterey. That means film rights, music rights — everything. If our name's on it, we want a piece of it and that's that. Our name is on the poster, the Dead's appearance is being advertised on radio spots, etc., so we want to be paid — *right now!*

People from Crosby, Stills and Nash are there, Warner Brothers is there, so is Mo Ostin, Jimi Hendrix's manager, etc. We're all jockeying for position: when do we get to play and so on and so forth. Hendrix gets top billing, natch. How's Sunday morning at six A.M., Jimi? And in between we're all calling the weather man because up in Wood-stock it is pouring down rain, it's already Mud Hill up there. While promoter Michael Laing is up in Bethel knee-deep in mud, we're all knee-deep in riders and appendices and parties of the first part. The cynics are saying it'll never work, but *we* know everyone in the world is headed for Woodstock.

We finally get it all hammered out; we get our deal signed, sealed, and delivered, and wide-eyed and bushy-tailed we leave in the middle of the night and drive all the way up to Woodstock. Well, not quite to Woodstock, because we get stuck smack dab in the middle of the mother of all traffic jams. I am in a wagon train of limousines with Bobby Weir and a bunch of stockbrokers who've just dropped acid and want to invest money in the Grateful Dead and be the next Woodstock biggies, promote concerts and on and on. The movers and shakers send me out to clear the road while they sit back and drink their champagne mimosas and snort their breakfast.

"Okay, we're coming through! It's the Grateful Dead!" I cry like I have the Holy Roman Emperor and his entourage behind me. Of course, it's only *one* Grateful Dead back there — Bobby Weir's stuffed in the back between two rich little stockbrokers' girls. Six limos coming through with *one* band member.

"Okay, clear the fucking road!" I cry (no more Mister Nice Guy). I end up walking a few miles up the road, but let's face it, I am the worst traffic cop that anyone has ever seen. For starters, I just don't *look* like an enforcer of Her Majesty's traffic laws. I am wearing Mountain Girl's pass, and the couple of hundred tabs of Sunshine acid that I've stashed in a silver Art Nouveau case are leaking out down my leg under the relentless rain. My pores are saturated with the stuff. My mouth is smeared with this Day-Glo acid, my hand a giant raw orange claw, my pants bright saffron. There is a river of orange acid trailing behind me and strange, mutant strains of vegetation are beginning to sprout in my wake.

We straggle into the backstage compound early in the morning. The band has already been there and gone. They tried to do their sound check but because of all the delays have gone back to their hotel, which is where I find Garcia.

A measure of the insanity level *before* Woodstock even starts is that Michael Laing hires, I'm not kidding, the Pranksters to do security! To assist in — you know — *the vibe*. Or maybe Michael Laing has had a premonition that the fence isn't going to be finished in time and people will try to sneak in. But, hey, what if there were a bunch of crazy outriders on the perimeters speaking in tongues and making unearthly rattlings? That would discourage a few interlopers, wouldn't it? So Ken Babbs gets all the Pranksters together, and they pile into the bus and drive all the way across the country to Woodstock, setting up their whole encampment down in this little gully with Wavy Gravy and his people. Freak Hollow.

In the afternoon Nicki and I go swimming. We are going to make love in the water, but all of a sudden there are magnets going in different directions. We are so high we can *see* the electricity, those LSD polarity warps, streaming through the water. We are tingling from head to toe as a thousand volts of ethereal electricity zap through us. Who needs sex?

Finally, it's time for the Dead to go on. We're getting ready to put our equipment onstage. It's all on risers, but our gear is so heavy it breaks the wheels off the risers and we have to move everything in by hand, which takes forever. In the meantime, incessant nightmare announcements are coming over the PA.

"Please do not rob the hot dog stands!"

"Please, everyone, get off the tower, someone just fell."

"Don't take the brown acid, there's bad acid out there, so don't take it." They don't say what the thousands who have *already* taken it should do (presumably get off the towers).

Ominous announcements, no music, everybody scrambling around. All of us looking tense and horrible and uptight. And then, that's right folks, it's time for the Grateful Dead to go on!

I make the mistake of thinking, What more can happen? And then suddenly, as if someone pulled a cord . . . darkness falls. Oh well, time for the light show — that should perk us up. Good old oily, spermazooic, polychrome globules oozing across the backdrop, and this screen is *huge,* a truly monstrous thing.

But no sooner is the screen in place than the wind picks up and the stage starts *vibrating*. Uh, *physically* vibrating, quaking. (And this is the largest stage you've ever seen, it stands thirty feet above the ground.)

Our beautiful giant screen has turned into a sail and is *moving* the stage through the sea of mud like the good ship *Marie Celeste*. It is starting to slide, it is, uh oh, *tipping over,* and Dicken, my brother, has to climb up the mizzenmast and slash the screen with a bowie knife. Not a good omen, Captain. . . .

The band looks petrified. The broken risers, the light and dark thing, the terrible announcements, the stage taking off on its own like that. And Garcia and Weir — all those guys — when they're in front of people and they're high and there's *fear* in the air, well, they become fearful too. It would take a lot less than half a million people zapping jangled, weird vibes back at them to spook this band!

And in the middle of their very first number, "St. Stephen," this crazy guy we know runs out into the middle of the stage and starts flinging LSD off the stage. After all those announcements! Okay, his acid is purple, but it *looks* brown. Oh no, it's the brown acid — the acid you're . . . *not supposed to take.*

When Garcia sees this mad, crazy guy throwing what looks like brown acid off the stage, something he might under normal circumstances have thought droll and antic now looks ominous. He is asking himself the question men zonked out of their minds on psychotropic substances should never ask themselves: "Why me?" God, he's turning into Captain Ahab! Any minute he's going to harpoon Wavy Gravy or something equally desperate. That *was* Wavy Gravy, wasn't it?

To make matters worse, the Dead are playing horribly. They just cannot get started, can't get it right. Not one song. And the sound is awful, and it is windy and blustery and cold. This, it occurs to me, would be just the perfect moment for me to flip totally out. Hey, why not? Why should I be left out? Letting myself go, I realize that the reason the music is so bad is . . . because I am here. It's so obvious, how could I have missed it? Jeez, I've got to get out of this place.

Yes, folks, just 500,000 people going through big old changes. A mini-revolution is taking place. Everybody's starving to death and there's not enough food because the mini-revolutionaries (all the socialists and communists at the top of the hill) aren't giving any out. People are begging food. And some maniac is actually running around robbing hot dog stands.

Other enterprising souls are out there selling glasses of water for a dollar. What do you expect when you put half a million New Yorkers in the middle of a cornfield and strand them there for three days?

We are all trapped in this quagmire (and grisly mind-set) when the State of New York declares the place a disaster area. With stunt pilots

buzzing the stage and army helicopters flying in with water, it's beginning to look like Vietnam. And it's a high old crowd, which is also like
Vietnam. Even the *music* reminds me of Vietnam!

Turns out someone dosed the water with hypodermics before they
even got it off the helicopters. So now even the army's water is loaded
with acid. It's reckless and not too mature of whoever did it, I must
say! Some of the chopper pilots are so fucked up that guides have to
sit in on every flight and talk them down (in more ways than one):
"Okay, now bring it down *gently*. Imagine you're a dragonfly and
you're landing on this giant lily pad."

Finally the Dead set finishes up with "Lovelight," but even Pigpen's surefire rabble-rouser can't quite pull it out. Thank God that's
over! We are walking across the area behind the stage, and we run into
one of the Dead's roadies, Jonathan Riester. I am talking to Riester
when all of a sudden all the paisley washes out of his face. Ah, nor-
malcy! I never thought I'd embrace it with such enthusiasm.

After all these years of mind-gumming psychedelics we are all actually beginning to *crave* the normal. We need something to ground us
— our hair is talking to us, our shoes have just presented a set of
demands, the walls are alive with the sound of intergalactic static.
Please remind us whereof we come? Our home planet is what?

And then one afternoon as we're lying on the grass looking out
into the ozone blue of a Marin County sky (with one cloud in
the shape of Conway Twitty) there appears unto us the word: B-A-K-
E-R-S-F-I-E-L-D.

Yahoooooooooooo!! Merle Haggard, Mel Tillis — anybody with
the first name of Merle or Earl or Travis or Porter or Conway — or
Buck for that matter. Just saying the words "Buck Owens and the
Buckaroos" causes a cool mist to sprinkle on our over-amped brains.
Shitkickers, rednecks, hillbillies and good ol' boys. Pickups and gun-
racks, pedal steel and hot wheels, white line fever and white lightnin'.
Roots, baby! Not *our* roots, mind you. None of us grew up in a trailer
park, chewed Skoal, or had ever even seen a levee — but at this point
who cares? The main thing is, it's *real* — the hundert-percent gen-
wine homespun Meriken article.

And using only slightly convoluted logic we convince ourselves
that these secondhand, down-home, grits-eatin' roots connect to our

youthful, folksy, bluegrassy, jug-bandy, coffeehouse selves. Our taste runs more to folky country stuff, moldy, down-in-the-mine-where-the-sun-don't-shine retro stuff. Bob Wills, Sons of the Pioneers Texas swing and cowboy songs, rather than hard-core Top Forty country countdown. Still, it's a start.

At Grateful Dead shows now, country music is beginning to act as that much-needed breath of hickory wind in the Dead's spiraling psychedelic jams. The Dead are so tuned into the wavelength of the audience and vice versa that there comes a point — several points, actually — at a Dead concert where you need to bail out. So precisely at the point when the space jam begins gyrating into the outer limits, the Dead cool everything out with a country song. These are subtle neural signals the band members send back and forth to each other on the stage so that when the center does not hold they can switch to another mode. During the Acid Tests this took the form of "Save us, Pig, it's time for the blues!" But at this point in time the blues themselves have become generators of ferocious noodling for Jerry Garcia and Phil Lesh. The blues are a hotbed of improvisation — jazz came out of the blues, for chrissakes!

By 1969 Garcia is beginning to fashion an electric version of country, a new way to do folk music that fits the mood of the times. Dylan, the Byrds, and Neil Young's band, the Buffalo Springfield, are already pointing the way. Jerry is listening to what other people are doing, and hanging out with Jack Casady from the Airplane and David Freiberg from Quicksilver. They came up the same way Garcia had, through folk music and jug bands, and are tinkering with the combine harvester currently chewing through the regional American songbook. Casady and Freiberg had merely dabbled in folkish country, but Jerry actually mastered traditional banjo technique and picked bluegrass music like he was Japanese.

Jerry is trying to experiment with electrifying bluegrass and country music in a rock format — with drums and electric bass. But this new direction is going to require even more coordination from the rest of the band, so the saga continues! Part of this struggle involves getting Bobby Weir to play a tight rhythm so that Garcia can pick. And in order to pick, Garcia needs Phil Lesh to play a strict bottom that will kick the band along; a bass line that the drums can hang with, that Kreutzmann can put his foot to and that can keep Pigpen interested in the rhythm.

Although it's just now becoming prominent in our shows, Jerry has been drifting toward country since the summer of '67, when he began teaching himself to play pedal steel at 710 in the little room at the top of the stairs. He would fiddle with it for hours on end in his tenacious way. It's not an easy instrument to master, but by '69 he has it down.

When he's playing pedal steel, Jerry can no longer comp rhythms any more than you can on a zither. Where the tightness of the band had previously been merely a consummation devoutly to be wished, it is now a necessity. By the end of 1969 there will be two sets at Dead concerts. An acoustic set and an electric set. The New Riders of the Purple Sage (another retro country outfit), with Jerry on pedal steel, are with us for all of these shows. We will do entire tours with them, all the way through 1970.

Eventually it becomes too hard for Garcia to go back and forth from the pedal steel to the electric. He also complains about the differences between an acoustic guitar and an electric guitar, how different the fingering is and how different the strings are and how tough you have to be on an electric and how gentle you have to be on an acoustic.

You can see the gradual progression from blues and rock into country throughout our shows in '69. The Hunter/Garcia ballad "Dire Wolf" goes back to the beginning of '69. Some of the songs from *Aoxomoxoa* — "Doin' That Rag" and "Dupree's Diamond Blues" — are just electrified jug-band tunes. But we're still doing old Pigpen standbys like "Hard to Handle" and "Lovelight."

We're also trying out new songs like "St. Stephen" and "The Eleven." And mixed in are pop country classics like the Everly Brothers' "Wake Up, Little Susie," which starts to show some harmony singing, and "Green, Green Grass of Home," which is pure high-octane country. It's ancient Celtic keening. Some Irishman who came to the United States and misses the forty shades of green in the grass of Killarney.

Even contemporary country hits like Merle Haggard's "Mama Tried" and Buck Owens's "Tiger by the Tail" are creeping in to the repertoire. But we're not getting that far from Union Station. You can see how many times the band closes with "Lovelight." Let it shine, shine, shine, shine on me. "Lovelight" is Pig's forte, along with his own song, "Alligator."

Jerry and Phil, however, are starting to get bored with pumping out "Lovelight." They're doing it the same old way they did it when it was a four-minute song, only now they're playing it for twenty-five minutes, maybe even longer! Pigpen can keep up with the first couple of verses, then Garcia takes it screaming into the ionosphere where it turns into something that isn't even close to the original end-of-the-party rave-up. It's now a thirty-minute jazzy, Sun Ra space orchestra improvisation. In frustration Pig turns his organ down and *pretends* to be playing! And believe me, pretending is a lot harder than you think. You see him reaching for his drink, bopping heads with the girls. But he isn't doing anything, and we all know it.

And because Pig doesn't do acid he can't get into that trippy frame of mind. By the time Garcia comes back to earth, Pigpen's three sheets to the wind — *uuuuhhhhhhhhhhhrrrr.* He's retired!

Then he has to come back and be right on the money and he has no idea what's happening and he's looking at Garcia and trying to figure when the vamp is coming. Garcia goes, *wooodooowromp-armp,* and then Pig goes, *bonnnnn,* and there's like two minutes of finale. Sometimes he forgets to turn his organ back up again and his feet go slamming down and the sound isn't there. The poor guy!

It has been a wet winter and spring, and from sleeping in that old school bus next to his house Jerry has caught double pneumonia. His breathing is still a terrible raspy wheeze, his eyes are watery, he looks peaky and frail. Jerry never wants to call off a show, but he's in no condition to tour. We have to cancel our upcoming dates. The man is in no condition to go out on the road. He's in such bad shape his doctor insists he be hospitalized.

Nicki suggests an alternative: Why not ask Rolling Thunder if he can do something? Rolling Thunder is a Cherokee medicine man who works for Union Pacific. He once smoked the Fillmore for us, a ritual designed to rid it of bad spirits. He's had a vision in which hippies are revealed to be the inheritors of the Indian destiny (which needless to say we wholeheartedly endorse).

First we have to clear the healing ceremony with Mountain Girl, and she definitely does not truck with this stuff. When she hears Nicki's plan, Mountain Girl pulls one of her long, crabby faces:

"Oh, come on, let him go to the hospital! Cancel the damn dates! Are you serious, bringing a witch doctor here? Get with the twentieth century, guys!"

Not that Jerry's too crazy about the idea either. In his wheezy croak he's saying, "Yeah, cancel the fuckin' dates, I'm dying here!" And he's taking little squeaky breaths that are truly alarming. Talking him into Rolling Thunder is a major undertaking, especially since Mountain Girl is a real cynic when it comes to Native American healing powers or holistic medicine. Since the beginning at 710 Ashbury we've been inundated with self-appointed mystics and acid casualties trying to convince us about pyramid power and the Lost Continent of Mu and Atlantis — trying to get us to *move* there! Actually, after enough of this everybody is getting a little bit weary. But bizarre as the idea of a Native American shaman chanting over Jerry is, going to the hospital ain't that appealing either. For one thing, Jerry hates doctors. We finally wear Mountain Girl down, and believe me it takes all of us — me, Nicki, and Rolling Thunder's son, Buffalo Horse.

"You guys are nuts, but, okay, let the guy come over. Once."

Rolling Thunder arrives. He surveys the house and says, "Yes, bad signs, we have to doctor the *whole place*. Rock, get down to market and pick up some chicken."

I get half a chicken cut up and bring it back. We put some stones in a circle and Rolling Thunder makes a big bonfire in the backyard under the redwoods. He sets the meat out on the ground between the fire and the french doors that open onto a redwood deck. Mountain Girl sees the raw chicken meat sitting out there on the ground and rolls her eyes, "I knew it, I never should have been so naïve."

"Just keep an open mind," Nicki's saying. "It may look weird, but it works!"

Mountain Girl goes upstairs and gets Jerry out of bed. He comes down in the ratty old terry cloth robe and shit slippers that he loves to wear when he's feeling sorry for himself. He comes trundling down, one arm on the bannister and one arm on Mountain Girl, and as pale as a ghost. He's got a fever, his hair's all stringy and matted, and his beard is growing in all straggly. Also, he's sweating like a pig. He looks as if he's about to keel over at any moment.

Rolling Thunder sits him down in a straightback chair in the middle of the room. Jerry looks so pathetic sitting there, I'm actually wondering how I could have subjected him to this nuttiness. I'm feeling sorry for the guy!

Buffalo Horse is here, too. He's outside drumming as Rolling Thunder starts to chant the greeting song, *"Ha-no-wa-na-ha-na-ho!"* a chant to cast the evil spirit out and make Jerry whole again.

I am holding an abalone shell full of sage and knickanick, which is Indian tobacco. Sometimes it contains tobacco, but mostly it's herbal, primarily sage, with a burning coal in the bottom to create smoke. I have to keep it smoldering. I am using a feather to fan the coals with the leaves on top of it to keep smoke coming off it. It is the same as smoking the Fillmore, except there I think we used coffee cans with holes poked in the bottom as well as abalone shells because it was a big room.

Rolling Thunder's holding an eagle wing — American Indians are the only people in the United States who are allowed by federal law to possess eagle feathers. The eagle's wing is attached to an eagle claw with intricate beadwork and a leather thong. Rolling Thunder lays it on his hand, using it as a giant fan. Every now and again, he asks me for the abalone shell and I pass it over to him so he can smoke some contaminated spot. He then asks me to go around the living room and smoke it, smoke the house up and down and come back. Meanwhile he's still chanting and praying and invoking the spirits.

He comes in the house and starts smoking Jerry, using the whole eagle wing, going — *schwooocccchhhh!* He walks all the way around him, wafting smoke down around his feet. He asks Jerry to stand up and smokes his hair, all the time wafting the air with the eagle wing. He stands in front of Jerry and hands me the abalone. He lays the wing with the claw down on his own arm and says a prayer. When he finishes an astonishing thing occurs. The claw *grabs* on to Rolling Thunder's arm and the wing stands up by itself! There are now little droplets of blood coming out of his hand where the claw has broken his skin, and he wipes them across his face.

Rolling Thunder makes a circular fanning gesture toward Jerry all the while moving us out the door and expelling the evil spirits, driving them toward the raw chicken and toward the fire.

In midceremony, right at the most crucial moment, in walks our cockamamie road manager, Jonathan Riester. Right across the path where all the sickness is being driven out the door, and — *wham!* —

that ball of malignancy wallops him and spins around as if he'd been struck by an invisible fist. All the color drains out of his face and he faints dead away.

Rolling Thunder, as if waking from a trance, says, "*What,* what, what? Who is that?" And then, seeing Riester, says: "Move him out of there right away!" Nicki and I run over and pull him out of the way. He regains consciousness, blinking his eyes and mumbling, "Wha' happened?"

"Riester, you got in the path of a healing ceremony. Why didn't you knock?"

"Knock? When did I ever knock? Anyway, I saw the fire and thought you guys were having a barbecue or something!"

Then Rolling Thunder says, "Go, smoke the room again, smoke it out of here, Rock, sweep it away!" And after the whole room has been swept, Rolling Thunder turns green, stumbles outside, and vomits his guts out. He has taken all Garcia's poison on himself.

Instantly, Jerry stops wheezing. "Well, fuck me, he's breathing again," M.G. says. Twenty minutes and Bob's your uncle! No more hospital tomorrow, in fact he's talking about playing this weekend!

Jerry's breathing and he can't believe it. None of us can. We're all struck dumb, which doesn't happen that often. Garcia had gone from being diagnosed with pneumonia and about to be checked into the hospital, to this utterly unfathomable recovery. We'd never seen holistic or alternative medicine really work, we didn't believe it, and I'm telling you, Garcia never for an instant believed it would work either. It was a mystical experience for him, a revelation that took the imagery of psychedelics into the real world. He suddenly realized that there were things out there he didn't understand.

We are at a loss as to how to thank Rolling Thunder. Nicki tells us it's traditional, when a profound service has been rendered, to offer the best you have to give.

"Well, hell yeah, he deserves to get whatever he wants!"

"Rock, go ask him what he wants, he's just cured Garcia and it's up to us to do the right thing."

I go over to Rolling Thunder and clasp his hands: "How can I possibly cover you for this, man?" I say idiotically.

And Rolling Thunder says, "Well, actually there *is* a way!"

I think he's going to ask for a bag of Indian tobacco because that's a traditional thing. You know, you give the medicine man a bag of tobacco and a dozen eggs and an eagle feather or a bear claw or some jewelry.

So I say, "Name anything you want, there's nothing I wouldn't do for you."

And he says, "I want your woman." Just like that.

Uh-oh! You could have knocked me over with a chicken feather. I go over to Nicki and say, "You're not going to believe what he just asked for."

"Try me! Right now I'm ready to believe in the Tooth Fairy again."

"Nicki, he wants, uh, you, honey." Nicki goes all quiet. She is caught off guard. No way was she expecting to be the sacrificial victim, the white Pocahontas.

"Uh, let me just think about this," she says and walks out into the redwoods. "This is a rough one," I say to Garcia. "Hey, you're the one he cured, shouldn't it be Mountain Girl?"

"Gee, thanks a lot, Rock," Mountain Girl says archly.

I decide to try sending a subliminal message to Rolling Thunder.

"Mountain Girl is Garcia's woman," I say (hoping that Rolling Thunder will be swayed by Garcia's being the great white leader of the Grateful Dead).

Right away he comes back with "Mountain Girl is too scary."

She's formidable, he's right about that! And Nicki is so good-looking, she even looks Indian. Olive-skinned and dark hair and dark eyes. Russian Jewish. Nicki comes back out of the redwoods and says, "Listen, guys, it's okay. I'll handle it."

◎

In the fall of 1969 I get a free trip to London courtesy of the band. The Rolling Stones' memorial concert in Hyde Park for Brian Jones has been such a success that the Brit hustler who produced it, Blackhill's Sam Cutler, is thinking of doing more free concerts. Maybe even importing some exotic types like the Grateful Dead from San Francisco.

"Wot abowt you bleedin' wankers commin' over 'ere and doin' a bit of jumpin' around wif guitars and other folly, eh darlin'?" Sam Cutler is on the line and wants to know what I think of the Grateful

Dead and the Jefferson Airplane doing some free concerts in Hyde Park. They'll pick up the hotel costs and airfare and take care of the technical stuff.

And why not? We have a meeting at the Airplane's place just before I'm to leave for England and I naturally run into some Merk pharmaceutical cocaine. Marty Balin gives me a small bottle filled to the brim, which I stick in my watch pocket. I go right from that meeting to the airport and fly to London with Bobby Weir's girlfriend, Frankie Hart, who once worked for George Harrison.

I am being sent as the front man, representing the Dead and the Airplane, to "suss out" (in the phrase of the day) how the money would work, if it could really be done, and whether it is worth doing at all. There are questions about staging and electricity and lighting, not to mention where the equipment is going to come from. Basically we would be going over there with just our instruments; amps, PA systems and all of that stuff will have to be provided.

On the plane I happen to look at the ticket Lenny Hart has gotten me and find it is *one way.* I take this as a somewhat ominous sign. I can't be flying to England with a one-way ticket and no money. Can I? I have no cash (I'm planning to sell some grass and tabs of acid I've brought with me to "finance" the trip).

At customs they see the one-way ticket and immediately ask: "And 'ow do you plan on supporting yourself 'ere, sir?"

"Oh," I say brightly, "Blackhill Enterprises! I'm working with Blackhill on a series of concerts, they're a very big concern over here and —"

He cuts me off midsentence: "Yes, we're well aware of Black'ill Enterprises. They just put on that fing in the park, didn't they? Big to-do about the lad 'oo died in 'is pool on drugs, right? What's's name, Percy?"

"Brian Jones."

"Yes, that's 'im. Right through there to luggage control, sir."

When I get to the baggage inspection all the customs officers are standing around reading the *Sun* or some other rancid Brit tabloid with 42-point headlines: "GRATEFUL DEAD PLAN LSD DRUG FEST HERE." Oh my God, they've been *waiting* for me. They actually greet me *by name!*

"Mr. Scully! How are you today?" Uh oh, they're being *nice* to me.

"My, my, what 'ave we 'ere, sir?" Well, let's see. Thirty-two hits of LSD in the film pack. I swear to them I didn't know it was there, but surprise, surprise . . . they don't believe me! They open the thing up and I am as amazed as they are to see it because I had actually forgotten all about it. Rule #1 in the Smugglers Handbook: When smuggling drugs, it is better not to *forget* that you are smuggling drugs. Pills are flopping all over the floor of the airport.

Plus I've got an American eagle feather, a bear claw, and all of this other earthy Native American stuff that I know the English are going to love: turquoise bracelets, turquoise jewelry, raw turquoise, all my Indian frou-frah. Just logging-in all this stuff at customs takes an hour and a half.

"Aha! What's this then, sir?" The customs guys are looking at each other very gravely and going "Morphine!" The pills happen to be purple Owsleys, but they look like the little jacks of pharmaceutical heroin that they give to addicts in England.

"Right, then, my lad, we'll see about you, then!" I'm whisked — literally lifted between two customs inspectors — right into one of those little interrogation rooms. Next thing I know, I'm standing there in my boxer shorts and they're going through my pants. There's two of them, a youngster and an older guy, and the youngster's going through my pants very efficiently. The older guy, however, is fascinated with the eagle feather.

"Why, that's a bald eagle feather!" he says. "That's a North American brown bear claw!" And this little colloquy momentarily interrupts the frisking of my pants. I am fully aware that in the watch pocket of these pants is this bottle of pure cocaine hydrochloride, which as soon as they find it they're going to know *exactly* what it is.

The next thing they find is my interobioform, which you take for the runs. The older gent says, "Why, sir, have you got a problem?" And I say, "Yes, I do, and actually I need to go to the bathroom *right now.*" So he tells the youngster to give me my pants back, and off we go!

I drop my pants in front of the kid and he says, "Go on, you can close the door." So I close the door and immediately — ha! — snort *all* the coke right up. Probably the worst decision I ever made in my life, because from then on I cannot speak at *all,* and the authorities begin to think I am playing tough with them. They take me upstairs to meet the C.I.D. in a very dark room with one bright light. They are interrogating me, but unfortunately I can't speak. I open my mouth and all that comes out is a strangled "Ahhhhghh. . . ." My larynx is frozen.

"Don't play tough with us, old son! The silent treatment doesn't work in England!"

When I get to the little jailhouse where they're planning to lock me up, they finally find the little brown bottle. I'd rinsed it out in the toilet, but hadn't flushed it. I didn't think it would go down. The copper takes the cork out of it and carefully sets it down on the table where he's logging my eagle feathers and stuff. He tips it over and gets this big drop of water on the end of it on his finger and sniffs! "And what might this be, then?"

"Toilet water," I say. "Eau de toilette."

In the john I'd also torn up Frankie Hart's ticket so they wouldn't connect us. She goes on to see Lenny Holzer to get the money to spring me, and also calls Keith Richards and Sam Cutler. Sam calls Chesley Millikin, who's currently vice president of Epic Records in Britain, and on Monday Chesley gets me out. Lenny Holzer supplies the money. He's filthy rich, living in London at the Dorchester. I'd met him and his wife, Baby Jane Holzer, when the Dead played on the roof of the Chelsea Hotel.

So I spend the weekend in jail and when I get out Sam Cutler takes me over to Keith Richards's house. I haven't claimed all of my baggage and one of my suitcases happens to be full of pot. When Keith hears of this he actually induces me into going out to the airport and collecting the bag! I know this to be completely insane, but I do it anyway. I have the taxicab drop me just before the underpass that goes into Heathrow. I'm wearing a suit and tie and I walk into the baggage claim whistling, trying to look like I've just arrived from America.

I can't believe it. I've just spent the weekend in jail and there in the big arrival hall all this stuff is still sitting there. I grab it and walk out. Nothing to declare and nobody checks. They assume I've already been through passport control, which is a good thing because at this point I don't even *have* a passport — they took it away when they busted me.

Nicki shows up to save my ass. She brings 3,200 hits of LSD and some pot so I can buy myself a lawyer. Selling the acid is not going to be a problem and Keith will buy the pot — fancy Big Sur top, the kind they really love in England. The dope is in Christmas candles, huge starform candles, with shrink-wrap Christmas paper around them and big red ribbon bows. The pot, wrapped in tin foil, is buried in the middle of each candle. So as soon as Nicki shows up, we go over to Keith's and sit around the living room at a Marrakesh copper table covered with a Tunisian rug, just *hacking* away at these beautiful Christmas candles.

I am in London two weeks before my trial (and deportation). Lots of time to cook up mischief. At Keith's house big plans are laid — concerts in Hyde Park, concerts in Golden Gate Park, concerts at Stonehenge and the Taj Mahal! Keith is turning us onto his Flying Saucer hash, we are turning everyone on to the bud and they love it. We sit around at night and Keith snorts crushed Nembutal. He neglects to tell me what it is until I've already got a big old honk up my nose and one eye is bleeding and my brain has gone to sleep.

"Ya know we used the 'Ell's Angels for security, don'tcha?" asks Sam.

"Yeah, it's brilliant, innit? Fuckin' Angels, man, they're beautiful!" adds Keith.

"One of these days you gotta come over and see the real thing, man," I say, and I start pitching the Rolling Stones on doing a free concert in San Francisco. And I'm sorry to say that Altamont came out of these raps. It's not exactly what we concocted, but it's what happened.

⑨

Drugs, constitutional bohemianism, chronic nosedives, horrible excuses for albums. These are a few of the things that the Rolling Stones and the Grateful Dead have in common, along with the ongoing enigma of how two such ragtag groups have managed to stay the course in spite of centrifugal forces that everyone assumed would have long ago rendered them asunder. They also share an uncanny feel for the zeitgeist. So it shouldn't be too surprising that the Dead become intwined with the Stones in cooking up that notorious end-of-the-era incident, Altamont.

By December we're back in San Francisco. We've gotten involved in trying to put a free concert together to try to bust the cycle of gang violence that has erupted in the last year in San Francisco. We have a mini–war zone on our hands, and we're trying find a way to end the gang warfare. There's the Brown Berets, the Chinese gangs, the black gangs, the Black Panthers, the Latino gangs, plus several different feuding biker factions: the Gypsy Jokers, the Hell's Angels, and Sons of Hawaii. All violently clashing with each other in what is really a pretty small town (San Francisco, the city itself, is only 750,000 people).

Everyone in the Dead agrees it would be a good idea if we could do something similar to what we did in Tompkins Square. We think maybe we could do it with the Stones, who are coming into town shortly. The idea is to involve every one of those gangs. Get a budget from the Stones to bring beer, briquets, the barbecue, the beer concession, T-shirts, Tex-Mex food, beans and rice, burritos, and so on.

We actually talk the Stones into doing a free concert in Golden Gate Park. The agreement will be the same one we always make with the Parks Department — no announcements about where it's going to take place until twenty-four hours before the concert. If anyone breaks that promise, the permit will be revoked.

The Stones have been in L.A. recording *Let It Bleed* and beginning their soon-to-be-infamous 1969 tour. Peter Tork's house becomes their headquarters, with Mick wandering around in a kimono and flip-flops shouting "Orderly!" whenever he wants someone to bring him a drink or a joint or a line of coke. I visit Keith and we stay up all night and watch the sun come up over the Hollywood hills, blasting like a fireball through these huge floor-to-ceiling windows.

Maybe it's because it's "Sympathy for the Devil" time and the Stones aren't getting much sympathy, or maybe it's because the Stones are getting flack for high ticket prices. Whatever the reason, one fine day Mick Jagger blurts out our plans for a free concert in Golden Gate Park and we lose the permit. Then the Stones want to save face by finding another place to hold their free concert. Also, they're making a movie of this tour — the aptly named *Gimme Shelter* — and a free concert in San Francisco would be the perfect finale.

So the frantic search is on for a new location. By now the whole world knows there's going to be a free Rolling Stones concert and people are pouring into San Francisco airport to be here for the Big Event. New location to be announced momentarily. We're on the phone to our reporter out at the site right now. Stay tuned!

Once the site at the Altamont Speedway is chosen, the original plan of bringing everyone together is totally fucked. How were Chicanos, blacks, and Chinese expected to get all the way out there? Take the bus?

The Stones had used Hell's Angels at their Hyde Park concert. *English* Hell's Angels, a far cry from the visigoths of the Oakland chapter. I see that the Stones' infatuation with the heraldry of the Hell's Angels could be the beginning of a *big* problem, but attempting to explain this to Mick Jagger is fruitless.

"Listen, man, you can't *hire* Hell's Angels. They're, uh, not for hire."

Mick quizzes me peevishly: "Wot you saying then, exactly?" Surely the Hell's Angels would leap at the opportunity to act as the praetorian guard for the Stones, wouldn't they?

Sam Cutler is equally smitten. "Oh, come off it, the Hell's Angels would be *perfect*. We used 'em in Hyde Park."

"Uh, Sam, those kids, excuse me, were *not* Hell's Angels. They had 'Hell's Angels' *chalked* on their jackets, for chrissakes! Like a costume party! These guys are red-and-white, real-time, Death's Head Angels! They went to Korea! Vietnam! They're fuckin' *killers!*" Mick and Sam exchange very noisy winks, and soon decide to "hire" the Hell's Angels for a truckload of ice and beer.

The day arrives and we take a helicopter out to Altamont. Bert, the roadie, drives Garcia's old school bus. The state of the Altamont site is unimaginably appalling. Mini-Vietnam of garbage and old car wrecks. The press arrive, but spin control is totally gone.

The mood is nasty and oppressive. There are fights breaking out everywhere, and just as we are pulling into the backstage area we see the infamous Hell's Angels'–motorcycles-getting-knocked-over incident. There are Hell's Angels beating up Hell's Angels. It is one hair-raising thing after another. Garcia and Weir are looking out the windows seeing all this horrendous stuff that they are soon to be part of.

We park the bus backstage. It becomes the Dead dressing room. Outside we pitch a tent, which becomes our hospitality suite. We figure we're probably going to have to camp out.

Once at the site our interaction with the Stones is minimal, to say the least. Mick and Jerry exchange about half a dozen words as Sir Mick's entourage bears him along. Something like "What time is the helicopter leaving?" The Stones have put the Hell's Angels in charge of security, but it turns out the Hell's Angels officers are absent, gone to a big meeting of the entire Bay Area governing board. The subject is turf, because the gang wars are all about drug territory and how to divide it up. This is the Yalta of gang powwows, Stones concert or no

Stones concert. The Angels are very turf-conscious, as territorial as a pack of wild boars in rutting season.

The only Angels there are "prospects" trying to prove themselves. They're out of control with no one to rein them in, and the hostility of the crowd is tangible. Its makeup is pure gelignite: East Bay rowdies on Ripple and 'ludes. This, combined with the steepness of the canyon slope, results in stoned people rolling downhill onto the stage.

Jerry, Mountain Girl, and I cower on the floor of the bus through the worst of the fighting — the Hell's Angels and guns and pool cues and all of that. We're watching the sun go down and the time going by and all the chaos out there — grisly and violent images replaced by others even more disturbing and incomprehensible — and we're *high* to boot.

Jerry is shaking and huddling with Mountain Girl. He keeps repeating: "No way am I playing, man, no fucking way am I going out there!"

Mountain Girl is going, "What about some fucking weed around here!" We've brought some opium, gummy opium, mescaline, and a ton of weed, but all the dope in the world isn't going to help a bummer like this.

Not until the Jefferson Airplane go on do we venture out of the bus. There is all this kinetic energy zinging about, and when Marty Balin gets into a fight with this Angel named (I'm not kidding) Animal, we fear the worst. Animal is wearing a grisly cowl made out of wolf fur. It is road kill, essentially, that he has shaped to go over his head, complete with snout, teeth and whiskers. All that's missing from his outfit are horns. Animal proceeds to smack Marty Balin in the face and has to be pulled off the stage kicking and screaming, still trying to smash Marty in the face with his boot.

It is a truly terrifying moment. Jerry holds up both hands in an involuntary gesture of keeping back some unseen host of demons. He is petrified. Speechless, and shaking like a leaf. He turns every shade of pale and whispers: "Oh, maa-aan, no *way* are we doing this. There is absolutely no way. The inmates have definitely taken over the asylum. Rock, go sort it out, man. Talk to the Angels or something."

Oh, sure, Jerry. If somebody would only just *talk* to the Angels, this misunderstanding could get itself worked out! Now, it's true I *am* dumb enough to go retrieve my suitcase after being busted, but I've got a little more sense than to intervene in foreign wars. It's not that Jerry fears for his life; he has a lot of friends in the Hell's Angels. What is truly disturbing him are the *bad vibes,* and let me tell you, they are truly ugly. Of course, being high as a kite makes things that much worse. The momentum is frightening, too.

"This show is like some kind of runaway train, and we best get the fuck *out* of here before it runs into us," Jerry moans, making a dash for the bus. And everybody else is running around and wailing and wringing their hands. Phil Lesh, who is even more jittery than Garcia, is peeking out through the saggy curtains giving us a running commentary of the savage sideshow outside.

"Jesus Christ, there's this three-hundred-pound naked guy, and — oh God! — the Angels are beating him to a fucking pulp."

"Phil, *stop,* please!"

Pigpen is huddled in the back of the bus too numb to react. But night must fall.

Healy pokes his head in the bus: "The Airplane are coming off-stage, what do you guys want to do?"

We had planned to go on just before the Stones, but things seem to be falling apart too quickly (including the band). It's essential, if more chaos is to be avoided, that the Stones play as soon as possible. A lot more bands have shown up than we anticipated, the show is going on too long, and if we go on now the Stones will go on way too late. It is starting to get dark, and there are no lights and no lit roads to find our way *out* of this godforsaken place. At least 350,000 people trapped in this demonic gulley!

Garcia tells me to get everybody together; he wants it to be a group decision. Well, turns out that Marty Balin's getting hit has made the band members fairly crazy; *nobody* wants to go out there and play, lights or no lights!

"Let the Stones go on, this is *their* madness," Phil says.

"No way we're going to *play* good, anyway," says Jerry (ever the philosopher-realist). "We're just gonna give our enemies more ammunition." Our enemies?

We don't even stay for the Stones entire set! We have to leave now if we want to fly out, because the helicopter has to come back for the Stones.

Teeth-grinding, amphetamine paranoia is rampant. Maybe Meredith Hunter got pulled into that undertow. He gets knifed by a Hell's Angel and the Angels pull him underneath Jonathan Riester's stake-bed truck. The very truck we were going to put our equipment in to take it back to our sound studio in Ignacio, but we'd have to pull the body out from under it first and we don't want to do that — don't want to go near it! Don't want to touch it!

And there are no police to be found anywhere! They are smart, they stayed away. They're drinking in some redneck bar somewhere saying, "Let those fucking Hell's Angels kill the hippies, the fuck do we care?"

We take off while the Stones are playing, and as we look down at the crowd it's as if we just caught the last helicopter out of Saigon.

The Grateful Dead are supposed to play at the Carousel, now called the Fillmore West since Bill Graham took it over. For some demented reason we figure we have to get back there. We're *booked,* after all, and it's Bill Graham. We go there thinking we are actually going to play, but everybody heard we were going to be at Altamont so nobody shows up. Sunday night, Jerry and Kreutzmann and I are sitting in this little dressing room backstage — our old hangout, it used to be *our* ballroom and now it's Bill's place but we're hanging out there just the same. We are all hanging with this tank of nitrous oxide. It's got octopus cords coming off it and a regulator with a shut-off valve so if you drop the hose it shuts off — innovations designed by the Pranksters. Each of us has a hose, you know, and we're sucking on this gas and . . . enter Bill Graham! Ranting and raving about Altamont and how the Dead are responsible for all the atrocities there.

"And you especially, Scully, you're a fucking murderer!" He picks me up off the floor and I freak totally out. I've just taken this huge hit, the whole band is there, and I'm blown away, pissed off, hurt — and high as a kite on nitrous oxide. So I, uh, *throw* Bill Graham down the dressing room's stairs. It's only like three steps, but he sails out of that dressing room and lands on his ass in front of everybody sitting in the big hospitality room where all the stagehands hang out with the family and kids.

The following day in the *Chronicle,* Ralph J. Gleason directs a similar indictment at us. The Dead's answer is Garcia and Hunter's "New Speedway Boogie":

Spent a little time on the mountain
Spent a little time on the hill
Things went down we don't understand
but I think in time we will

Woodstock and Altamont are seen as polar opposites in a mass-media-generated parable of light and darkness. Woodstock is peace, love, and the triumph of Woodstock Nation. Altamont is guns, drugs, and the end of the world. But they were just two ends of the same mucky stick. The same fuck-ups, the same cast of characters.

Woodstock and Altamont were the result of the same disease: the bloating of mass bohemia in the late sixties. The Haight worked because it was a small, closely knit community where everybody knew each other and shared a common vision. Then came the attempt to re-create the vibe on a larger and larger scale. At that point, Mercury, the patron of merchants and thieves, took over and they started setting up bleachers out on Highway 61.

A couple of days before Altamont, Emmett Grogan left a message scrawled on the blackboard at the Dead office: "CHARLIE MANSON MEMORIAL LOVE DEATH CULT FESTIVAL." We should at least have read the writing on our *own* wall. . . .

11

Two for the Road

IN THE FALL of 1969 the band begins recording again. It's an existential moment for the Dead — this is another who-are-we-anyway? album and at this point there *is* some confusion. Let's see, the Dead are: ex-jug-band folkies who (a) went electric, (b) became a pizza pub blues band, (c) took acid and played long noodling psychedelic sets, which they then (not too successfully) (d) attempted to fuse with conventional songs on their two last albums, *Anthem of the Sun* and *Aoxomoxoa*.

At this point, Garcia, Mountain Girl, and Robert Hunter are sharing a house over on the creek in Larkspur. Janis lives right down the road, Stephen Stills is a neighbor, and David Crosby lives only a few minutes away in Novato. The atmosphere is real neighborly and before too long there are actual kitchen jams going on again, like from the very beginning of the Haight when people were banging on pots and pans and playing kazoos and guitars and staying up all night — the ur-pot and red wine parties that the Haight began with.

Garcia has been friends with David Crosby since the days of the Byrds and the Buffalo Springfield. The Byrds' version of "Mr. Tambourine Man," even more than Dylan going electric, was the pivotal event for California folkies. The instant they heard it, they knew they'd found their sound. It merged folk, rock, and Beach Boys' harmonies. Crosby was the first folkie on the West Coast to go electric. He had no boundaries. In a sense, David Crosby had been an example for the Warlocks in their move from folk to electric music, and he was now showing the Grateful Dead a new way of doing folk music.

And, of course, Crosby and Garcia also like the same drugs. Crosby and Garcia went through major pot-banging, pot-smoking, wine-drinking, playing-at-coffeehouses episodes, and have recently graduated to the high plains of coke-snorting, high-tech, and neo-bluegrass (so there's a lot of common ground). They can sit around all night, do a few lines, play some old saws on acoustic guitar, and go into the studio totally wired. They do some beautiful stuff in the studio together.

With David Crosby, coke frenzy comes to the Dead camp like a Peruvian blizzard. Along with ice-bag pot, this is the fuel of the new era. Smoking ice-bag pot you don't even know you are high until you're breaking out in a sweat.

One day Hunter is working with Jerry on some new songs, Mountain Girl is making dinner, and I've just stopped by on my way to Mill Valley. There's a knock. It's David Crosby and Don Lewis, our advance man in Hawaii. David hands us a vial of some colorless liquid — some close relation of LSD. Like a character from a fairy tale, he looks us in the eye and says, "Ah-ha!"

Shortly thereafter, the meal turns to sculpture and the Rev. Crosby is sliding around the room. He's a miracle of enthusiasm. A Serbo-Croatian *griot* reciting the Epic of Ned Hey — imagine what Mussolini could've done if he'd had good drugs!

"Stories, man, *stories!*" he's saying. He's getting up on the table, painting little Expressionist watercolors in the air.

"Song stories, story stories, stories with *guitars.* That's what the whole fuckin' thing's all about. Think back to what got you into this stuff in the first place."

"Not wanting to get a job?" suggests Jerry.

"Yeah, but *besides* that. What was the *song?* The first song that ever took you out of your fuckin' teen angst and told you about *life,* man, as it's lived on this earth?"

"'Irene Goodnight'?"

"Well, anyway, all of those songs, they're our holy scriptures, the folk bible."

"Hallelujah!" (Hunter)

"Ah-men!" (Jerry)

"You guys are wigged out, you're going too high-tech — crashing microphones and flashing this and compressing that and phasing your voices and all this synthetic stuff. Forget all this electronic shit, it's the sound of *voices,* dudes, singing together, the high-lonesome harmonies of the Everly Brothers, that got us hooked in the first place. Just try to settle down, get back to your roots! Get back! You don't need to be all weird and slick and fancy electronically."

So Crosby is the evangelist of our long-lost folk heritage and we are the sheep who've gone astray. Not that Jerry has ever forgotten his folk roots, but Crosby's reminder stimulates him to look back and set out on a new path, which of course is actually an old path (an axiom needless to say implicit in the nature of folk music itself). What we really need is a new beginning, new words, a new direction for our sound — and here it is! The avatar of our new era come to us in the unlikely form of David Crosby.

Workingman's Dead and *American Beauty* begin with David Crosby. The Dead are no longer living communally in the Haight, and in a fundamental way Garcia and Hunter, inspired by Crosby, transpose the loss of community (the band and the Haight) into a universal metaphor. And to complete the circle Garcia ends up doing pedal steel on "Teach Your Children."

But it isn't just Crosby. All the Dead's gurus have been urging them to go back to simpler stuff, even Kesey. Fortunately, just at that moment Hunter begins coming up with songs that allow the Dead to get back to doing some simple storytelling and still maintain their integrity as an electric rock 'n' roll band. Which is how songs like "Friend of the Devil" with its fablelike confrontation of good and evil come about.

Garcia and Bob Hunter go off by themselves to write the songs for the new albums. They isolate themselves from the rest of the band so they don't have to deal with months and months of waiting around for Bobby Weir and Phil Lesh to come up with songs like "New Potato Caboose" and "Born Cross-Eyed."

The songwriting relationship between Weir and his lyricist, John Barlow, is considerably more volatile than that of Garcia and Hunter. During the first writing session on "Playin' in the Band" over a bottle of Wild Turkey sitting on Bobby's living-room floor, Weir and Barlow almost come to blows. Bobby isn't quite as diplomatic as Garcia, and when he tells Barlow: "This stuff is too stilted, it doesn't flow and nobody's going to understand it," Barlow becomes enraged and chases Bobby around the house with the now empty Wild Turkey bottle. Weir hides in the bathroom with Barlow trying to break down the door, shouting: "If there's one literate man left in America, I'm writing for *him*."

Out of this intense period of collaboration, Hunter and Garcia come up with the New Book of the Dead. They're on the same wavelength, they have a lot of the same history. Both had been in the army. Used to bum around together. Back in the old coffeehouse days they slept in their cars — I think they actually lived in the *same* car for a while! That'll bring you together.

Hunter is somewhere between beatnik and hippie. A fifties collegiate hipster, basically. Kingston Trio coffeehouse humor as opposed to black Mort Sahl coffeehouse humor. More Ivy League. Hunter and Garcia share a taste for melancholy ballads and cosmic ironies. Garcia loves Mexican waltzes and little-girl-on-a-train-going-to-visit-her-dad-in-prison-as-told-by-the-conductor ballads.

In place of the long psychedelic jams of the previous albums, Hunter is coming up with knit-together lyrics that work as songs. Fables, storytelling, down-to-earth adages. The forms of traditional American music as opposed to the jazzy outer-spaced breaks.

The way Jerry works on these songs is a moldy, dank process — it's very organic. There's no plan, there isn't even a point in the early stages where he consciously sits down and works on it unless Hunter or one of the band happen to be around. It's a *very* vague, ambling, protracted business. He usually starts by putting a sequence of chord changes together. Then he'll begin sketching a melody over the top of it. Once the basic melody is floating there, he'll just let it sit for a few weeks and let it ruminate. Gradually he'll flesh out this backbone by attaching a few melodic phrases here and there and at this point he'll walk around the house humming it to himself. When it's got some shape to it he'll start playing it on the guitar to whoever's around and then get together with Hunter who will write some lyrics to the tune.

If Hunter shows up with a finished lyric Jerry will scratch around for loose melodic phrases from three or four different songs he's been playing with until something fits. This is pretty much what happened with "Casey Jones." Hunter had the words together. It was a perfect song, all Jerry had to do was pick up the guitar and play and the song came out fully formed in one session.

But Hunter's initial experience was as a poet — word magic — and it took a while for him to craft strings of words that were singable. Vowels sing a certain way and consonants another. In the beginning of their collaboration Jerry had to adjust the phrasing, to edit and *tune* the lyrics. This was the case with "Truckin'," which was never intended as a song; it was Hunter's own laid-back on-the-road-ography of the Grateful Dead, fast thoughts and snapshots of life on tour. It didn't flow as a song and had to be dismantled and reassembled, which is why the chorus and the verses sound like two different songs.

Although apparently as plain and simple as a sampler, the message of *Workingman's Dead* and *American Beauty* directly addresses some of the quandaries that now face the Dead and their audience: the loss of community and the intense existential isolation that psychedelic drugs can bring on. The recurring sense of dread and dislocation that can arise from doing shows for thousands of people *while high on acid!* Your psyche tends to get peeled — mortification of self-confidence, Healy calls it.

With the decline of the Haight and the waning of the counterculture these anxieties became more intense and the new songs speak to those basic fears. The mood of these Dead albums is healing and philosophical, even at the risk of appearing sentimental and clichéd.

Like all traditional music, the new Dead songs are designed to console, enlighten, and bring the good news. It's quite a feat for a hipsterish band like the Dead to deal with this kind of material without sounding preachy or mawkish. Hunter manages to pull this off by casting his homilies in the parabolic language of the late-sixties Dylan and the Band. His tone is that of a drifter's ironic lament. The kind of advice you'd get from a singing brakeman or a philosophical gambler. On *Aoxomoxoa* Hunter's lyrics were inspired but *baroque,* and the music that went with them didn't quite work. Now Hunter is paring down the lyrics as Garcia makes the melodies simpler.

Workingman's Dead and *American Beauty* are twins. The essential difference is that songs that were in finished shape at the time went on *Workingman's Dead* and the ones the band hadn't yet played in front of an audience went on *American Beauty.* Both are unlike anything the Dead have done up to this point. This is not just electrified folk music, it's folk music that has taken LSD and come out the other side (and then taken the Greyhound bus home to Indiana). A line from an old song, like "Sometimes I feel like a motherless child," which in the past seemed merely quaint, now leaps out at us with new meaning, and Hunter is learning to craft his own lyrics with that same elemental, profound edge to them.

It is also a time of personal reflection for members of the band. As recording progresses into 1970, Jerry's mom dies, as does Phil's father, and Pig's, and both of Bobby Weir's parents. All in 1970.

As Jerry says, "It was raining down on us the whole time we were working on that record." Amid the hassles about management and money, the group retreats to the studio as the only calm place in the storm and hunkers down.

Despite the losses, it is a magic time where everything feels right. The relationships between the members of the band are positive, and everybody is trying his best to make things as easy and smooth as possible. "Uncle John's Band" is the major group effort on *Workingman's Dead*. By the time we go into the studio, the music is there. It leads to two very smooth, flowing albums. After the experimental music saga, the band wants to boogie. After spending some eight months and $180,000 on *Aoxomoxoa,* there is a real effort to keep costs down and these constraints — more rehearsals, less time spent in the studio — in themselves help give *Workingman's Dead* and *American Beauty* their immediacy and tightness.

One of Jerry's worries in the studio is always the sound of his voice, which he is never satisfied with. Graham Nash solves this problem by teaching the Dead how to blend their voices in the studio by stacking them. Stacking is a device whereby you can put layers of vocals on top of each other and merge them in such a way that it creates a wall of extremely smooth sound. English groups like the Beatles and the Hollies did it to perfection.

Stacking is not just three guys singing harmony. It can incorporate reverb and echo along with the overlaying voices. Stacking is especially appealing to a singer like Jerry, who may be insecure about laying down a good vocal track that day. With multitracking, if the first take is shaky you can sing the same part over again only this time a little higher (listening to the first vocal on a headset along with a mix of drums and bass).

"Pretend you're in a nightclub on a stage or in a folkie grotto-type place, man," says Crosby, creating a little mental movie for Jerry. "And you're doing bluegrass and you're singing with your buddy — only your buddy is yourself! You just fuckin' *cloned* your sorry ass and now you're harmonizing with the ugly little fucker."

Stacking is an ideal technique for a band who are not too confident about their harmonies. The voices of Weir, Lesh, and Garcia don't blend all that easily. Unlike Crosby, Stills and Nash, the Dead have widely divergent vocal personalities and pitches, but stacking helps smooth those wrinkles right out. You just keep adding tracks to your own vocals until you get it where you want it. You only have to do a few passes and it comes out sounding like butter.

But when the Dead use stacking it doesn't sound all that slick — how could it? — it's like a pizza pub band version of Crosby, Stills and Nash. Despite the fact that we follow Crosby's advice to the letter, the only track that resembles a Crosby, Stills and Nash song is "Uncle John's Band."

One of the paradoxes of the band's return to their roots is that it is achieved through advanced technology. It is the new 16- and 24-track studios that made stacking possible and it's through stacking that Jerry emerges for the first time as a distinct vocal personality. Instead of the thin, reedy (and phased) vocals on previous albums, we now have Garcia literally *multiplied* into a mellow crackerbarrel Buddha entity.

Pig plays pretty well on *Workingman's Dead* because these songs are simple, the kinds he always could do. It was when the music got psychedelic that he began having a hard time. And there is still the Bobby Problem. Betty Matthews Cantor Jackson, our recording engineer, is shouting at him: "Weir, I don't care what you think is gonna happen when you pull that string, just believe me, it *ain't* — so tune up, fucker!" Garcia is a little more charitable — initially. He laughs it off.

"Aw, c'mon, maaan, leave Bobby alone. Weir's got his own way of tuning." Most of the time Jerry's real casual and just lets it go, figuring Weir will work his way around. That way Jerry won't have to put on his hard face — which he absolutely hates to do. But at some point even Jerry gets frustrated and he starts going, "Dammit, Weee-ir, tune the little sucker *up!*"

Workingman's Dead and *American Beauty* are the first Dead albums that we think of as having any commercial potential. Our previous approach had been that of lysergic storm troopers: "We think the world should get cosmic so we're gonna force this psychedelic shit down your throat." But the spaced-out psychedelic and blues jams on *Anthem* and *Aoxomoxoa* weren't working even on their own terms, and there are fewer stations that want to play the sort of music the Dead used to play at all-night shows at the Fillmore. FM radio itself is moving from the middle-of-the-night gonzo thing that it had been when it started out. They're going into daytime programming, for chrissakes! Long cuts get played when the deejay has to go take a leak and that's about it. They no longer play a whole side of an album. Now even FM needs songs under five minutes long!

With the new material we don't have to think about banding (arbitrarily putting spaces in the tracks) because for the first time since our first album we are dealing with *songs* rather than jams. And these songs are all three-and-a-half, four minutes long! There are actually a lot of songs that could get radio play, so we try to arrange the order in such a way that it will be easy for deejays to cue. The song we think will be the most popular is the first track of the first side, the next most popular is the first track of the second side, third choice is the last track of the first side and the fourth choice is the last track of the second side.

"Truckin'" (from *American Beauty*) is Jerry's favorite. It was very timely since, coincidentally, the R. Crumb cartoon has just come out. The word's in the air. "Truckin'" was a Haight expression, it's what we did down the avenue. Everybody is moving around a lot at the time, that truckin' down the road momentum is part of the times. "Truckin'" has a similar rhythm and narrative (tribulation with straight society) to John Lennon's "Ballad of John and Yoko," which had been a hit the previous summer.

"Truckin'" is in part about a drug bust in New Orleans:

> Sitting and staring out of a hotel window
> Got a tip they're gonna kick the door in again
> I'd like to get some sleep before I travel
> But if you got a warrant I guess you're gonna come in

"Truckin'" is the first song we think could be a hit so we hire the best "hit men" in the business. First we hire Chesley Millikin away from Epic Records to help us make "Truckin'" a hit. The Byrds, CSN, the Airplane, all our friends have had hits. I figure, fuck this, let's get one too, we're good enough (and we're sure taking enough *acid*).

And through Chesley I meet a guy who is one of the most successful record pushers and AM radio fixers in the business (he ends up a beer distributor in Florida). And this guy manages to get "Truckin'" played on "heavy rotation" — some sixteen times a day on the major AM stations. As a result, we actually have a mini-hit. "Truckin'" gets into the Top Twenty and the album gets into the Top Ten fueled by all this AM airplay. We are amazed. Fuck me, it actually works! And to think all you have to do is lace the deejays with an eight ball of blow, a few luncheons, and the occasional new Cadillac. Capitalism at its finest! And you can always bank on the dinner being inexpensive because by the time that blow hits, the ol' appetite has gone south of the border.

We push "Truckin'" like crazy. Listen to this record, man, just listen to thirty seconds of it! Okay, now do another line and listen to it again.

◎

Workingman's Dead is released in May of 1970, *American Beauty* in November. Both albums, by far, outsell the Dead's previous LPs, which usually ran around 175,000 to 200,000 records. *Workingman's Dead* sells some 250,000 copies and *American Beauty* more than doubles that.

◎

In 1970 the craziness begins. One hundred and forty-five gigs this year alone, not counting a large number of free shows.

◎

January 22–26. We play the Civic Auditorium, Honolulu. Wow, Hawaii in January, man! Sun, sand, *wahines,* and a little Maui-Wowie — what could be wrong with that? Well, the promoter, for one thing. He is a little wigged out and has chosen to proclaim his celestially anointed lunacy at a Grateful Dead concert. Don't get me wrong, we *like* lunatics, some of our best friends are lunatics, but crazy in *promoters* makes us nervous. You know, like who's minding the store? And this poor kid (an acid casualty, obviously) plans to throw his entire inheritance out into the audience during one of our shows. I mean, does this sort of thing ever happen to the Bee Gees?

Lenny Hart has set up this gig and it turns out he's known about the throwing-away-money business all along but kept mum about it. What the kid has neglected to tell Lenny is that he's planning to throw out his daddy's fortune in *one-dollar bills.*

The gig is absolutely mobbed. We've never had a crowd like this, nor such a big space, and it's packed to the rafters. Kids are climbing the walls.

"Gee, I guess we must be pretty hot in Hawaii, huh?" Weir observes, quite pleased with himself.

Then we see the headlines in the paper: "SHRINKWRAP HEIR PLANS TO GIVE AWAY FORTUNE AT ROCK CONCERT." According to the article, the kid plans to dump $400,000 in singles into the audience during a Grateful Dead concert.

"Shit," says Weir, "this is worse than throwing away bad acid at Woodstock."

Jerry is utterly revolted: "Aw, maaan, it's so fuckin' *demeaning*."

"Yeah," Kreutzmann adds, grinning. "If it'd only been in *twenties. . . .*"

After the last show Tom Constanten quits in high dudgeon. He's had enough. Nobody tries to stop him.

January 31. The New Orleans police bust the Grateful Dead for possession of pot — a fine way to begin the seventies! Off-duty cops (our own security!) see the crew smoking grass and search the band's rooms while the Dead are onstage. Their excuse is the allegation that the Dead have underage girls upstairs. They smell pot in the hallways, and that gives them the right to search every room, which they do. And guess what they find? That's right, folks — drugs! So they leave the various stashes in the rooms, wait for the band to come back to the hotel, and then bust 'em. All they find is a little marijuana residue — in *every* goddamn room!

Pig, not being a partaker of drugs per se, is outraged. "Rock, am I doing time over this?" he wants to know.

"Yup, I think you're gonna have to bite the big one over this, Pig."

"Jesus fuckin' Christ, Rock, this ain't funny!"

He lives right down the street from me in Mill Valley, and when he gets back home I go over and see him. Poor Pig's totally freaked.

"We're all fucking busted! And I don't even use drugs. What am I gonna do? Please get somebody on the phone, I'm not kidding, *anybody!*"

"Calm down, Pig, it's no big deal. Just tell me what happened and we'll sort it out, okay?"

"Well, there was some drugs around, I guess. And, you know, sex with little white girls . . ."

"Oh no, not *that!*"

"Aw, c'mon, Rock, you know the story. 'Mom, I'm having a sleep-over at Judy's house, tonight.' Meanwhile Judy's supposedly staying over at Elizabeth's house and the two of them are actually down at the Grateful Dead Hotel. And these chicks are *lying* to us about their age." Like *he's* the injured party.

There were to be more than a few close calls, but thanks to the institution of de rigueur I.D. checks and full-body searches, they never, suffice it to say, caught us with underage girls or pot again. Ever.

◎

May 24, Newcastle-Under-Lyme. An outdoor festival with Traffic, Black Sabbath, Mungo Jerry, and Ginger Baker's new group, Airforce. Also a bunch of wankers like Demon Fuzz, Titus Groan, and Screaming Lord Sutch (& Heavy Friends). It's a good opportunity for us — the Dead have never been to Europe — and Sam Cutler, being the old bucca-neer he is, extracts loads of loot for it. It's essentially a Brit version of Woodstock, and with all the same problems: way too many kids, too few facilities, lots of rain and even more mud. Also, they don't get the fences up in time and there's nobody there to collect tickets (like most of these events in the late sixties and the early seventies). Sunday they give up and make it free. We give 'em "Casey Jones," "Uncle John's Band" and close out with "Lovelight." Take that, ya Limey fops!

◎

June 27–July 3, 1970. The Festival Express, a five-day train trip across Canada with the bands playing at various points along the way. Pas-sengers include: the Grateful Dead, Janis Joplin and her Full Tilt Boogie Band, the New Riders of the Purple Sage, Delaney & Bonnie & Friends, Buddy Guy and his band, Ian and Sylvia and the Great Speckled Bird, Eric Andersen, Tom Rush, James and the Good Broth-ers, Robert Charlebois, and Rick Danko, bass player for the Band, along with assorted managers, promoters, writers from various rock rags, friends and relations, and a film crew.

"Welcome to Camp Lagunitas!" says Jerry, breaking the ice, and everybody laughs. There's a sense of foreboding about being couped up together for five days. The creeping panic is voiced by Sam Cutler:

"Who do I have to fuck to get *off* this train?" He's a recent addition to the Grateful Dead family, but 130 people is not what he bargained for!

Still, there's a miraculous intermingling of musicians on the train. The bar car is going twenty-four hours a day, and there's an endless exchange of country, rock and blues. Pigpen's in there with his harmonica and steel guitar jamming with the guys from Buddy Guy's band. Jerry is playing an energetic "Wake Up Little Susie" with Marmaduke, a.k.a. John Dawson of the New Riders.

Janis and Jerry trade a couple of old coffeehouse favorites, "Whinin' Boy" and "Walk Right In."

"I heard you sing those songs down on Grant Street in 'sixty-one and 'sixty-two and you blew me away," says Jerry. "I remember asking people, 'Whatever happened to the chick from Texas with the big voice who used to sing country blues?'"

"Oh, *honey!* Well, see, I had to get a little more crazy before I came back. An' that crystal meth, darlin', was just burnin' out my brains."

Jerry offers a toast: "To the bad old days!"

Janis sings a few bars of "Careless Love." Jerry backs her up and harmonizes.

"And all this time I've been thinking of you as a blues singer," says Pigpen when the song's done.

"Hell, I'm from Texas, ain't I? Home of George Jones!"

I've never seen Jerry drunk like he got drunk on that train. That goes for Mickey Hart, Bobby Weir . . . all of us are seriously hung over, sitting on the railroad tracks holding our heads.

The Festival Express is supposed to go all the way to Vancouver, but the promoters run out of money and the last gig we do is Calgary, after which we take a little side trip up to Banff and stay a couple of days in the Banff Springs Hotel overlooking the Rockies — cue the Byrds' "Blue Canadian Rockies"!

And now for a brand-new experience: mountain climbing — on acid! After a huge barrel of Sunshine acid, people start holding forth on how mountain climbing is *easier* on acid, dig? First you become a mountain goat. . . . With steely determination we set off to climb the North Face but we all get hung up on the alpine flowers before it gets very steep.

Meanwhile, back in Calgary the stampede's about to happen and there ain't gonna be too many beads and Roman sandals seen around this old town come Monday, you can bet your 4x4 on that one, Merle.

As it is, our crew gets into a major fight with the cowboys who are staying at our hotel. Bull wrestlers and bronco riders eating raw eggs and sharing the same bar with our always excitable crew. The evening ends with brawling and throwing beer mugs and smashing the saloon mirror. It's right out of the old rock 'n' roll days. A mite *too* authentic for dudes like us.

Everyone decides it's time to get out of town. Still, it's been a perfect time, the best time any of us ever had. Five wild and woolly days and nights together on a train across Canada. The totem whiskey bottle raid, the missing compartment, the mad runs into strange little wilderness towns, and the longest-running rock 'n' roll jam in the history of the world. A little reprise in miniature of the high ole days of the Haight, captured in Garcia and Hunter's ode to that train ride.

> Never had such a good time in my life before
> I'd like to have it once more
> One good ride from start to end
> I'd like to take that ride again
> Again
> *"Might As Well"*

12

Box of Rain

‹‹

OCTOBER 4, 1970, *Winterland*. Janis Joplin O.D.s at the Landmark Motel while the Dead are doing their set at Winterland. Later, somebody figures out she must have died during "Cold Rain and Snow." We decide not to tell the band until the show is over. Maybe they'll want to do "Death Don't Have No Mercy" or some other blues dirge as an encore. But as I break the news I can see there ain't going to be any encores tonight, everybody is too broken up.

She didn't take acid, she yelled at us a lot, but if anybody embodied the high-spirited, larger-than-life energy of the Haight, it was Janis.

I can see that Jerry is blown away, but at moments like this he always manages to summon up his philosophical side. "She was on a real hard path. She picked it, she chose it, it's okay. She did what she had to do and closed her books. If you had a chance to write your life . . . I would describe that as a good score in life-writing, with an appropriate ending."

◎

In October *Vintage Dead* and, shortly thereafter, *Historic Dead* — tapes of 1966 Avalon Ballroom shows — come out on the Sunflower label. The first in a long line of unsanctioned Dead albums. Deadheads, naturally, don't care whether their albums are bootlegs or not — in fact they refer to the officially released record company records as "pedestrian" albums. But *Vintage/Historic Dead* are not bootlegs per se, since through some crafty legalism they pre-date our contract with Warner Brothers. And they come not from obsessed Deadhead tapers but are the brainchild of Mike Curb at MGM. The same Mike Curb of the Mike Curb Congregation who had all the acts believed to be dopers thrown off the MGM label. All the bands using drugs or *singing* about drugs, bands with names like Lavender Popcorn. Then he goes and puts out two albums by the most notorious drug group on the planet! He's spent all this money on these albums and he's putting them out even if we all have needles sticking out of our arms. Business as usual, folks.

Speaking of which . . . around this time I happen to ask Joe Smith at Warner Brothers what we have to do to get our latest advance payment, and he says, "What are you talking about, we paid it *months* ago. Ask Lenny. I've got the canceled check right here. A hundred and eighty thou. What kinda bookkeeping do you guys have up there anyway?"

Well, Lenny Hart is nowhere to be seen. I knew we were fucked when he had the Dead renegotiate their deal with Warner's. But now he's actually run off with the whole advance, the money that was going to be used to — sob! — pay our taxes. None of the stuff that he scared everybody to death with has been accomplished. Once more, we're totally broke. I go back to Warner Brothers and hit on them yet again.

I hire the famous San Francisco detective Hal Lipsett to find the motherfucker, but by the time we get to him he's spent most of it. Gambling up at Lake Tahoe and spending money like crazy. They find some money in a bank in South Shore Lake Tahoe, Nevada. He's named it the Sunshine account! There's only thirty thousand dollars left; the other hundred and fifty thousand dollars is gone. All the money from the renegotiation with Warner's. Lipsett eventually finds Lenny in San Diego, baptizing Born-Again Christians in the ocean. The poor man dies in jail a year and a half later.

⑨

November 23. Sandy Alexander, head of the New York chapter of the Hell's Angels, is a good friend of Pigpen's. At Dead shows at the Fillmore East in New York, Sandy always drops by and puts a bottle of Southern Comfort on Pig's organ. By and by they begin talking about the Dead doing a benefit for the New York Angels. Mickey Hart signs on first and when Jerry says okay, the rest just falls into place.

Since Bill Graham isn't about to let the Angels hold their benefit at the Fillmore East, they decide to use the old Anderson Theater. The Anderson is a broken-down palace if ever there was one. It's beautiful inside but it's been closed for a while and has no power — it is pitch-dark inside. The Angels rent a huge generator and run the cables right smack down the middle of the aisle. The generator is so loud that it has to be set up outside on the street, but every time the door is opened this terrible thumpedy-thump just about obliterates the band. Noxious gas fumes blow in, too (somewhat masked by billowing clouds of marijuana smoke). Sandy has gotten hold of a couple of pounds of pot, and the girls have been rolling it up for days. He proceeds to pass the whole thing out into the audience. Pigpen peers out at the crumbling baroque decor of the Anderson through the smoke and fumes and says: "If there was ever a Sistine Chapel in hell, this is it!"

The Anderson is right down the street from the Fillmore East, and Bill Graham is doing his damnedest to kill it. He's fuming. There are Angel choppers lined up and down both sides of Second Avenue — but there isn't anything he can do about it. It's a major bargain. Graham is charging eight, ten dollars a head at the Fillmore, while over at the Anderson you get the Grateful Dead, the New Riders, Traffic, and Ramblin' Jack Elliott for two bucks (plus all the grass you can smoke). I think in the end the Angels only make about $1,300. Almost everybody gets in free.

Shortly after this, Jerry lends the Angels the money to make the movie *Hell's Angels Forever.* Sandy promises him: "I give you my word you'll get your money back whatever happens." And he does. The movie actually ends up making money!

◎

Jerry is putting a band together. It is variously billed as "Garcia & Saunders" and "Jerry Garcia & Friends." They play at some little clubs around Marin, but mainly at Whitey's place in San Rafael. Old Whitey, the owner, is a character. He decides to open a psychedelic club called Pepperland (as in Sgt. Pepper).

Portrayed on the cover of *Shakedown Street,* it's a seedy place with several different names because Whitey is fighting with the city council of San Rafael over his liquor license and meanwhile selling beers under the bar. It's a homegrown joint. Nobody from San Francisco comes to these gigs, just people from Marin County — everybody from Huey Lewis to John Cipollina and Janis Joplin, mostly musicians and their friends. I'm sure half the audience is on the guest list.

The Dead are on a killer schedule, but if we have a night off, Jerry gets antsy and wants to go out and play. He mostly wants to play in a smaller group and try songs in places other than the ice arenas and big halls.

The main reason for all the splinter bands Jerry puts together — the Garcia band, the bluegrass band, Old and In The Way — is that he just doesn't feel good if he's not playing. Jerry's got fierce energy, an insatiable appetite, and endless curiosity. If he doesn't play for a day or two he feels he's going to get stale. That's why he's always doing his scales and practicing his chords.

"I'll just sit home and rust if I stay on a Grateful Dead schedule. The Dead want a week off? Fuck 'em, I'm going to go out and play."

Kreutzmann's saying, "I'm pooped, man, I'm not coming out." So Jerry calls Lesh or Weir or Hart. And David Crosby, whom Garcia's been snorting coke with up in Novato, is (naturally) always up for a gig. Soon Garcia's got a little band together. They can go back to their coffeehouse days and just hammer out those old bluegrass and folky tunes till the cows come home.

This is a wonderfully vital and energetic time for Jerry. He's developing his skills on the pedal steel, performing with the New Riders of the Purple Sage and recording with them. The Grateful Dead are getting all crazy about this: "Is he leaving us?" "Is he deserting his electric guitar for the pedal steel?"

Pepperland is the ideal joint to hole up in. Just soak up the gritty vibes and . . . evolve. It's one of those rowdy, wonderful places. There are three bars, a cast of rogues, and fisticuffs in the parking lot. The cops are there almost all the time, sirens wailing throughout the set. Things just spring up out of nothing. Everybody is drunk and crazy (hippies just don't handle drink well).

"That's why Leo Fender made his electric guitar with a solid body, folks," says Jerry. "To deflect beer bottles."

☺

February 19, 1971, Capitol Theater, Port Chester, New York. Dr. Stanley Krippner has created the Paranormal Institute Dream Laboratory and he wants to do an ESP experiment. His friend Mickey Hart has suggested he do it with a Grateful Dead audience, and the day has finally arrived. Krippner's plan is to project psychic shapes onto a screen in back of the stage and then everybody in the audience is supposed to glom onto them with little intercortical tendrils and project them to various psychics who are sitting around in their wigwams in New York City.

The results turn out to be shady at best. Krippner perhaps thought that the Grateful Dead audience would be an especially psychic group of people, which might have been true if the experiment had taken place in Panhandle Park or Olompali. But the Port Chester audience is eighteen- and nineteen-year-old kids who've hopped over the border from Connecticut to get drunk and are all screwed up on beer and hard liquor.

Krippner is saying: "Now, ladies and gentlemen and paranormals, I want you to project these pyramids and squares. *Con*-cen-trate . . . let the images sink deep into your inner recesses like pebbles falling into a deep well, sending out concentric circles of psychic energy. Now, here, my friends, is a circle. You will please concentrate on the *round-ness* of this circle, on it's infinite resonance."

Meanwhile people are literally falling down drunk, drunk on their asses: "Say what, man? Circles? I'll take three. How much do I owe you?"

Jerry is more or less laid back about the whole thing. He's standing with his arms folded looking at a giant occult eye, a bemused look on his face.

It isn't just an incidental, light-show-type thing, either. It's a full-blown lecture complete with admonitions to do our "best work."

"Now, class, all during the show we want you to think of pyramids, circles, squares, and rectangles. And you will please use *all* your mental power, right *and* left side of the brain, or your test results cannot be officially coded." Hey, is that a promise?

Jerry is pissed off mainly because he wants to be one of the psychic *targets:* "The receiving end is where it's at, man. Hey, why not let the psychics project those doodads onto *us* while we're playing? Now *that* would be an experiment!"

After this concert Mickey Hart temporarily quits the Grateful Dead. He is so embarrassed about his dad running off with all the band's money that he doesn't come back for five years.

March 5, Black Panther Benefit, Oakland Auditorium. This is pretty political for a nonpolitical band. Just one of those out-of-the-blue things
that are always happening to the Dead as they travel down the path of
least resistance! We meet Huey Newton on an airplane coming back
from New York and we get along famously. When he tells us he's
holding a rally at the Oakland Auditorium, we offer to play. Why he
would *want* a honky, psychedelic outfit like the Grateful Dead to play
at a Black Panther rally is not clear. Maybe he's just being polite.
Maybe it's the martinis.

Anyway, when we get to the gig our soul mate from the plane is a
great deal frostier. As a matter of fact, we don't even get to talk to him.
He's surrounded by crazy-eyed bodyguards with big Afros. You know,
black CIA/FBI types. And everybody's packing pistols. They are all
over the place, and they're looking for *bombs* and stuff! We are the only
white guys there, and we're getting real bad vibes from everyone. The
crowd barely tolerates our presence. It's scary, and we are in no mood
to linger. I don't know if it's our decision or theirs, but it's pretty
obvious we best go on *early.*

The Dead do a *very* brief "Lovelight" — about six minutes (as
opposed to the usual twelve) — strictly the R&B version. We do our
gig and get the hell out of there.

When we play the Fillmore East on April 27 we get a very different
reception. We're heroes! A motley cast assembles to cheer us on. Emmett Grogan shows up with Ewa Aulin (who plays the eponymous
Candy) naked under a raincoat, assorted debutantes, tycoons, and
none other than Bob Dylan himself. With the arrival of Dylan, Bill
Graham runs totally amok, rushing around in his wake offering him
champagne and virgins. He gives him one of those dopey fake balconies and — I'm not kidding — a *throne.* And there sits Sir Bob with
hat and gloves on — immobile, pale, otherworldly, like Franz Kafka at
a wedding in Prague, observing the players below on the stage.

Garcia plays the pedal steel on "Mama Tried" and "Bobby McGee"
and a few numbers with the Beach Boys: "Riot in Cell Block #9,"
"Okie from Muskogee" and "Johnny B. Goode." That night, Rhonda,
the wife of our roadie, Johnny Hagen, is giving birth all by herself in
the wild west of Marin County, so we hook up a phone to the mikes
and the Dead sing her "Help Me Rhonda" with the Beach Boys. It's
all being broadcast live, plus we're recording the whole concert on a
16-track in the basement.

We are meeting the movers and shakers. Dealers are dropping off bags of coke to get backstage, pimps are pulling up in gold Caddies. In their shambling way, the Grateful Dead are suddenly stars. Girl-of-the-Year Baby Jane Holzer wants to throw a party; Hilton heiresses and lox importers' daughters are inviting us up to penthouses. And we know we're in the big leagues not because of all this, but because Bill Graham has started treating us with a wee bit of respect. He's not offering us thrones in candy-box balconies exactly, but still. . . .

You always end up talking about Bill Graham no matter what the subject is. In the rock 'n' roll world, it always comes back to him because he's at the center of that universe. I love that quote in the beginning of Bill Graham's book where Grace Slick says, "He is one of us and he is one of them." Peter Coyote said he was part Mother Teresa and part Al Capone.

With Bill you always have to earn your money the hard way. He loves to scream and shout and get you screaming and shouting. (There you go, we're family.) He hustles everybody on *principle.* The poster artists are getting fifty bucks a poster and Graham is selling thousands of copies of the damn posters for a dollar each.

The Dead start out getting $150 a show from Bill and work their way up to $300 (with Bill chewing on the carpet over every extra fifty bucks). It's a riot.

Eventually we get smart and start counting up the crowds who come to the Dead shows at the Fillmore, so when we go in to negotiate he knows we've done our homework. He says: "I know next week you're going to ask for more money and I got an idea what it is, so I'm going to write it down on this piece of paper and I'm going to seal it up and when you come back see if I'm not right." So he does that and when we come back he asks us what the number is we've come up with and I say, "Three hundred dollars." And Bill says, "Three hundred is fine." Then he reaches in his drawer, pulls out the envelope and opens it up. But instead of showing us the piece of paper on which he's written his estimate, he pops it in his mouth and eats it. A real charming guy that way. You really have to work.

Hardball games are Graham's specialty, and eventually we get into it too. It's necessary if you want to survive the Graham *Anschluss.* It isn't very long before we figure out what his principal delusion is and we play on it mercilessly.

The Dead finish their set and leave the stage. Into the dressing room dashes the breathless Bill. He's a little electron of undischarged energy zinging about the room. "You guy's are doing an encore, right?" And Jerry says: "Bill, we'd do anything for you, Bill, but it's been a long night, man. . . ."

"*What?!?* You've *gotta!* The crowd isn't leaving." We'd make him promise us trips to Hawaii and color TV sets for the whole band. We get him on tape promising us all kinds of outrageous things.

What's he going to do, go out and tell the audience that Elvis has left the building? No, no, he doesn't want to do that because he thinks of himself as in control of the situation. Santa Claus always delivers the goods. Graham isn't just a promoter, he is an *impresario.* Ever since he started giving away apples in barrels at the early Fillmore shows he'd been promoting an ambience, a vibe. Brought to you by . . . ta-da! . . . *Bill Graham!*

The Dead would've done an encore anyway, but the maestro is too wound up in his role for this to occur to him. Those long jams are the very air the Dead breathe. They can do half of *Anthem of the Sun,* "St. Stephen," "China Cat," and then it's like "Holy shit! we just got started. What time is it?" We get outside and it's *daylight.* We walk up to Gem Spa at six A.M., buy a newspaper and go have breakfast at Ratner's.

◎

June 21, Château d'Herouville, France. The Lost Boys quest for a new broken-down palace goes on. For some time we've been looking for a *big* place, somewhere we can all move into, 710 Ashbury on a monumental scale. An old hotel or an abandoned summer camp where we can each have our own log cabin with our names carved on pine shingles above the door: "Black Jack" (Garcia) and "Scockrully" (these were our pseudonyms in the hotels on the road).

I decide to scout New Mexico. We have this idyllic idea that we ought to move to someplace sublime and cool, so I go down for a week or so and visit the New Buffalo commune and other people we know down there. But New Mexico is a bit *too* cool. The winters are terribly harsh down there. Everybody is living in mud and adobe houses that they made themselves. They are very smoky, and the one I happen to be staying in has an unfortunate thing happen to it — I have nothing to do with it, I swear! The builders hadn't exactly followed the Indian adobe process; they put too much straw in the clay, and when somebody leaves a roach on a windowsill the wall catches on fire and we spend the rest of the night shivering under blankets out in the desert. Not exactly a great place for the Dead to live.

Then comes the French château fantasy. I've recently hired John McIntyre as a baby-sitter for the Dead, and while reading them their bedtime story one night he happens to mention that there is a château over in France that is available and would be just perfect for the hairy simians. What's more, it has a recording studio right there in the old dungeon *and* its own winery. This feature nearly drives Lesh wild. He'd be able to roam around all night in the cavernous wine cellar with his sommelier's key on a gold chain around his neck, checking out mythical vintages in bottles covered with ancient dust.

When the owner offers to fly the Dead over for a gig and to check out the joint, the band goes for it. A week or so later the honky château is a fading postcard and we are looking into something nearer home.

"Hey, the only hamburger you can get over there is fuckin' *raw,* man."

In the worldwide quest for a Grateful Dead rest home, we've all conveniently forgotten we weren't all that good at holding it all together when we *did* live communally. And it drove the women crazy. None of us could be pleased enough, no one was doing the jobs that needed to be done, you know, and we couldn't keep our women. . . .

◎

August 8, Gaelic Park. The Bronx is where the graffiti artists have their spray-can parties, living on paint fumes, cocaine, and red wine at the end of the subway line. Everywhere burnt-out buildings and signs of defamation: "Fuck the Pigs!" "Kill Whitey!"

After our show there, Pigpen gets really sick and checks into the hospital for three months. But there isn't a lot that they can do for him. He isn't even drinking much anymore. Jerry is doing far more poisonous stuff. But with Pigpen, the damage had been done a long time ago. He began drinking with a vengeance at the age of thirteen and never let up. He would drink a couple of bottles of Ripple just to get started and then on to the harder stuff. Wild Turkey, Bushmill's Irish Whiskey, and later, with Janis, Southern Comfort. The two of them would drink half a gallon of that stuff a night.

Before Pig goes in the hospital, Jerry has been getting schizophrenic about him. Pigpen had once been the mustard on the sandwich — the guy who held the Dead together — but now he is getting left behind. He just can't keep up with Garcia. Pigpen fucks up more and more, and Garcia gets less and less tolerant of him. The more Pig drinks and misses rehearsals or drops out at gigs, the more impatient Jerry becomes. And the more coke Jerry snorts, the shorter his temper.

At the end of September '71 we start rehearsing with Keith Godchaux. His wife Donna Jean has been calling me. She'd heard that Pigpen is sick and that we might need a piano player to take his place. We are getting a bunch of calls from keyboardists from all over the place. The vultures are beginning to circle.

Donna Jean comes to me with such a soulful rap about her husband that I tell her we're holding rehearsals over at 20 Front Street, let him come down. He comes in late and bedraggled. A few other piano players show up, but Keith is the one Jerry connects with. He plays a very soulful piano the band can groove with. So the poor fellow signs on with the Ship of Fools. He takes over while Pig is in the hospital and then when Pig comes back, it's Pig *and* Keith.

Keith plays his first gig with the Dead at Northrup Auditorium, University of Minnesota, on October 19. Unfortunately for Keith, his personality and his habits lock in effortlessly — and for him, disastrously — with the Grateful Dead and their well-developed drug habits.

Garcia sees Godchaux as fatally addicted to medications: "Here's somebody that's been taking medication all his life for a variety of childhood illnesses — asthma, hay fever, whatever — he's a medically imbalanced child who has the misfortune to hook up with the Grateful Dead who are self-medicated up to the eyeballs. Almost immediately he becomes strung out on cocaine, which in turn wrecks his stomach so he has to drink Mylanta constantly — he always had Mylanta mustache around his mouth — and soon he's into the Chinaman, too, and that's the beginning of the end."

We've had one double live album, *Live/Dead,* and now we have another two-record set of live material that we've just convinced Warner Brothers to put out, promising them to come up with a dynamite title, one that's *guaranteed* to boost sales.

In October we take the entire Dead family with us to the Continental Hyatt House in L.A. — "the Riot House" we used to call it — for the great unveiling. Everyone shows up: the band, the crew, the whole outfit. Dan Healy is there and Bob Matthews, also girlfriends and wives and children and dogs. The entire Grateful Dead cosmos.

We rent a conference room and have the meeting catered with sandwiches and refreshments. Just like a Florsheim Shoes sales conference. A big Hollywood production.

All the Warner execs show up: Clyde Bakemo and Joe Smith and Mo Ostin with their secretaries and accountants, and they say, "Who are all these people? We thought it was just going to be —"

"This is our family," I explain. "The Dead family."

"What is this, a bar mitzvah?" they want to know.

We've set up the tables with the Warner people on one side and us on the other. It's the North and South Korea Unilateral Treaty Conference. Release all prisoners!

And then we present them with our brilliant idea of calling the new album *Skull Fuck*. Dead silence. Mo Ostin's eyeballs blink like a pinball machine at full tilt. Bakemo is so stunned he has to repeat the words just to make sure his ears haven't deceived him. "*Skull* Fuck?"

"Yeah, what do you think?"

Great shuffling of papers, whispering and nervous snowball-making motions with the hands. Clyde Bakemo opens the negotiations: "I think I see what you guys are getting at but what you're forgetting about is Sears. Sears are never gonna sell it if we call it *Skull Fuck*."

This is their biggest argument: that *Sears* won't buy the record. Sears, Roebuck, for chrissakes. And they have all their accountants and demographic gnomes waving statistics and charts at us, trying to convince us that this album title will not work.

"Well," say I, "how many Grateful Dead records has Sears sold anyway? You got a demographic for that? How many kids go to Sears and buy Grateful Dead records?"

"I hear ya, but there's also J.C. Penney to consider. They won't take it either."

Oh, wow, we hadn't thought of *that*.

"Clyde," I say, "Grateful Dead fans don't go to Penney's! They go to the Salvation Army, man, that's where they get their clothes! And they buy their records at Sam Goody's. Get a grip, they don't go to Sears, Roebuck for records!"

Everybody puts in their two cents' worth. Phil waxes eloquently about the philosophy behind *Skull Fuck:* "We have to shake up our listening public once in a while. We owe it to them to keep our edge."

"You see, we are targeting the 'crazy' market," explains Garcia patiently, "and they *expect* this kind of thing from us." He's grasping at straws.

"Now, fellas, I acknowledge that you know your target audience better than we do, no one's disputing that. But what you gotta bear in mind is that we're the one's who've gotta *sell* the album and if we don't —" Mo Ostin's speech is interrupted by loud snoring sounds.

Joe Smith wants to know what's going to be on the cover! What's the *artwork* going to be? He has visions of this skull eating a big cock. It's too fucking funny!

We know we aren't going to get away with *Skull Fuck,* we are just trying to have some fun. It's the funniest meeting we ever have with those guys. *Skull Fuck* eventually gets called *Grateful Dead.* Hello?

Now, believe it or not, Jerry is very squeamish about anything to do with skulls and skeletons in connection with the Grateful Dead. He is very anti-bones of any kind. Jerry's idea of the name had more to do with the death of the ego, Lao Tzu, and the letting go of the self under psychedelics. But almost as soon as the name is coined, the Dead's first promoters are putting the band in graveyard tombstones that say "The Grateful Dead." Or racks of skulls from the catacombs under Paris. Halloween shit that Jerry absolutely hates.

But his aversion to the boneyard theme is a losing battle. The skull with the lightning bolt insignia is thought up by Owsley and executed by Bob Thomas. (Owsley now has the skull-and-lightning-bolt concession at Grateful Dead concerts.) Jerry is nervous about it from the minute he sees it. His biggest fear is that it might be used in a satanic ritual or a ritual killing and the karma ascribed to the Dead.

Also, Jerry just doesn't like *definitions,* never has. He doesn't like being pinned down. He never wanted any part of that Captain Trips business. It came out of a Prankster thing, Captain Trips, and he hated it. He's sorry he ever put on that damn Stars and Stripes hat. But in those days we didn't know we were going to be featured in *Time* magazine.

In November '71, *Grateful Dead* — forever to be referred to by us and countless legions of Deadheads as *Skull Fuck* — is released. It's a throwaway album that, to everyone's surprise, goes gold. Imagine what it could've done with a good title!

The Dead don't make any studio albums in 1971, and being at loose ends everybody decides to make solo albums. On *Garcia*, Jerry plays all the instruments except for the drums, which Billy plays. We get a separate deal for Jerry — extra money! *Garcia* is done at Wally Heider. Beautiful songs mixed in with weird electronic music. The maddening thing about it is that some of the best cuts are banded with Insect Fear craziness. "To Lay Me Down" is a gorgeous little song, but it's surrounded by "Eep Hour," which is just scary, and the interlude, "An Odd Little Place." I don't know why he's even putting it on there.

"Why don't we just drop it, Jerry," I plead, "and improve the quality of the recording, because the album is already eighteen minutes a side — and the bands that separate the tracks are *so* skinny you can hardly see them, never mind putting a needle down on them."

"'Cause it's *my* album and I like it just the way it is. Haven't you ever heard of *juxtaposition?*"

"Yeah, I've also heard you can go through a day without sex and drugs, but you can't get through a day without rationalization."

"Fuck you, Scully."

The biggest crime is that the one obvious hit on *Garcia,* "The Wheel," is hard to isolate. A deejay would need a microscope to find it.

It's Jerry's ultimate ourobouros song. So other-worldly and wonderful, but almost impossible to find (even though it is the last cut on the album). That nutty "Odd Little Place" bleeds right into it.

"I'm not playing for the radio here," Jerry tells me patiently. "This is my own album, I don't have to be commercial here, I can do what I want."

"Of course, but you do want it to be heard, don't you?"

God, we go around and around on that one!

Garcia is released in January '72 and the Dead begin to work on Bobby Weir's *Ace* the same month. Weir sees Jerry cutting his album and asks me to get the lawyers to come up with a contract for him, too. I sell it on the basis of two songs (and Bobby being the good-looking one).

If Bobby had been working alone it would have taken five years to do, so everybody pitches in. The Grateful Dead come in and pretty much do everything for him. Bobby writes the songs, but only under duress. I even have to come up with the name of the album, not that Bobby likes it. I have to twist his arm to get him to call it *Ace*. Bobby has come up with some *very* convoluted titles:

"Hey, Rock, how 'bout *Eight-Sided Whispering Hallelujah Hatrack?*"
"Too Strawberry Alarm Clockish."
"Okay, how's *Seven-Faced Marble-Eyed Transitory Dream Doll?*"
"Nurse!"

I manage to convince him by demonstrating how graphically the title *Ace* works on the cover: an inverted horseshoe with a lady swinging in it and holding cards.

"It's a good luck thing and it's *recognizable*, Bobby. And look how beautifully it fits in with the Grateful Dead's roll-the-dice-and-see-what-happens philosophy."

⑥

The band has got its groove together onstage but since Owsley went to jail at the end of '69 our sound system has fallen into sad repair. It's in very tatty shape when in December of '71 Dan Healy stops by the Felt Forum to catch one of our shows and . . . hell, Healy, you tell it:

I hadn't seen the band for almost two years and I couldn't believe it. It was just awful. I mean, the setup was terrible, the sound was terrible, the whole production was muddy, the music was all fucked. It had all degenerated to nothin'. I was appalled. Whatever it was that I saw in the Grateful Dead had by then completely evaporated. The music was disgusting, Pigpen was passed out, the whole thing was just down. Even the vibe was weird — that was the night that Kreutzmann punched out Bob Matthews. I was in tears, I couldn't believe it. I just went and sat in this audience and at the end of the gig I went up on the stage and made some comment and Garcia immediately challenged me, in this inspiring kind of way. He has this way of making you want to say, "Oh, watch! I'll show ya!" He has that way of encouraging people, you know, he can always get ya to do your best, because he has that way of demonstrating faith in you.

So I say: "You guys finish your tour, we'll finish our tour, I'll meet you back home." I tell Ramrod and Jerry, "I'm comin' back. I can't stand this. Ya know, I'm comin' back unless you tell me right now not to." And neither one of 'em said a fuckin' word, so I go, "Okay!" And I came back and at the beginning of '72 we began building the infamous Wall of Sound.

The Grateful Dead now believe that in order to hit the big crowds they're playing to, they *need* a wall of sound. This colossal Dead sound system, born in Owsley's brain and materialized by Dan Healy, is a critical component of our shows. Bands had pumped out huge amounts of white noise from Marshall amps long before the Dead Wall of Sound, but these PA systems were pushing raw blues power riffs — where distortion was a plus. The Dead have another philosophy that has to do with the kind of music the band plays. The idea is to get into amplitudes of sound that can render delicate sounds cleanly and powerfully, so when Garcia plucks a string it fills the room.

The band also wants their system to be in stereo. They don't want monitors that feed back, so a microphone system has to be developed that will not feed back, which means we need a computer system to create what comes to be called digital delay. Digital allows a fraction of a second space between speakers, and this eliminates feedback.

Soon I am spending a fucking fortune on this stuff. They're wondering where all their money is going, and I'm telling them, "Look up!" We're buying thirty-two feet in the air of speakers and amps and scaffolding. Then there's logistics. How many guys is it going to take to move this stuff and set it up? We have to figure out how to get it up there without breaking backs and what the insurance costs are going to be and where we can get the pneumatic hoists and cables to put the system up. You can't get a union guy anywhere in the United States to do this kind of backbreaking precision work. They don't want to know about it. And as soon as we start using the system, we have kids throwing things at the speaker towers and then we have to figure out a way to cover them. This is when we get the psychedelic coverings made.

The difference between how the straight world approaches sound and the Dead's approach is night and day. For years Dan Healy would go into halls all across America where we're playing and they're expecting one little speaker here and another one over there and he has to tell them that they're going to have to practically dismantle their hall and reconfigure it so that we can play in there.

It represents a radical, radical change. Before the late sixties musicians carried their own instruments and there was this little teeny amplifier on the stage and that was about it. The existing systems we encounter all date back to our parents' generation and before. Their groove was the Dorsey orchestra and the Goodman orchestra, and getting them to adapt to our way of doing things is really uphill. The venues we're playing don't want to hear about us bringing this mountain of scaffolding for the Wall of Sound. It's like, "Fuck you, you long-haired punks!"

Dan Healy and the crew guys get that every day of their lives. It'll jade you, all that abuse, but at the same time, we witness things in live performance that nobody has ever witnessed before. We've seen the audience all stop, stand dead still, two thousand people in a little old theater not flinching, not moving a muscle because what was going on was so electrifying. I remember after those wonderful shows at the Fillmore East where it would be almost a spiritual thing and people wouldn't even be clapping. I've seen audiences get up and walk out without saying a word. What is there to say?

It's during this year that Dan Healy contrives the first of his many ingenious broadcasting schemes: a quadraphonic simulcast of a Dead show using two FM stations and a TV channel. So . . . if you happen to have two radios and four speakers you can hear the Dead in Surround Sound, plus see them on your TV. Virtual Dead.

$$\circledS$$

The sixties are well over (for most of us) — it's a time for reflection, for getting back to the land, the sea and the sky. Jerry and Mountain Girl find a comfortable 1950s suburban house near the Tamalpais Mountains, overlooking the Pacific. Jerry is twenty-nine. He's happy and beginning to see the Dead take off at last. "At first we stumbled, then limped along and started flying with one wing and bumping into trees. But after six years, what the fuck? It's still groovy for us."

He's at the height of his powers. In an era when every rock star is (or is supposed to be) a spokesman, a philosopher, a model mutant New Being, Jerry really is all these things. When I bring Jann Wenner, the publisher of *Rolling Stone* magazine, and Charles Reich, the Yale law professor who wrote *The Greening of America*, out to Jerry's place, they are blown away. "Shit," says Jann, during a break in their taping the interview, "he is the real thing. A profound fucking rock star!"

And sitting on the grass looking over the ocean and listening to Jerry effortlessly explain the mysteries of the universe, you know Wenner isn't just saying this about some blues superstar who's managed some easy cosmic tautology. This man is seriously deep. As the smoke from the joint makes tiny clouds against the azure blue sky I hear Jerry's creaky rocking chair voice drifting across the afternoon:

> The information we're plugged into *is* the universe itself, and everybody knows that on a cellular level. It's built in. Just superficial stuff like what happened to you in your lifetime is nothing compared to the container which holds all your information. And there's a similarity in all our containers. We are all one organism, we are all the universe, we are all doing the same thing. That's the sort of thing that everybody knows, and I think that it's only weird little differences that are making it difficult. . . .

Fuck, this might actually explain everything. Maybe Jerry is the Buddha after all.

13

We're All Bozos on This Bus

THE GRATEFUL DEAD Tour of Europe '72 is undertaken with the usual alarming casualness. The truly nutty, *demented,* part of it is that the reason this entire venture (monster sound system, twin buses, three-album live set, and ensuing madness) got rolling is because "some of the dudes in the band wanted to check it out." *It* being Europe. The Big It.

Europa: ancient warehouse filled with unimaginable junk, abbeys full of saints, reliquaries containing the Virgin Mary's toenails and the foreskin of J.C. himself.

To the Deadheads *Europe* means the three-record set (*Europe '72* Warner Bros. 3WX2668). Chartres, the Sistine Chapel, Rimbaud, Stravinsky — the great, gilded panopticon of European history comes down to *this:* a triple live album.

Look out, Ye Ancient Fingernails, the barbarians are coming. Open the gates! Saracens with 5,000-watt amps will soon be storming the Bastille. Not that the Dead are *just* another band of uncouth rowdies, motel-demolishing loons, or shark-copulating deviates on the road (boorish *Schweinerei* like Grand Funk or satanic deviates like Led Zeppelin). Our crusade is basically, uh . . . molecular!

And by now we are rolling headlong down the track, drivin' that train high on vitamin C and cocaine. We're stoked and working like dogs. Seven nights in a row at the Academy of Music in New York, doing two sets a night. A week later we're playing City Hall, Newcastle.

And this isn't like a couple of guys with guitars and a pignose amp

going on a tour of folk grottoes. This is the Persian army on the
march! There are seven musicians and singers, five managers, five
office staff, ten equipment handlers (handling 15,000 pounds of PA
equipment), four drivers, and seventeen assorted wives, old ladies,
babies and friends.

We don't have that big a sound system on this tour compared to
later expeditions, but still it is *tons* of fucking gear. In addition to all the
PA stuff, we take our 16-track recording machine, which is as big as a
wall — it is monstrous! Part of the reason for all this stuff is that we're
recording every concert on this tour — twenty dates. We need to
make an album just to pay the bills on this one. Our gear is getting
bigger and bigger and heavier and heavier. So much doggone stuff it
is out of hand. The logistics of travel and gigging, multilingual press
conferences, and live recording are mind-boggling. Costs are going
sky high and thank God (and Joe Smith) Warner's is paying for it all.

I have to go down to customs at Kennedy Airport to pre-clear and
sign for it. Seeing it all stacked up in one place is a chilling sight. A
mountain of gear in this huge bonded warehouse — like the last scene
of *Citizen Kane*. The customs guy has a giant book with our stuff
inventoried in it. He says, "I want to see box four-hundred-and-
whatever-it-was." Ay, Carumba! The problem is I don't know where
the fuck that particular crate is. "Look, the best thing you can do, man,
uh, sir, is pick a box from the boxes here, and then look at the inventory and check it out." In the end they inspect one box and one
speaker cabinet, get fed up, and say screw it.

The thing about European tours for American bands is that they
get everyone pulling together in a slightly different way than American tours for American bands. A sense of community, if you like,
develops out of it. Almost two months crammed together on a bus
will bond any group together — or end in mayhem (see below).
These epic bus journeys weren't the most efficient way of doing
Europe, but with all the drugs it was still safer than using commercial
airlines because of the radical nature of policing at European airports
in the Baader-Meinhof era. Also, it gave us a chance to see the coun-
tryside!

At first we are just going to do it with one bus, but we're a two-
headed beast at best. We'd forgotten about the yin yang of the Dead
(or any other group of people on the road for a prolonged period of
time). Factions rear their ugly heads. What if someone wants to go one

way and someone else another? What if I don't want to sit next to Pig? So, folks, we get *two* buses. We have the British soccer team's bus and the Danish soccer team's bus, which turns out to be Pig's favorite bus. He takes over the whole back row of seats, but unfortunately this bus has a wooden suspension and every jolt and bump in the road knocks him onto the floor. Poor Pig gets badly damaged landing on the floor so many times, only worsening his bad kidneys and horrible liver.

Everybody assumes identities and picks a team. All of the squares are on one bus and all the hipsters are on the other, and the pair of buses comes to be referred to as the "Bozo Bus" and the "Bolo Bus."

"The Bozo Bus was for people who wanted to be tripping out and raving all the time," says Robert Hunter. "The Bolo Bus was people who preferred to sink totally into their neuroses, or just sleep."

Thing One and Thing Two. The other bus, or the other person, is always the one to blame. So it is with the Bozos versus the Bolos. One can hardly improve on the account by the Choirmaster (a.k.a. Robert Hunter) who described their mysterious qualities and mythology thusly:

> The Bolo bus had a john in it and its seats faced forward. The Bozo bus had a refrigerator and some of its seats were installed facing back, to accommodate four tables. And to look back. The subtle difference in the character and import and atmosphere between the two buses was so profoundly hidden and enigmatic that you could not possibly understand it. The Bozos wore masks, and the Bolos showed their faces.

But who gets on what bus just as often has to do with who gets out of the john last or who dallies longest buying postcards. We are the people we worried about yesterday!

◉

The tour sets out, appropriately enough, on April Fool's Day.

EXCERPTS FROM MY EUROPEAN TOUR DIARY

April 7–8. London. The gig is Wembley Empire Pool. They don't exactly *get* the Dead in England. Screamin' Jay Hawkins, Tiny Tim, Kinky Friedman and the Texas Jewboys they get. They have a lot of different slots. But they don't have one for the Dead. It just staggers me that the band has never really cracked England when they're so popular in America and Germany. Get wif it, you Marmite-eating wankers!

An historic encounter: William "Randolph" Kreutzmann, swing drummer for late sixties dope band, meets Christine Keeler, who brought down the government by fucking both a Russian naval attaché and John Profumo, the British Minister for War.

Staying at this weird salesman's hotel on Kensington High Street right on Hyde Park and just down the road from the Queen Mum's house (palace). A bunch of us get the crabs. No connection stated or implied.

April 11. City Hall, Newcastle. I'm fucked if I can remember *anything* except for "the room." It's a famous rock 'n' roll gig — the only gig you *can* do in the Northeast. Everybody's played here. The Beatles, the Who, the Stones. Actually, it's an all-around shit gig. A municipal concrete dump, with a balcony all the way round and big, fucking, concrete pillars that interfere with the sight lines. Still, the place is *packed.* Thousands and thousands and thousands. Perhaps we're finally catching on.

April 14–15. Copenhagen, Denmark. On the waterfront, and crew walk into a rowdy sailors' bar. Straightaway, get into a fight. Sample dialogue as later reported by the roguish roadie, Rex Jackson:

"This is your day in a barrel, jarhead!"

"Yeah, right, I fucked your momma."

Big melee breaks out. I can hear it all the way over at hotel. Go out in hallway to see what's happening. Corridors pitch-black. Fuck! Crew have knocked out all the lights in hallway. Out on the street, I freeze my tits off. Cold, midnight black sky. Must be dark half the year here, it's so far north. Fuckin top of the world.

Gig at Tivoli Gardens. Like an old Fox Theater–style place. Our tour happens to coincide with the state visit of Queen Juliana of the Netherlands. Danish TV plans to segue from live broadcast of Her Majesty straight to the first-ever live broadcast of a band on Danish television. The anchor at the station goes, "Schoolie-de dowvaglub-gub-de-gubbly-gub, the Grateful Dead." Cut to the Grateful Dead show. But the fucking camera can't find the guy who is emceeing the show. The steady cam *searching* the stage. Can't find him because he's right behind Garcia's huge amp. In order to get seen over the amps, he dumps out a garbage can on the floor and stands on it. Just as he says "The Grateful Dead!" Steve Parish, our biggest baddest roadie, knocks him out. On the monitor all you see is a big fist coming sideways through the screen, *CRUMP!* Watching this, Jerry doesn't know whether to laugh or cry or tear his hair out. The producer in the sound truck falls in a frenzy on all the knobs. He's in tears, saying, "I'm ruined, I'm ruined, ah, this is a disaster."

Hotel Nyhavn. Right on the harbor — open up your window and watch the ferries coming in and out — but designed for midgets. Duck head to get into the room, and once inside you duck-walk to avoid smashing head on wormwood-riddled beams.

Our favorite day-off activity: what stuff can you buy in this country? We all come home with three, four, ten of everything. Boredom + money = much junk. In Vancouver it's sheepskins and Anacin codeines. In Copenhagen we descend on a costume store like locusts. Buy up all their clown masks, big fake noses, Groucho Marx glasses, and orange, green, and purple wigs.

April 16. Aarhus, Denmark. Pull into Aarhus, heading down main street. It's *Fasching,* a sort of Scandinavian Halloween. Streets lined with locals, we end up at tail end of some parade. So . . . we all whip out our masks, put them on, and stare out the windows at town population. Orange hair sticking out to *here,* Bozo noses and the orange and green hair, Groucho Marx glasses and mustaches. The effect is great. Aarhusians vote us best float in the parade!

April 17. Copenhagen. Take ferry from Sweden back to Denmark. Suddenly we're at the border. Bus in a fog of marijuana smoke. Realize we're exposed! Buses stink of California pot. Bus driver in panic. "Must do something *fast,* Herr Scooli!" Everybody is shouting "*Spray the bus!*" We soak the place down with Ozium spray, but we have to wait hours to go through customs. Driver has nervous breakdown.

"I'm going to jail! My children will be grown up before I see them again!"

We're all still in masks, with red noses and green hair. "Should we get them to take costumes off?" asks the driver.

"Hell, no, let's *confuse* them to death." Sure enough, a nonplussed customs officer pokes his head in and lets us through. No one would be stupid enough to carry drugs looking like that. . . .

April 21. Bremen. The Beat Club, a kind of disco joint managed by straightlaced, technical little German shits. "You vill do it zis vay!" The Grateful Dead follow the rules? Good fucking luck, dudes!

April 24. Düsseldorf. Phil flips. This must happen at least once on each tour.

"Düsseldorf, *this* is Düsseldorf?"

Now, I know from hard experience when Phil asks a question this way it means either (a) I am an ignorant swine for not knowing that this happens to be the birthplace of Ditters Von Ditterdorf or (b) Phil needs his medication.

"That's right, Phil, Düsseldorf. What's it to ya?"

"See that building over there?" Is this a trick question?

"Yeah, the Reinhalle. We're playing there."

"Well, my friend, Hitler built it. DO YOU SEE THOSE MA-CHINE-GUN BULLET HOLES?"

"Phil why are you SHOUTING?"

"DON'T YOU CARE THAT THEY USED TO LINE INNO-CENT CIVILIANS, WOMEN AND TEENAGERS, UP AGAINST THE WALL — *THIS* WALL — AND SHOOT THEM! MUR-DERERS! BUTCHERS! WAR FUCKIN' CRIMINALS!"

I start to say "Phil, I think those are bullet holes from where British aircraft strafed the place. You know, *The World at War,* the night bombing episode?" But I realize this is not going to be a historically accurate conversation anyway. Let him blow off a little steam. Fire cannons at will!

Tonight the Dead died. Smack in the middle of dimwitted coal-mining area nicknamed *"Sturgebiet,"* meaning the dense region. At the concert we see why. Front row looks at us with weirdest cross-eyed expressions, scratching their heads and rubbing their tummies. Who *are* these guys? Nobody knows how to take it. *No* applause. No reaction, period. Baddest gig nightmare ever. Fortunately, electronic composer and Lesh-idol Karlheinz Stockhausen comes to show with some of his students. They're the *only* ones that have a clue what the Dead are doing.

April 26. Frankfurt. Am in big trouble here. As front man for the band I go ahead and — theoretically — smooth out all the problems. But life being what it is, sometimes it turns out the other way around, you know what I mean? Fail to measure the entrance doors to the Jahrhundert Halle, which is not good because we are traveling with *huge* equipment. It won't fit through the doors! And if we can't get the equipment in, the band can't play. A fact that should be obvious to a child. Boy, do I take some shit for that! Everything has to be taken apart and pulled through sideways. You know, do we put it up on end or do we cut it in half? The crew, needless to say, is not happy.

Fire marshals getting noses out of joint about fans dancing in the aisles. These guys are a little high-strung if you ask me. Audience mainly American servicemen. Have to make announcement in my katzenjammer German to a bunch of American GIs: "Bitte stayen zie aus die aisles, mein dudes, die Feuer Führers are zer pissed off und die will sand throwen on du." Not much humor there. These guys have been krautized; stationed here too long — some of them remember Elvis!

April 29. Hamburg. Enthusiastic crowd at Musikhalle. After show, groupie comes into the room. Lost (I guess). Lights dim, Mott the Hoople *All the Young Dudes* on tape deck. "I love the big guys who have taken the lysergic dope from island of California," she says in lisping broken English.

Phil takes side trip to Externsteine. Bizarre stones of Teutonic priesthood, inspiration for Nietzsche, Wagner, and Germanic pagan intellectuals. Phil's mystic attraction for standing, stone, megalithic monuments, ley lines and plain old rocks: Stonehenge, the Pyramids, the Red Rocks Amphitheater in Colorado.

May 3–4. Paris. Olympia Theater in Paris just like the Fillmore East; if anything, a bit more funky. Tradition-riddled place. Everyone keeps saying how special it is because of who's played here: the Stones, the Who, Piaf, Aznavour. . . . Hallowed ground, but with insufficient electricity.

We stay in Le Grand Hôtel. Big, big place. You can get lost in the hallways. Single rooms start at $35 a day. Comes with balcony and small automated refrigerators that dispense liquor and beer and champagne at ridiculous prices.

As we check in: "Are you 37-piece orchestra we are expecting?"

"Sure, why not?"

Room 4600 is nerve center of Dead operation. There, Sam Cutler, a one-man borsa and private bank — changes German marks into French francs and hands out road money ($10 for chicks, $15 for dudes — hey, we eat more!). Lesh's old lady, Rosie, prepares the *Bozos & Bolos News*. Others man the telephones.

Yes . . . we have our own newspaper! In each new country so far, a copy of our own Xeroxed newspaper, the *Bozos & Bolos News,* had been slipped under our hotel room doors. Tuesday's issue reads:

Today is a free day. In the evening, Warner's is hosting a dinner for all of us (and a few very discreet press people) at a very fine restaurant located in the Bois du Boulogne (the city park, but what a park!). It is called La Grande Cascade, and holy shit, is it ever neat! You might even feel like dressing special for it, although you don't have to. It's just that kind of place. . . .

La Grande Cascade, oval glass walls look out onto a lawn of blossoming chestnut trees. Dinner lasts three and a half hours. During the serving of liqueurs we turn on the waiters. Not a pretty sight.

May 5. Lille, France. We're meant to do gig in Lille, however. . . . One of the equipment guys thumps a fan. Irate youth returns, puts sugar and pisses in gas tank of truck, sticks potato in exhaust pipe so the truck breaks down. Equipment never leaves Paris. Being followed around by radical French students who want us to put on free show. French promoter goes out on the stage to tell crowd that the Dead aren't gonna play. Hall goes ape shit. Band freaks out. Situation getting ugly fast. Real concern there's gonna be a serious riot. Sneak out to the buses and make ignominious dash for it. Have to lower Donna Godchaux out back window of the place. Put her down on the top of the equipment truck that's parked right underneath the window then down onto the tailgate. Ridden out of town on a rail by frog revolutionaries, who are *still* after our asses. Have to reimburse promoter and promise we'll come back to do free show.

May 7. Wigan, England. Bickershaw Festival. *Pours* with rain. Then brightens up when the band plays! Band does four-and-a-half hour gig.

> Play list: (1st show) Truckin', Sugaree, Mr. Charlie, Beat It on Down the Line, He's Gone, Chinatown Shuffle, China Cat> I Know You Rider, B.T. Wind, Playin', Next Time You See Me, Tennessee Jed, Good Lovin', Casey Jones. (2nd show) Greatest, Big Boss Man, Ramble On, Jack Straw, Dark Star> Drumz> Other One> Sing Me Back Home, Sugar Magnolia, Lovelight> Going Down the Road Feeling Bad> Not Fade Away

NRPS and some weird other bands play too. Nobody had ever seen anything like them. Happy birthday, Billy (26 today)!

May 10. Amsterdam, Netherlands. Gig in Concertgebouw. Pigpen has a go on an organ that Johann Sebastian Bach played. Built in 1640 or something. Whole hall recently renovated to traditional 18th-century grandeur. Gold leaf all over the place, under the railings, on balconies, around proscenium arch. Only been on there for about a week. Our cables everywhere in hall held up with gaffer's tape. Go to fold up cables after show and roll up yards of gold leaf with them. Sheets of gold pull right off the wall. Whoops! Better than the '49 California Gold Rush! They freak. Their $250,000 gold flake job on the balcony is going to hell in a handbasket. It wasn't like we were trying to steal it or anything. We were just gonna throw it out. None of us was paying attention. Ramrod gamely trying to stick it back up again! We have to pay to have it put on again. It was a real innocent mistake, dudes, and Amsterdam is a very forgiving town. They're used to crazies and freaks. But they never had a rock 'n' roll gig in that place again.

May 13. Lille. Free concert outside Lille Opera House. Cold, foggy. You gonna remember us when the revolution comes, *mes enfants?*

May 16. Luxembourg. Radio Luxembourg at midnight. Dead concert broadcast around the world! Radio Luxembourg is huge. The power emanating from there is so strong the hair on your head stands straight up from the electricity. They make you wear hats so your hair doesn't

fly off and get into things! And white lab coats and little booties just as
if you were going into the operating room.

Outrageous fucking equipment. And, you know the Dead's fascination with equipment is second only to that of the Frankensteins'.
All of us agog. Standby generator room with two huge diesels. You
could eat off the floor it's so clean.

All mumbling "Wow!" many times in different time signatures. The
engineer is saying to his co-worker, "What to do with these freaks
that are looking so admiringly at such equipment?" I speak German
so I answer: "Could you start the fucker up?" Tubes fire up. Huge
megawatt Klesitrons each in its own glass bell jar. Oh, my God. Tubes
as big as people.

Matthews says, "Ask him what all these other transmitters are
doing at the hour that the Dead are playing."

He says, "Nothing."

"So how can you, uh, get *into* those transmitters?"

"Easy does it. Just patching from here into master control."

"Okay, Rock, ask him if he can patch in all these other transmitters
and broadcast the signal worldwide."

And they look at each other and say, "Yes it is! *Ja wohl! Ja wohl,* Herr
Matthews!"

Matthews totaled up the power of wattage that we were getting
halfway around the world and estimated this was the largest single
radio transmission of a single source ever.

May 18. Munich, Germany. Great drug drought. Visit Deutsches Museum. Lose Garcia to world's biggest coke crystal.

May 23–26. Lyceum, the Strand. Our last gig. Still dragging 16-track
motherfucker tape machine around with us. Had it mounted in an
aircraft pod inside sound truck. Parish throws five rowdies out of gig.
They come around to back alley of Lyceum. Betty Jackson, our recording engineer, is in sound truck — little metal tin can packed with
blankets to keep it from reverberating like crazy inside. Betty's higher
than a fucking whatever, she's on the next planet. Truck starts rocking,
rowdies banging on the sides. The whole thing turns into a bell. Calls
Rex on intercom *HELP!! I'M INSIDE BIG BEN AND IT'S RING-
ING OFF THE HOOK!* Rex to the rescue! Takes theater fire door
off — one of those ten-by-twelve-foot heavy metal jobbies — picks

it up off its track, throws it to the side — Hulk mad! Hulk not like! — and proceeds to wipe up the alley with these five guys beating on the truck.

Sam Cutler brings his mum and stepdad to show. Seats them in the balcony right by mixer unit. Mum insisting she has to leave. Music too loud. "What's that, Mum?" Introduces Mum to Garcia at intermission. "Garcia, Jerry, I'd like you to meet my mother." Jerry looks at his mum, looks at Sam and says, "I didn't know you had a mother!"

Acid madness of epic proportions in full swing. Play here for three days. It is a high old gig. Mecca Ballrooms owns the Lyceum. Has all the fucking bouncers in dopey red jackets with black lapels and bow ties. All get dosed *without exception*. All immediately disrobe and get rid of their bow ties and red jackets as fast as they can and want to get naked with the girls and roll down the aisles and yodel. The place is supposed to close at eleven o'clock or something stupid but it goes on until one-thirty in the morning. *Every night*. And every night they have to bring a whole new bunch of bouncers in, because the ones from the previous night are never seen again.

14

Ship of Fools

SACKS AND SACKS of mail are piled up in the Grateful Dead office in San Rafael. Thousands and thousands of letters — printed, paisleyed, typed, scrawled, carefully lettered in Celtic uncials — all in response to Garcia's plea on the inside of *Grateful Dead* (the *Skull Fuck* album):

DEAD FREAKS UNITE Who are you? Where are you? How are you? Send us your name and address and we'll keep you informed.

"25,000 fuckin' letters, wow!"

"Deadheads, maaan!"

"You know what this is, man? It's a" — *snoooooort* — "*mailing list*. We can now contact Deadheads *directly*. Tell 'em where we're playing and shit like when the next album's coming out."

"Cool, maaan!"

Let's-do-it-all-ourselves fever is running dangerously high. We can do anything! All kinds of plans are laid on glass-topped tables.

"Fuck, man, with a list like this we could even" — *snooooooort* — "sell our records, do it through mail order, headshops, at the gigs and stuff."

"Distribute them in Grateful Dead Good Humor trucks!"

"Hell, yeah! Let's cut out all the record company bullshit and make our own records. *Without* producers being foisted on us. No more Ed Thrashers and Joe Smiths. . . ."

"Free at last!"

The only question is "Who's going to put the bell on the cat?" For this we need a certified adult. Someone who understands the arcana and secret handshakes of the Bureaucratic Order of Suits and Ties. And then . . . heh, heh . . . along came Jones, or Ron Rakow, to be more precise. Actually Rakow has been here all along; it might even have been his idea. Rakow had been involved in running another business venture with a similar megalomaniac — the Carousel Ballroom — which, through no fault of his own, we hastily add, had ended disastrously.

At the Securities and Exchange Commission, Rakow photocopies the financial statements of the major record companies and using these cabalistic tracts he compiles a ninety-three-page report called the "So What Papers" to convince the band that putting together their own record company is the only way to go. On July 4 — (heh, heh) — 1972 he formally presents his proposal to the band.

With the release of *Europe '72* in November '72 our commitment to Warner's effectively comes to an end. *Europe '72* is the Dead (mostly) live at their furry finest, but it isn't a purely live album. The "live" sound is partially re-created in the studio by playing studio tracks back over the same equipment that the live stuff was originally recorded on, thus generating an approximation of the original ambience. Got that?

Garcia and Hunter regret that some of the new songs on the album — which could have been tuned up in the studio — are buried amongst the covers and live versions of earlier songs.

Hunter: "To me, all that material was the kicker follow-up album to *American Beauty*. Instead, we put out this three-album thing that sounds good, but it spreads out the material so thin we never get to hear what those songs might have sounded like on an album of their own."

Garcia: "I concur. Instead we dribbled some of that music all the way up through *Wake of the Flood*."

There is also a lingering resentment that Warner's gets most of the bread because the Dead won't let them charge a whopping twelve bucks for the album. Consequently the Dead end up with a greatly reduced royalty.

All of the above having fueled Jerry's revolutionary zeal, he is by now wildly enthusiastic about the possibility of Grateful Dead Records: "What are we gonna do now that we're enjoying amazing success? The nice thing, man, would be not to sell out at this point and instead come up with something far out and different, which would be, y'know, sort of traditional with us."

I am a little more jaundiced. Where I see the whole business as a huge red herring and waste of time, Garcia, bless his ever-optimistic hippie heart, sees it as subversive action. Bypassing official channels had been central to the Haight's Declaration of Independence, a strategy Jerry would like to see extended to the whole process of making records. The seductive thing for Jerry about starting a record company is that — on the surface of it, at least — it seems to be in the tradition of underground, guerrilla activity.

In Garcia's "So What?" utopian vision, Grateful Dead Records is a way of reconstituting the lost community of the Haight by other means. A closed circuit of heads and freaks owning their own company, distributing through their own channels to other freaks. A Deadland of airwaves and albums and concerts that would supersede the first, literal (and doomed) attempt at a hippie community in the summer of 1967. This new plan would no longer necessitate everyone living together or starting our own country or seceding from the union; we would be a community of like-minded souls linked electronically. A *virtual* Haight-Ashbury! It's a typical Garcia sci-fi fantasy of stoned, *Village of the Damned* children with "earphone heads and dirty necks" tuned to the same wavelength.

There is one major flaw, however. The day-to-day requirements of running a record company are the very things we've spent our whole lives *avoiding*. Going to offices, monitoring pressing plants, making out bills of lading, checking inventories.

For hippies, the straight world is the domain of our parents: clipboards, memos, office hours, bosses. The day gig, for all intents and purposes, *is* our parents. Are we going to become just like them? But nobody wants to hear my objections; they're all too hopped up on getting rid of the people who tell them what to do. Off with their heads!

Rakow makes the band these giant promises and a year later, on April 19, 1973, they give their go-ahead and Grateful Dead Records enters history — along with Round Records for the more dubious solo projects of band members.

And so the Dead get into the record business. The creation of

Grateful Dead Records dissolves the original communal bond between members of the Dead family. This agreement had divided shares in the Dead pie equally among ten members: six band members, two managers (Danny Rifkin and me) and two roadies (Laird and Ramrod). The new arrangement is a straightforward business partnership between Rakow and the band for Grateful Dead Records projects and a partnership between Garcia and Rakow for Round Records, the spinoff projects. So, onward we go into the deep, dark and dreamless wood.

On March 8, 1973, Pigpen dies after a long illness. He is twenty-seven, and our first casualty. His loss is devastating to the band and forever alters the chemistry of the Dead. As Garcia says at Pig's funeral, "We can go on calling ourselves the Grateful Dead but after Pigpen's death we all knew this was the end of the original Grateful Dead."

In August the band, family, and crew move into the Record Plant studios in Sausalito to start work on the first Grateful Dead Records release, *Wake of the Flood,* named for the first line of Hunter's lyric to "Here Comes the Sunshine." According to Hunter it is about living in other people's homes in the aftermath of the great Vanport, Washington, flood of 1949, but it could just as well apply to all of us.

The opening track of *Wake of the Flood,* "Mississippi Half-Step Uptown Toodeloo," was written over a year earlier. The band first played it in concert at Dillon Stadium in Hartford, Connecticut, shortly after the '72 tour of Europe. It's one of Hunter's full-blown Western fantasies: loaded dice, cups of rock and rye, powder charges in the silver mine. All life for Hunter in this period is couched in this wonderful gambling vernacular of the Wild West. "Half Step," "Dire Wolf," "Friend of the Devil" (among others) are all card-playing, down-and-out, mission-in-the-moonlight, out-of-luck-gambler-stumbling-around-on-red-mountain-Burgundy songs. Song after song after song about playing your cards right, keeping 'em close to your vest, laying 'em down, folding 'em — not that Hunter's actually a gambler, it's a literary folk thing with him, deriving ultimately from Dylan.

The *Wake* sessions go pretty smoothly by Grateful Dead standards, but it's the first of many Dead albums where half the record is great, the other fair-to-middling. *Workingman's Dead* and *American Beauty* work so well because they are consistent in tone and style and full of crafted Garcia/Hunter songs. But band members are beginning to object to Garcia's getting all the publishing. They feel that these albums are really Jerry-Garcia-backed-by-the-Grateful-Dead records. This is partly true, but only by default. Jerry not only writes most of the songs, he's the only one in the studio every day.

In response we are actually creating financial spaces on these records for the drummers by incorporating them into the arranger's royalties based on very little effort on their part. The way record royalties are divvied up is between the writer and the arranger, basically. And so all along Garcia has been cutting the band in as arrangers, but it amounts to a symbolic gesture that is getting more and more ridiculous because no one else is coming up with songs. And Garcia is not only teaching them to the band, he's doing virtually all the arrangements himself. The band's contribution is in helping shape the material at live performances, which in turn determines what it's going to sound like on the record.

Weir and Lesh start to write songs again. Eventually everyone in the band wants to be included, but because their contributions are all in different styles and of uneven quality, a process of fragmentation sets in. On *Wake of the Flood,* Keith Godchaux gets his own track, "Let Me Sing Your Blues Away" (written with Hunter), and Weir gets his own song cycle, "Weather Report Suite," a sort of mini-opera that takes up close to half of side two. It is grandiose and unlike anything else on the album.

And record company business is constantly intruding, seriously distracting Garcia, interfering with the making of the albums, adding on hours and hours of studio time. As a consequence, Jerry isn't able to look after Weir and help him pull together his songwriting projects, which are by now becoming extremely ambitious. Jerry comes back from two weeks of looking after record business shit and finds Weir's song still not ready to go into the studio. Just a few chords, no words, and a very loose concept of what the song is going to be.

Weir's songs take the longest, come together at the last, and are usually the most critically received by the band. It's like pulling teeth to get a song out of Lesh or Weir. We'll have the whole record together except for that one track and it's come on, Weir, would you get this together, *please?* You have to get out the cattle prods. Finally he shows up and all he has is a bunch of chord changes. I am usually desperate by this point, saying, "Let's call John Barlow, let's call *somebody.* Chesley, go find somebody. Is Bernie Taupin busy these days? Why don't you see if Van Morrison has a couple of songs at the bottom of his sock drawer."

You hear people saying oh, dear God, it's a Weir epic, oh no! After months of agonizing over his magnum opus he comes up with something about gotta go down by the river and see the water on the rocks (again).

But in spite of everything Jerry and Bobby Weir have always had a special bond, although politically Weir is the diametric opposite of Jerry. There's no one more conservative than Bob Weir when he's on a bat. One time Weir comes up to me in the studio and puts his arm around me and starts parroting some right-wing newspeak. I look at him and say, "Weir, hey, it's me! Who do you think you're talking to? Get a grip, buddy." Despite occasional frustrations, Jerry almost always defends Weir, even during that grueling period when Weir is learning slide guitar *onstage*.

When he gets on his soapbox about something, Bobby's the world's greatest expert. Jerry teases him unmercifully. "Where'd you read *that,* Weir?" he'll say.

The distractions of running our own business are bad enough, but almost immediately *industrial* problems raise their ugly head, critical manufacturing-stuff problems we'd never even *heard of* before. Shortly after our new album is released on November 15, 1973, sleazy counterfeit copies of *Wake of the Flood* start turning up on the East Coast. As a form of self-protection we begin manufacturing our own jackets with invisible color codes, scratching arcane symbols on the pressing templates and working hand in hand with the FBI (!) to foil the bootleggers. By the time the counterfeiting subsides, we have lost valuable weeks that we could have otherwise spent promoting the album (or even working on a new one!). Still, despite the "evil twin" album, we are able to sell a healthy 400,000-plus copies of the real *Wake.*

One thing's for sure, we're certainly rolling out the product! In March of 1974 the Dead start recording *Grateful Dead from the Mars Hotel* at CBS Studios in San Francisco. It is the straight old corporate professional recording studio scene, complete with CBS company engineer Uncle Roy (Seigel). *Mars Hotel* is intensely rehearsed at S.I.R. (Studio Instrument Rentals) across the street before we go into the studio every day. All the tunes are pretty much arranged. The band has been playing them for almost a month before the sessions start.

Mars Hotel has some similarity to *Workingman's Dead* in that there are fewer instrumentals, more songs, and the album as a whole is more centered on the lyrics. It is even laid out better for airplay — four tracks on each side. It's jumpin' and hoppin' and poppin', but compared to the live performances the studio versions are flat. The eternal Dead dilemma. "Scarlet Begonias" and "Loose Lucy" really pump in concert. "Ship of Fools" makes the hair on the back of your neck stand up. "I cannot share your laughter, Ship of Fools. . . ."

Phil Lesh gets to do *his* song cycle this time round on "Unbroken Chain." With its sound effects, soul breaks, and jazzy interludes, you feel like you've walked through half a dozen hotel lobbies. On "China Doll," Hunter and Garcia's infatuation with desperate plights, low-lifes, angels, and the raw edge continues in a wonderfully eerie dialogue with Jerry's compressed vocal sounding like a ghost voice arguing with itself.

There's a lot of tension building among band members, but much of this comes from the pressure of running their own business, flying to plants in Santa Rita and Santa Whatever, and not seeing each other — not practicing that much. Jerry gets his stuff done in a snap of the fingers, but after the Garcia-Hunter compositions are done the record languishes waiting for the other songs to come together.

Grateful Dead from the Mars Hotel gets its name (and cover picture) from the old Mars Hotel, a sleazebag hotel in the Mission District that is torn down the same year as we made the record. Where "Scarlet Begonias" materialized from is less clear.

"Where the hell did *that* one come from?" asks Garcia.

"Yes, and who were we before we were taken over by pods?" asks Hunter. "They've left us with just enough memory to get by on: social security number, that sort of thing."

If some aspects of the song are enigmatic, the Caribbean poly-rhythms, according to Jerry, have a more terrestrial origin: "I think I got a little of it from that Paul Simon 'Me and Julio down by the schoolyard' thing. A little from Cat Stevens — some of that rhythmic stuff he did on *Tea for the Tillerman*."

Jerry is still experimenting with voices — Paul Simon, Paul McCartney, Gary Brooker (Procol Harum), Rick Danko's phrasing, and (with the help of mucho voice compression) evolving a vocal persona. The big advantage of recording in Columbia's Studio A is the capacity to synch-up two 16-track tape machines and record on up to thirty tracks that all manage to fill up and create an effect Garcia describes as "an acoustic feel put into an electric space." They make your voice sound good, too!

Somewhere in the middle of recording the album we have to stop and order vinyl, book time at pressing plants, and figure out how to get the airplay necessary to push the album — all this, combined with pressure on the band to finish the album fast enough. Must take advantage of specified Killer Time Periods to sell records. Jesus, we've *become* Mo Ostin.

15

Barbarians in Europe

ON SEPTEMBER 9, 1974, we start our second European tour with a three-night gig at the Alexandra Palace in London. The depraved blueprint for this tour first reared its ugly head about a thousand years ago when a middle-aged Cockney suffering from cocaine dementia knocked at the door of the Grateful Dead offices in San Rafael. His name was Tom Salter, and he had a grand plan. He had a briefcase full of blueprints, wads of five- and ten-pound notes, and more blow than we had ever seen.

He's pulling out papers, diagrams, bank drafts, snapshots of the family, the house, the dog. A torrent of barely intelligible babble pouring out of him: Cockney rhyming slang, building codes, Queen Boadicea, *mise-en-scènes,* weather reports, tincture of cannabis. We're all caught up in this vortex of words, paper, money, drugs. He's a force of nature.

Tom Salter had taken acid late in life and it did something very peculiar to his head. He acquired a huge empire in London, leapfrogging out of Carnaby Street and gobbling up desirable properties. His little brush with LSD had fortified his business acumen (in the beginning at least). He now has houses, cars, the beautiful wife and kids, but his leapfrogging system has taken on a messianic quality; he can't see why it shouldn't be applied to anything at all. The Grateful Dead, for instance.

Jerry, Bobby . . . everybody is charmed by him. He is mesmerizing in that maniacal sort of way Jerry has always found irresistible. And like Charles Dickens on a coke binge he keeps on repeating "Wait till you see the Ally-Pally, lads! Blow your bloody little hippie minds, it will. Wot's left of 'em. Ha! Ha! Ha!"

"Say *what?*"

"The *Alexandra Palace,* man, don't tell me you never heard of the Alexandra Palace, supreme jewel of the British Imperial Wank!"

We are confused. Does he live in a palace? Is he some sort of Cockney aristocracy? Is he trying to sell us Buckingham Palace? A South London hustler high on cocaine is capable of anything. We finally realize he wants us to *play* the Alexandra Palace, which turns out to be a nightmare Victorian railway station.

He's as bald as a badger and tenacious as a terrier. Salter can steamroll you to death, and we don't at this point have that kind of stamina. The man is there at eleven o'clock at night and he's back at nine the next morning all bubbly and cheerful and still raving on about this trip to Europe. Out of desperation we give in. We agree to do it (whatever it is).

By the time he's been there four or five days everyone is completely fried, even the roadies are starting to worry. The only way they can talk to us is to come to the office after eleven o'clock at night.

This isn't a major tour — three nights in London, one gig each at the Olympiahalle in Munich and in Dijon, and two nights at the Palais des Sportes in Paris to wind it up. Still, the preparations are going to be complicated. After all, we are carting around the 38-ton Wall of Sound.

After the last East Coast gig at Roosevelt Stadium in New Jersey, the band is (briefly) to go home to California while I head straight off to London, followed at regular intervals by crew and equipment.

The advance setup is made more agreeable by Tom's manner of conducting business in the wine studios on King's Road. We start at lunchtime and go on till five, then it's across the street to the Queen's Arms and then back to his house for some major lines and maybe to smoke some hash. Then out for dinner! And all the time talking about the show and what needs to be done. Adding this, subtracting that . . . but mostly adding!

The enterprising little maniac wants to — single-handedly — bring back the sixties. We're to be the spearhead, he tells me, of his crusade.

"Tom," I try to say, "let me explain something to you. We already *did* the sixties once. O Lord, why *us?* Why does everyone treat the Dead as if they were a fucking Haight-Ashbury diorama?"

"It shall all come to pass, old son," he says in a mysterioso Cockney whisper, "it shall all come to pass!"

September 5. Band members start coming in early. Where's the party, man? Jerry, Billy, Bobby — they've heard about the madness going on at Tom's house and can't wait to get through customs and check out the scene. I take them right out there from the airport and they don't ever want to leave. I book the band into Blake's Hotel, but Garcia is over at Tom Salter's from early morning to late at night.

The house has the astonishing name of St. John of Jerusalem and it becomes the Dead's nerve center of operations until we get offices set up out at the Ally Pally. Night and day, day and night, the party that wouldn't end goes on and on. Jim Carroll of *Basketball Diaries* fame is passed out on the floor of the library; Christine Keeler is sprawled on the couch; Top of the Pops deejay John Peel is curled up on a Jacobean sidetable; the guys from *Private Eye* have taken up residence in the pool room. It is like an immense pub in which all life is represented: deviants, bookies, flacks, starlets, rock dogs, minor aristocracy, assorted wildlife, and babes. The Grateful Dead coming to Londontown begins to seem an event of unparalleled anticipation — like the arrival of Halley's comet. This Ally Pally thing is starting to heat up big time. And in the general atmosphere of reckless camaraderie and stimulants, it all starts to swirl.

And just when the band begins to think that — for once — they did the right thing even *doing* the damn tour, along comes . . . the dark element. It's the first full day after a night of serious carousing and we're introduced to Tom's crew and their leader — a giant with a bent nose out of a fairy tale. He's called Johnny Binden, an absolutely fiendish character who wraps me in his arms.

"Hel-lo baby!! Qu'est-ce que c'est?"

He's an ex-con with, I am soon to learn, a monster reputation around town. The man is covered with scars and tattoos (and speaking the occasional French). Wonderful guy, but *scary.* A stock villain straight out of Ealing Studios, I figure this guy's gotta be an ex-cop or something. Much later I start hearing the stories. About the time he's spent in prison, how many blokes he's done, how big his dick is. He's not shy about it at all.

"A donkey dick, mate, eighteen inches — at last measuring." The man is famous for going into a pub, laying his dick down on the bar, and balancing six shots of whiskey on it. Colorful, but not exactly Knightsbridge.

I've hardly met the dude when he launches into a true-crime story of how he killed this bloke after the sneaky bugger had stabbed him fifteen or sixteen times. And who do you think is going to be in charge of security, making sure that the money is safe and all of this stuff? None other than my newfound friend, Johnny K. Binden.

Now this Johnny does not exactly come off as a cheerful LSD-hippie-who-loved-Woodstock kind of guy. You get the feeling he'd stick you in a flash. You know, right after he says: "What are *you* looking at?" And England is so polite.

An English gangster! What had possessed Tom to hire this guy? The only thing I can think is that Tom heard stories about the Grateful Dead and the Hell's Angels and — as a special favor to us! — hired the closest thing he could find.

Tom Salter is the kind of guy who would love to get into a Socratic discourse as to whether there's honor among thieves, but it's been my experience that if you put more than two thieves together you can forget about law and order. Our London run is a disaster waiting to happen; the only question is when.

On and on goes the never-ending party. Endless lines of cocaine and huge Bob Marley ice-cream-cone hash spliffs. I am as coked up as a Taiwan freighter, and the vibes are getting just as quaky. When your brain crackles and your eyeballs burst out of their sockets, it's usually a sign that you're overdoing it just a wee bit. I have to do something, but what?

We are exhausted, overamped and stretched to the max. None of us is eating properly. Not that there isn't any food. There's pheasant in aspic, pâté, cold cuts, and cakes, but who's hungry?

It's at Tom's house that I first meet Lady Carolyn Christie, an English aristocrat and wild child who'd gone to art school with Jimmy Page, grown up in a crumbling baronial manor with her eccentric mum, and now works for Atlantic. It is a measure of the prevailing insanity that in no time we are married, an incident I somehow think I can explain away to my common law wife as simply a means of obtaining a green card for Carolyn. You know, so she can join the Led

Zeppelin tour of the States at the beginning of next month! You can understand that, can't you, Nicki?

At this point we're getting ready for the gig to happen. There are buses to take us down from Blake's to Tom's and from Tom's to the Ally Pally and back again. We play baseball on the cricket pitch, American football on the soccer grounds, soccer on the cricket pitch.

The top floor of Tom's house is the most exclusive club of all, the inner sanctum reserved for high rollers, rock stars, and dealers. He beckons me to his bedroom, to a monster closet, the *sanctum sanctorum*. It has huge doors like those on the Houses of Parliament. They open to reveal an Ali Baba's cave of drugs: kilos of hashish, pounds of coke, and plenty of jars and baggies with interesting-looking little colored pills in them.

The only thing that really shocks me, however, is the suitcase full of tickets *that aren't locked up*. It freaks me out and I tell him so. How in God's name are we ever going to keep track of all these tickets? Whereupon Tom proudly shows me a log he has of all the tickets going to the brokers — which is all very well, but what about the rest of the ticket sales? He has people constantly running tickets out to ticket sales locations all over the place. It is terribly loose, because the only way we have of determining how we are doing is by ticket count, and you need that daily.

It really bothers me, and it is probably another reason I have to get out of that house. I can't stand living there knowing there are thousands of tickets upstairs — all in the same closet with the coke! Tom doesn't really know what he is doing and his right-hand man, John Morris, isn't really looking after these things either. I'm afraid the only person who is paying close attention is ol' Johnny Binden.

And the cocaine frenzy has escalated way beyond even California-style excess. It is beginning to spiral, spinning faster and faster, fueled by jet lag and monster lines of cocaine. As the party goes into hyper drive, the pirates begin to come aboard one by one. Binden is in and out of the house all the while, like Long John Silver, assembling his own scurvy crew. He is giving people jobs who hadn't had a job since they last got out of jail. Lining up these old sea dogs, like this is fucking *Treasure Island*. A splendid crew for you, Jim lad!

There is some question, too, as to exactly how seaworthy the good ship Grateful Dead is at this point. In my infinite wisdom (and after countless tours), I have calculated that exactly seventeen days is the longest we can sail *without serious incident*. This estimate is based on the flash-point potential of the most volatile member of the group, Bill Kreutzmann. Anything beyond seventeen days at sea puts us in grave jeopardy.

And here the band had been in London barely *five* days and the smell of mutiny is already in the air. Due to a mass of aggravations compounded no doubt by coke. Too much good coke. Even for drug veterans like ourselves, it is just too much. The stuff is sitting around in *bowls,* for chrissakes.

Everyone is having a wonderful time at Tom's house but as soon as we begin to turn to what we are actually in London to do, things begin to go haywire. Part of the problem is we haven't worked to-gether for a while. Garcia says if he's off for three days he gets rusty, and we have been off for a *month.* Everyone is out of practice and dislocated and wrecked. We've been on the road almost nonstop since 1967 and the schedule for the last few years, especially 1973 and 1974, has been just brutal. We are at the end of our rope.

Gremlins have now set to work on us! Not only is equipment never where it is meant to be, we are now beginning to lose *people.* Everyone is torn and frayed, bickering and fighting over nothing. And of course I'm getting it from all sides, it's part of the job description. Telltale whining noises coming from band members usually means so-and-so's not getting enough attention. Where are the interviews, then? That type of thing. They bitch about having to do interviews, and even more when there aren't any.

There isn't a whole lot of press set up because there isn't really a whole lot to talk about. That's how it is in London when you don't have a record out: "Wot's the angle then?" Not to mention the atti-tude the British press have about the Dead anyway. It's a little beyond their grasp — like egg creams.

On top of everything else, everyone is dropping acid at all hours. So some of us are peaking, some coming down, some are on the rag, some irritatingly ecstatic. The ones on the rag develop murderous feelings toward the ecstatic ones, and the ones that are ecstatic are grinding down on the ones on the rag. Crew members are threaten-ing to go home. Things are getting outrageously ragged, and we haven't even gotten to the first show yet. Mutiny!

Finally it reaches a point where it all reels out of control. The coke demons have gotten us. The air is filled with hydrochlorous fumes.

Toxic psychosis! A shouting match erupts during sound check the night before our first show. Just the band and the crew is there, and our head roadie, Rex Jackson, challenges us all to just "give it up." Gives this impassioned speech.

"We're tearing each other apart. The band hates the roadies, and we have had it up to here with them. It's a fuckin' horror, man, it's a nightmare. It's too dangerous to be carrying around contraband anyway. And after the Ally Pally we're going to fucking Germany, mates. We can't be carting this stuff across borders." Everybody agrees, but it's so theoretical — what's a poor boy to do? Then Ramrod says something about "if you sorry sons of bitches think you can quit, let's see your stash on the floor!"

Everybody kinda agrees with that too, but naturally no one wants to go first. Ramrod takes out his stash and empties it on the stage, and after that I guess everyone is too embarrassed to hold on to theirs (besides, they probably have some back at the hotel). It starts out as a trickle, but ends up the Mississippi River of cocaine. The stuff pours out, baggies full. It's like a Moscow show trial — people start denouncing those who haven't come forward or those they feel have just made a token contribution to the pile. I, for one, only have a tiny glass jar, so I am under suspicion.

When it is all piled up, it has to be at least a few ounces. Rex sweeps it all together and then Ramrod puts lighter fluid on it and sets it on fire. We have a bonfire going made out of cocaine hydrochloride and lighter fluid, and it melts down into this lovely waxy blob. Hey, dudes, I think we just invented crack!

No sooner have we finished burning the coke *onstage* than the GLC (Greater London Council) shows up with the fire department. Mercifully they miss the conflagration ceremony, but we are still in big trouble. The fire department isn't going to allow us to play.

So we use all that displaced energy on the fire department. They are trying to unplug us, and if they succeed everything will really blow sky high. I get Dan Healy, because he's a natural diplomat. And he charms the shit out of them. Shows them the state-of-the-art circuit breakers, our monster transformers. Everything has to be by the book and it takes forever, looking up the bylaws and codes and regulations.

Will this fit? Can we bend it? And the whole time the band is backstage, waiting to go on. The GLC guys are in awe of our equipment, but in the end it comes down to Healy greasing the fire brigade captains with their hard hats and their slickers. "Hey, tell your kids to come, we'll take you to dinner, and I can explain it all to you in much greater detail."

The act of burning the stash and finally playing together (along with a fairly decent show) has broken the tension. It isn't that all future dissension ceases, but it does get us through the night. Once the band is playing, everything is fine. When we get down to what we're supposed to be doing, the bond is there again. But this is far from a complete renunciation of drugs, and later that night Garcia and I sheepishly run into each other at Tom's house (after all, we're all out of blow).

When Lesh and Kreutzmann show up it's ostensibly to discuss the concert.

"How many people do you think showed up?"

This is a pretext but it's still a good question. By now I have a pretty good eye for how many people it takes to fill the Albert Hall. What Salter tells me he's sold is off *by half* according to the band's estimate.

I don't know what to think, and I can't face dealing with it that night. We do one more show, and it's the same damn thing all over again. Now I am worried. The second night I prevail on Salter to check the deadwood (unsold tickets) and by morning it's obvious he's missing many, many tickets.

A good half the tickets for our shows are going to the London underworld. Sold in pubs, at the door. There are tickets available *everywhere.* We ask people, "Where did you buy your ticket?" and they say, "Oh, at the Arms." The pirates have taken over, and they're underselling our ticket price! Now, who do you think is going to sell more tickets? By the last night in London we have a packed house, but the number of tickets sold stays the same.

@

On our last night in London, the crew comes fleeing back to the hotel. They've just escaped with their lives from an East End whorehouse — panties, garter belts, and lethal-looking spiked heels in tow. They're crestfallen.

"Fuckin' hell, man, all we did wuz ask ta see the donkey-stickin'-his-dick-in-a-chick act and they got all hot under the collar and threw us the fuck out! Called us a bunch of Yank pervs!"

These beefy crew guys like bumpkins from a Shakespeare comedy have come to Europe to see the sights and they're not going to be disappointed. They scour the ancient cities of the continent in search of their holy grail, the quasi-legendary donkey-fucking-whore act last seen in Havana circa 1958. But they're simple lads. None has graduated high school, and geography was obviously not their strong point. They know we're going to Munich next. Time to brush up on their Spanish. *Mira, donde es el burro, señora?*

Never mind, I tell myself, it's only the beginning of the tour. On to Munich, dudes!

◎

September 14. We soon find that Munich is crawling with American expatriate rogues, a seething little colony of scoundrels, dope-runners and hippies on the lam, and the arrival of the Grateful Dead is an occasion for them all to congregate for a grand ol' *faites dos dos.*

We have barely set foot back at the hotel when who shows up but the most infamous Haight-Ashbury smuggler of them all: Ken Connell, a.k.a. Goldfinger. We all know that he has just escaped from the most dire jail in Greece: Hanja prison in Athens. So we are all just a wee bit apprehensive about him, especially since there are warrants out on him in a dozen countries. Goldfinger is typically devil-may-care about the whole thing. A wonderful pirate; big red beard *and* a hook. Traveling on a German passport, while still learning the language . . . a redheaded Irishman with one hand.

Goldfinger soon becomes a very popular dude, mainly because he has his own drugstore: a large traveling salesman's suitcase with compartments rather like the ones DEA agents bring round to schools to illustrate the evils of drugs. You can have anything you want from his medicine chest on one strange condition: You have to do a hit of acid first.

We've had problems with fire departments all over Europe, but Germany has to be the worst by far. Everything is by the book, baby, by the book. We are no longer dealing with the Greater London Council and their matey inspectors. No, the men of the München Stadtliche Feuerwehr are sticklers for details. They weren't really inspectors at all, they are *demons!* Fire trolls! Terrible grey specters in, I'm not kidding, World War I German troopers helmets. Their leader: *Hauptmann* Zahngrunder, Herr Toothgrinder! A perfect maniac, a cabalist misplaced in the Munich Fire Department. Books filled with columns upon columns of kilowatt registers, amperage variants, resistance oscillations, capacitor scales. Endless bone crunching digits. Computation taken to the point of numerology.

Now according to Herr Toothgrinder, the transformers for our amps do not comply with Statute 248B, Section 14, paragraph D of the Munich Fire Code. At first, we patiently attempt to explain that our amps aren't listed in their book because they'd been *custom-made for us, you asshole!*

But it isn't really a disagreement about amps and transformers, it is more in the nature of a theological dispute. They can't believe that these unshorn guys in Harley T-shirts can possibly know what they're doing. There had to be an error somewhere and they're going to find it!

But despite the zealotry of the München Feuerwehr, their principal method of dealing with fire is positively Babylonian. *Sand!* In America where you would normally see a fire extinguisher, in Germany you see: a peg on the wall and hanging from that peg, a *bucket of sand.* After five thousand years of human thought on the subject of firefighting, this is the conclusion they have come to. There is something very elemental about this sand and fire business, very, uh, *basic.* Fire knows its enemy is sand, *ja?* All over this ultra-modern building . . . buckets of sand. Now the Grateful Dead (like most red-blooded Americans) when they see a bucket of sand they stub out their cigarettes in it. So every bucket of sand in the Olympia Halle featured at least two dozen Marlboros with their butts in the air.

This "fire anxiety" (apparently one of the four basic *angsts* of modern Germany) is exacerbated because the Olympia Halle is not so much a building as a gigantic postmodern pop tent. Built for the 1972 Munich Olympics, this oddity is basically an enormous butterfly shape made by stretching canvas over a cable roof. Consequently it is very vulnerable to fire, but it is the Bavarians' pride and joy, their Sacred Tent. And here these barbarians, these hairy, alien beatniks are, out of ignorance of basic wiring, threatening to burn the place down.

Unable to find any legitimate objection to our equipment, the fire brigade had to come up with this new menace. So they are going to double their crew. Where once there had been forty firemen, now there are eighty. Wherever you look there are Fire Trolls, always in the way, casting a pall over everything they gaze upon. At least one of

The band with Dave Nelson (far left) and John "Marmaduke" Dawson (third from right) of the New Riders of the Purple Sage at Mickey's ranch in Navato. That's the recording studio in the background, 1969.

The haunted eyes of Bob Weir.

Goin' country western. Garcia and Weir backstage, 1969.

Jerry in his element: rehearsal hall, 1973.

Hired guns: Rex Jackson, Scully, and Sam Cutler at the free concert in Lisle, France, 1972.

Am I adorable or what?
Weir, 1987.

The drummers get their
graduation pictures
taken, 1987.

A touch of gray, 1987.

An uneasy Brent, 1987.

Lesh, the preppie look.

Kreutzmann, 1983.

Weir at a free concert, Golden Gate Park.

Lesh, when he still played four-stringed bass.

The three gunslingers on stage.

Jerry on his way to the Us Festival, 1980. Note briefcase made for Jerry by Fender to look like a sawed-off guitar case.

them outside each of the dressing rooms, like uniformed guards out-side Buckingham Palace. Six of them directly behind the amplifiers, another six next to the mixing board. And each Fire Troll, I'm not kidding, has his own bucket of sand. And should there *be* a fire, my friends, they're going to *dump these buckets of sand on our sound equip-ment,* the great multimillion-dollar electronic Pyramid of the Dead.

We eventually get most of them back against the wall where the clusters of cable from the roof come together. Still, this army of weird fascist loonies in gray is a nightmare. . . . Every time the band looks over their amplifiers, there they are, an unflinching phalanx of gloom. They won't smile, won't even look at you, they just stand there, like rabid Norns protecting the Well of Urd. A very uncool situation.

Meanwhile, the acid we took back at the hotel is starting to come on, and with it we realize that our heads are being fucked with — a far more grievous transgression than the hassle with the permits. They have broken the most sacred taboo of all, they are threatening the vibe! This is a violation that the Grateful Dead, as its consecrated guardians, cannot permit.

The vibe: that quivering, numinous essence of the Haightgeist, which the Dead had singlehandedly brought with them, like the Ark of the Covenant, out of the sixties. These infidel Fire Trolls have unwittingly brought a *jihad* on themselves. It is time to resort to some serious voodoo.

And so we do what hippies always do in moments of indecision: we throw the *I Ching.* We are all quite high and the outcome seems divinely inspired. The hexagram reads: TWO PATHS OVER FIRE LAKE.

"Wow, man! Uh, what does it mean?"

"It means the kraut firemen and us are on very different trips."

"And?"

"The key is to get everybody on the same, you know, wavelength."

"Uh, oh!"

In a shaft of light appears . . . Goldfinger! With the instincts of a haruspex and a buccaneer's sangfroid, he knows just what to do:

"Hell, let's dose 'em!"

Of course, persuading the Munich Fire Brigade to drop acid is a daunting proposition, but for a man who had just evaded the air forces of five countries this is child's play. Goldfinger finds out when they take their break and goes out and buys ten cases of the best Bavarian brew. When they come backstage, there he is waiting for them with the refreshments.

"Complimentary beers, *meine Herren!*"

In Germany there is no social stigma to having a beer on the job. If you've got ten minutes off, you go and have a sandwich and a beer. There's so much beer-drinking in Germany it's like oatmeal. And so, after much *clinken und trinken* and singing and yodeling, the Fire Trolls return to their posts.

And Germans just can't handle that acid! During the course of the evening the Nazi fire brigade simply falls apart. Slowly . . . those neat rows . . . crumble. Shirts get pulled out, hats askew. Faces pouring with sweat begin to strobe through a staggering succession of expressions, tears running down their cheeks as they contemplate the incandescent enigma of the light bulb, memories of past existences, their own shoes.

As the Dead Dead Dead play play play on on on, a few of the Fire Trolls begin doing jerky little dances, like those tiny wooden figures who trundle out of cuckoo clocks. Others conscientiously follow the movements of the notes that hover like invisible flies above guitars, while still others stand transfixed as the meaning of the words, G!R!A!T!E!F!U!L D!E!A!D, dancing before their eyes like tiny bones, begin to dawn on them.

I don't think the fire brigade has any idea what happened to them, except that this is a wild and crazy American band that is so nice to give them all free beer. Some leave their posts and are dancing with the hippie girls in the audience, but the tough ones never budge — they've been told not to move and they take it quite literally. They are still standing at attention, that's true, but with zippers undone, uniforms unbuttoned, helmets cockeyed. One of them is standing in a pool of piss.

God, you have to hand it to them! When the heavens opened and out poured a host of nubile angels singing hosannas, they simply sat down on their buckets of sand and watched as the apocalypse passed by. By the end of the night they are sitting in corners with these big shit-eating grins, and they are letting just about *anybody* backstage. You could see paisleys radiating out of them — the hippie at the bus stop could see it and the little old lady could see it too.

But its not over yet. *Someone* has nicked one of the firemen's brass Napoleonic helmets for a souvenir and they're hopping mad. They call the cops and the lieutenant says, more or less, if that helmet isn't in my possession within the next five minutes you're all going to get nicked. That's the implication. I round everyone up and say, "I know one of you dudes has it, but they're going to throw us in the clink so let's give them their funny hat back and they'll go away and maybe not notice all the drugs floating around backstage." Rex, very sheepishly, produces the thing from an equipment box and we restore the helmet.

We've just got this latest crisis damped down when Herr Tooth-grinder catches sight of Jerry, who's a veritable walking bonfire, and goes haywire. Again. Garcia's smoking a huge, fat, badly rolled hash joint, which is coming apart and spilling burning chunks of tobacco and hash onto the stage and he's got another joint and two cigarettes burning away on top of his amp. Smoke is curling up into the kleig lights, ashes are cascading off the amp, and the amp itself is slowly simmering away.

"*Achtung! Achtung!*" the forlorn troll cries and promptly throws a bucket of water over Jerry and a second one on his amp. All of a sudden it's all blacked out. Everything stops, the whole place goes pitch-dark. The audience begins flicking lighters and lighting matches, which, of course, drives the fucking firemen even more bonkers! And that was it, no more juice. Luckily, the band had played a couple of hours by then so it doesn't, thank God, develop into a riot. But there is one more little glitch. Our transformers have shut-off circuits, but the electrical surge is so massive it backs up into the municipal power system and we end up blacking out half of Munich that night.

☉

The band had asked if I could find some girls and bring them backstage, so this morning I obediently talked to the promoters, who gave me a few phone numbers. Do any of you girls want to come down and meet some American rock 'n' roll stars? We actually pay them to come to the show. We end up with about fifteen girls and put them all in the front row. These are not street hookers, they are almost-elegant call girls. There are also a couple of girls from Lippman & Rau, the promoter's office. I am planning on having all these assorted women come back to the hotel and join us at the bar. But when they get backstage, the first people they run into are the crew, and the crew being who they are begin trying out their katzenjammer German on them, basically variations on *Fraulein, sucken mein Dick*. They're a little rural that way. The women flee back to their seats in horror.

So now the crew is confused. What happened to the chicks, man? Well, what do you think happened? Oh come on, you can get them to come back. But I couldn't, really. They were seriously spooked. In their entire professional experience — Bulgarian football teams, restroom suppliers' conventions, Black Forest pigs' trotters fairs — they had never met such animals, such *Schweinerei*.

Meanwhile, the crew has turned surly. It seems their feelings are hurt. They're actually threatening me: "Well, Garcia can't play if we don't get laid." This moronic talk goes on and on throughout the show, and after the show it is still going on. They're so pissed off they decide to go out and buy some with their own money (now that *is* serious). And only some ardent Bavarian *Mädchenfleisch* will satisfy them. Big healthy girls alone will soothe their savage souls. It is the firemen who direct them to the local whorehouse.

This is something of a relief to me because the band will now have the hotel bar to themselves. I figure that with the uncouth element out of the way we can look forward to a somewhat civilized evening. But it turns out that with all the dosing and leftover craziness from the grisly London coke bash, we are all crazed, crew or no crew. We've also been using more psychedelics, which have their own kind of wired tension. Now suddenly . . . we're in beerland. Beer and acid. . . . Let's just say there is no stopping it.

By the time I get back to the hotel, everyone is at the bar, plastered and rowdy. The band is not used to the 14 and 18 percent alcohol content of German beer. Munich pilsner beer served in, well, *shoes*.

At one end of the bar, Kreutzmann and the portly bartender in leather shorts are trading dirty jokes: "What's the difference between pussy and parsley?" At the other end Garcia has mesmerized Weir and Lesh with the vision of the 350-pound coke crystal. He has them crazy. He's actually trying to figure out ways to *steal* it. Topkapi!

Meanwhile, the bar is beginning to lose its patience with the loudness of these Americans, these *Ausländeren* who *can't handle their beer*.

At some point the manager comes in and announces that if we don't keep the noise down he is going to close the bar. I am trying to hip Kreutzmann to this since he is shouting the loudest, but he is on a bender and it is too late for subtle hints.

And here comes, oh no, Goldfinger. With a couple of the call girls on his arm. The man of the hour! A round of applause from the boys in the band. He bows and bangs his hook on the bar. Downs a few shots and starts doing — what is this? — charades? Grim face, clockwork gait. A soldier . . . a wooden soldier . . . uh, a Nutcracker . . . rhymes with pole — a Fire Troll! The Fire Troll examining something very carefully. His hand, I believe. It's just dawning on him that this strange extremity is *attached* to him! A Fire Troll on acid! Goldfinger slowly miming hypnogogic horror as the fingers of the Fire Troll begin to s . . . p . . . r . . . o . . . u . . . t!?! His hand is changing into a huge fleshy tarantula! His own fingers are turning on him!

Soon all the Ugly Americans are doing imitations of Fire Trolls on acid, spastically marching around the bar, banging into each other, kissing the furniture. Beer and acid! Beer and acid!

Eventually they close the bar down on us, but by this time we are all too drunk to leave the hotel and go anywhere else. It's too late for that; people are staggering. And then suddenly, out of the blue, I hear Kreutzmann's voice booming through the bar: "YOU . . . STOO-PID FUCK-IN' . . . KRAUT-EATING JUGHEAD!" Jeez, he seems to have taken the closing of the bar very personally.

"WHY WHEN YOU WERE STILL IN DIAPERS, MY DAD WAS . . . MY DAD . . . *BOMBED* THIS TOWN! *CREAMED* THE FUCKIN' PLACE! YEAH, THAT'S RIGHT! AND KNOW WHAT? I'M JUST SORRY HE DIDN'T DROP ONE ON *YOU!* AND THIS STINKING HOTEL. SHOULDA DROPPED THE WHOLE LOAD ON THIS FUCKING BAR!" He's yelling this terrible stuff to the bartender. I'm trying to think.

"HEY, SAUSAGEHEAD, MORE BEER! MORE BEER! AND BOMB THIS WHOLE TOWN IF YA HAVE TO. WIPE THIS CRUMMY JOINT RIGHT OFF THE FUCKIN' MAP!"

The worst part about this is that Kreutzmann's dad or some other American actually had bombed this hotel. Pretty much obliterated it, in fact. There were only a few precious souvenirs left of the old hotel, which the owners treasured. They are all very proudly displayed, like pieces of the true cross. Throughout the hotel there are little plaques identifying the various objects that have survived.

"In the family since 1800," "Survived two world wars," etc. Shards of cable, china, tables, lederhosen, doorknobs, toilet pull chains, ceramic donkeys — anything that survived has a little plaque next to it.

In the elevator is their *pièce de resistance,* a massive Gothic mirror. It is a masterpiece of Bavarian woodcarving kitsch. Carved antler horns, alpine climbers making their way up the frame, stein-hoisting peasants, little girls in dirndls offering posies to their pet goats — no cliché has been omitted. All framing a hulking old beveled mirror (it, too, has a little plaque on it). I think Kreutzmann read it out loud to us earlier as we were on our way up to the rooms (and still sober).

As Kreutzmann walks into the elevator the mirror faces him, so over his shoulder he can still see the bar. And what the still bellowing Kreutzmann sees is the bartender making a face and giving him the finger! Instead of turning around, Kreutzmann addresses his final threat to the bartender in the mirror, presses the button for his floor, and then takes his fist and *thwaaack!* The mirror shatters into a thousand pieces just as the doors are closing. Time to go!

We all adjourn upstairs to the Dead suite, and after a few more beers I decide to call it a night. Everybody is accounted for except the crew, but they are big boys and can take care of themselves. I am tired, I want to relax, take a bath, watch late-night TV in German, but no sooner have I lain down on the bed than the phone rings. It is the police. Something about "Grateful Deads." Seems some hooker burnt Sonny Hurd for all his money, the crew got mad and, uh, raided the whorehouse, refused to pay, pillaged the place, and have taken, wow, souvenirs. I figure ashtrays and towels with the name of the whorehouse on them.

I run downstairs just as they are straggling in, drunk on their asses. About eight of them. One has a bannister handrail complete with brass attachment, another is waving a big piece of velvet felt wallpaper. It is huge and he is carrying it like a banner in triumph. They proudly show me their trophies: chamber pots, lampshades, atrocious paintings yanked out of the wall complete with picture frames, screw holes, etc. All the big guys, Rex Jackson, Sonny Hurd, Peter "Craze" Sheridan . . . chanting through the lobby:

"DON'T FUCK WITH US! WE WON THE WAR!"

The next morning I go down to the desk to settle up for the

devastations of the night before. The *Rechnung* is the size of a small country's war reparations — which in a sense it is.

◎

September 22. Jerry and Phil are looking over Paris from the balcony of the Dead "hospitality suite." From the Paris Hilton you can see the whole city laid out below you. The lights are twinkling from the houseboats on the Seine, the Panthéon and the Place de la Concorde are exquisitely lit up. In the distance the sound of laughter and Gallic oaths, an accordion playing in a cobbled street, a Charles Aznavour record blasting from a bistro.

For once it's just like in the brochure, when out of the inky black velvet night comes a creature of alarming savagery. It's thrashing through the Tuilleries shouting, *howling* its feral agony. There's a trail of devastation in its wake. Statues are toppled, pieces of bushes are ripped off and thrown in the air, chairs are flung into fountains.

"Crazy fuckin' frogs!" I say. "What do you think happened to the guy?"

"Maybe he just found out that the *Nouvelle Larousse* permitted 'le weekend' into the dictionary?"

"Nah, there's crazies *everywhere,* maaan," Garcia offers philosophically. It's a reasonable enough statement as far as it goes, but as this particular madman comes into earshot it becomes obvious we are not dealing with a native.

"Oh no! It's a fuckin' *American* loon, for chrissakes!"

"Too much *vin ordinaire,*" Phil suggests.

"Omigod! *Omigod!*"

"What's the matter, Rock?"

"Shit, it's Kreutzmann."

Kreutzmann on a moped crashing into lampposts, trash cans and pissoirs pursued by a horde of screaming Arabs also on mopeds.

A wild-eyed Kreutzmann throws open the door. He's all cut up, he's bleeding from the knuckles, he's bleeding from the nose, he has a split bloodied lip. He's been punched out and God knows what. There're glass cuts all over his face, and his jacket is covered with shimmering shards of glass.

"That must've been when I threw the fucker's moped through the window of the Bon Marché department store," he explains.

"Kreutzmann, maybe you should start from the beginning."

Turns out he'd walked into the wrong club — an Algerian disco as it happened — and in the fucked-up state he was in he got sorely pissed off that there were all these gorgeous girls there and none of them would dance with him. They were only interested in the Algerians.

"Fuckin' A-rabs, man! I wuz so mad I went out and knocked over all their mopeds. And then I took one of them and threw it through this store window and called them a bunch of niggers and split. And then *they* got real mad and the fuckers started a high-speed chase all over Paris."

Cut to later that night, and Kreutzmann is still mad as hell. He spends hours going up and down the hallways poking the lights out and taking shoes left outside rooms down to the next floor and leaving them outside *other* rooms. Childish, I know, but at least these are *cheap* thrills on the Grateful Dead hotel destruction scale. A few francs and a suggestion we stay somewhere else next time we visit Paris.

Could things possibly be about to calm down? The thought barely crosses my mind when the promoter of the Palais des Sportes concerts introduces us to a new drug. China White heroin. We only do it once, but it's the shape of things to come. Although smack of any kind used to be *the* taboo drug among hippies, it seems times have changed. To the Dead it's just another drug, and I seem to have gotten over my reservations about it too.

16

Blues for Allah

IT'S ALL BEEN too much. We've been slipping deeper and deeper into drugs. Since 1970 we've been doing close to a hundred gigs a year, and made four studio albums (not counting the two live albums). The band is at the end of its tether, a whirlpool of inner events is swirling, our nerve endings are close to the surface. The band is stagnating, we don't have any new songs, we're worn out, it's been ten years without *one* break. We all agree it's a good idea to take a year off.

The last official engagement of the Grateful Dead juggernaut is to be the five-night "retirement shows" at Winterland, October 16–20, 1974. Followed by a one-year vacation.

Just before the last concert, Mickey Hart had appeared on the scene. It's not that anybody at this point — including Mickey — thinks he's coming back into the band for good, he just wants to jam with the Dead one more time. The problem is Kreutzmann, who isn't all that crazy about having him back in the band.

Rex Jackson has a plan. We move Mickey's drum kit into Winterland and hide it at the bottom of the stairs. On the last night at Winterland, Rex asks Kreutzmann if Mickey can jam with the Dead. Kreutzmann has no objection to playing with Mickey — "problem is, we don't have enough drums." To which Rex answers, "Oh but we do, we've got another trap set just down the stairs here." Mickey's, that is!

Kreutzmann can't argue with that. We're all standing there and Rex can be very persuasive. And that's how Mickey came back into the band. After that night, Kreutzmann just accepted him. It is such a shiny evening with two drums again. Even Kreutzmann is slightly humbled by the power of their combined energies. The Grateful Dead need the rolling thunder of sound that the two of them generate — and it's stayed together ever since.

◉

The break in touring enables us to extricate ourselves from a $100,000-a-month overhead for trucking around the Wall of Sound, paying a crew of forty people to maintain it, and meeting a monster payroll.

But nobody is on retainer, and we are all fairly heavy into dope. Did I forget to mention that? China White is eating up more and more of our money. Up till now we've been relying on our per diems to pay for our habits. We break up at the height of the drug frenzy, so naturally we all decide it's time to quit dope as well. And of course there's also the vague thought that it might even be a *good idea* for everyone to get off drugs and take a deep breath.

But what to do with all this time? And how to make some bread? For Lesh and Weir and Hart and Kreutzmann it's a complete burn, because Garcia immediately — the next day! — has a new band. He has this physical need to play, so bang! he makes a few phone calls and has a band together, is out booking nightclubs and going to work.

Everybody's hustling to keep up with him, and soon junior versions of the Grateful Dead are sprouting up everywhere you look. There's Ace and Kingfish with Bob Weir, there's the Garcia & Wales, Jerry Garcia & Merl Saunders, Old and In The Way, the Diga Rhythm Band, Keith & Donna, and on and on.

◉

With the band broken up, there's no regular income anywhere: People are dropping from $500 a week to zip. The Grateful Dead has been a gold mine, and none of us is prepared for the abrupt downturn in our finances. A month ago we had fat salaries and all of a sudden . . . laid off! Any plans involving money are shelved, and here am I struggling to keep my head above water. Gotta do *something* to make money, man. I mean, I have bought things — *large,* money-devouring things. I own cars, even have commitments for chrissakes! I owe my soul to the company store, and I don't have a pot to piss in — it's an outhouse, actually.

Oh yes, I am also strung out. So I need money to do what any self-respecting hippie in my position would do: get involved in a (far-fetched) marijuana-smuggling scheme. My slithery cohorts, Tyler and Bruce, are bringing in three hundred pounds of pot from Mexico, which I plan to hide in a cunningly contrived stash in my barn. I will sit on it and the dealers will come over to my house and get what they need. I am to be the marijuana troll sitting under the bridge. What could be simpler?

Well . . . the plane runs out of fuel (they forgot to take out the seats!), is forced to land on a highway and . . . they get popped. Unfortunate, but thank God I am not in any way connected with it.

Shortly afterward Tyler calls me up. He's desperate, crying to me over the phone: "They've got me dead to rights, man, you gotta help me get out of the country. You think you can get me some phony I.D.?"

When we meet downtown I see this gold Dodge across the street from the phone booth with a guy in a shiny jacket staring at me. So I have the good sense from my Hell's Angels training to take twitchy Tyler through a car wash in case he's wired. Nothing in the paperwork I give him has been touched by anything other than rubber hands. I take a hankie and pull the envelope out of my pocket. It's got the Michigan driver's license, the social security card. He can get a passport with this shit. I'm saving the motherfucker's life, but he's sandbagged me, called me from a federal building.

The next day who should come across my bridge but three DEA agents. I happen to be growing pot in my front garden, trying to disguise it with corn stalks, but the grass is getting higher than the corn. They see it, but that's not what they're here for. I'm in my car leaving with my kids for school when they come up the driveway. They look like barrio L.A. thugs: leather jackets, greasy hair — you can smell the grime on these guys, and they're clearly packing guns. At first I think they might be Hells Angels (!) but when I take a closer look I know they're cops. It's the white socks. Immediately I put the car in reverse and back up to the house, run in, take everything I find and throw it into an ammo box, which I stash under the house. The only thing I miss is a string of peyote buttons that is up on the top of my bookshelf, but the rest of it, they will never find. I get back in the car as if nothing has happened going five miles an hour and as I come up to them they pull out these big silver .44s. I know I'm sunk, but manage my best "Is anything wrong, officer?"

He says, "Get out da car wid your hands on your head, mudderfugger!" and I know the little creep has nailed me. This, my friends, is what happens when you get laid off from the Grateful Dead!

⊚

The hiatus may have been necessary, but stopping a juggernaut like the Dead creates many problems. There's far too much time to brood and get fucked up. Another casualty of this period is Jerry and Mountain Girl's relationship. They officially separate in 1975. She had spoken about her frustration over life with Jerry as far back as 1971, but they stayed together and had a second daughter, Trixie, in 1974. After Mountain Girl leaves, Garcia begins to lose his bearings. Kreutzmann and Suzila break up around this time, too, and shortly afterward he gets married for the third time, to Shelley, with whom he will live for the next fifteen years.

⊚

I'm out on bail. My court case won't come up for another year and I put it in the back of my mind.

The band goes back in the studio at Weir's house in Mill Valley. So far, for Grateful Dead Records they've cut one fair-to-middling LP (*Wake of the Flood*) and one solid album (*Mars Hotel*) with actual tunes on it that could've got radio play had we so wished. Really. Now it's time for something completely off the wall. The band is in a speculative mood, a Zen frame of mind, and they have lots of time on their hands. Hence, *Blues for Allah,* their last studio album for the Dead label.

Garcia has always been a big fan of Beat spontaneity — "first thought, best thought." Now Chairman Garcia announces the ground rules for the new album: "We're gonna go into the studio with no preconceptions, and with no material. We bring nothing in. It's a chance to let us hang out together and let ideas evolve from absolute coldness, from absolutely nothing."

This sort of talk always makes me nervous, but I'm aware that part of Jerry's motive is to heal the rifts and get back to where the band makes the main contribution to the evolution of the material. This approach can lead to advanced noodling, which it soon does on the drum sequence at the beginning of "King Solomon's Marbles" and the aptly titled "Milkin' the Turkey." There are way too many instrumentals. This kind of stuff'll work at a concert, but on a record it is wasted time and space. It goes on so long you are almost relieved when this bright and bouncy country twangin' tune of Bobby's comes along (even though it doesn't exactly fit with the Near Eastern theme of the album). But then, Donna Godchaux's solo on "The Music Never Stopped" doesn't quite blend in either.

Donna's voice works better in the studio than it does in performance. Her voice has never harmonized well with the Grateful Dead live. She has a beautiful voice; the only problem is that it doesn't blend that well with Garcia's and Weir's. Jerry has a sort of Americana take on a song. Like Dylan, you can't argue with it. And why bother, it sounds great. But put a *glorious* singer like Donna next to him, and it's like putting a Meissenware figurine next to an old whiskey jug.

Bobby wrote "Sage & Spirit" while my daughters, named Sage and Spirit, were jumping on his bed and generally trashing his hotel room. He was trying to play his guitar and came up with the rhythm for this from their jumping. The flute mimics their laughter.

"Help on the Way," "Slip Knot!" and "Franklin's Tower" are actually all part of one long song. "Franklin's Tower" is great in performance, but on the album it sounds too neat and tidy. Garcia's guitar is far punchier live. It sounds a wee bit flat. The truth is these guys have never developed a persona for themselves in the studio. Their attitude is "Nice suit, let's have it cleaned and burned."

Since the band isn't touring, the guys now have all the time in the world to spend on the album, a prescription for serious mucking about. Such as collecting five hundred crickets in a cardboard box, sticking microphones inside it, slowing the tapes down, speeding them up, and playing them backward at half speed so they end up sounding like whales and chirping birds.

These crickets chirp on the bass track throughout the second side of *Blues for Allah*. But this shouldn't be mistaken for a simpleminded exercise in decorating the track with sound effects. It's in aid of a far more mystical quest: *giving voice* to the desert. The Dead asked themselves the ancient question: If the desert could talk what would it sound like? To answer this truly mind-boggling question, Hart and

Garcia construct the talking sands. Garcia engineering, Hart in the studio playing all his little percussion things — bells, metal, glass. So that when Jerry says "In'sh'ALLAH" it's not a human voice that you hear pronouncing the name of God but the brittle desiccated voice of sand being blown across a hot moonscape.

"I think that's the first record we've made in ten years where we really had fun," says Garcia. "Also had the chance to get weirder than we normally do." Now that's saying something.

The off-the-cuff approach may work well for musical instruments, but it doesn't transfer all that well to language. It's a nightmare for Hunter, who prefers to sit back and toy with things a little bit more. "Blues for Allah" with its long melodic phrases and twelve notes (or more) to the bar is hardly made for impromptu versification.

"Okay, Hunter, we're ready for the words for this one about now."

"Well . . . it's not in any key and it's not in any time. And the line lengths are all different. How in the hell am I supposed to get a scan for that?"

"Dammit, Bob, stop stalling, just give it to us hot off the brainpan, whatever it is."

"How about 'Here comes that awful funky bride of Franken- stein'?"

"Right length, wrong country."

"How about: 'Arabian wind, the Needle's Eye is thin'?"

"That'll do, got any more?"

On the other hand, "Crazy Fingers," with its loping camels and bells, comes together in a blinding flash of satori, just leaps off a page or two of haikus Hunter has been scribbling in a notebook. Jerry spots these random jottings and recognizes them for what they are: lyrics!

But by the time *Blues for Allah* is ready for release, Grateful Dead Records is floundering financially. From now on United Artists will manufacture and distribute Grateful Dead Records. *Sic transit gloria mundi* (that's how the cookie crumbles).

Over a period of four years, Grateful Dead and Round Records have put out no fewer than fourteen albums. But the *Grateful Dead* have only made three albums: *Wake of the Flood, Mars Hotel,* and *Blues for Allah,* stretching themselves to the max in the process with loans from the Bank of Boston.

In 1976, the Dead close down Grateful Dead Records for good —

after *Steal Your Face,* the double live album culled from recordings made at Winterland in 1974 — the so-called retirement shows. This record is called *Steal Your Face* for good reason. Ron Rakow had assured everybody that there was plenty of good material on these tapes, but as Lesh, who mixed the album with Owsley, eloquently puts it: "Rakow wouldn't know good material if it came up and pissed on his shoe." Let's face it, this album would never have been released if we hadn't needed money for the film.

Did I mention the film? While the Dead are on hiatus, Garcia is also embarked on a new career, moviemaker. He's working on *The Grateful Dead Movie,* a documentary of the retirement concerts at Winterland, filmed every night with six cameras and nine crew members (and a whole lot more money taken out of the Grateful Dead coffers to pay for it). Besides doing his band projects, Garcia, with Dan Healy and Eddie ("big black leopard") Washington, commutes down to L.A. every week. Garcia is the director, Healy the engineer, and Eddie the director's assistant. Eddie is crucial to this project because he's the only one who was involved in shooting it. He monitored the filming on six screens in the mixing truck and he also knows the songs backwards. The directing of the film is essentially an editing process, so it's from Eddie's notes on the sequencing that the film is spliced together. He also acts as a kind of crew boss for these two loose hanging wires named Garcia and Healy.

While the three of them are hunkered down in Burbank, the rest of the Dead have forgotten they ever *made* a movie.

Garcia spends two and a half years working with Healy on *The Grateful Dead Movie,* editing some 150 hours of film, painstakingly synching the footage to the music, during which time no one in the band ever asks what it sounds like, what it looks like, or what Jerry is trying to do with it. He works like a dog on that film. It isn't until it's almost done that anyone else in the band takes the slightest interest. And then — all at once — the chihuahuas of paranoia begin howling.

Phil freaks. He insists that I take him and a committee of Grateful Dead band members to Los Angeles. I call Garcia down at the lot: "Um, get ready, there's a small palace revolution going on here, and they all want to come down *tonight* and see what you're doing with *their* movie."

Sharp intake of breath from Garcia: "Oh, no, please. Not the Grateful Dead. I've been working on this thing for a year, and they want to come *tonight?*"

"Well, Jerry, I think that, uh, on the other hand, man, it might be a mistake to put them off. They're starting to think something's amiss and it's only going to get worse if we avoid them."

"Oh, maaan, that's gonna interrupt my whole work schedule! Tell 'em there're no rooms down here."

Which happens to be true. I call the Grateful Dead travel agent, and the best he can do is to book the band into this newly finished old folks' home. It has aluminum bars next to the toilet and red handles to summon the nurses in case you fall down. The beds have railings around them like big cribs for giant babies. Phil takes one look and says, "I don't care for this room, Rock."

"Tough, there aren't any other rooms. You wanted to come down here on one day's notice. Hey, you can't do much better than this, man, there's a Kiwanis convention in town!"

Goddamn if Jerry doesn't charm the shit out of them! He could always do that. But it was a shabby thing for them to do. And Phil as the instigator ends up spending all of about twenty minutes looking around and watching a little bit of the movie and then wants to go to a fancy French restaurant and drink some wine and have a nice dinner.

A year after my bust, my case comes to court. I get eight months and probation, and thank God it's in a minimum-security federal corrections institute where I have the good (?) fortune to get to know H. R. Haldeman, fresh from his Watergate exploits, cooking his heels in the room next to mine and cursing Richard Milhous epithet-deleted Nixon. Screaming with rage.

"That cocksucking S.O.B.! Sick little shit!" He's telling me all these nightmare stories while I'm trying to eat that cold toast and awful mush that they make in the joint. His epithets about his former boss are *scorching*. Otherwise, he's a mild-mannered, well-spoken company man, a Southern California promotion man who became the Assistant to the President. He tears Nixon a new asshole — daily.

"Jesus, Scully, it's lucky that they booted the fucker out when they did or the world might've *ended* with his presidency. Damned lucky!

The goddamn raving lunatic was hell-bent on bombing *somebody.*"
Then H.R., shaking imaginary jowls, does his Deputy Dawg imitation of Nixon: "'Or shoooooould we make peace with them? I dun-
nooooo.' What a fucking dimwitted nerd!"

◎

When I come back to work with the band I wind up doing carpentry,
putting in a new floor at 20 Front Street, the Dead rehearsal space in
San Rafael. How art the mighty fallen!

Jerry is still working on the *Grateful Dead Movie* down in Burbank.
It now has fantastic animation sequences by Gary Gutierrez, film clips
of the 1960s, concert footage of the band and audience, and interviews with band members, crew, and Deadheads, including one in
which a stoned fan objects to the whole idea of filming on ontologi-
cal grounds — i.e., it interferes with the concert in progress, to which
one can only agree, adding: "*Om Sri Maitreya,* dude!"

It's meant to translate the Grateful Dead experience onto film,
"coming from what it's like for me — in my head, as abstract ideas,
nonspecific images — and what it's like for anybody." But the roiling,
mind-fusing cauldron of a Grateful Dead concert is not something
you can really bottle, and the effort of this quasi-mystical venture is
taking its toll on Jerry. Wearily he is beginning to call his endless
sojourn in the studio "two and a half years of doubt." All those days
and nights running into one another in that huge sublunar studio in
Burbank. Lobsters scuttling at the bottom of the sea. A high floating,
detached mood pervading everything as Garcia settles into a permanently stoned state of mind, getting heavier and heavier into dope.

And we aren't only smoking just pot anymore. By 1976 we've
moved on to a new drug. Persian base heroin.

In the beginning nobody quite knows what it is. And they haven't
taken it long enough to get strung out. Like Alice, we are satisfied that
since the bottle wasn't *labeled* "poison" it must be okay. And, hey, it is
organic!

The Persian has come to us from a guy I'll call Ashram Harry.
Ashram Harry was an old friend of Garcia's, a swami with a long
white beard, turban, and flowing robes who had his own ashram. And
one day a devotee who had been in Iran studying Sufism brought
him some Persian as a gift. He tried it and loved it and turned Garcia
onto it.

At the time — the fall of '77 — Jerry is very involved in the studio, mixing down his third solo album, *Cats Under the Stars.* He's in the studio twenty hours a day and the Persian creates this single-purpose intensity that allows him to focus for hours on end during the incredibly tedious business of mixing.

The Grateful Dead had quite a bit of experience as drug guinea pigs. It was on us that the alphabet psychedelics, MDA and MMDA, had first been "tested." A lot of our experience with drugs had, in fact, been as white mice. "Let's try it out!" is our approach. We are the original experimental animals.

Persian is an innocent by-product of our guinea pig mentality where any new drug is okay with us as long as it feels good, and the Persian is unbelievably dreamy stuff.

My first brush with smack had been so grisly I had nothing to do with the insidious opiate family until the '74 Tour of Europe when the French promoters offered the China White heroin.

We had also used certain drugs like cocaine and speed as road tools. Sleeping four hours a night, a different town every night. The band, the crew, everybody was using coke to get going. Working until four in the morning, crash, wake up with a line, hit the road. Even after we'd been through the coke mill in London, we put it down to, uh, just doing a bit too much. You know, nothing to do with using it for ten years!

For some reason we figured that Persian is recreational — like coke! We believe that coke is something you don't really get strung out on, anybody knows that. How can it be harmful — I do it every day!

Anyway, worrying about getting strung out farther down the line is not one of our major concerns when a new drug comes along. First of all, there is the myth of the Invulnerability of the Dead — a myth the band devoutly believes in. And the Persian is so hard to find that it doesn't seem like any of us will ever get a *chance* to get hung up on it. Weird logic, I know. After we try it for the first time, it is a long, long time before we can find any more. Eventually we run into a couple of Iranian playboys whose father had been the chief of police in Teheran. They own a car dealership in the East Bay, and they do a little side business in Persian.

And, hey! Persian is so cosmic, it even comes with its own mythology. It had been used in the fourteenth century by Persian warriors who heated it on the blades of their swords before going into battle. Now who could resist a drug like that?

What Persian turns out to be is a very refined form of Iranian opium. Not so refined that you can't get addicted to it, though. It is also very volatile; has to be mixed with cocaine so that it won't evaporate completely when you heat it in tinfoil. Mellow rush, especially mixed with cocaine — known as a "speedball," long a favorite of jazz musicians.

And Persian has the advantage of no telltale smell. A smell so faint that cigarette smoke would cover it. Plus you can't identify it. On the other hand, it isn't something you can nip in some place and do real quick. It takes some preparation, and the crinkling of the tinfoil makes it extremely hard to do on the sly. But once you start smoking it, well, that's all you *ever* want to do. All thought of life beyond the foil soon vanishes. Oh great. . . .

17

Zeno's Lullaby

<<<<<<<<<<<<<<<<<<<<<<<<<<<<<<<<<<<<<<<<<<<<<<<<<<<<

I AWAKE IN terror. I have been abducted by aliens. Wherever I go, they reconstruct the same absurdly kitschy room. I recognize the same painting of windmills, the folksy curtains with the poodle-and-Eiffel Tower pattern. All cunningly designed to reassure me, this is clearly an extraterrestrial's idea of human habitation (culled, perhaps, from episodes of *The Mary Tyler Moore Show*).

But, as Jean-Paul Sartre once said, "Everywhere is the same place after two weeks." A pretty funky perception for an old speed freak who never had the experience of spending seventeen consecutive nights in seventeen different towns — all in *exactly* the same Ramada Inn room. Identical sleeping pods pumped out in some factory in Dubuque.

With trembling hand I put out a big rail, get on the phone. Must make contact with others of my kind.

"Good morning, Jerry! [pause] Jerry . . . ?"

"You've got the wrong room. And who is this, anyway?" Click. Omigod! They've replicated Garcia!

I make one last attempt. I knock on Healy's door.

"Go away!"

"Healy, open up, I think I'm going insane. For God's sake, man, answer me one question."

"Make it snappy, will ya? We're busy doing nothing here!"

"What was the name of Garcia's dog?"

"You mean Lady?"

"Thank God, Healy. They haven't cloned you yet."

"Jesus, Rock, you still got some of that killer blow! I'll be right in."
The world is pulling into focus. Slowly. Soon I will forget last night's
dread.

Healy stumbles out of his room: "What do you mean you thought
aliens had taken Garcia? Garcia *is* an alien." Healy always has a re-
freshing point of view — go with the madness!

I call The Alien's room again and this time he's more like his old
foggy self:

"Ooooh, maaan. . . . Who's in charge? Accept loss forever. And
where's breakfast?"

"I don't know. Hold on, I'll call the desk."

"How soon do we have to be out of here?"

"I'd say an hour, tops."

"Excellent, excellent, an hour is always good. But unfortunately,
whoever you are, my clothes are wet. . . ."

"Wet?"

"Don't ask."

"I'll call room service."

"No! Don't you understand? *No one* can come here!"

Strange goings-on chez Garcia.

Call the desk, lines busy. Probably ten other "guests" asking where
the hell *they* are. Out the window I see we're on the main square of
whatever city this is, but that's not much help — some generic patriot
in bronze trousers, the cannon and pile of cannonballs. I open the
night table drawer. Aha!

The Providence Chamber of Commerce brochure informs me
that "In the northeast corner is a statue of General Ambrose E. Burn-
side, a Civil War General and Rhode Island statesman who popular-
ized burnsides, the forerunner of sideburns." From this I deduce (a)
we're in Providence, and (b) this is Tuesday.

Jerry once told *Rolling Stone:* "The Grateful Dead is like one dumb
guy, instead of five, you know . . . dumb guys, it's like one dumb
guy. . . ." My job is to put this one dumb guy back together again
every morning. This is a laborious business that takes several hours.

I start dialing the Dead Kindergarten Class of '77. I have thirty
rooms to call, including crew. Two and a half hours on the phone,
sipping orange juice, watching my eggs turn into rubber eyeballs.

"Weir. . . . *Weir?* WEIR!"

"*Drrrrrrrrzzzzzbbbbbbzzzzzbbbb.* Wha. . . . What?! What did you say?!

"Bobby, turn the fuckin' hair dryer off!"

Bobby will not leave the hotel without doing his hair. Every morning, like the adherent of some esoteric cult, he performs the same rites: shampoo with placenta of unborn yak, then condition with ergometric kelp extract, blow dry, and, like Rapunzel, endlessly comb the glossy locks. Now he's wondering where his hair went! I told him a few years ago, it *blew* away, Weir!

Anyway, Bobby needs the most time to get ready. After the hair ritual comes the choosing of the outfit. Will the faded minty cargo pants go with the Guatemalan poncho?

"Bobby, we're outta here in forty-five minutes, dude."

"It'll never happen. Sorry, old man."

"Why can't you do this stuff at night, Weir?"

Same lame excuses every morning. They don't even have the common decency to think up new ones.

"Kreutzmann, wakey, wakey!"

"You silly asshole, do you know what time I went to bed?"

"I really don't care. And don't call me silly."

"Gee, I give up. What time *is* it?"

"Time to *get the fuck out of bed.*"

Most band members I have to call two, three times. Second call to Garcia.

"Don't you want some breakfast? It's two hours to Jersey City, man, no food on the flight. Why don't you have something right now? I'll call room service for you, okay?"

"No! Absolutely not!"

"Okay, Jerry, okay. Jeez."

"I'm not dressed. I *have* no clothes. . . ."

"Try the black T-shirt."

No breakfast for me either, hope to catch a bite on the plane. Make a few more calls and I'm out of here.

As usual, everybody wants something. Window seats, vegetarian food, a dog leash, newspaper, Tampax, guitar strings, backstage passes for little friends, the area code for Frankfurt, shoelaces, and plane tickets for whoever they're fucking.

Head downstairs and deal with the hotel bill, make sure the limo drivers are there and everybody is ready to go. Naturally, there is no sign of Jerry.

"Anybody seen Garcia?"

"Nope."

"Ha ha."

"I know nothing. I was only obeying orders."

I better check on him. I get off the elevator on Jerry's floor and make my way to his room. Squish-squish-squish-squish: I have a sinking feeling that the Incredible Swamp Creature has been at work again. The ground grows spongy as I approach his lair and there's that telltale smell of burning horsehair, one of his trademarks. No smoke detectors are going off, no fire department, no crime scene tape. It can only be He! It's getting wetter and wetter as I approach Jerry's room. By the time I reach the door, the carpeting shudders away from me like a moray eel. The stench is overpowering.

I knock on Jerry's door. No reply. The key's still in the lock, so I walk in. It's like some aquatic creature's house on a Saturday morning cartoon, an Okefenokee diorama with resident creature emerging from his burrow. He has mournful, sheepish eyes and wet whiskers. And there is Swamp Dawg himself, perched on the one dry place left in the room — his bed! Wet socks, knees pulled up under him like a flood victim sitting on top of his house on the six o'clock news. He's finally had to get into bed. He's burned up the couch, he's burned up the easy chair, there's nowhere else left to go.

There are towels everywhere. Jerry's made a valiant effort at sopping up the flood, but it's like holding back the Mississippi. The carpet is *floating* eerily several inches above the ground. Obviously at some point the sprinkler system came on and deluged the room. The putrid smell of burning horsehair from the still smoldering furniture is enough to choke you.

Jerry has taken great pains to make the room look normal — for him, an act of sheer desperation. It would require a blind, olfactorily impaired chambermaid in wading boots not to notice the devastation. It's an endearing side of Jerry's character. Even under the most dire circumstances he wants to make everything better again. He's turned over the cushions on the couches in the vain hope that the burn marks on the other side will not be noticed. The indomitable optimism of his nature! Little touches, like a corner sofa cushion with the white side up. When you turn it over it's got a half-bushel-size crater in it, and it *reeks* to high heaven. It's just recently been put out with a bucket of ice (now melting on the floor). A horrible way to come down from the blissful opiated dream state induced by Persian.

He is in the 3:00 A.M. nod-off zone — out there! Bali, perhaps. The temple bells are tinkling in the distance, a balmy wind stirs the palms carrying the monkey chant across the hills. And then — suddenly! — Krakatoa! The walls crumble, tidal waves roll over the acrylan shag beaches of Oroboro, a vicious rainstorm deluges the faded plaid landscape. The gods are angry with the Akond of Swat.

I go along with Jerry's ludicrous charade of tidying up. We raid the laundry carts for towels to sop up the flood and pray that the maids don't get to this room before we duck out of the hotel. Freshen the place up as best we can by throwing some of those little sweetheart soaps they give you under the rug to make it smell better. Also drop a few down the hallway for good measure as we skank our way downstairs. I'm hoping we can squeak out of the hotel by our tail feathers.

But the chief maid has figured it out. How could she not? The hallways are *squishy*, for chrissakes, and the smell is overpowering. There's been a spate of complaints to the front desk from irate early risers who have awakened to find soggy newspapers and waterlogged shoes outside their doors.

The minute we leave the room the head maid lady sends her little stoolie upstairs to take a bunch of quick Polaroids. He's a nifty little bugger, apparently, because he manages to snap them fast enough to get them down the service elevator in time to reach the desk as I'm checking out. While trying to maintain standard checking-out banter I'm furtively wiping my shoes on my pants legs to get the moisture off and hoping I don't smell like burned-up furniture. But alas, all semblance of normality is shattered when the Polaroids appear. Ooops.

"That'll be three hundred dollars for the easy chair, Mr. Scully. . . ." *Ka-ching!* the terrible punctuation of the kindergarten cash register.

"Three *hundred* dollars?" I say, searching for the snooty British accent I can sometimes summon up in drunken emergencies. "*Please!* For that moth-eaten thing? Why, it's all burned up and everything!"

"Look, bud, the maid says she found a hole the size of a frying pan in one of the cushions." I know we're in trouble when the previously fawning desk clerk starts calling me "bud."

"Very well," I say, "let's be civilized about this, shall we, and not *dwell* on the sordid details? How much for the couch?"

"The couch . . . ?" *Tic-a-tac-a-toc-a-tic* go the menacing little Chiclet keys of the calculator. "Eight hundred dollars." *Ka-ching!* "We paid twelve hundred for it new."

"That piece of shit?!" Oops. There goes the British accent. "Didn't I see a sign that you were gonna be renovating this wing pretty soon?"

"And of course we'll have to replace the carpet."

"Madame, I could argue that on the basis of these pictures, this could have happened some other time." I get the pained expression of someone whose patience has been sorely tried by having to cope with a blithering idiot. "And the carpet doesn't *look* wet in the Polaroid. Does that carpet look wet to you?"

"Shall we go upstairs and examine it at first hand, Mr. Scully, or perhaps I should call in the National Guard? It's a disaster area and you know it."

Shoved under my nose are frightening close-ups of (a) a coffee table so tattooed with cigarette burns crisscrossing its surface it looks like a crude diagram of a railway marshaling yard and (b) an unblemished nightstand except for a long thin oblong where a just-lit cigarette has fallen out of the ashtray and burned a full-length portrait of itself in the glassy fake mahogany top. In the wake of the flood, indeed!

We've only been on the road a week and already I have American Express charges of roughly twenty-five thousand dollars. This is just rent-a-cars, hotel rooms, and airfares. Including those frequent unscheduled flights where Mickey Hart or Phil Lesh picks up a girlfriend and wants to fly with her from Indianapolis to Providence (which is an expensive little flight) and then make a quick run out to the Cape.

"Just cover it, Rock." I do, and it adds up alarmingly. Now with the overcharges at the Providence Hilton, we've spent our *entire* allotment on Jerry's furniture. A little episode that costs almost five thousand dollars. Nodding off at night does get expensive.

"And of course the hallway will have to be redone. The cigarette receptacle will have to be replaced, and also the bench."

"Why don't you repave the New England Freeway while you're at it?"

The furniture isn't exactly Chippendale — it isn't even Monty

Hall — and it isn't as if we've burned down the west wing of Versailles. If they had any imagination at all, they'd auction it off to Deadheads — someone out there would pay handsomely for items like this.

"This is where Jerry nodded out, man, I swear to God."

⊚

Flight 719 to Jersey City. Jerry's immersed in a science fiction novel. You always know when Jerry has a good book because he'll share it, quote from it, give you a synopsis. By the time he snaps it shut, everybody wants to read it next. The Dead are a literate group of guys. Hey, this isn't the Allman Brothers with everybody reading comic books.

These are the days before full stereo, television, a choice of six movies and a meal. Jerry regales everyone on the plane with the ongoing plot, the whole storyline in a few paragraphs:

"See, Captain Zeno and his expedition — they're, like, the good guys — land on the red desert of Planet Morg. They don't have much time, because Morg has been subdued by vicious Klaggon raiders. Zeno and his crew must reach the Intergalacticum Chamber. But Klaggon warlock, Mordred, has atomized the Intergalacticum Chamber — it's *invisible,* man! The only way it can be located is if Captain Zeno can remember the words to the lullaby his mother sang him to sleep with, but Zeno has been suffering from amnesia. . . ."

"Sounds like last night's show," says Weir.

"Man, how could you forget the words to 'Jack Straw'? Didn't you write the fuckin' thing?"

"Uh, maybe I did, but that doesn't make it any easier to remember, y'know."

Weir can remember the words to the most complicated Dylan song and then he'll forget the words to "Truckin'."

⊚

August 1. The gig tonight is at Roosevelt Stadium, Jersey City, an old baseball stadium. We're looking forward to it. The Band's on the bill, too, so it's going to be a great show. It's Jerry's birthday and my birthday — I'm a year older — so it's an auspicious day by any standards. I've told the promoter, so there's bound to be a little surprise waiting for Jerry after the show. As we get off the plane, a light rain is falling. It's nothing, just a spring shower, but the very idea of water is making me jumpy.

We're in that open area behind the stage at Roosevelt Stadium — everybody's there, all the guys from the Band and the Grateful Dead, Dylan. There's a circle forming around two people fighting, shouting at each other. Backstage is a volatile place. Tiffs flare up over nothing, and with the coming of heavy blow it happens more and more.

Except this isn't a couple of roadies fighting over lading dock protocol this time, it's the legendary Albert fucking Grossman, manager of Dylan and the Band. He's apparently gone mental, fucking lost it. In his gray ponytail and granny glasses he resembles an enraged grandma, but Maude Frickett he ain't. He's a very belligerent guy under normal conditions, and right now he's screaming wild, unaccountable things. He's foaming at the mouth, threatening Sam Cutler with dismemberment: "You cocksucking little limey sonofabitch, your mother fucks sailors in a . . . Buick."

Cutler is pluckily riposting with the old Brit sangfroid ploy: "Now, look here, old man —"

Albert's lunging at him — the beet red maniac Grossman, a deranged hyena right in his face. There's an aura of savagery about this altercation that the dispute in question hardly warrants: the Grateful Dead are being paid more than the Band for the gig. Hardly a global issue (even for a manager). Grossman is accusing Sam Cutler — who is the booking agent for both groups — of dark deeds: flagrant bias, fixing . . . *graft!*

"How much did they slip you under the table, eh, shithead?"

My God, it's so over-the-top! Rick Danko is shaking his head in dismay: "Oh, man, this is so embarrassing, I can't believe this is happening. Somebody's got to get him out of here."

Sam's a cool fry, but he's been pushed too far this time. He's about to clock Grossman. Then I spy Weir's girlfriend, Frankie Hart, giggling uncontrollably in the corner and the *Aha!* buzzer goes off. I grab a ball-point and scribble on the palm of my hand "FRANKIE DOSED ALBERT" and hold it up to Cutler. A big smile comes over his face. "Did I ever tell you wot a wonderful 'uman bein' you are, Albert?" he says as they drag a blithering Grossman off into a limo.

The promoter, John Scher, wasn't counting on rain for August 1; he's neglected to put a roof over the stage. It's sopping wet and starting to pool up. In places there are four inches of rain on the stage. Hmmmmm. Maybe the water demon has pursued Jerry from the hotel. . . .

It's an extremely hazardous situation, one in which someone — namely one of the band — could easily get electrocuted. Thousands of watts sitting in puddles of rain. The band members *very* gingerly creep up the stairs to the stage. If one of them so much as touches the railing on the way up, they're going to get zapped. Don't touch ANY-THING metal! Or it's Jersey-fried Dead! The whole band could end up looking like one of our posters — lit-up skeletons jangling at the end of a high-tension wire. Phil manages to ferret himself up to the microphone, he's speaking into it from a good foot away so he doesn't arc it and zap himself with umteen volts of electricity. "YOU WOULDN'T WANT TO SEE US ELECTROCUTED-TED-TED, WOULD YOU-YOU?" It's a rhetorical question, but this is Jersey. The heartless little fuckers yell back:

"YEESSSS!!!"

Metaphysical Phil tries again. "WE CANT PLAY-AY-AY IN THIS RAIN. DO YOU NOT UNDERSTAND-AND?"

No, they do not. They *will* not. And so begins their terrible sullen zombie chant:

"GRATE-FUL DEAD! GRATE-FUL DEAD! FRY! FRY! FRY!" Jesus! Cold-blooded little bastards, aren't they?

"That's it!" Phil unplugs his guitar and walks off the stage shaking his head, his hair spraying everyone in his path like a wet dog: "I ain't getting electrocuted for those little shits! I ain't plugging back in for those animals and that's that! Uh, you go out and tell them, Rock."

So yours truly goes out to the lynch mob and attempts to read an announcement. "May I please have your attention? I regret to inform you that the Dead —"

"FUCK YOU!"

"Thank you. As I was saying, uh, where was I? In a few moments you will be informed as to where rain checks may be picked up. Thank you for your —"

"ASSHOLE!"

As I run under the stadium bleachers toward backstage, I see at first hand the black heart of the mob, throbbing with fantasies of vengeance. I am the lame-brained sheriff's deputy from some late-night Western — not paid enough for the job and never given any backup. Except here, there are dope deals going on around the poles, and gangs of weirdos congregating — ugly jangled vibes zinging through the charged air.

I find the promoter in his usual manic state. "Soo? So it rained, big deal."

He can't be that stupid. Probably just doesn't want to say anything that could be *used against him*. I'm saying, "How could you not put a roof on? What are we gonna do with like twelve, fifteen thousand people."

"That many, huh?"

"Just count the stubs, man."

"Jesus, Rock, I'd love to but . . ."

Omigod! Of all the lowdown, dirty tricks in the promoter's hall of shame, this is the lowest. He's had some sick child puke on the ticket stubs.

Jesus, he is *so* tacky! First *vomit,* for chrissakes, and now, for Jerry's birthday he's ordered up one of these cakes that a stripper jumps out of. As Jerry catches sight of the hideous thing, a throttled cry escapes his throat.

"Aaarwwwgggggggg!" It's so awful. The girl is weird, the cake is nasty — *and* it's been left out in the rain — cue "MacArthur Park." The icing is melting under the torrential rain and dripping onto the floor, the stripper's blubbering, her mascara's dripping onto the cake like great black tears, and the whole thing is turning into a great greasy glob.

Also, Lesh has gone weird on me. He is walking about backstage with that glazed look that the Boris Karloff mummy takes on after he's eaten a few *tana* leaves.

Phil is very deliberate about his drinking. He'll drink wine from lunch till showtime in measured doses, eating just enough food to stay sober. During the drum break, he'll start getting seriously soused, polishing off a half liter of some gorgeous French wine. And then, backstage after the show — before we even leave the building — he'll have that one drink too many and just *snap*. Fall apart big time, and have to be looked after. From punctilious musician to wild-and-crazy guy ready to party. Which is the state he's in right now. Randy as a dog, ready to tear the clothes off any woman within range, and one sip away from a blackout.

But this time Jerry saves the day.

"Hey, Rock, get over here. We've got a neat little riot on our hands." The crowd is a roiling mass of discontent. They've already told Phil to go electrocute himself. They're going for a general admittance version of *Suddenly Last Summer.* The only safe way out at this point is the giant rear service doors, which haven't been opened in years. They're rusty and ancient and *stuck.* We have to pop them off their hinges using a backloader. And there, outside, is *another* mob. Garcia is freaked.

"I ain't leaving. You take the first car out, Rock." Well, I do have a beard just like Garcia's, my hair is black with a touch of gray and Jerry's still skinny enough for me to pass for him. I make a dash for the limo in this big black (wet) T-shirt with a little hood. I've already primed the crew to initiate Jerry Garcia frenzy. "Yo, Jerry!" "Hey, Gah-ceea!" "Jer-rreee! Jer-rreee!" I jump in the car as a decoy to make the crowd think Garcia's gone, and at the bottom of the ramp get out the other side and run back in to get Garcia.

"Get me some rent-a-cars or we'll all be killed," I shout (so cool under pressure).

We take the crew cars, the band slinks down in these DEA-type four-door Dodges and Chryslers. All the same, there's a ton of people running after the cars. I catch a glimpse of red, beady ratlike eyes fired up on battery crank. A gnarly, vicious mob who'd like nothing better than to crush the car like a beer can.

◎

With underage girls and dope in virtually every room in the hotel, logistics are a crucial part of my job. The Grateful Dead can't afford too many busts like the one in New Orleans. We carry a lot of incense with us, use wet towels under the door, and pay off everybody concerned to let us know if the cops come looking for us.

For those of you considering Rock Group Management as a career here is the basic speech. It should be delivered to the desk clerk in an even tone without the slightest whiff of panic. You don't want to alarm anybody or trigger anything. What you are asking of them is perfectly reasonable. You are sincere and, above all, you are official:

"We have *many* fans, and as you know we've taken a lot of rooms in your hotel and, just sometimes, these kids get excited or their parents come around. Here's what I'd like to do, Bruce. It is Bruce, isn't it? I want to know if there's any trouble, any trouble at all. Oh, here's fifty bucks for you, because you're gonna have some extra work tonight, too, and I want to make sure you can go out and buy some breakfast in the morning. Now I want to know *immediately* if there's *any* problem. If the police come looking for girls or *whatever* happens, I need to know about it right away. Have you got that? Good man! And, um, if you don't mind, I'd like to leave some money for the telephone operators tonight because they probably won't be around in the morning and it's gonna be a demanding evening for them, too. I'd like, with your permission, to give them a set of instructions. I want to know about unusual phone traffic. That way I can keep an eye on my clients."

And now try giving this speech with a rottweiler wrapped in a bunch of local newspapers that you are pretending contains reviews of tonight's concert. Mickey's decided he can't go out on the road without his little dog. A puppy, actually, that isn't exactly house-trained so it has to be walked every half hour, and then comes in and goes right on the carpet. It's got to be *smuggled* in and out a dozen times because the hotel naturally isn't crazy about having an un-trained puppy peeing all over its carpets. At the gig, the promoter hires a security guard to look after Mickey Hart's puppy — it's now a part of our standard contract. In Boston the long-suffering guard takes Nipper Jessica for a walk and she immediately pees on his leg and poops on his shoe. He sits there outside Hart's dressing room good as can be, with piss on his leg and rottweiler puppy shit on his shoe.

We aren't yet hip enough to know to change our names or to disguise where we are staying, and anyway the band and the crew have already given all the girls our address. Weir always gives them my room number. We get home from the gig and there're a hundred people lounging in the lobby lying in wait for us.

I come in and the guy at the desk is very flustered: "There's all these kids asking for your room, Mr., uh, Rock." I try to calm him down, making it seem routine.

"Didn't I tell you there were going to be a lot of people? We get this kind of thing wherever we go. But you're handling it like a trooper, Bruce."

"Don't worry about a thing. You can count on me, Mr. Rock!"

"Next thing you know, Bruce, *you'll* be managing a rock band."

No sooner have I got up to my room, smoked *one* joint, turned on the news and called room service, than the desk clerk is on the line.

"Oh, the police are here? Is that so? I'll be right down." Use some eyedrops, take another snort, wipe the crust off my nostrils, put on my sportcoat, and spring downstairs.

"What seems to be the problem, officer? Can I help you?" The essential thing is to be as polite and official sounding as possible under the circumstances. Theater of the Absurd is constantly required of me. My most demanding role is that of a model citizen. I'm here as an illusionist, essentially.

(1) Bring on the smoke and mirrors. It may look like a gang of hairy men on drugs are dragging underage girls up to their rooms to ravish and corrupt them, but it's just the other way round, officer. These fans are harassing my clients — always use business lingo — and I'm doing my best to see they aren't disturbed.

(2) Change the subject as soon as possible. Do you know that the Grateful Dead are the thirty-ninth biggest corporation in the State of California? (I didn't either.) I can't afford to have a bunch of out-of-control kids endangering our situation. *Whatever* it is, remember: It can be explained away.

Out of sheer fear, I never get to bed before four o'clock in the morning. If it's not the cops it's irate parents, and *they're* threatening to call the cops. The desk clerk calls me up: "There's an older couple here, Mr. Scully, and they're looking for their daughter, Chelsea. They say that she was supposed to be spending the night with her girlfriend, Tiffany, only her girlfriend is not at home either. They say that the girls went to see the Grateful Dead show, and they want to know are they by any chance *upstairs* with the Grateful Dead?"

First line of defense: Deny everything.

"Well, there's no one of that description here, I can guarantee you that. As a matter of fact, we have no *girls* upstairs at all (I always go too far). And then again, uh, the band have all turned in for the night. Yeah, plumb tuckered out, they were. Have to get up in the morning for an early flight to Washington. But allow me to run downstairs and I'll see what I can do to help." Whatever happens, brazen it out. Should a band member appear with a nubile groupie in tow simply say: "Ah, there's Mr. Kreutzmann now, with his lovely daughter, Molly."

On the way down I make sure band members are locked into their rooms from the outside and that any Chelseas and Tiffanys get dressed and down the back stairs pronto.

In the lobby I ask the parents how old their daughter is. "Fourteen? Oh, I have a daughter just about her age (give or take about eight years) and I know how you must feel. I bet she just went down to the mall with her girlfriend and by the time you get home she'll be there.

Please don't hesitate to call me anytime should you desire, uh, tickets?"

Our list of demands — presented to travel agents, hotels, and promoters — escalates with the years. Lesh has a bad back and has to have supplied in every room he sleeps a bed board of a certain thickness and resiliency (this is in the rider to the hotel). Also French wines, specific vintages. Weir wants his preferred shampoo, Jerry his favorite flavor of Häagen Dazs.

The nerve center of on-the-road operations is the "hospitality suite," which I usually share with Dan Healy in the other bedroom or with the bookkeeper (or whoever is traveling to semi-keep the accounts straight).

I'm checking our airline reservations on line one, Mickey Hart's on the other line. He wants to smuggle a girlfriend — without his old lady knowing about it — to the next place we're playing. We're constantly adding tickets, disguising the room numbers so that there won't be coitus interruptus with a phone call from the old lady. Most calls instead go to me; I'm the old-lady switchboard. Rock wives — that supremely contradictory condition — live a perpetually paranoid existence. How do you think they got to be rock molls in the first place? They're a suspicious bunch and must be handled with care. Deliver these lines as affectlessly as possible: "Oh, you just missed him. He went out to get some strings for his Gibson." Or try: "I left him five minutes ago. He was practicing." God, I have mortgaged my immortal soul to a rock band!

The phone rings constantly till four o'clock, and if we were on the East Coast, all night long — because of the time difference. When it's four o'clock in the morning here, it's only one on the West Coast and it's "Hey, you guys back from the gig?"

"Yeah, about four hours ago."

Hmmmm, 4:18. Maybe I can grab a couple of hours of sleep before my wake-up call. There's just one thing I have to know before I go to sleep.

"Hi, Jerry, it's Rock. No, everything is peaceful and serene here at the Ritz Carlton. All the Jacks are back in their boxes. I'm just wondering . . . did Captain Zeno ever remember the words to that lullaby?"

18

Trouble Behind

"HEY, LISTEN TO this, Weir. 'ROCK GROUP IN PANTY RAID AT LOCAL GIRLS' COLLEGE. New Bradford police department reported that the rock group, the Grateful Dead, raided Yarrow Stalk Women's College last Thursday night. They broke into the senior dorm chanting "Trouble ahead! Trouble behind!" and removed numerous pieces of women's underwear and hosiery.'"

"Jeez, how did I miss *that* one?"

"We weren't there, dude. We were all in California last week, remember?"

"So what are you saying? That there's another rock group called the Grateful Dead?"

"Now that's a chilling thought!"

We call the New Bradford constabulary and find out it was actually the Grateful Dead *Motorcycle Club*. Wow, Grateful Dead one-percenters, man!

Sandy Alexander, the president of the Manhattan chapter of the Hell's Angels, is at the gig tonight and Jerry asks him if he's ever heard of a motorcycle club by the name of the Grateful Dead. No, he hasn't, but as president of the Manhattan chapter of the Hell's Angels he's very interested in any new clubs starting up, especially any who would deign to usurp the glorious name the Grateful Dead.

"I'll look into it," he says and you know you've got his word on this one. He's *very* protective of the band. And this is fraternity house stuff. You can't have a bike club named the Grateful Dead going on *panty raids*. It's embarrassing!

The next time I visit Sandy at the Hell's Angels clubhouse on 3rd Street, there's a Grateful Dead MC patch pinned up on their patch wall.

"Yeah, we pulled their patches," Sandy says laconically. "And then they prospered and became righteous good Hells Angels." Glad to hear those boys grew up to be Angels. Still, a Grateful Dead biker club would've been cool.

May 7, 1977. Boston Garden. Speaker of the House Tip O'Neill is coming to the show tonight and bringing along some Kennedy kids. Tip O'Neill, Deadhead — who would have thought! We're getting famous now, boy. Everything is rolling along smoothly. Too smoothly, apparently, because we have now done something guaranteed to upset the apple cart. We have appointed Peter "Craze" Sheridan, a world-class berserker, as the advance man for the crew. This is a truly deranged idea, but fun! You never can tell what might happen when you let a gin-soaked, acid-addled yahoo from Chevy Chase, Virginia, loose on an unsuspecting world, but you know it's going to be *interesting.*

He began turning up at Dead concerts a couple of years ago and the crew and the band took to him immediately. Jerry loved him. We recognized him at once for what he was, "a true aristocrat of Freakdom" as Hunter Thompson called him in *Fear and Loathing on the Campaign Trail '72.* He had all the mad drive and Zen instincts of Neal Cassady, but where Neal was short and wiry, Sheridan is *colossal* — 6'4", 250 pounds of haywire energy.

What makes Sheridan utterly compelling is *the story.* (How he single-handedly derailed Ed Muskie's whistle-stop campaign.) Jerry loves this hippie Paul Bunyan fable, a tale of a freewheeling freak creating havoc in the camp of the sanctimonious and hypocritical.

Sheridan boarded Muskie's "Sunshine Special" in Key Biscayne using a press pass borrowed from Hunter Thompson (ha!), downed ten martinis before the train even left the station, and proceeded to terrorize the passengers all the way to Miami, threatening to throw anyone who crossed him off the train at the next bridge and calling an esteemed correspondent from the *Washington Post* a "greasy faggot and a Communist buttfucker." The only passengers he had any time for were the Muskie cheerleaders in their boaters and red, white, and blue hot pants whom he importuned relentlessly: "Come on over, my little beauties, and sit on Poppa's face." Any other campaign would have thrown him off the train, but these were quaking liberals who apparently would go to *any* lengths to avoid a scene.

Then came his pièce de résistance. Reeling off the train in Miami he mercilessly heckled Muskie from the tracks (alongside Jerry Rubin shouting, "You're not a damn bit different from Nixon!"). As a finale, Sheridan grabbed Muskie by the pant leg and shouted, "Get your lying ass back inside and make me another drink, you worthless old fart!" At which nadir of public humiliation Muskie burst into tears in front of a host of network news cameras, effectively ending his campaign.

With credentials like this, how could we resist? We hired him on the spot. For the Dead there's a perverse pleasure in letting such a fiendishly loose cannon demolish the business-as-usual, we've-got-everything-under-control pretenses of the straight world. "Craze" was guaranteed to run amok, and in this he reminded us of our past and of one of our fundamental principles.

"Formlessness and chaos lead to new forms," Chairman Garcia has always said. But what demented impulse possessed us to elect him advance man for the crew, I cannot now recall. He liked riding in trucks. I suppose that may have been it.

Anyway, by the time I get to Boston all hell has broken loose. Everything is at a standstill. Nothing is moving in or out of the hall. We've a mountain of stuff. Crates of equipment are piled up outside the Boston Garden, knots of surly guys in hard hats are hanging around the entrance kicking the air. The crew are sitting dejectedly on the gear drinking beers and inside, alone in all his glory in this giant ice arena, is an exultant Peter "Craze" Sheridan. In his eyes I detect the maniac's gleam of lunatic resolve. He's done it, the crazy fool! Seems he's *fired* the unions, and very proud of himself he is, too.

"You *what?*"

"Fuckin' worthless sacks of shit!"

"Craze, let me see if I've got this right. This is the *union* we're talking about, the stagehands' union?"

"Yeah! Good riddance!"

"Yeah, well, man, guess what? They just fired us right back. And without them you can kiss any Grateful Dead show goodbye."

"Hey, we don't need 'em. The crew'll shift the gear. They're doing all the work anyhow."

"Yeah and we'll end up with tire irons through our speakers."

"But they're not *doing* anything!"

"That's their job, dig, *showing up.*"

For such beefy guys, the stagehands' union is a notoriously touchy bunch; they won't let you even screw in a lightbulb without being on site and picking up an astronomical hourly wage to do so. It's true they don't show much interest in hoisting two-ton speakers forty feet up onto our scaffolding, but unless they're paid they're not going to let anyone else do it either. This is going to be a *very* expensive show. All of these guys, the Master Unplugger and the Assistant to the Master Unplugger, are going to have to be greased big time. We're going to have to "buy them all breakfast" in the quaint lingo of their guild.

The set varies, but Dead shows by the late seventies have evolved into a deep groove, taking on the form they will always have. Sometimes they do a little more country, sometimes longer jams, but tonight's show is fairly typical of their current song list. Three songs from our soon-to-be-released-order-your-copy-today! album, *Terrapin Station*: "Samson," "Estimated Prophet" and the eponymous "Terrapin." There's "Friend of the Devil" from *American Beauty,* "Eyes of the World" and "Mississippi Half-step Uptown Toodeloo" from *Wake of the Flood,* a couple of numbers from *Skull Fuck* (a.k.a. *Grateful Dead*), "Wharf Rat" and "Bertha"; "U.S. Blues" from *Mars Hotel.* Also two numbers from Jerry's first solo album, *Garcia,* "Deal" and "Wheel." Almost all the songs are Garcia/Hunter numbers but there are three Weir/Barlow songs: "Cassidy" from *Ace* and "The Music Never Stopped" from *Blues for Allah* and "Estimated Prophet." Plus "Jack Straw" from *Europe '72,* which Bobby wrote with Hunter. Some oldies — Chuck Berry's "Around and Around," Johnny Cash's "Big River" — and a handful of folky favorites: "Peggy O," "Samson" and "New, New Minglewood Blues."

Nineteen numbers! (plus "Drumz>") all lasting seven, eight minutes — *minimum.* A Grateful Dead concert is by now like a folk-rock version of Wagner's *Ring* cycle. Shows routinely run four to four and a half hours. Intermissions barely give them time to recharge. Even for the resilient, chemically fortified members of the band, some respite is needed, especially by the second set.

Hence the dodgy rite of the drum solo, introduced into rock concerts in the late sixties. Or, in the case of the Grateful Dead — drum duets, customarily catalogued in the Deadbase as "Drumz>."

Drummers are touchy guys. In their heart of hearts they all want to be guitar players and lead singers and strut and fret their hour upon the stage. They resent their Igor-like status: hunched over their drum kits at the back of the stage, shunted out of the limelight like second-class citizens. Some of them (Chairman Hart, for example) are actually into issuing statements to the press on the subject: "The real role of drums in the twentieth century is not to be relegated to the backbeat all of the time. I'm not into speed-drumming. Both Billy Kreutzmann and myself feel that we are long-distance drummers, able to see the sights along the way."

Naturally Hart and Kreutzmann liked the little "Drumz>" show-cases, and they soon became — for very different reasons — wildly popular with the band. The drummers remain onstage, the band splits to go get high, crack a beer, have a glass of wine, take a leak, take a snort, smoke a doobie, chat up a groupie. A little break — lasting anywhere from four to fifteen minutes — a much-needed oasis in the dauntingly long Dead sets. It got to be so important for the band to have this drug/beer/wine break and still keep the music rolling that "Drumz>" gradually became a fixture at Dead gigs.

"Drumz>" usually comes about five songs into the second set. The song the band is playing (tonight it's "Eyes of the World") gradually loses its melody, the rhythmic beat picks up along with synthesized drums. The "Drumz>" sequence crawls into the set and suddenly it's there. Billy drifts from the drums to the congas. The spotlight comes on the drummers while the rest of the stage becomes dark and skampy so you can't see Jerry skulking off to do himself a line or Phil running off to air out a bottle of chardonnay. Just the two drummers under the key lights with their giant iron wing. "Drumz>" is played on "the Beast," a giant iron pot rack built for them by this guy Willy at Bill Graham's backstage facility down on Folsom Street. On which is hung all these kettle drums and gongs and bells and chimes. A veritable Marrakesh bazaar of percussion instruments from around the world collected primarily by Mickey Hart. Once he broke out of the confines of military-style drumming and started exploring other rhythm patterns, he went *tribal*. We no longer had just another drummer in the band, we had an *ethnomusicologist*.

"Drumz>" is a theatrical event. It's the drummers' moment to shine. The two of them get up there with soft wooden mallets and begin striking the hanging drums — *brrmmmmnn-buburrrmmmmnn-brmmm-brmm-brmm* — locking eyes with each other, moving back and forth, creating hypnotic, lizard's-heartbeat, Shinto tintinnabulations. There're the small hand-held Talking Drums, and on another rack there're the clear plastic tubes with sheepskin on one end, each tuned to a different pitch. You can play them almost like you would a xylophone. They're called Talking Drums because you can change key by squeezing them. From *de-de-de-de-de-doom* to *zhe-zhe-zhe-zhe-boom,* if you get my drift.

The Beast's first incarnation came in the mid-1970s with improved broadcasting technology, and along with the new technology came Kreutzmann and Hart's ever-increasing appetite for buying equipment. Bigger and bigger drum kits. The gear starts to pile up and soon they need bigger and bigger risers to set up on. Mickey is constantly tinkering with the Beast, acquiring new exotic percussion instruments. Tiny Zanzibari chimes that hang from a mahogany spindle, cost a fortune, and have to be hung precisely. Hart becomes extremely agitated if they aren't miked *just* right. This sort of thing drives the crew up the wall. These chimes that he only plays for maybe two or three seconds in the whole show — one *swash* through — *vvvwwwwwwwsssshhhh* — like water splashing on a stone but, *man,* if Ramrod hasn't got that thing miked right or some instrument isn't there when Mickey decides to use it, he's a holy terror. Miking this stuff is a nightmare. There are already sixteen mikes on his stuff alone. They're *everywhere.* They're hanging down, they're clamped, they're inserted and taped on.

But it's not just the temperamental nature of the setups that makes the crew nuts. "Drumz>" happens to come along right at that point in the show when all Ramrod wants to do is go have a Heineken and smoke a doobie and now he's got to be there hovering with this microphone. Take it off of one of the drums that isn't being used and *rush* it over to the Zanzibar waterfall chimes.

A few years ago another kind of musical interlude was introduced, Phil and Ned Lagin's — what to call it? — Insect Fear Interlude. Phil saw Jerry sitting in with various guest bands and thought to himself: If Jerry can play *his* bluegrass licks with the opening act, why can't I play *my* music during intermission? This led to the Assault of the Grisly Outer Space Noises. And very expensive noises they were.

When Lagin signed on, Phil convinced us to spend a ton of money on his equipment, way more than we had spent on any instrument before. An incredible array of shit that we had to cart around, a ton of keyboards and electronics, and all of it very high-tech.

Ned Lagin was another of Phil's brainy friends and the two of them — Lesh on bass, Lagin on electronic keyboards — would come on toward the end of the intermission, and their performance would segue into the second set. What Lagin and Lesh played was excruciatingly dissonant electronic *musique concrète*.

But it did have one saving grace. It lengthened the break and was an excuse for everybody to go off and get high and drink and party and have a sandwich — even the drummers.

But, dear God, it was driving the audience nuts. People'd take acid to see these shows and Lagin, the little demon, would be playing this bone-chilling stuff! For a bunch of high hippie people that just want to boogie, this *nouveau* noise was just frightening. You could see people's faces crumbling: "*What* the *fuuuuck* was *thaaaat?!?*"

When the Lesh-Lagin interlude ceased, its place was taken by the Space Break, a sort of benign fusion of electronics, feedback, and weirdness where the guitarists come back and join Godchaux in playing interstellar sounds — no direction, no melody — that gradually turn into a melody and the rest of the band join in and the set continues.

Dead concerts are an ongoing mystery to news commentators, sociologists, and other uninitiated busybodies. Why, for instance, would anyone want to attend *every* date on a tour? It's a standing subject for jokes among the unDead. But, dear unenlightened ones, don't you know Deadheads go to these shows just to see what will *happen*? There's no set playlist at a Dead concert; the band just go on and "follow the vibe." This makes for a suspenseful set, at least! Did I just hear a hint of "St. Stephen?" Yeah, I'm sure of it. Jerry wants to go into "St. Stephen," but Weir's not following his lead and the band drifts off into "Sugar Magnolias." Now we're moving out of "Sugar Magnolias" into "Scarlet Begonias" and then on into Bobby doing a rocker, "Around and Around," and then mysteriously we're back into "Sugar Magnolias" again — the "Sunshine Daydream" sequence.

The workings of the Grateful Dead group mind is what creates this pervasive uncanniness at Dead shows: the inescapable feeling that

Jerry somehow knows you, that he's plugged into your wavelength. There's an almost tangible wash of feedback at a Dead show. It's as if GarciaLeshWeirKreutzmannHart — that One Dumb Guy up there — is tracking the slightest quiver in your synapses. Okay, we know this is dynamite acid, but still. . . . *You* — Brian Williams — are somehow signaling the band telepathically. Or are they beaming the vibe out at you? Ah, fuck it! It's all so deliriously unfathomable who would *want* to figure it out?

And, hey, ring them bells, boys, it's Kreutzmann's birthday today! Happy thirty-first, Billy! And no chicks jumping out of cakes this time. But as soon as there's a break in the set the assembling of the harems begins. This ancient tradition began with Pigpen, Pig being the most upfront about his needs when we were all quavering little schoolboys. But the rest soon caught on. Bobby's usually the first to hit on me in my role as pimp to the Dead.

"Have mercy, Weir," I cry to no avail, "I just got out of the box office. Let me listen to a couple of songs before sending me out there." He's indifferent to my plea and unrelenting.

"No, you go out there right now! That chick's getting antsy — she's gonna leave if you don't nail her. See if she wants to lose her date or if she wants to bring along a girlfriend. Oh, and, Rock, if she says she doesn't have a ride home, tell her we'll pay her cab fare home."

I submerge myself in the shifting tides of the audience, my ears barely tuning in cries of "'Shrooms! Mud! Tabs!" I'm on a mission to the interior in search of nubile talent on behalf of His Weirdness. Hmmmm, what will my line be to these sultry young *wahines* tonight? "Would you like to have a glass of wine with Bobby?" That's always a good one. Then there's the all-purpose "We're having a party in my room, would you like to join us?"

The groupie shuffle gets to be a real hustle when the show ends because as soon as the crew gets packed up they start hitting on girls, usually by the tried-and-true method of trashing band members, *viz.*: "Y'know Weir's got an old lady. Hell ya, it's serious! He's even started talking about having kids. You don't wanna break that kind of thing up, do ya?" Or the pathetic country lads routine: "The band guys get all the girls. We're just poor boys from Oregon. Only been working for the Dead fifteen years."

Meanwhile Lesh and Weir grab the wine bottles and potted shrimp and run off before the crew is finished. On a particularly randy night, they even get in a quick one in one of the small bathrooms or stairwells.

Back in my suite at the hotel, the calls start coming in. "Oh, are you the blonde with the date or are you the redhead with the girlfriend? Oh, Cindy! I remember you, you're the one that Weir likes so much. Yes, we *are* having a party. Why don't you c'mon up? Suite 618."

Lesh generally goes for the trashy type. Bleached blonde, tight butt, small tits. Weir gravitates to the classic hippie chicks, but after about ten minutes Weir'll see the wisdom of Lesh's choice and start hitting on the girls Lesh has invited. Groupie musical chairs goes on until six in the morning.

In my suite the band members can socialize their way into their own rooms, sometimes coming back to the groupie pool as many as three or four times a night.

One of Lesh's lines to these girls is that he's sterile and therefore can't get anyone pregnant. I guess there must be some truth to this because I never have to deal with any paternity suits for him. And then, miraculously, late in life he is blessed with two sons, Brian and Graham.

Now, I don't want to imply that it's *all* down to sexual pairings chez Suite Scully. Often we'll sit down and listen to tapes of that night's concert — a practice begun by Owsley — and the band members will critique each other's performances. *Then* we'll pair off.

⑥

The Kennedy kids have followed us to, uh, where the fuck are we? Okay, let's just call it the next gig. *With* their Secret Service guys in tow. And now President Carter is coming into town with *his* Secret Service army. The place is *crawling* with these guys. They're easy to spot: drugstore shades, bad skin, psycho eyes, and wires coming out of their ears. There's Secret Service guys stationed in the lobby, up and down the hallways, in the stairwells . . . all *over* the damn hotel, talking to each other on their Motorola radios, the same ones we use to talk to the crew and the lighting guys.

I've brought Jerry and Bobby into town early to do an interview, and go back to the hotel to set it up. It's a remote with whatsisname? That very strange velour guy, you know, Casey Kasem.

Nice reconstructed old hotel downtown we're staying in. Considering the toney crowd booked into the hotel, they've given us a nice big suite. Two rooms opening onto each other and a third room at the end — with a key dangling in the end door. Ah, my bedroom, no doubt. I open the door and I walk in and there on the nightstand is a small snubnose .38 hammerless in a leather holster, a badge, and a Motorola radio with an antenna. And standing next to the bed, almost nude, a vision straight out of a Mickey Spillane novel.

"Oh, is this *your* room?" I guilelessly ask. "Hi! I'm Rock Scully, manager of the Grateful Dead. I'm next door." I take the key out of the lock, but make her walk over to me to get it. Gorgeous mulatto, late twenties, with the light behind her in a flimsy evening gown that leaves little to the imagination.

"Are you, uh, here to look after us and everything?"

"No, I'm the First Lady's bodyguard. Mrs. Carter arrived in the hotel an hour ago and, now, if you'll excuse me, I have to get dressed."

The Casey Kasem interview is standard issue: "So where do you guys see yourselves going from here?"

"Nowhere, fast."

The Kennedys desperately want to lose their Secret Service tails and the Secret Service are so inept that they eventually manage to lose both of them (with a little help from us). We create a diversion by throwing some cherry bombs into the swimming pool. The S.S. guys rush down there and by the time they've figured out it's a hoax, Caroline has vanished. You lost the princess of the realm? Major panic sets in. Paranoid dreams of ransom notes! A possible national crisis! Maybe they've been abducted by Arab terrorists! "No, worse! They're with the Grateful Dead!"

Soon I'm getting very imperative voices on my Motorola.

"Code Oscar! Code Oscar! Where are the kids?"

"Who *is* this?"

"Garth Wasserwinkle, sector two special service branch. Confirm whereabouts of Kennedy children at once!"

"I thought that was *your* job, dude. How did you get on this radio, anyway?"

"How did *you* get on this frequency? This frequency is reserved for the exclusive use of the Secret Service. You are in violation of Code 3026A of —"

"Healy, what the fuck's going on? The S.S. guys are all over our radios."

Big wink from Healy: "I *know.*"

Healy's swapped radios on them or maybe switched frequencies.

Meanwhile the guys with the wires coming out of their ears have lightened up a bit. They're talking to the lighting director over our radios. A little more purple on Garcia, yeah, that's *nice.* Now how about a little red and green wash on the drummers. . . .

But hey, they're human, too. We invite them back to the hotel for a little post-gig shindig. Now half the hospitality suite is Secret Service guys in their Ken-doll suits and the other half are Grateful Dead family, friends, and dealers in characteristic tatterdemalion splendor. In other words, a bunch of very antsy hippies surrounded by guys who look like plainclothes dicks.

In walks Garcia. Everyone in the room turns and looks at him, but Jerry is oblivious. He is *very* focused right now. The guys in suits he's seen before. Record company flacks, probably there to have their picture taken for *Billboard* with one of those dumb gold records (which, by the way, when you play them all have Trini Lopez's *Greatest Hits* on them). Casting a searching eye about the room Garcia says:

"So! Where's the drugs?"

A great shuffling of feet. I'm trying to whisper to Garcia: "See that guy over there with the shiny shoes . . ." But his mind is on other things. The first likely guy he lays eyes on he grabs. "I know *you* have drugs," and he yanks him into the bathroom. You can hear big old honks — *huge snorts* — from within. I want to shrivel up and die.

The little knot of dealers who've come back from the concert just *freeze.* The color drains out of their faces. You can spot the ones who are holding — they're the ones as pale as ghosts. These guys may not officially be cops, but they sure don't work for the record company either. A little thuggy looking and running on that high-octane fuel mix of fear and paranoia — in that habitually tensed *pounce* posture.

But not to worry. Tonight they just shrug. These are *special* cops, you know? Speaking of which, I know there's a beautiful one right next door and where is she? If we're going to have a suite filled with S.S. operatives, let's at least have one or two that are easy on the eyes. I go out in the hallway and leave Jerry wallowing in the bathroom, knock on the door, and invite her in. She comes with all of her off-duty buddies.

To top things off, Jerry has invited Jimmy Cliff's entire band to the party. You don't need to be told they're staying in the hotel — the whole place reeks of pot! You get in the elevator and it smells like a skunk got run over. Soon the room is filled with Rastafarians in knit caps, blowing *huge* spliffs, pot smoke curling out of their dreadlocks.

⊚

We're staying at the Navarro on Central Park South in New York, a hotel the Who have been trying to sell us for years. They own a third of it or something. We've got adjoining rooms. Jerry and I are spending a quiet evening in the global village, working on our hobbies: recreational drugs and watching TV. The eternal, endlessly shape-shifting *box*. Its nature changes with each new drug. With grass you want to turn the sound off and play records, on acid *everything* that happens on the set is uncannily calibrated to each fleeting thought. You *are* TV. With coke, you talk over it, talk back at it, shoot it dead if need be — it's *alive!*

Tap-tap-tap-tap.

"Did you hear that?" I ask.

"Yeah, man, what *was* that?"

It's . . . something . . . outside the window!

The thing about blow is it breeds paranoia. It's *contagious!* There are enough demons flapping through our brains as it is without some alien entity crouching on the windowsill forty stories up, tap-tap-tap-ping on my casement window. I don't want to engage Garcia's alarm system over nothing, but this is, let's face it, a critical situation. It's one of those dread occasions where you need another human being to tell you you're imagining the whole thing. I know from bitter experience Jerry isn't that guy, nevertheless. . . .

Knap! Knap! Knap!

"Jesus! There it is again."

"Turn the set off, man, so we can hear the damn thing." Good! Jerry's being very sensible about the whole thing.

"It's probably a pigeon," I suggest. "It could be anything."

"It could be *anything?*"

BANG! BANG! BANG!

"Holy shit! It must be fuckin' *huge!*"

"Jerry, we're on the forty-first floor!"

Jerry's not taking any chances. He assumes "the shield position" from the high school manual *What to Do in Case of a Nuclear Attack,* crouching down on his knees under the writing desk.

"You go check it out, Rock."

Oh, thanks. And if you see my head getting chewed off by a fucking gigantic mutant mantis be sure to call the front desk and inform them so it doesn't disturb the other guests.

What, me worry? It's a game. It's something the Imp of Blow has cooked up in our overscorched brains. It's just going to be some bird with a broken wing or something. And when it sees me — a bug-eyed teeth-grinding giant human — it's going to be scared out of its wits.

I pull back the curtains with a dramatic flourish. And, there, outside the window I see — the fearsome popping eyes! the demented predatory grin! — the fiend itself!

"*AAAAAAAAAAAAAAH!*"

That *Clockwork Orange* orb of a face could only belong to — Keith Moon! The demon drummer of the Who is blithely grimacing back at me from his precarious perch. I pull open the window and let him in.

"Keith, what the hell are you doing out there?"

In a barely recognizable imitation of the Bard he drones: "May I *pleeeeeease* crawl in your window, baby."

Because he's so paranoid from doing blow in his room alone all night he's double-bolted his door, forgotten that he's done it, and is too stoned to figure out how to open it. Calling the desk in this state might arouse unwanted questions and quite logically he decides to inch along the ledge between our connecting rooms.

"Come in and do a few lines, maan," Jerry says sweepingly. The euphoria of relief and surprise in the room is intoxicating.

"Don't moind if I do."

Snoooooort!

"Wot abowt goin' out an' creatin' some, uh, *havoc!* eh, lads?" The eyes of Moon are like asteroids of Saturn whirring in their own lunar orbits. They're independent entities, a sort of coke-crazed pair of quasi-human agents — an amped-up Tweedledee and Tweedledum — and *both* of them want to go to Studio 54, *now!*

Jerry generally never wants to go out once we get to New York. He likes to vegetate in his room with the big color TV until showtime. New York is way too much input, it's abrasive and intimidating to Californians — especially Californians as high as we are. But Moon is fearless. He's a force of nature, he's unstoppable! Jerry loves Moon. He has an abiding affection for maniacs, Kerouackian roman candles: "The mad ones, the ones who are mad to live . . . exploding like spiders across the stars," etc.

In the company of Moon, all apprehensions about New York vanish. Hey, don't mess with us, we're with the Tasmanian Devil!

Garcia's suddenly very animated: "Oh, we're going out? Cool! I'll just go get my coat." He leaves.

Moon's wheels are spinning. He wants to go out to that discotheque, Studio 54, but he's forgotten his stash. And he must have the stuff. It's his *familiar.* So he goes out in the hall and uses his key in the door but naturally it won't unlock. All that coke has frozen his memory cells.

Out in the antiseptic hallway with the carpet with the matching deep-pile burgundy borzoi pattern, the Mad Hatter of the Who ponders to himself: "How could this have happened? Hmmm, let's see, I'm out of the room but yet it's bolted, you say, from the *inside?*"

Chief Inspector Moon voice: "One o' them locked-room mysteries is wot it is." He comes back to my room.

"You climbed along the ledge, remember?" I remind him.

"Fuck yeah! But wot to do, eh? I'm not goin' owt on that bloody precipice again, I can tell ya that!"

It's a quandary all right. While I make a few phone calls, Moon disappears into the bedroom. More tapping! This time it sounds like a giant rat caught in the walls and clawing its way out, which, when I go in there to see what's going on, turns out to be pretty close.

There he is, the giant rat of Sumatra, busily gnawing away — *nrrr-nrrrr-nrrrr-nrrrrr* — in my clothes closet. There's dust all over my clothing, lumps of the wall all over the floor.

"What the hell you doin' in there?"

"My room's right next door, mate."

"You're goin' through the *wall?*"

"Wot uvver alternatives do you recommend?"

"Jesus, Moon, it's only drugs!"

"You should hear yourself, Scully."

"Can't we get more of whatever it is, man? I mean it's not *ibogaine,* is it? Or extract of Madagascan tree toad venom?"

He doesn't hear me. He's a man possessed. He's stripping the plaster off the wall with a buck knife. He's got that mad Jack-Nicholson-with-the-ax look — here's Johnny! He's a miracle of enthusiasm. Now he's got the plaster off and he's down to the lath and bricks.

"Won't be a moment," he says and splits. Am I being too optimistic to think he's abandoned his nutty project? Gone to raid Pete Townshend's stash, most probably. But no, it's too good to be true. He goes downstairs to the basement and comes back up with a chisel and a hammer! He's taking the bricks out *one by one*.

"I *own* a third of this hotel, y'know," he says by way of explanation. He's going, "God, I'm gonna get in so much trouble for this!" But he doesn't care, he's pounding away at it! He's determined to get back into his room and get his drugs.

Jerry comes back and goes in to take a look. He's standing there looking at this devastation. "What!? Jesus! Moon's turned into some kinda human mole!"

Finally the hole is big enough. Moon wriggles through it, gets his stash and crawls back through the hole, once again forgetting to open his door. He's now covered with dust from head to toe, like a ghoul recently exhumed from a graveyard.

Later on that same night . . . Captain Gas shows up with one of his monstrous tanks of nitrous oxide. A G-tank. It's over six feet high and is so heavy it has to be wheeled in on a hand truck. How, you may ask, would you get such a massive thing through the hotel lobby — it looks like a small bomb — without someone stopping you? But he's had years of experience at this, wheeling G-tanks into hotel lobbies covered up with a raincoat and a hat on the top, pretending it's a drunk friend, hugging it and getting it into the elevator before anyone notices that it's not a human being. I can't picture it either, but somehow upstairs it goes.

We all suck on the plastic snakes until it's almost dry and starts to freeze over. At this point you've got to heat the tank up again. So we drag it into the bathroom, which we very rapidly destroy — the fucking thing is so unwieldy! The shower rod has collapsed, the shower head is bent, tiles are smashed. . . .

Finally we get the shower on it, full on hot, and it starts to defrost. It's a little precariously balanced (the bottom of the tank on the edge of the tub) but no matter, it's working again, dudes!

Whew! Going out on the town with Moon is like spending an evening with Harpo Marx. He's a magical creature. Perhaps it's that clown face of his. Like the Lord of Misrule, wherever he goes he turns the world upside down.

Here he is pinching girls' bottoms, requesting autographed panties from them — stuff that had Jerry or I tried would provoke a smack across the face. But Moon gets just the opposite reaction. They *love* it. Telling their girlfriends, *boasting* about it.

"You're not gonna believe this, Cheryl, but Keith Moon just pulled down my panties and bit my ass!"

There is at this very moment (in all probability) in another galaxy far, far away, *another* Garcia. Jerome van Rijn Garcia, renowned painter of mindscapes. His microchip masterpieces are implanted in all the most discerning brains. For relaxation he plays the fretless moon lute.

Jerry paints, you knew that, but you may not know how deep the graphic vein runs in the inscrutable Garcia. Not everybody is aware of the life-or-death struggle that went on within the anguished breast of the teen Garcia. Painter or musician? Filigree mandolin player or savage *tachiste?* Let the fates decide! And, of course, they did. But it was touch and go there for a while.

Painting's not a mere hobby with Jerry the way some guys put ships in bottles — it's the *second path*. His double life began at Balboa High, attending sessions at the California School of Fine Arts in the North Beach Section of San Francisco on weekends and during the summer. And, every now and again that urge, that apparition of his lost other, Jerry Garcia, painter, rises to the surface.

Garcia fondling an ostentatiously embossed invitation: "Is this for real? This Salvador Dalí thing?

Lesh, the culture vulture, comes to full attention: "What about Salvador Dalí?"

"Salvador Dalí Requests Your Presence at his Exquisite Corpse Brunch in Suite 210 at the Pierre Hotel. Sunday June 2 at 1:00 P.M. RSVP."

How did we get on *this* guest list?" Weir's impressed.

"Well, hell, *however,*" says Garcia, "let's respondez, shall we?

John McIntyre, our booking agent, is the Dead's resident art enthusiast, and knowing that Jerry is a painter manqué, Phil a culture maven, and Weir up for any bizarre scene, he has made arrangements. It's going to be a formal scene, this we know from the overdressed invita-

tion. Although these things rarely impress Garcia, he has conde-
scended to throw a black sportcoat over his black T-shirt for the
occasion.

We walk over to the Pierre to pay our respects, and are greeted
effusively at the door by whatshername, Mrs. Dalí? Gala!

"Gratefully Dead, are we? Darlings! We are so honored you are
coming. Come, meet Da-*lí*." We are at the center of the universe.
Another genius has recognized the Dead as one of them (and about
time, too!). Phil is creaming his jeans. Brunch with Salvador Dalí!
Here he is *in the flesh!* Popping up straight out of the Skira coffee table
art book. One of *the* guys of modern art. Picasso, Matisse, Mondrian,
Dalí — the *berserkers* of modernism who drove the great freight train
of art right through the museum walls.

Dalí approaches Garcia with rapid little bullfighter steps, pushing his way through a thicket of art maven frou-frous, doddering
aristocrats, art-collecting investment bankers and scene-makers and
— Tom Wolfe. Yes! *Him!* Significant! Taking it all in, writing it all
down on his custom-tailored — by Mr. Ferencsi on 53rd Street —
extra-wide shirt cuffs.

Wolfe makes the introduction. "Señor Dalí, this is Jerry Garcia
from the Grateful Dead."

"Ah Gar-*thi*-a! *Nombre Español, no?*"

"*Si, señor,*" says Jerry, trying to humor him. But Dalí intends to take
the game a little further.

"*Como Antipodi cuando usted los volvermos a verme?*" Dalí asks in
Edward Lear Spanish. ["How were the Antipodes when you last saw
them?"] — a prankish question but Jerry gets the joke.

"*Bueno, maestro.* But nippy."

"*Bravissimo!*" says the Dalí, cuckoo-clock eyes bulging in chronic
self-impersonation — Dalí does Dalí does Dalí.

"I first met Jerry," Tom continues, "when I was writing about the
Kool-Aid Acid Tests. . . ."

"Ah, *Zambristi!* Kool-Aid lime green is most sublime color in the
cosmos," declares Dalí. But now the hierophant is puzzled. "What is
Acid Test?"

"It's where young people take LSD and dance to rock music and
colored lights and . . ."

Dalí makes the sign of the cross, rises to his full height with ferociously bristling mustaches: "I do not take drugs," says he. "I am drugs!"

Phil hangs on every word, he's too intimidated by the scene to say much. After a statement like that, there isn't much you *can* say.

Jerry mentions the melting watch in *The Persistence of Memory.*

"I'm always knocked out when I see it. It's like all of science fiction is in that one painting." No response from the maestro — the compliment is evidently beneath him, so Jerry tries another approach. "It's like Einstein's theory visualized, as if time —"

"Time . . . ," says Dalí in his oracular tone of voice. The room turns to hear the pregnant aphorism. "Time is the interval between rhinoceroses."

Jerry asks what kind of brushes he uses to get such microscopic detail.

"Tiny brushes. Tiny baby hair, soft as Gala's bottom, made from the pubic hair of capuchin monkeys."

It's exhausting being geniuses together, and Jerry goes to the bar to get himself a Bloody Mary.

I ask Dalí if maybe the Grateful Dead could play sometime at his museum. I've heard other groups have given concerts there.

"To *play?* No, they must *live* at *Museo Dalí!* A *tableau vivant,* yes? Then I can say, 'The Dead are *living* at the palace of Dalí.'" Uh oh, time to go. Again.

There may be any number of Jerry Garcias on alternate universes, but there are also quite enough of them right here on earth. It's a look that's not that hard to achieve. Black beard, aviator glasses, rumpled black T-shirt over a rolly-polly belly. Sometimes this can be a problem, like when we check into a hotel and they say, "*Sure* he's Jerry Garcia, tell it to the guy in room 513!"

We now have a sinister Garcia lookalike dogging our steps, lurking around the parking lots at the shows, staying in hotels near Grateful Dead gigs out on Long Island, luring young boys and little girls — *very* little girls — up to his room.

We call the police about it, but they say unless they catch him in the act there isn't much they can do. We've reported it so many times. I am getting calls from irate parents that *Jerry Garcia* has violated their daughter. They want to string the old pervert up by his balls and then. . . . It's developing into a serious problem, and sooner or later it's going to get into the papers.

I go and consult Sandy Alexander.

"Yeah, man, I heard about that," Sandy says shaking his head. "It's a fuckin' crime, man. Some creep's abusing my friend, posin' as him and doin' evil shit, which is a total wrong, man. Jerry's got a heart of gold, he's a good man. I love Jerry dearly, man, *you* know that, and if somebody's jeopardizing his career, trashin' his name . . . well, let's just say I'll take care of it." And that, as they say, was that. Never heard of the guy again.

"Cockadoodledoooooooooooooooo!"

It's Kreutzmann! He's jumping on a forklift and driving it at warp speed toward the loading gates.

"I'm *outta here!* So long, suckers!"

"Open the doors!" I'm shouting "He's gonna smash into them!" *Krrrunnnge!* The doors are bent like a giant greeting card, but Billy's still in one piece.

Yesterday he used the forklift to pick up rent-a-cars and park them up against a phone pole. Three wrecked rent-a-cars, TVs in the pool, rooms smothered in shaving cream. As a manager you start getting worried about whether he's gonna piss off a cop or maybe even clock somebody.

Kreutzmann likes to be outdoors. Ride his horse, feed his cow, be sort of the local squire and go to the bar and hang with his guys. He has the energy of a bull (he is a Taurus, actually) and he can go on forever — he thinks. It's just that on tour there's always that irreparable psychological abrasion taking place day after day until eventually you get down to the bare wires. Kreutzmann can only put up with this citified stuff so long and then he turns into a mutant barnyard animal ready to pull down the statue in the square.

Drummers have a tendency to flip. It has to do with how much energy they put into it. They work themselves to death. They have to punch the band into gear. It's a lot more demanding than playing a guitar.

Anyway, he's always the first one to snap. In the old days it was the

Pigpen Factor, now it's the Kreutzmann Krunch. He's made up his mind he's going home even if it means going by golf cart. We all know we were pushing it this time, but these great offers for more and more money keep pouring in.

Twenty-four days ends us up in Syracuse, upstate New York. Uh oh, we've gone over the K-line! When Kreutzmann starts pissing on his Eggs Benedict in front of the maid, it's just too many days!

A Terrapin on Shakedown Street

GARCIA HAS ALWAYS had a soft spot in his heart for a certain melancholy type of folk song. He loves the mournful death-besotted border ballads with their climate of doom and mist. Once touched by the keening airs and plaintive words of ancient folk-begat songs, they'll follow you all your born days. On the 1977 album, *Terrapin Station,* in the "Terrapin Suite," Garcia and Hunter entirely surrender themselves to ye olde melancholy airs. It's full of ghosts and shipwrecked sailors and pining maidens fair, broken hearts and sighs and newborn moons and ancient mazes, tumbled stones and apparitions floating out of flickering fires.

Terrapin mysteries aside, making a Grateful Dead album these days is not entirely a conceptual matter. It's all very well for Garcia and Hunter to swoon off in realms of aerie, but there are others to consider and their insistent voices grow louder with each successive album. There are, at last count, four other band members plus the Godchauxes to be considered. As usual, when we start cutting up the pie, everybody has to get a slice. Weir gets two tracks, Lesh one, Donna Godchaux gets one, Hart and Kreutzmann two, and Hart one to himself.

At this point the Dead are splintered into many factions on the recording issue. Since our track record — especially the albums on our own label — hasn't been that great, there's always a vocal chorus saying what we should have done. If Lesh had his druthers we'd be doing *le rock electronique.* Weir's monitoring the FM stations; basically he wants to be a rock star and see the Dead going in a more commercial direction. And then there's Garcia, who is looking for a more natural course; he wants to develop the *American Beauty / Workingman's Dead* approach, closer to the Eagles and tunes and Americana: telling stories musically in three- to five-minute songs.

The reason *Wake of the Flood, Mars Hotel,* and *Blues for Allah* are so fractured sounding is that there are too many cooks. Phil gets to produce his part, Jerry gets to produce his songs, Bobby gets to produce his part, and the drummers get to produce their part, and we end up with this hodgepodge of sound. It's really manic-depressive — the first one'll be zippy, the next one plodding along.

However, nobody but Jerry is willing to deal with the *longueurs* of the recording studio. Jerry is the only one who has that decisiveness and the stick-with-itness to stay at it all night long. Phil just wants to go home to dinner and a glass of wine. He never sticks around, but when he shows up in the morning and listens to the playbacks he's the first to make objections. I've never seen him hole up with Jerry and spend all night hovering on the mixing board, painstakingly listening to every take. Phil is very adept at intellectualizing and criticizing but he never wants to actually do the work or make the decisions. He'd get a cassette of the mix and as often as not never play it. I'd hear Jerry saying, "You didn't listen to the cassette? You know, we stayed up all night editing this tape. I'm going to bed."

So the band has come to an impasse, where nothing is getting done. The obvious compromise is to hire an outside producer. The only producer the Dead will put up with is someone they respect more than themselves, which ain't all that hard. Jerry is always saying: "We ain't that great, man, we make shitty records. I don't know why ya like us."

The decision to hire an outside producer for the next album is more a political than an artistic choice. In part it's to defuse a growing concern among the members of the band that the Grateful Dead are not able to produce themselves. After *Wake of the Flood* and *Mars Hotel,* it's all gone pretty much asunder. We aren't plugging in, we aren't selling records. So we hire Keith Olsen to produce *Terrapin Station.* He's recently produced *Fleetwood Mac,* that group's break-through album, which has made its way to the top of the charts and gone gold and there are more than a few among us now who would like to get their hands on that gold. Lesh is very happy with the choice, as is Weir. Weir idolizes Fleetwood Mac, he's in love with the whole L.A. thing. He wants to see the Dead get a giant hit record. Garcia never thinks in terms of hit records.

The band begins recording in January 1977 at Sound City Studios in Van Nuys with additional overdubs at Automated Sound Studios in New York City. All-night recording sessions. We take over a shoddy motel on the Strip as a day sleeper crash pad. Addams Family housekeeping arrangements, with maids coming in at night when we Dead awaken.

Jerry as usual hunkers down for the duration, the rest of the band come in and put down their parts and leave. Garcia and Olsen sit there at the board into the night with Jerry coming up with new lines and new ideas — it's a joint effort. The rest of the band has little to do with the making of the album. Sound City is a particularly sterile environment. Even the food comes out of vending machines.

Keith Godchaux's habit is going full blast during these sessions. Heavily into downers, Quaaludes, and Percosets, he's becoming a space case. He's using China White. He'd asked me to turn him onto my connection in Los Angeles for pills and found that this guy could also get him heroin. He comes to L.A. addicted to Percodans and slides almost immediately into heavy addiction.

After the sessions are over, Keith Olsen takes the 16-track tapes to London to "sweeten" them — add horns, strings, and choral singers — in an impeccably hip way, we're sure, but still the prospect causes alarm. Where's Keith?, where's Keith? He's gone, it's a done deal. WHERE ARE OUR TAPES? WHERE ARE THE MASTERS? WHAT?! THEY'RE IN LONDON?! WHAT ARE THEY DOING *THERE?* THEY WENT THROUGH THE METAL DETECTOR AT THE AIRPORT?!? IT COULD HAVE *WIPED OUT* ALL THIS WORKKKKK!!! Phil is incensed. How dare he do this and not *tell* us??? Jerry, ever laissez-faire, says, "But we *hired* the guy to produce us, lets see what he does with 'em. If we hate it we can always, like, write 'em off."

"The Terrapin Suite," one entire side of the album, ends up being orchestrated by Olsen with Paul Buckmaster, who'd worked on similar projects with the Stones, Elton John, et alia. It is recorded at Abbey Road studios in London by the Martyn Ford Orchestra using almost a hundred musicians and singers.

Terrapin Station is released on July 27, 1977, and goes gold a few months later. Critics and Deadheads find it overproduced. Jerry's initial reaction is "What are they complaining about? The performances are much better than we were ever able to flog out of ourselves — it actually sounds like a record! People aren't going to believe it's us." To accusations that the Dead, especially on "Dancin' in the Streets," are becoming blatantly commercial, verging on "disco-Dead," his attitude is "Fuck 'em if they can't take a joke."

But the proof of the pudding will be how many of the songs are going to make it onto the live playlists. That's usually the real test of where the commitment is for the Grateful Dead on these things. If the Dead enjoy doing it for an audience that enjoys it, it'll stay, and the rest is just chaff, it's gone. Only a few of the songs from *Terrapin* ("Estimated Prophet," "Dancin' in the Streets," "Samson and Delilah," and "Terrapin") end up really working in concert. Privately, Jerry and Hunter both think the album is too manufactured, too un–Grateful Dead–like.

◎

During these days, Jerry is still deeply involved in the band's business and comes into the office religiously. He gets to the Dead office in San Rafael early in the morning, even before the secretaries get there, always the second or third one in. The usual schedule has Rifkin showing up around ten, Sam Cutler bounding in not long afterwards, and around eleven I amble in. Frances Carr and Annette Flowers are there by then to answer the phones. We go into an inner office and . . . start snorting coke. Great plans are made on coke. Jerry is there to make sure the plans happen. This is *his* office and at this point, it's a vast complex. Weir's girlfriend, Frankie Hart, is running the travel agency, Fly By Night Travel, and Sam Cutler has a major booking agency going full steam. He handles Doug Sahm, the Sons of Champlin, Cipollina's band, Copperhead, and New Riders of the Purple Sage. We have an awful lot of people and stuff out on the road including roadies, trucks, PA equipment. Sam is hiring people right and left and they're all drifting in and out.

Garcia sits in this little back corner office and anytime we need to check in with the boss, we run back there. A secondary inducement to consult with him is the blow. He'll shake out a pile of coke on the tabletop and there's always a rail two and a half inches long on it. And this is just the coffee break. Lunch is at three o'clock. We order miso soup, something we can digest, maybe some noodles and vegetables if the blow was really bad.

Jerry likes to bring his guitar and sit in the corner of my office. I have the deepest darkest dungeon of an office in the building. Turns the phones off and sits there in splendid isolation — nobody else knows he's there. And as soon as we're dispatched to look after these various matters, Garcia settles down with his coke and his pipe and plays his guitar and practice his guitar books, with us dropping in from time to time to check in with him and he says, "Okay," or "Forget it."

"Well, we got an offer from Pittsburgh, we got an offer from Cleveland, we got an offer from Cincinnati, and we're trying to put together a Midwest tour. . . ."

Jerry dispatches Cutler to check out the distances, how long the crew would be out there, how long it takes by truck to drive from Pittsburgh to Philadelphia.

Sam Cutler runs out of the room and comes back with the timings: "It's five hours to here and three hours to there, and then we have to figure in how long it's gonna take to set up, so let's add that on to the travel time."

Meanwhile I'm hacking away on my calculator, working off of a formula that looks like the Ohio tax system. I push in "Ohio" and it spits out exactly what it's gonna tax us. Every community, every city has a tax, every county has a tax, the state has a tax. Then I have a bottom line and at that point I go after the promoter. It's still a theoretical proposition — after all the logistics and statistics, we present it to the Dead.

Cutler, as the booking agent, has to deal with the mileage and the temper of the crew. When asked to travel 250 miles from Syracuse, New York, to Philadelphia, you can bet they're in a foul mood. Everything on the road is designed to aggrieve and torment the crew. Because of union hours and codes, they've only got a certain number of hours when they can come into a hall and unload all the gear. They often have to get up at five, get over to the hall, and they've only gotten into town two hours ago, traveling all night, one guy driving, the other guy sleeping. And then they've got to deal with surly union stagehands, the most uncooperative group of people on the planet.

And if you don't grease them, forget it! So there's the grease money to be discussed.

And Jerry is paying attention to all this stuff! He's into it! God is in the details, babe!

"I don't want a surly crew," he says. Well, good luck on that one, Jerry. They started out surly and the road has honed their boorishness to a ferocious edge.

Until we brought Sam Cutler on board in January of '70, it was my job to manage this sullen lot. The crew is a much more pigheaded, intransigent, willful, and sulky quantity than the band members. Most people who do manual labor have the same attitude: they think any other kind of work is shirking. They're also ungrateful; the band takes great care of them and the crew just shits on them. The Dead think of themselves as tough-minded, down-to-earth guys, but man, are they easy. They are ruled by a bunch of kids who never got out of high school and have never worked for anyone else in their lives.

Trying to see Jerry backstage is like getting through Gadhafi's Iron Guard. The equipment guys are jealous of the band's meeting any-body that might ask them to do something that would involve the crew having to move some equipment. Garcia hates it but does noth-ing about it.

The Grateful Dead are the only band I know of that has such an obnoxious crew. The Eagles, the Jefferson Starship, they've still got that family thing going, everything is just so *easy* — the one drawback being the music. Everybody looks after each other, not like the back-stabbing Dead crew, where everybody's territorialized and paranoid and job insecure.

One of my principal jobs is dealing with another scaly group of individuals: promoters. Promoters are all gamblers and most of them lose big time at the tables. We're always running into these guys with both thumbs broken — "Oh, this? I fell off my bike." There is no end to the nefarious schemes of promoters. Reselling tickets, adding fold-ing chairs, and on and on. My main concern is not getting screwed out of our money, an almost nightly struggle requiring cunning, ruth-lessness, and nerves of steel.

We run into a promoter in the South who has used our ticket

money to buy a large quantity of bad cocaine. We'd been warned that he was planning not to pay us and was going to try to pass off this bad blow on us.

We're sitting in the promoter's office with the roadies, Messrs. Ramrod and Rex and Peter "Craze" Sheridan and Hurd, and representing the band: Phil, Weir, Kreutzmann, and Jerry. They've come along, too, because they know this promises to be an amusing episode. The promoter walks in with his briefcase, the one that should contain money.

I say, "If there's blow in that briefcase, don't even open it!"

The guy goes pale — twenty shades of gray. He was gonna flash me with this cocaine and have me take it instead of the money.

"Let me tell you something: Contrary to what you may have heard we don't take cocaine in payment for concerts. We've already got your advance, now we want the rest of the money. We have a deal. You owe us another fifteen thousand dollars."

"I don't have it, I don't have it!" Wringing of hands, grimaces of despair. But we're not impressed. "Here, this is all I got, take it or leave it." And he gets his goon to open the briefcase and sure enough, there's the bad blow, the whole room fills with this awful cat piss, kitty litter smell.

Hurd and Rex pick this guy up and shake him down — literally — in front of the band. Pick him up by his ankles and shake him and money comes *pouring* out of his pockets, big *rolls* of it that he's been collecting from the concessions and the head shops. There's almost the whole amount right there — but not quite — so Ramrod says, well, let's go over and look in his desk! Ramrod rummages through all the drawers of the desk and comes up with another five thousand dollars — we got it! Maybe. We're going to have to count it. We take it back to the hotel, stick it on this queen-size bed, and spend the night snorting coke — better than his! — and counting all this money. The bed is covered with bucks, rolls and bundles and tied-up fives and twenties. We double-check and double-check and double-check and the higher we get, the less we are able to keep track so we just say, fuck it, we're going to the bank in the morning! But, not to worry, the roadies have the promoter held hostage, handcuffed to a radiator in a room down the hall. Charming.

We go down to the bank in the morning with all of this money and send it through one of those canning machines to count it. We make our nut with a few bucks to spare, which we give him back. Just to show him we're nice guys.

⊚

All right, for our next album we're not going to fall into the mistake we did with *Terrapin Station*. None of this cool professional attitude in fully automated studios. This time we're going to use someone certifiably funky — Lowell George of Little Feat — to produce.

Lowell reminds the Dead of Pigpen and their roots and Jerry loves him for that. We love his inspiration. Lowell says: "I like the old Dead, let's get *that* sound. How did you used to play 'Good Lovin''? How would Pigpen have done it? Guys, let's boogie."

The dude is laid back, for sure. Wears his Oshkosh overalls, a big baggie of coke hanging out of his hammer pocket.

On *Shakedown Street,* Lowell records the basic tracks live, which is really the only way the Dead can get a good basic track — playing together, not with the drummers isolated and Jerry coming in later and adding his guitar. Just do it full-on.

Lowell takes this one step further. "We're not going into the studio, period," he announces. "This is where you rehearse, right? We'll do it right here. We'll get some baffling, put up some curtains and deaden it down a little bit, hang some stuff from the ceiling, and we'll get it right here."

And that's where the band cut *Shakedown Street,* at the Dead's rehearsal studio, 20 Front Street, which is nothing but a big old garage. Shakedown Street is Front Street, a particularly seedy area of San Rafael. The general lowlife ambience is well depicted on the cover of the album. Jerry loves this sort of scene: pimps and hookers, dealers, greasers, garages, Angels, winos, the impeccably seedy Bermuda Palms Hotel and Whitey's masterpiece of a sleaze lounge, Pepperland, right across the street.

One day I'm making my way through the parking lot of the Bermuda Palms when there's a very loud explosion, followed shortly thereafter by a long-haired hippie chick flying out of a second-story window holding a 'base pipe. She lands on her fanny still holding the pipe with a what-the-fuck? expression on her face, unscathed but for a few scratches. She'd been up in her room making cocaine 'base using ether and must've left the cap off the ether bottle when all of a sudden the gas wall heater kicked on, ignited the ether fumes, and blew her, the window, and most of the furniture from the room into the parking lot. A classic Front Street tableau.

The Dead have played "Good Lovin'" forever but in the old days when Pig was still alive, they did it in more of an R&B style. Lowell wants to record it that way, to bring back the old vibe of the Dead as a dance band and short circuit the warbles and woofs of *Wake of the Flood* and *Blues for Allah* and *Terrapin Station*.

We already have one 16-track machine at Front Street and we hook up another one up to it. The soundboard is separated from the rehearsal area by curtains and sonotubes, these being giant round cardboard tubes that serve as a breakup for the sound. Since there's no booth, we communicate with headsets. If Lowell wants to discuss something at length with the band, he gets up and runs around the sonotubes.

They play as a band to get the basic tracks, then they augment them — at this point, we're talking thirty-two tracks, so there's *plenty* of room for all kinds of overdubs. Some of the vocals on there are double-tracked. Mickey Hart's a perfectionist. You often find him down at Front Street; he'll stick around all afternoon but by six or seven he's worn out. Jerry will just be getting going, playing his guitar with his headset on, Lowell's doing his thing, getting the drum mix right, and Jerry's playing along with it. His guitar is just wonderful on *Shakedown Street*. Although Lowell doesn't play on the album the fact that he's a rhythm guitarist means he can run over to the piano, or pick up Jerry's guitar and say, "How about you do a comp, rhythm thing here *chukka-cak-chukka-chak-chukka-chak* because Bobby ain't nailing it." He can just take his guitar and do it. He also does wonderful things with the vocals. Weir sounds like Howlin' Wolf on "Good Lovin'."

Normally when you go into a recording studio you hear the play-back blasting out over these big booming Altec Lansing speakers at ear-splitting level. But Jerry's method of mixing a record is unlike anyone else's I've ever seen. He listens to the playback over tiny six-inch Bose speakers. You can barely hear it. He turns them way down and sits right in the middle sliding up and down the console in his roller chair making his adjustments. You come in to Front Street and it's like a library. *Shhhhh! He's listening!* Garcia's hunched over the console *scanning,* insectlike, with antennae twitching. He has this undying belief that if you hear it quiet and it sounds good, it will sound good loud.

Healy, God bless his soul, sets up a little radio station out of 20 Front Street. He searches around for a channel that isn't being used and broadcasts from the board so Jerry can drive around the neighborhood and hear what the tracks sound like in his *car*. "If it sounds good in my car, it's gonna sound good in someone else's!" Jerry cruises around San Rafael, picks up his laundry, goes to the grocery store, scores, and listens to the mix on his car radio. Only Jerry and Healy know the frequency!

Healy ends up doing this at concerts where we're sold out and have a huge crowd of fans who can't get in. I go out to tell everybody, "Tune in to 95.5!" People could turn on their car radios and listen to the Grateful Dead *live* right from the sound mix. He'd broadcast it right out of anywhere, any football stadium. We did it in Philadelphia a couple of times, we did it all over the place. He'd find an available niche and blast it out there.

◎

We now return our souls to the creator and as we stand on the edge of eternal darkness, let our chant fill the void, that others may know: In the land of the night, the Ship of the Sun is drawn by the Grateful Dead. . . .
Egyptian Book of the Dead

That was the *Egyptian* Grateful Dead, dude, you see we took our name from . . . oh, never mind. Even if the band's name had nothing to do with the mysteries of Ancient Egypt, this was fun stuff and eventually the band started talking about doing a concert at the pyramids. In 1978 we decide to just go ahead and do it. We've been touring continuously all year and we're right in the middle of *Shakedown Street*. We manage to convince ABC to cover the event and get an offer of full cooperation from Jihan Sadat, the wife of Anwar Sadat, the president of Egypt, who asks us to make it a benefit for one of her charities.

But once planned there is the age-old dilemma: How are we going to get our drugs in? We've heard that Egyptian customs are extremely strict and no one wants to risk getting caught bringing Persian into

Egypt or relishes the idea of getting off the plane and looking for needle park in downtown Cairo. The only other solution is to take a bunch of pills along. A *lot* of pills. From our experience of jonesing on European tours, you could take sixteen Percodans and two Dilaudid and still feel uncomfortable. Itchy and scratchy.

And then there is a breakthrough. One of the guys from Kingfish, Bobby's band, knows someone who knows someone who's recently ripped off a pharmaceutical supply house and sells me a bunch of pills. So I'm sitting on top of Percodans, Percosets, Demerols, Dilaudids and on and on and on. I stuff them into official-looking little brown medicine bottles, get a bunch of labels from a pharmacist, and in my capacity as drug embalmer to the Grateful Dead begin typing "Take one every ten minutes. Do not operate heavy machinery." Make up a doctor's name, type this shit out, peel it onto the brown plastic bottle, and we have enough downers and narcotics to keep everybody straight enough to play. In order to get anywhere near a Persian high, you have to take like four Percodans every couple of hours. It's very strong stuff.

Now that that's taken care of, there's one minor problem. Nicki and I both want to go and there's only one ticket. Being a gentleman I let her have it. I'm to follow later, on the Led Zeppelin plane, which is now carrying a bunch of Brahma bulls to Addis Ababa and has been converted from a sybaritic flying rock palace into cattle pods. Not the most appealing method of travel, but I don't have much choice. When I get to Texas to meet up with this flying cattle car, I find it out of commission due to engine failure. I'm strung out, and I've stupidly sent all the pills on ahead. It's all I can manage to catch the next plane back to California.

The Dead played three nights (September 14–16) and the third night had an eclipse of the moon, the full moon in eclipse. There was the usual hippie folly, trying to wire the Great Pyramid to a pedal that Jerry was supposed to play with his guitar, with Cutler & Co. crawling all over the pyramid trying to find the little vent holes so they could drop the wire right down into the king's chamber. But they couldn't get enough wire to go all the way around and into the gallery and eventually had to give it up.

After Egypt we were supposed to do a tour of Europe, but we still have to finish mixing and overdubbing *Shakedown Street* so we cancel the concerts. The album's release is slated for November 1978 to coincide with a national tour, so the pressure is on. It's the first time we ever coordinate a tour with the release of a record.

The album is never really finished. Lowell had a problem and he didn't know it. We didn't know *we* had a problem — we're all using the same damn drug and he was overweight and died before his time — seven months after *Shakedown* was released.

Shakedown Street gets mixed reviews but it has three great songs on it: Hunter/Garcia's "Shakedown Street" and Hunter/Hart's "Fire on the Mountain" and "Good Lovin'."

⊚

It's around this time that Francis Ford Coppola is working on the soundtrack for *Apocalypse Now,* looking for jungle music for the up-the-river sequences, when he comes to a Dead New Year's Eve gig, hears the drum break, and knows at once that this is exactly what he needs.

The soundtrack for *Apocalypse* is done with Hart and Kreutzmann and a panoply of other musicians including the Diga Rhythm Band members and Airto and Flora Purim, a famous duo from Brazil — he's a percussionist, she's a singer. Garcia basically does the engineering himself at Club Le Front.

Coppola installs some twenty-five thousand dollars' worth of sound and reflecting gear and a big screen onto which sequences from the movie are projected. The sessions go on into the night and Coppola ends up living at 20 Front Street, getting to know the wonders of the Bermuda Palms and Garcia's live-in recording style. Many nights he sleeps over, Jerry and he at either end of one of the couches. I come in the morning and there are the Smith Brothers. I can't tell which is which. They are both huddled under their Bekins moving van covers with their big bushy beards sticking out.

⊚

There was one more Dead album in this streak, *The Grateful Dead Go to Heaven,* released 1980. Give me a minute, I'm trying to recall the shapeless thing. I hated the name of the album to begin with. *Go to*

Heaven was Bobby Weir's idea. *Go to Hell* would have been better — and more honest! No one liked the lay of it. They're just too namby-pamby in the white suits and the smoke and you've heard all the songs already at gigs. I rail on about it but to no avail.

Go to Heaven is produced by Gary Lyons, who's worked with Aerosmith and Foreigner, yet another attempt to somehow weasel our way into the Top Ten — the Grateful Dead do Aerosmith's greatest hits! But *Foreigner?* It has to be a studio album — because of a stupid clause in our contract with Arista — and it is cheap to make. It takes longer to do the cover and make the vanilla ice cream suits that they wear on it than it does to cut the album.

In April 1980, the Dead perform "Alabama Getaway" and "Saint of Circumstance" on *Saturday Night Live* to coincide with the release of *Go to Heaven*. But despite the heavy airplay "Alabama Getaway" gets as a result of the *SNL* appearance, the album is another stumble for the Dead, squeaking — only just — into the Top Twenty.

The desire to go commercial tends to backfire with the Dead. The long break between studio albums is not just by chance. From 1977 to 1980, the band put out three consecutive studio albums using outside producers — *Terrapin Station, Shakedown Street,* and *Go to Heaven.* Designed for commercial airplay, they are in many ways less successful than the albums they were meant to supersede.

Following *Go to Heaven* there are seven years during which the Dead don't cut a single studio album. After *Go to Heaven,* there is nothing going on. Can't get them to record. It's coming apart, but I always think that even when things are falling apart it's especially important to keep material coming out. The Dead ride on the same old songs for the next seven years.

And *In the Dark,* which came out in 1987! I mean, have you seen the cover? You can't see a thing on it. You know the Beatles' white album — well, this is the Dead's black album! It's also the biggest album they ever did, because it had "Touch of Gray" on it, which I'd been trying to get them to release for years. They'd been doing it in concert for five or six years before they took it into the studio. It was everybody's favorite song, it was just a natural.

It tells you something when there are seven years between recording sessions. Something is wrong with the process. Jerry doesn't see performing and recording as separate activities. He tends toward what the Dead can do live, trying to generate that locomotion sound that they create onstage. The crowds keep coming back and back and back and back, but they don't buy that many records.

The live/studio dilemma reaches its ultimate compromise solution on *In the Dark:* playing in the Marin County Veterans Auditorium without an audience for that "almost-live" feeling. The basic tracks were laid down at the Vets Hall and then the recording and mixing were done at Front Street where all of the vocals and sound effects were added on. Finally! An album that has neither the energy and spontaneity of a live performance or the polish of a studio album!

20

Up in Smoke

<<<<<<<<<<<<<<<<<<<<<<<<<<<<<<<<<<<<<<<<<<<<<<<<

MAMA CASS IS dead, you say? God, that's right! And, fuck, Keith Moon's gone, too, so it's at least 1978, right? Oh well, right now exactitude isn't our main concern. These days we're trying to become *more* confused (and succeeding admirably).

At least I know *where* we are. UC-fuckin'-LA! They've finally broken out the home team dressing room for us. The *sanctum sanctorum*. It has taken us five concerts at Pauley Pavilion to get in there. Previous to this we'd been banished to the visiting team's locker rooms, which are crummy compared to the home team's. The home team's dressing rooms are carpeted, with killer showers and big beautiful lockers and a *lounge*. We're getting the royal treatment on account of Bill Walton, the UCLA star player. He has shoehorned us in. He'd made the Bruins number one and now he's put UCLA on top. He has persuaded the coach, John Wooden, to let the team practice to Grateful Dead music, if you can believe it!

And we have, as usual, made ourselves very much to home. Caterers out in back are barbecuing steaks; sauternes and Chablis and champagnes are chilling in buckets. And there are blonde college girls in shorts and tank tops running around, which is always nice. Who needs New Year's Eve?

Hey, there's Captain Gas! Without whom no party would be complete. He's got a long gray ZZ Top beard and a captain's cap with the anchor and scrambled eggs on it. And he's got his G-tank of nitrous oxide with him — complete with eight plastic hoses, each equipped with a dead man's cut-off that shuts off if you pass out and fall over. Let's not waste natural resources!

With eight people sucking on a tank, it freezes up fast and becomes a giant frozen bomb so frosty you could write your name on it on a Tijuana night in August. To free up the gas there're only two things you can do. You can turn it over, in which case the gas becomes liquid and dangerous — it'll freeze your heart and your lungs. Or you can drag it into the shower and heat it up, which is what Peter "Craze" Sheridan has just done.

The whole team showers together so there're like sixteen shower-heads per wall. Craze turns them *all* on. It's a rain forest in there with this frozen tank of nitrous oxide that is *slowly* thawing out. Meanwhile the roadies have talked a few coeds into entering the shower. This *Playboy* pictorial wet T-shirt thing going on. One of the girls has taken her shirt off. Their bras are gone and they're frolicking in the showers, falling *down* in the shower, *lathering* themselves up with the soap and the bubbles and sucking on the octopus — each one has her own clear plastic hose. Another five minutes and everybody is stark naked. I'd like to join them but I have other things to do.

I'm charging down the hall when the promoter runs up to me and says, "Rock, man, you better get it together. The Regents of the University of California at Los Angeles are here."

"Ha! ha! ha! Ha! Hey, that's not funny, dude."

"I'm serious. They're right behind me!" he says, and I look over his shoulder and — fuck! — there they are, these *stern* overlords of the executive caste in little Benjamin Franklin glasses. *Very* tucked-in, watch fobs, and discreet lapel pins entitling them to a personal cryonic crypt. Even the women are in three-piece suits.

A phalanx of pinched faces walking in tight formation, their next destination is the team locker room (our dressing room for the night) and just beyond that the showers where bacchanalian revels are in progress. Dr. Gas is stark naked except for that dopey captain's hat, which he wears even in the shower. People are passing out from the steam and the nitrous.

I know there's no way I can stop the dour army of Regents. They stride into the lounge. The leader of the delegation is like Rosemary Woods, a librarian from hell. Casting a beady eye around, briskly making a few marks on her clipboard. "The lounge and dressing rooms seem to be in order," she says. "Now, let's move on. We'd like to inspect the showers next."

"Uh, you mean, like —"

"Now!"

"Um, I don't think that's advisable just now, ma'am. I've got some crew in the shower, ma'am, you know, um, we're moving out of here tonight, would you mind coming back another time?"

"That's out of the question."

One of the gentlemen in the delegation pushes ahead of her. "Belinda, why don't I just go in there and take a look." He goes into the locker room, peeks into the showers, and stops dead in his tracks. He's speechless, riveted to the spot. His mind is split in two. Half of him wants to tear off all his clothes and join them, but the other half (the half that owns four thousand shares of 3M) is appalled.

It's the *way* he stops that alerts the rest of them. What could it be that has so paralyzed our Mr. Metalfatigue? The Regents want to know. They all rush in — including this woman.

Half a dozen healthy Southern California Valley girls cavorting with a bunch of degenerate beer-swizzling, gas-breathin' crazies. And this naked guy wearing a captain's hat passed out on the ground with a big hard-on. Reader, we blew their minds. I'm told some later moved to Denver. Would you be surprised to hear that we were booted out of there that very afternoon and told we'd never play there again? Or not for another year, anyway.

We are now *definitely* dependent on Persian, and I think it's safe to say I can add "drug courier" to my résumé. I make arrangements for packages to be sent to the cities we're playing. We divvy the stuff up when it arrives. Jerry gets his, I get mine, whoever else is partaking gets theirs. The idea being that this is your *daily* ration and that's all you get. Garcia, of course, always runs over his quota.

We develop these foil pipes that hang up the tar on its way up. The more tar that builds up on the inside of the foil pipe, the more you have left when you run out. You melt it and then chase it down a little runway with a ramp — the pipe. We call this residue "rat," and it is strong stuff. You know if you haven't opened up the pipe and smoked what's inside, you still have some left. In lean times we get by on rat.

We use the airlines to ship dope. I have somebody run it out to the airport in an envelope, put it on a plane, and it gets there like clock-work until some weird hippie at TWA recognizes Jerry's name on the package and takes it. The first time it happens, we're in Philadelphia. I'm jonesing in the Philadelphia Airport waiting for the shit to arrive and it never shows up. I know it got onto the plane, but somewhere along the line somebody stole it. This little glitch leads to a day and a half of the shakes. Garcia is too junk sick to perform the following night. Prescriptions from the hotel doctor help, but we use up all the pills the first night to get rid of the shakes. In Washington, a desperate Garcia decides to do a radio interview in the middle of the night and "put the code out."

Garcia's nodding into the mike during the interview. On air he asks fans — in code — to bring their stashes down to the station and he will sign albums for them. He says, "Uh, anybody *down* with Garcia out there tonight? You wanna come *down* to the station? I'll come *down* from up here and sign autographs, but bring me some *down*."

Thirty kids show up at the station reception with grass, 'ludes, uppers. Uh oh, the *wrong* drugs! Oh God, now he wants to get more *specific* on the air, spell out what precisely he needs. We send kids out to get downers and tranks to get us through the night.

◎

Jerry and are I easily doing $700 a day of this stuff. A gram costs $700, and it never sees the end of the day. When we can't get dope, Jerry goes onstage full of Valium. Bumping his nose into the microphone, tottering around and dozing off midsong. And the songs are all dirge-like and *sloowwww.*

In Boston, Garcia refuses to come out of his dressing room unless he gets some dope. Even when we're not on tour, I am now roused in the middle of the night to get packages off planes for Garcia.

I've also become the band paramedic. Since we can't risk consulting local doctors about drug-related problems I develop an over-the-phone description of symptoms with Dr. Weisberg: the color of urine, dilation of pupils, etc.

Jerry's the only band member with a specific attachment to Persian. The others are fairly indiscriminate. Billy Kreutzmann does it whenever it's around, but he's never strung out. He's into everything: drinking, Persian, cocaine, pot . . . *whatever.* He just wants to get to a certain state of mind and it doesn't matter to him how he gets there. Hart gets totally strung out, as does John Kahn (the bass player for Garcia's band), and Keith Godchaux is in the worst shape of all.

Phil Lesh is addicted to wines. Never did Persian; has never been addicted to anything illegal as far as I know. In his youth he used speed, dropped acid in his eyeballs, tried everything he could lay his hands on, and then settled into French wines.

Bobby Weir had a brief encounter with heroin with the Kingfish band and that was it. He'll use a pill now and then to go to sleep or wake up, but he never becomes dependent on any of it. He has more self-control than anybody else in the band. Which is interesting because looking at this spaced-out kid one might think that he'd be the most likely candidate for addiction. The only drug he's ever been addicted to is LSD, which gave him a good frame of reference.

Jerry, on the other hand, when he finds a drug he likes he never wants to be without it and will go to any extremes to get it. The other guys in the band know this about him. They're crashing and they know that he has it, so they beg me to go get it off him.

"Hey, you don't want Jerry to get sick, do you?"

"Well *I'm* sick, too," Mickey Hart is claiming.

Kreutzmann's on my case, too: "I'm fucked up, I've got the shakes."

"God, you guys, why didn't you tell me about this before we left?" Keith Godchaux is the worst, a nightmare. He never lets me know and never makes plans and then hits on me constantly. *Heavy* leaning.

"C'mon, man, I'm the piano player, I can't play this messed up!" Meanwhile Donna Jean is saying, "Don't give him any, Rock."

"Don't worry, I don't have any."

Donna Jean doesn't do any of this stuff. She smokes grass, of course, but grass in the Grateful Dead camp is just like a salad — that you smoke.

Keith Godchaux is daily getting more and more out of it, nodding out at the keyboard. His forehead, midset, just collapses — crash! — onto the piano. He actually gets lost between Atlanta and Buffalo. When you're this fucked up, anywhere can become the Bermuda Triangle. Constant, terrible fights in hotels with Donna Jean. In Buffalo, I find her huddled behind the soda machine out in the hall, shaking and crying.

The fighting gets so extreme that Donna Jean and Keith Godchaux each have to have their own limos. Keith is becoming increasingly demanding and grandiose. He insists his own *tuner* go on tour with him, and Donna Jean is telling me she can't travel without her rocking chair! We have a case built to transport it.

Things get worse than they already are when Donna Jean and Bobby Weir start having an affair. Keith is now kicking in doors, punching people. We begin auditioning new piano players, and by the end of '78 we've pretty much agreed on Brent Mydland as Keith Godchaux's replacement. He's from the band Silver (and had played with Bobby and the Midnites). The Godchauxes are asked to leave the band. It is quite an accomplishment to be so strung out and weird that you're actually asked to leave the Grateful Dead! Or so I think at the time.

Just over a year later, on July 21, 1980, Keith, after two days in a coma, dies as the result of an automobile accident.

New Year's Eve, 1978. The Dead have been doing New Year's Eve bashes for a couple of years now. It's become an institution and a very big deal. But at this particular one, Graham is not allowing the Hells Angels in wearing their colors. What does he expect them to wear, blazers? Anyway, we've already invited the New York Hell's Angels and a bunch of other chapters to come and they all show up at once — of course! — on a hundred and fifty motorcycles. They want in the back door (with their mamas), which, at Winterland, is one of these huge metal gates that clanks open like a rusty drawbridge. It has a little door cut into one side of it, and outside knocking on this door is Tiny — Tiny, of course, is as big as this room.

"Let us in!" says the giant. The door opens and through the open door the whole hall can hear the roar of the motorcycles. Everyone knows the Angels are here.

It is just bad timing on Graham's part, but he's smart enough not to deliver his edict in person. We have a powwow in this little cold storage anteroom right next to the back door, where we store the Heineken. Angelo from Richmond and Badger and Sandy Alexander from Manhattan are standing around waiting for Graham to show up, but Bill has more sense than that. The Angels have fiendish plans for him.

"We may have to hang him out the building or take him up to the air ducts and, you know, and gas him."

I interrupt their reveries: "Let's cool it with the serious bodily harm, dudes, the Grateful Dead will refuse to play if Graham doesn't allow you guys in! For one thing, you're on the guest list. . . ."

And just at that moment this freak takes off his clothes and starts running around — a naked freak flying all over the concessionary in the back of Winterland. All the security guards are black and not one of them will touch this white boy with a hard-on, so Graham's lieutenant, Jerry Pompili, asks a Hells Angel to help out. The Angel *yanks* the guy up and throws him into the Haight-Ashbury free clinic. There's always a medical unit at Grateful Dead concerts, to deal with the kids who take too many downers or too much wine.

And right at that moment, while Pompili and the rest of Graham's honchos are distracted, Sam Cutler opens the door and a motorcycle *runs* into the building and zips right up the ramp and onto the stage and then we park it and bring in another one. We're going to have them rev up during the Rhythm Devils set.

The show starts with a screening of *Animal House* followed by Belushi and Ackroyd doing their Blues Brothers routine, then the Flying Karamazov Brothers juggling act, then the New Riders. Kesey & Co. join in on the "Drumz>" sequence — pot-banging being a Prankster specialty. John Cipollina jams on "Not Fade Away" and "Around and Around" at the end of the second set.

Bill Murray and Franken and Davis come out to join the festivities. We have a roadie standing at the top of the stairs to the stage. If you want to get backstage — where the action is — or even *on*-stage, you have to get a drop of acid put in your soda or beer. Black and white 7'2" monsters from the Portland Trailblazers (Bill Walton's team), Golden State Warriors, and Washington Redskins lumbering around on acid backstage along with the dealers and hipsters, while the Dalai Lama, Francis Ford Coppola, and Herb Caen from the *San Francisco Chronicle* watch the festivities.

The Dead stage has a maze of alleyways underneath it, an incredible netherworld of cables covered with rubber padding so that you don't trip over them. The only way out to the audience is usually from under the stage. There're other parts underneath that are like little clubhouses you can go down into. Nitrous oxide isn't allowed on the stage, but no one said anything about *under* it. When the band isn't playing, you can hear the gas running and the people laughing down there. There's a scene in *The Grateful Dead Movie* where everyone is sucking on the nitrous octopus. That's belowdecks at Winterland.

Janis's old dressing room has been converted into the Nose Room. Bill Graham has glued plastic noses from Groucho Marx masks all over wall and wired the room with speakers with sniffing sound effects.

Around midnight the Dead start playing. It's now time for Nicki and me to be lowered from the ceiling dressed in our skeleton costumes. Just part of the job! I have the top hat and Nicki has the crown of roses. We are two scared-shitless guys.

A long, *long* show. Three sets, two encores. Last "Dark Star," O ye mystic Deadbase watchers! When they start playing it, the however-many-days-since-the-last "Dark Star" banner goes flying off the balcony. During the encore — around 7 A.M. — the band put their arms around each other to sing "We Bid You, Goodnight." At dawn Bill Graham puts on a breakfast for seven thousand, and after that Ray Zimmerman has rented a boat to take everybody on a cruise but it never leaves the dock because he's afraid we're going to get seasick. We're fucked up enough already.

New York, September 1979. When we played Madison Square Garden in July we'd broken all attendance records. We've come back to do another sold-out show. But there's a price for success of this magnitude. Twisted minds in lonely bedsits are plotting even as we sleep. About six hours before the set we receive an ominous note:

"Jerry GARCIA dies 2NITE!!"

A Jerry Garcia death threat! I'm impressed. With this, he's officially a star. Elvis, Jagger, Dylan, Wayne Newton have all got them. Well, Wayne Newton even I can comprehend.

During the sound check we get a phone call from the creep himself, asking in a garbled voice if we received the note. The cops trace the call, break into the sender's house. They find a gun permit, but no gun.

We still have a good relationship with the police these days. We hire off-duty cops as our limo drivers and never have a problem. I'm telling everyone we meet on tour that I never found a better cop than in New York City. The precinct that deals with the Garden is Midtown South, which is a pretty heavy beat. They handle a lot of scary shit and are glad to get assigned to a rock concert. And there's never a problem at Dead concerts. This is still the old days (they don't waste their time busting kids for acid). The cops like working Dead gigs because the audiences are so easy to deal with. It isn't a rowdy AC/DC crowd. Grateful Dead fans present them with the fewest problems they have ever encountered.

"Gee, what is it that makes those kids so mellow?" they ask.

Jerry's reaction to the death threat is almost medieval: "That laughing Jap! I knew it would create problems for us sooner or later. *Baaad* fuckin' karma, baby!"

He's referring to the Grateful Dead skull with the lightning bolt icon. That's what he thinks has done it. He's always been afraid that some ritual killing is going to take place because of it and the Dead will be blamed. He doesn't, thank God, say this to the police captain. He just tells him: "Hey, you protect the *president,* just do the same thing for me."

The police strategy is worthy of Monty Python. The first twenty rows are cops disguised as Deadheads in yellow tie-dyed T-shirts and shorts. Our one proviso is that they not bust anybody for drugs during the show. Healy goes out and buys a bunch of infrared scopes and has the roadies scan the audience continuously. The would-be assassin never shows — so far as we know.

During the set Garcia remains remarkably calm, but after the gig he goes absolutely berserk. He goes back out onstage, I assume to thank everybody for rallying around, and over the PA system begins *ranting:* "WHO THE FUCK STOLE MY STASH? Where's my BINDLE? I left my bag here and you guys STOLE all MY DRUGS! I'm not leaving until one of you motherfuckers turns it over!"

In front of the promoter and the union crew — and the place is still crawling with cops! He's describing his fucking bindle of Persian in shockingly gory detail *so they can look for it.*

On this 1979 East Coast tour we get tight with John Belushi and Dan Ackroyd from *Saturday Night Live.* They've bought a neighborhood saloon down in the meat market in the bowels of Manhattan, opposite a nude bar called the Sweet Shop or something. It's their own private bar where they can party all night long with their friends, and no one can stop them! It's almost invisible from the outside. All boarded up with steel roll-down gates in front and not a single neon beer sign to indicate that anything is going on there.

It's ancient, built in the 1800s with old wide plank floors. And behind the funky old bar there's a wooden trapdoor that you can pull up and walk down steep wooden stairs into what might be a dungeon. Stone walls and a low ceiling of old wooden tree beams. Here the serious partying goes on. Jerry spends most of his time down here in a cloud of white dust. There are huge friggin' lines laid out on top of cases of Heineken. Sometimes there's a rail of coke on every stair as you go down.

Garcia's most recent obsession is Kurt Vonnegut's *The Sirens of Titan*. He's bought the movie rights. It's playing — right now! — in his head. "Hey, maaan, if I may: A man and his dog are about to" — *snoooooooort!* — "materialize out of thin air by way of the chrono-syn-clastic infundibula on the lawn of a large estate. . . ." The intercortical cameras are rolling.

Vonnegut's premise is one that would naturally appeal to Garcia's sense of the absurd. The world's great monuments are simply *very large handwriting* meant to be read from outer space.

Garcia explains it all: "See, Salo, this Tralfamadorian, is stranded on Titan waiting for news from his home planet about a spare part for his spaceship and — dig this! — the reply is written on Earth in huge stones — Stonehenge! And the meaning of Stonehenge in Tral-famadorian when viewed from above is: '*Replacement part being rushed with all possible speed.*' The meaning of the Great Wall of China is: '*Be patient we haven't forgotten about you*' and so on."

Few could resist the lure of the Blues Brothers' club. One night Francis Ford Coppola shows up and we try to interest him in doing the film of *The Sirens of Titan*. He's astonished anyone would even try. "You can't make a movie of that, it's *philosophy*." But Garcia is con-vinced it *must* be brought to the big screen! He begins casting about for screenwriters who'll take it on.

In order to goose the project, a major meeting is held with Garcia and Ackroyd and some of the *SNL* writers about raising development money for *The Sirens of Titan* using some of their connections. Jerry hates meetings, so to keep his attention we invite the delectable Amy Moore down to the bar, and between Amy and *piles* of cocaine we figure we can get him through it. At this point Tom Davis and Michael O'Donohue begin writing the screenplay. It's an almost impossible task, the book is a satirico-cosmic tract. The funny bits aren't really filmable, they're *verbal,* and without them the plot is a preposterous interstellar chicken without feathers. As far as I know they're still trying to get the shapeless thing to fly.

Local precinct cops love to come down to the Blues Brothers' bar because they can always talk to someone from *SNL* or a visiting rock star. They like to hang out and drink and observe these people close up. TV stars! Rock legends! In one of the funkiest saloons in lower Manhattan.

Ray Zimmerman, who's Belushi's manager (and runs the bar), has an amicable relationship with the First Precinct. In other words, they leave him alone. They know Ray doesn't have a license, it's a private bar. When the local precincts come around, he gives them bottles of Johnny Walker Red and glasses of ice and they're happy to turn a blind eye to whatever else is going on. Some of the guys even come in uniforms. It's a bit of an alarming sight to see a Hells Angel snorting cocaine off a bar with a uniformed cop right next to him drinking, and the band all doing drugs in the basement.

After Grateful Dead gigs — and especially after they do *Saturday Night Live* — there are mondo jam sessions there. The usual logjam: seven guitar players, four keyboard players, Kreutzmann on drums and Rick Danko from the Band on bass and, occasionally, a sax player named Mars Williams who is starting a band called the Psychedelic Furs.

All the musicians squeeze into one tiny corner of this little bar. There is a PA system and a drum kit — that way people can just come down and plug in and jam. Belushi always sings with whomever is playing. He loves all the Stax-Volt bands and he has the jukebox loaded with Otis Redding, Booker T and the MGs, Sam and Dave. He gets Garcia to teach him Otis Redding licks. A lot of the Blues Brothers schtick came out of Jerry's little tutorials. Belushi has a hard time remembering lyrics, but he can always make up spectacular ones on the spot.

Sometimes we go over to Belushi's apartment and hang out. One night Belushi and Kreutzmann and I go over to a recording studio where the Firesign Theater guys are recording and Belushi decides to see how many microphones he can steal (we have, needless to say, been drinking all night). Eventually Belushi's pockets are so full he falls down and can't get up again. He lies there thrashing on the floor with his clown face a mask of desperation, the shiny mikes and black mike cords spilling out of his pockets like giant mechanized spermatozoa.

"Do you know why it takes fifty million sperm to fertilize one egg?"

"No, why?"

"Cause none of them will stop and ask for directions."

The Blues Brothers' club is where some of the great *SNL* routines develop. It's their lab. They can try out riffs in a very receptive environment. The samurai dry cleaner, Ackroyd doing Mick Jagger or Nixon. Ackroyd's Nixon skits lead to us doing a radio spot featuring an intense Richard Nixon trying to scam Grateful Dead tickets.

August, whenever. One of those really hot days in Oregon. They do have them, you know. It reminds me of that day in '72 we spent at a benefit for Ken Kesey's brother's creamery at the University of Oregon, in the woods on the Long Tom River. Hottest day in Oregon's history. It was so hot the *redwoods* were sweating. Twenty-five thousand people were coming through the woods, taking their clothes off. Half the crowd with tops off, the others stark naked. Garcia got hit with heat prostration and passed out onstage. Bobby Weir was puking. People were dropping like flies, ambulances screaming through the woods. The only islands of relief from the unrelenting heat were under the parachutes on old telephone poles (or one of Ken's gin and tonics).

Today is even hotter. 110 in the shade. We're on our way back to the motel in a VW Bug, Garcia, Page Browning, and myself and a G-tank of nitrous oxide slung in the backseat. We're breathing gas and driving at the same time, which is really a no-no, and, due to some, uh, distraction the Bug skids off the road and turns over on its side. As it does so the fucking top flies off the G-tank in the backseat and immediately the entire inside of the car freezes up — this is in 110-degree weather.

We get out of there just in time! Or we would have been found frozen inside like an exhibit: "Three hippies in a VW Bug, late twentieth century." They'd put us next to the Woolly Mammoth from Siberia in the Museum of Natural History.

Once outside everybody's going, "CLOSE THE DOOR, close the fuckin' door, SAVE THE GAS!" Volkswagens are supposed to float in water, the idea being when you close the doors, the car is airtight. The

Bug fills up with nitrous oxide in seconds. It is frozen solid, a furry ball of frost in the middle of a hot summer night. It's so frosty you can write your name in the ice! Which Page has the presence of mind to do. He writes: "WILD THING, I LOVE YOU!"

A few minutes later the highway patrol shows up just as I'm pissing on the door lock to get it open. The frozen Bug is all fuzzy with frost like it just came out of the freezer.

"And what happened here exactly?" the highway patrolman asks. I'm not saying a word. I let Page do the talking.

"Waaall," says Page, "as a matter of fact we have no explanation for it, officer. It's like spontaneous combustion or somethin'. It's a god-damn mystery."

Jerry senses this is not a good tack and picks up the slack, beginning with a supposedly rationalist approach: "Oh, officer, we must have hit an icy spot." Right.

"An icy spot!" says the incredulous cop. I'm standing behind the good officer trying to signal Garcia to cool it. He's still trying to explain a completely iced-up VW Bug in a heat wave.

"We don't have any idea how it happened, officer. Just came round the corner, slid off the road on this, um, vestige of ice." The patrolman walks up and down the road. Of course you can't see this icy spot, but were all obviously sober. We're come down *fast*.

Eventually he leaves, scratching his head and muttering: "Damndest thing I ever saw. . . ." We're pissed off that all the gas is sealed in the car and we don't have a clue how to suck it up. Do you open the window a crack? Can you fill a balloon from a Volkswagen full of nitrous oxide? Let it melt is what were gonna do!

☉

June 1980. A short tour of the Northwest and Alaska. It's the Summer Solstice in Anchorage, Alaska, which means it's dark for about five minutes a day. None of our kids can go to sleep. Even with blackout curtains, the rooms are bright as day. An ideal place for people like us who never want to go to bed, anyway. Two in the morning and the sun's still blaring right overhead like it's noontime. And the bars are humming. We sit up watching the sun sink two-thirds below horizon.

Grim Hilda, the archetypal pain-in-the-neck groupie, follows us up to Alaska. There's nothing more fearsome than a Garcia-smitten Deadhead with credit cards. No sooner do we get into the hotel than the desk clerk says, "Mrs. Garcia already picked up the key and went up to the room."

Grim Hilda is the most notorious in a long line of "Mrs. Garcias," and she's tenacious as hell. I thought we'd shaken her back in San Jose where she was sitting by the pool making goo-goo eyes at Jerry. As we checked out, Parish, our roadie, nudged her into the pool and filled her handbag with shaving cream. Once she was in the pool, *bang!* we were gone. It slowed her down some, but she just jumped on the next plane. The morning after the last gig Garcia opens the door to his room and there she is! He's on the phone to me screaming. "HELP ME! Grim Hilda's HERE!!! Get down here *IMMEDIATELY!*"

"How the hell did she get in?"

"I DON'T CARE IF SHE CAME IN ON A FUCKIN' BROOMSTICK. GET HER OUT!"

Jerry doesn't like confrontation. He'll never tell anyone himself to get out. He wants to be the nice guy. Instead he'll call a bouncer (like me).

When I get up to Garcia's floor, I find him out in the hallway. Grim Hilda is in the room refusing to budge. I call management and they send up security, who pry her loose. She's relieved of the room and taken downtown and booked (for harassment, or maybe impersonating a rock star's wife).

We get on the plane to Hawaii and *damn* if the last person to board isn't Grim Hilda! She has gotten out, paid her fines, and is on her way in the time it takes us to get out to the airport. But — *aha!* — she doesn't have a ticket! In other words she's bogused her way on the plane saying she is with the Grateful Dead ("Oh, the road managers got my tickets") and gotten on the plane just before takeoff. I inform the captain and they keep her on the plane for the return flight to Anchorage.

⊚

June 7–8, 1980. Concerts at the University of Colorado at Boulder celebrate the Grateful Dead's official fifteenth anniversary. Fifteen years of the good ole Grateful Dead! There's a time, sayeth the preacher, to rejoice and a time to reflect. And upon reflection it's clear that it is around this time, late seventies, early eighties, that things begin going seriously awry.

Previously there'd been a clear-cut line between those who made things happen and those who were just kind of there. And there were only one or two band members who were actively involved and initiating stuff. A lot of momentum came from people like Owsley and Dan Healy and Rex Jackson. The others were all nice people but they didn't really have that much to say. For years they didn't even write songs. The day it began to dawn on them that you get more royalty money by having your own songs on an album, they began writing. Unfortunately it was around this time that Jerry got strung out and lost his ability to steer the band.

If I were to pinpoint where it began I'd have to say around the time of *The Grateful Dead Movie*. The Dead movie was made wholly and solely by Garcia and Healy with a little help from Eddie Washington, but everybody else that was anywhere near it was either trying to scam something from it for themselves personally or — if they weren't involved — were jealous of Jerry's spending all that time on the project. And, with Jerry down in L.A. much of the time, little wheels began to turn.

One of the myths of the Grateful Dead is that it's a democracy. That's an admirable ambition; unfortunately, it's not true. The Grateful Dead has always been and always will be Jerry Garcia. And when the king abdicates — as Jerry does constantly — the kingdom falls into the hands of manipulators and thieves. Garcia's never been really good at being in charge, has he? He passes the buck any time he can. Jerry will squirm out of *anything*. He can't deal with unpleasantness of any kind.

What E. M. Forster said of *Tristram Shandy* might equally have been said of the early Dead: "There's a god at its center and its name is MUDDLE." In those first rambunctious years we would have taken this as a compliment. As our fearless leader once said: "Formlessness and chaos can lead to new forms. And new order. Closer to, probably, what the real order is." This was the high, cosmic energy of the Acid Tests and the early Haight.

For a long time anarchic mischief propelled us. It was a magic force. But now the Dead have become engulfed and paralyzed by those very forces of chaos they once rode like a wave. What we have now is no longer Taoist chaos or fertile anarchy but the default. And we all know what flourishes in the default.

That Garcia was being held hostage by the Grateful Dead had been obvious for years. Jerry wasn't blind, he could see that the Dead were stagnating, turning into a Haight-Ashbury version of the Buffalo Bill and the Indians show, but any murmur of taking a break — as we did in 1974 — to rethink and revitalize the Dead was met by laying a huge guilt trip on Jerry. The babies, the kids, the hospital bills. "We've all got families!" Big wringing of the hands and weeping. There's a huge jones there for the money. Everybody who works for the Dead has been so well paid for so long they can't let the cash cow go to pasture. They've got mortgages and car payments and God knows what, and all this has swamped the original ideals of the band.

Nothing captures the mindless maliciousness of the default frame of mind like Robert Hunter's Five Commandments of Rock 'n' Roll:

(1) Trash the people that are gone.

(2) Trash anybody around you that's doing anything you're not.

(3) If you don't understand it, it's fucking with you.

(4) If somebody's got something better than you, go out of your way to take it away from him.

(5) Don't volunteer for anything.

The Dead had the chance to be different. In the old days, adventure was our mission. Let's try it! Healy always wanted to take the band to the Grand Canyon and play, but it seemed as if the more years went by, the harder it got to do anything besides go to the same old places.

It seems like everything that starts out as genuine in America eventually hits the road and starts selling tickets to itself, turning into self-parody in an amazingly short amount of time. And, let's face it, *authenticity* is just about the most marketable thing going. Still, I never thought I'd see the day.

(◉)

August 31, 1981. We're playing the Aladdin Theater. Vegas, babe! Hippies invade the polyester capital of the world! VW buses full of hair pulling up in front of the Flamingo and Caesars Palace, clouds of marijuana smoke trailing after them. Droopy guys in tie-dyes and cutoffs. And the Bobby Darin lookalikes in sharkskin suits observing this Furry Freak Brothers intrusion can't believe their eyes. Whaddafug is this ovah heah? Serious infractions of the Italian-American dress code. Lounge lizards are *sharp* dressers, you better believe it. Sprayed trim jobs, immaculate hair, pussy ticklers, tanned — *perfect!* All night long, one crazy low-camp high drama after another. Dacron vs. tie-dye.

It's probably a hundred degrees outside, we're in this air-conditioned mausoleum with bells going off every few seconds, the slot machines in the background going *ping! Pa-chung!*

I'm trying to check the band as a mountain of hippies and hippie chicks pour into the lobby. We've reserved the whole fifteenth floor — except for maybe *twelve* rooms — and I hear next to me at the front desk this guy in patched Levi's and a string vest going, "Yeah, give us something on Floor 15." I'm going to myself, "Oh, no, we have hippies on the floor!" These are some of the grubbiest-looking guys in the world. Long dreadlocks and beards that have never been washed, reeking of smoke — it permeates the whole lobby — and they're pulling out gold cards and *rolls* of cash.

Weir's going, "Man, where did they get all of that money?" This is before we realize that there is a lucrative side business going on in the parking lots at Dead concerts and in the hallways — grass, LSD, and cocaine. Whatever they think the band is doing, they sell.

The hippie chicks are already over at the gambling machines throwing away fifteen cents and getting complimentary drinks. Meanwhile through the mirrored ceiling men in suits are watching the scene at the front desk with avid interest. Hippy-dippies with gold cards! Deadheads in ragged jeans and sandals and Guatemalan shirts checking in with rolls of hundred-dollar bills! When Las Vegas sees rolls of hundred-dollar bills, they just go apeshit. They are saying to themselves, "Hey, we got ourselves some high rollers!" They don't, of course, understand that these people are not going to drink. They're not gonna have *one* drink the whole night and if they do, they'll ask for a free one with a roll of nickels, s-l-o-w-l-y throwing the nickels into the nickel machine while ten Deadheads *partake of the experience.* This isn't Vegas's idea of high-rolling.

Wait a minute! What are those freaks doing over at the craps table! There must be fifteen, twenty of 'em, at least! But when the camera zooms in it'll turn out to be only one Deadhead from New York, the one Deadhead who knows craps (he's been to Atlantic City). Meanwhile, every time he wins something all his friends are reaching across the table, grabbing the chips and the croupiers are beating them back from the take.

"No, no, no! That's not your money!"

"But we won! It's ours!"

The croupiers have pencil mustaches and after-shave and hair so slicked it looks painted on. They are profoundly *shocked* — not at the tatterdemalion clothing, the hairy armpits, the tits showing in see-through blouses, the reeking beards and torn jeans, but at the breach of etiquette. Ain't they got no respect? The sacral solemnity of the gambling tables has been violated!

Deadheads are sweeping the money this way and that and the croupiers are whacking their knuckles with their canes. "Aw man that *hurt!*" Deadheads aren't used to pain!

It's an anthropological misunderstanding. The croupiers can't comprehend the Deadhead thing at all. The group mind. One big unification party at the Grateful Dead concert, where we take you now. Backstage to the Great One's dressing room.

"Rock, I'm falling asleep here, where's your stash?"

"Don't look at me, I don't have any."

Between sets, when he doesn't have what he needs, Garcia sends me out into the audience to score.

"Go out and find somebody. If he's got any, bring him back, now!"

No sooner do the other band members see me going out into the audience than I start taking orders for various chemical cocktails. Kreutzmann goes, "Know anyone with blow?"

"Yeah, it's all over the building."

"Well, GO GET ME SOME!"

"Okay, but you're gonna have to put up with the guy that's got it."

"Aw, I'll sign a drumstick or something. Here's some passes!"

It's easy to spot them. The guy that's nodding off in his coffee has downers, the guy with big birms around his nostrils like he's been eating donuts is obviously the coke freak. Usually I don't even have to look; they come up to me.

"Scully, Scully, can you get me backstage?"

"You got any?"

"Hell, yeah! A solid eight-ball, man!"

"How is it?"

"Best you *ever* had, I swear, man."

"Sure, sure. Okay, come with me."

I loop a plastic pass on and it's full speed ahead and don't spare the horses.

"This is Jerry Garcia. . . ," I say, opening the door to his dressing room, but Jerry doesn't have time to socialize.

He goes, "BREAK IT OUT!"

Scronnnkkkkkk, aaahhh-hhhhhhaaaa-ha. And that is the end of the audience.

I go, "Say goodbye to Jerry." The kid's happy just to have been in his presence. He can go around the hall saying, "Jerry's doing my blow!"

We get back from the gig and there're people camped out in the hallways, with shower curtains pulled over them. People turning blue in the lips. There's loose pot on the coffee table and lines reeled out to the bathroom. Drugs on every surface.

Deadheads are bribing secretaries at our travel agency in San Rafael to find out what hotels we're staying in, greasing the phone operators with fifty-, hundred-dollar bills to spill the room list and then book hotel rooms on our floor. One Volkswagen full of hippie people spend all their money to find out what floor we're on and then sell that info and squatter's rights to other Deadheads and they all pile in. It's like Calcutta, fifteen, twenty people to a room, sleeping on the floor, in the bathtub.

We end up with Deadheads like Sunshine and Tex having rooms on our floor and inviting all their friends up. "I'm on the same floor as the Grateful Dead!" They leave their doors open and there's pot smoke everywhere. And here comes Captain Gas wheeling his tank of nitrous oxide into the hotel and onto our floor. Filling balloons with nitrous — *bzhhhhhhhht!* Balloons are exploding. All the doors are open and everybody's camped out on the floor of the *hallway*. It's their living room!

And we're in a sense protecting them. I've hired ex–New York narcotics officers to look after us (we're greasing them good). They've just gotten acclimatized to the Dead thing (sort of) and now this. They're asking, "What's with these guys, are they with the band?" Obviously I'm not going to snitch on them, but I'm in constant fear of getting busted.

There's Fat Freddie who's stashed three hundred sheets of blotter acid — with zonked Mickey Mouse icon — under the bed in a glassine Zip-loc envelope and forgotten it. And then suddenly realizes there's thirty thousand hits of blotter acid under the mattress and the room is in his name. It's a bust! So he sends an underage girl to go up to the hotel room and get it. But the maid's already found it when she made the bed and the cops are waiting there with the rubber gloves. "Oh, is it yours, sweetie?"

Not long after we move into the big outdoor arenas, Grateful Dead concerts become the focus of serious police harassment. And the little creeps have the nerve to start getting political and high-tech! They're up there in the booths using binoculars and walkie-talkies. These guys in the stands sitting up there where John Madden used to report on the football games, and they are all the FBI and the CIA and the DEA and the BNDD, Bureau of Narcotics and Dangerous Drugs for the State of Nevada, are watching our audience and any roach that gets passed is a bust! Down amongst our fans are the hippie-looking cops — they're about as convincing as hippies on *Hawaii Five-O* but somehow it still works. A guy in a headband sees somebody smoking pot and says, "Oh, can I have a hit?" And, *bang!* Sudden little flurry of activity right in front of the band. Where it really starts to make a dent on us is at the Nassau Coliseum. That's pseudo-Nazi country out there. Another fascist enclave being Milwaukee.

Now not only are we in Las Vegas, it's Las Vegas, *Nevada*. The State of Nevada doesn't tolerate loose change. Whatever loose change is around *they* want it. Anything that they can't control is dangerous to them. You can have a career as a hooker at any state-accredited pussy ranch, but no freelance *anything*. They have ads in the newspaper for bordellos: Sex workers sought today, come on down now. No prudes need apply.

They especially don't want drugs. Most of the money in Las Vegas *comes* from drug money in New York and New Jersey and so on. And the Deadheads come here in all innocence smoking weed — these Volkswagens full of hair, bringing their stash with them, roaring out with this pile of smoke and they have no idea that they can be sent away for life in Carson City, Nevada, where the state pen is. The laws are incredibly harsh for anyone caught with even a joint. It's worse than Texas.

Deadheads have to be warned specifically. We are such a magnet for dopers that our audience becomes a target for police enforcement surveillance. They're rounding people up in the parking lots and setting up sheriff's substations to photograph everybody. They lock up these kids briefly and then let them loose until they have to come back for the trial. We are getting letters from parents whose kids have gone to jail for eighteen months for holding one square of window-pane acid. That's when we start sending out letters to fans warning them.

The Dead realize that they are major bait. We get really careful about how to book our hotel rooms and who knows where we're staying. I often put Jerry on another floor to keep him away from the fray. The major action is generally happening on the crew floor. Depending on whether or not there's an old lady along, Kreutzmann likes to stay down on the crew floor to check out the talent. The hallways are just parked full of little hippie chicks.

Deadheads occasionally find Jerry sitting in the hallway. So do I. In the morning on my way downstairs I'll come across a forlorn Garcia sitting on the floor outside his room. He's been there all night waiting for me to wake up.

"Garcia, what are you doing out here in the hallway?"

"I can't find my key."

"Well, why didn't you go down to the desk?!"

"I'm scared."

"Jerry, you're the reason we're all here! We've got thirty rooms in this hotel and everybody else has booked the rooms because of you, what *you* do. You're the Great Barcia!"

Actually, he doesn't look like the immortal Ludwig van Garcia this morning, I'll tell ya. Jerry's trying to make himself very small because he thinks he's the weirdest-looking guy in the whole hotel. Our fearless leader has apparently taken too many drugs. Too much blow and you get paranoid. You're afraid what the guy at the desk is going to think of you for losing your key. You're so far ahead of yourself you're thinking his thoughts for him and — just maybe! — transferring them to him.

What if I go down to the lobby and the desk clerk doesn't *believe* that I'm Jerry Garcia? After all, everybody *else* has tried to check in as Jerry Garcia (or Jerry Garcia's wife). So he just sits in the hallway. It's typical of Jerry's character to keep it all under the hat. Jerry's just like one short flight away from the Deadhead dormitories. He could've gone down there and found instant bliss. Deadheads *prayed* for occasions like this. They would have moved out of their rooms for him. "Oh, you want a dry room?" "You want two, three girls to bundle up with?"

The meek guy sitting in the hall not saying a peep is the same guy who has no qualms about running out in front of thirty or forty thousand *straight* people and asking who stole his dope.

⟡

November 17, 1981. The Jerry Garcia Band are in Chicago to play a gig at the Uptown Theater. We're having dinner with Geraldo Rivera at our swanky hotel in Chicago on the edge of Old Town. We've laid on champagne and caviar, the whole bit. He wants us to be on his show, a *20/20* segment called "Not Too Old to Rock 'n Roll." They've got Grace Slick, Mick Jagger, Jerry Garcia, and one of the Beach Boys to do it.

Mick does Geraldo in, in the way only Mick can. Trashes him. ("So, Mick, in the last ten years or so you, me, our whole generation have gone through these immense changes and —" "Wot changes?") Now it's our turn. Mid-dinner Jerry nudges me. "Did ya bring your Visine with you?" We travel with LSD in eyedroppers, Visine or Murine bottles. Good for easy dispensing, too. A drop is fifty mikes, a hundred mikes. Two or three drops is a major hit. Jerry points out to Geraldo a fictitious rock star on the other side of the room, say, Rod Stewart. "Where, *where?*" Geraldo is frantic. Hmmm, let's see, about five drops in the bubbly should do it. The incredible thing is after this *huge* spike Geraldo doesn't seem to realize he's been dosed. I don't know if he knows to this day. But he is certainly acting strange. He's a basket case by the time of the interview, but the makeup people make him *look* really good. They have to keep stopping the interview because he is sweating so much! Garcia makes him smoke this big roach just before the show so his eyes are all red. The producer keeps saying, "Geraldo, are you all right?" He is so wonky they have to make cue cards for everything he says and even these he keeps flubbing. The card says something like "How long have the Grateful Dead been together?" Which comes out "How are you grateful?" It's hilarious. But the show turns out great.

⟡

December 31, 1982. Oakland Auditorium. The Mother of all Dead New Year's began with our buddy the deejay Jack Ellis asking Etta James if she's ever been to a Grateful Dead concert. Etta James is a legendary

R&B singer and a big bad woman of the blues and she naturally says, "Now why the hell would I want to do that?"

"Because," says Ellis, "at a Dead show you can be anything that you want to be." And what can you say to that? If you're Etta you say, "Huh!"

Next, Ellis and his wife, Sue, drop by the bad pad that Jerry and I are sharing up on the hill in San Rafael. The four of us are listening to an Etta James tape playing in the background and Jack says, "Jerry, you gotta listen to this chick sing, man, you won't fuckin' believe it! She does an imitation of a fucking *trombone* in there." Three or four tunes into the tape, Sue and Jerry are talking and all of a sudden, Jerry says, "I *know* her, I've played with her before, like a benefit for a clinic or something." Jack says he wants to get her a backstage pass after she plays *her* gig because she's never seen the Dead.

"Fuck getting her a backstage pass, maaan, let's have her *play* New Year's!"

"Too late. She's already booked somewhere." No reaction for a minute, then Jerry goes bonkers.

"Do whatever you have to do. *Whatever!* Get Tower of Power as her backup band, I don't care." And that, as they say, was that.

Etta James has a reputation for being a no-show, and she's already late for the New Year's lesbian ball at the top of the Sir Francis or the St. Francis or something — the gig she's playing before ours.

Her husband has just been released from jail and they've stopped at a motel, but she calls and says — dig this — a plane has landed on the highway and they can't get around it! That's just for starters. The next reason she's late is that they won't let her out of the Fairmont. R&B Queen Held Captive by Lesbians!

It's getting close to midnight and she's still at the ball so we send over Leon, our Arab limo driver, along with the biggest black roadie we can find to yank her out of there, along with Jack Ellis as baby-sitter. Finally, she is released and dives into the limo. They're doing seventy across the Bay Bridge and Etta is yelling, "Slow down, baby, I'm not ready to die for you. Hell, I ain't even heard you play yet."

By twelve fifteen Bill Graham's people are panic-struck, but Graham himself is mellow. He climbs up on a ladder and — turns the clock back! Uh oh, he's obviously been dosed. Talk about fluid, man! He's like that Oldsmobile transmission — the Power Glide!

She's two hours late. Weir and Lesh get the keys to the songs down. The Tower of Power are primed. I send them in there and say, "You guys decide on the songs, Etta'll be here any minute." She saunters in about twenty after midnight. I holler to Lesh and one-two-three, they go into a tune.

Right before Etta goes on, Jack asks her if she needs anything. "A beer, a line, a joint?"

"Yeah, your fuckin' Niner jacket!"

Etta does a walk-on, about three-quarters of the way through "Lovelight." Bobby is totally plugged into her, Tower of Power love her, she is heartfelt and great with the band. They steamroll through Bobby "Blue" Bland's "Turn on Your Lovelight," Etta's own "Tell Mama," Jimmy Reed's "Baby What You Want Me to Do," Otis Redding's "Hard to Handle," and Wilson Pickett's "Midnight Hour."

It's something in the nature of a tribute to Pigpen since these are all songs Pig used to do. The Wicked Pickett's "Midnight Hour" is the only song they screw up. She can't get a handle on the lyrics and flubs them.

Etta comes offstage, raving about Hairy Garcia. "That mother-fucker Hairy in there, that blew me out, man, the motherfucker can play!"

I say, "Etta, it's Jerry, *Jerry* Garcia."

"*Harry?* Fuck you! Fuckin' Harry can play, man. He's bad, man, I never sang with anyone who could play five notes at once. He's some magician, I'm tellin' you!" She's ecstatic, but she can't get his name right to save her life. She's calling him "Berry," Berry Garcia and Bobby Garcia. And in her overbearing way she makes it *his* fault!

"Harry Garcia, Berry Garcia, Jerry Garcia, make up your fuckin' mind! What are you Latin or somethin'? You a Mexican, Jerry, I mean your folks?"

"My dad was Spanish."

"Aw, that's what they all say! Garcia sounds like a fuckin' beaner name to me. What you ashamed of, man? Mexicans, they got big dicks." She's almost got him convinced that his father wasn't Spanish!

Still, it's one of those moments when the Grateful Dead transcend, when everybody feels it.

"We're really honored, Etta. This is the first time that the Dead have backed a woman — aside from Janis, that is."

Veronica, Pigpen's widow, comes into Jerry's dressing room where we're all hanging out. "Honey," she says, "thank you, for bringing Pigpen's spirit back into the hall."

Mickey Hart comes in to pay his respects: "Where's that black queen o' yours, Garcia?" It's like the visit of the Magi, everyone crowding into the dressing room to share in the glow. Then Kreutzmann comes up and does his salutations. "Thank you, thank you for playing with us, Etta." He's laughing, he's tripping and cutting up a little bit with her but I can see he's been bit.

Bobby and Etta hit it off big time. I'm sitting next to her in Garcia's dressing room and in the middle of Weir's pledging-my-troth-upon-bended-knee speech she grabs my hand: "Get this white fool off his knees! Get this boy outta my face! What is he *doin'*?"

"Etta, he's part of the band and this is his way of welcoming you. We're hippies, you know."

"He's a goddamn white boy! Get this fool off his fuckin' knees! No one is on their knees in front of me."

Soon Bobby's sitting cuddled up next to her, like mother and son. Her father died last night and Bobby, who lost his parents a few years ago, is getting her through it. Or maybe it's vice versa. She could have put a blanket on him and he would have taken a nap right there.

In her Pentecostal quavering voice, Etta gets up and testifies. "I *understand* now, I come to *church,* I'm back in church for the first time in my life. Now I knows what you mean. I'm gonna go out there and thank Jack, but I want to thank you all for bringing church to me again! This is church music, baby, my kinda church, y'all understand? Tonight I gave myself back to *God!*"

And we're all saying "Hallelujah!" (and meaning it).

"This is the church's music, healing music. This is the Holy Spirit at work. Who would have fuckin' thought? From a bunch of stoned hippies. Now I know the Pentecostal flame can burst out *anywhere!*"

On the way home, in a gas station, Cipollina sings "Silent Night."

21

Before I Get Old

1981. LUFTHANSA FLIGHT 607 to Munich. It's just a short hop. May-be forty minutes. What could possibly happen on a forty-minute flight?

The minute the FASTEN SEAT BELTS sign goes off (accompa-nied by that mystic *ping*) Garcia is unbuckled, up and into the aisle. At 230 pounds he's a miracle of agility. His whole being is focused on *one thing:* getting into that first-class john before anyone else. And once in there, nothing on earth can get him to come out. I'm trying to catch his lunging eyeball as he nips into the aisle.

"Jerry . . . no, man! Jerry! JERRY! It's only a FORTY-MINUTE FLIGHT. *Please* do not DISAPPEAR."

"Say, what? Yeah, I'll take two."

Shit!

After Garcia has been in there about twenty minutes and a great long line of rich, irritated passengers has formed outside the first-class toilet, the stewardess approaches with a pained expression.

"Izt yer friend all right?" That's the first thing she asks.

"Nothing to worry about," I say, "just a bad case of the runs. We only got here a few days ago and he's not used to the food."

There's a high insanity quotient at twenty thousand feet, and folks get far more wiggy on commercial airlines than is generally conceded. It's a number of things: the thin air, the 3-D food, cabin fever, free-floating lust, fear that the thing in which you're traveling will hurtle to the ground and burst into flames, and the usual unremitting horror of having to make small talk with monomaniac synthetics moguls. All these tense, sexually aroused passengers locked in a metal tube careening through space at five hundred miles an hour. It's a fucking tinder-box of snarly petulance and acrophobia. The whole thing is as unnatu-ral as hell, and any sane person's basic instincts would tell him that the best thing to do is to get as high as possible and stay that way until landing. Which is just what Garcia does.

He has locked himself in the john with his tinfoil pipe and his Bic lighter, his bindles of Persian and coke. No kraut stewardess is going to lure *him* out. He might as well be in Morocco. Through the door I think I hear him talking to Neal Cassady down by that Mexican railroad track.

Another twenty minutes and queue frenzy begins to mount to fever pitch. Mutiny is in the air! It is a formidable mob. Serious multinational guys on their way to summit meetings with dire global consequences and they *can't get into the john!* The Great Khans of business and industry in Pierre Cardin suits and Jacques Fath ties, hothouse women on shopping safaris clutching fabulously expensive tiny handbags. All made to wait because of *him!*

A savage mood begins to take over. Smooth well-groomed faces are buckling under pressure. Becoming vindictive, seething, ratlike. A sort of alternate face — the real insect within — is bleeding through. Rage of the undead! It's an ugly sight. This could just be the moment when they snap. They're itching to get out the fire axes! They want that bearded weirdo in the john!

Get the keys to the emergency tool kit! Break out the hinge bombs, the pneumatic lock drill. . . . ROCK STAR FOUND DEAD IN PLANE TOILET. Emergency landing at an American army base. They'd love that! Waves of hysteria beating out. They're getting *high* on this shit. To what lengths, I wonder, will straight people go to avoid taking drugs?

"Lotte" — our stewardess — is coming down the aisle. Some tank driver's daughter but who cares, I find her efficiency sexy. I want to take her legs into a 24-track studio and record them. She's miming exasperation. It seems this is not the Lufthansa way.

"Would you mind asking. . . . Please!"

I unbuckle and go up and knock real loud, making sure everybody can hear.

"JERRY, ARE YOU ALL RIGHT IN THERE, MAN? THEY'RE GETTING A LITTLE *CONCERNED* OUT HERE." Some rumbling and cursing from within.

"He can't keep anything down," I explain to no one in particular.

Eventually the stewardess makes an announcement over the PA system: "We have a man in the forward lavatory who is sick. Please use the toilet at the rear of the plane." We aren't popular in first class and we know why. We have sent them to a pitiable fate, the tourist-class loo.

The suction drains in the bathrooms of commercial airliners are very convenient for smoking dope. Lean on the drain handle with one hand and smoke dope with the other; blow the smoke down the sink and the suction pulls it right out. This method works fine for taking the odor out of the bathroom, but the smoke clings to your clothes, and your hair reeks of marijuana as you walk down the aisle.

This is Persian base, however, and there is no telltale odor. Persian is an opiate, obviously, but it's more refined than heroin. It's more in the morphine category. The method of smoking it is called "chasing the dragon." You melt the brown powder with a little flame under a creased piece of tinfoil until it puddles into a golden honey brown liquid which you let roll down the tinfoil gulley (called "the runway") by tilting it. As it burns, the Persian gives off smoke that you inhale through another piece of tinfoil rolled up into a pipe, which we named "the ramp." You constantly move the burning Persian back and forth in the tinfoil runway so it doesn't get hung up on particulate matter. When the smoking puddle of liquid Persian gets to the end of the runway you tilt it back the other way. You go after the smoke, staying right behind it, picking up the smoke as you go down to the end — hence the name "chasing the dragon." You then quickly turn the runway around, holding your breath and getting ready for the next run because now it's up at the top of the hill again.

The drug, combined with the method of smoking it, is a totally absorbing business. All life is in that little Sisyphean pool of Persian rolling up the hill of foil and down the other side giving off its mind-numbing fumes.

On the Concorde — where there's only *one* bathroom for the whole plane — the situation has been known to become critical. International incidents develop. Unlike your standard flight with your usual assortment of subnormal Eurofreaks selling each other ball-bearings and condoms, on the Concorde you have your seriously important people in a state of severe agitation. Heads of state, overpaid deejays, ex-kings of Yugoslavia, Sonny Bono's grandmother, Grand

Viziers of the Exalted Order of Elks, the man who invented Baggies. Not to speak of your actual Hollywood celebrities. All banging on the door of the loo, demanding that the captain turn the plane around . . . and who but Garcia, in there for the whole three-and-a-half-hour, harrowing transatlantic flight.

Today's flight to Munich is forty minutes, tops, but the band has settled in for the long haul. Like we were going to, say, *Australia*. Lunch, a movie, maybe a few cocktails to start. I'm trying to figure out how to get us all "deplaned," especially Garcia, who is, I'm not kidding, still in the bathroom. I'm slipping frantic notes under the door: "Landing in ten minutes" (first note). Then "Jerry: Come out NOW!" Goddamn sonofa*bitch*.

We're being told to secure our trays in the upright position, and Garcia is still in there. Never mind the illuminati, none of *us* can get into the bathroom! A quiet panic is setting in. Wait just a fucking minute! What am I going to do with my *drugs?* Gram and a half of coke, half a gram of Persian, little under one ounce of grass, 120 hits of acid (approximately), twenty Quaaludes. . . .

All through the cabin the same thought is popping into everybody's head: "What am I going to do with what I'm holding?" How the hell are we going to get into Germany with our stashes? No one is copping to anyone else that he's still holding. The only thing I don't have to worry about is *Garcia's* stash: that is definitely gone.

Usually there's a group effort to stow the goods really carefully. Drugs get to our next tour stop *way* before we do, so we can always count on having something waiting for us when we arrive. We haven't been in this situation since we used to travel around the U.S. on commercial airliners. When we went through the metal detectors back then, it was always a surprise to see who was holding what. Jerry used to carry his stash in a small round metal tin and every time he'd go through the metal detector it would go off. They'd open it up and there would be thirty-four bindles inside. But they had no idea what these little cardboard packages were. They never examined them. Probably figured it was something hippies were into. Origami, maybe. But Germany is going to be a different kettle of fish. They're very serious about these things (and just about every *other* thing). We are all in the icy grip of Border Angst.

The minute the plane lands we peek outside just to reassure ourselves we are being paranoid, and lo and behold up on the observation deck (where families and friends normally gather to watch the planes and wave) we see . . . *sandbag emplacements.* Everywhere there is the German military in gray uniforms and very weird helmets with long tonguelike flaps going down the back of the neck. The place is bristling with automatic weapons. It's World War Two! Turns out the Baader-Meinhof gang and the Red Brigades have recently given the Germans an excuse to arm themselves to the teeth!

Band members creep off the plane tight-lipped, glum, and not a little apprehensive. German security troops stand around rocking their machine guns as the bags are off-loaded. Even the baggage crews are packing pistols, and they march out in a *column.* The passengers file out of the plane in two neat rows.

The German's love of orderliness is well known. Never having gotten over the straight line, they are a tidy, obedient people with a desperate horror of chaos. Everything according to plan! But they are about to meet anarchy itself in the shape of a gonzo juggling act called the Karamazov Brothers. We'd run into the Karamazovs in London and asked them to open for us in Munich. A scraggly outfit to begin with, after three weeks on the road they have gotten seriously ragged.

The Karamazovs get off the plane wearing clown costumes and top hats and swinging bowling pins. The Cats in the Hats at the Munich Airport! The only thing the Germans have ever seen that looks anything like them are the local chimney sweeps.

The Karamazovs' luggage consists of suitcases with no handles, taped together with rock 'n' roll tape and stickered all over with labels reading: NUCLEAR DANGER ZONE! and CONTENTS UNDER PRESSURE.

In the customs hall there are two lines. If you have nothing to declare you go to the green zone, otherwise to the red. Naturally we make a beeline for the green, but the zombies are having none of that. They beckon us over. Let's face it, we are as red zone as they've ever seen. Unkempt, degenerate, acid-eating beatniks.

It's as if Genghis Khan had arrived at the gates of Vienna. Could we possibly be Lebanese bombers, PLO operatives? *Warum nicht?* People who look like us are capable of anything. All other business stops. They wave most of the passengers through — and brace themselves.

For once the Dead are the sedate ones — trying to make themselves as inconspicuous as they know how. Creating the usual ruckus are the Karamazovs, who can afford to act as outrageously as they please since they aren't holding. They have pot waiting for them in Munich, so they don't give a hoot.

They begin juggling! Stacks of top hats, ashtrays, and airline cutlery are whizzing through the air. In the end they create such a scene that the Dead breeze through customs. The Customs Officials from Hell are busy obsessing on the Karamazov circus. Everything about the Karamazovs fascinates them. The authorities turn all the top hats inside out, prying loose the felt, peeling back the headband. Feeling up and down the pants, taking the heels off shoes. *Nothing* is going to get through. They actually take samples from the Karamazovs' "flaming objects act" and send them off to the lab.

But nothing fazes the Cats in the Hats. They are actually feeding off the adrenaline rush. They are inspired. In the middle of this incredibly intense search of their luggage one of the Karamazovs cuts the tape off this black beat-up suitcase, flips open the top, pulls out a gun, and — before anyone can stop him — pulls the trigger. Out the barrel comes a big red flag with the word BANG! on it. The Karamazov Brothers are held for hours. Everything about them is suspicious. A box full of hatchets, bundles of old deutsche mark notes printed between the time of the Weimar Republic and Hitler's rise to power (one-mark notes to which zeros had been added with rubber stamps). These are just the basic tricks of their trade.

I see Garcia sail through and I say a little prayer. Now all I have to worry about is myself. I have one of those money belts with a zipper, and it's stuffed with assorted tiny packets. As the customs officer frisks me, the metal detector goes off. I remove the belt and place it on the inspection table. To my horror, there, for all the world to see, is the raised outline of all those little packets. The inspector takes no notice, however. He's looking for sticks of dynamite or plastique. Hey, maybe my luck is changing.

⌾

After we've all gotten sufficiently high back at the hotel, Bill Kreutzmann and Mickey Hart go out busking in the town square with the Karamazovs, passing all those hats around, the same hats they mesmerized customs with. Kreutzmann and Hart have hand-held Nubian drums called *tars*. They're made of goatskin stretched across a fine wooden frame and made taut by heating over a flame. While the Karamazovs juggle, Kreutzmann and Hart walk out into the middle of this hail of lethal objects: flaming hatchets, carving knives, saucepans. To the audience it looks absolutely hair-raising, as if some deadly missile were going to take their heads off at any moment.

But they're drummers, of course, and they're counting. And like drumming, juggling is done on a count. The hatchet flies on a two count, the bowling pin goes on a four. The crowd cries out every time a flaming ax skims the drummers' heads. It is wonderful street theater, and it gives me an idea.

Later that night. . . . The Karamazovs, in the middle of their act, are hurling a typical assortment of deadly weapons back and forth when out walks, my God, Jerry Garcia, apparently very stoned and completely oblivious to the carving knives, irons, and flaming hatchets whirling inches above his head. He strolls absentmindedly over to an amp, plugs in his guitar, and, as he tunes it, slowly backs up . . . right . . . in the path . . . of great, lethal hunks of flaming metal. The audience are out of their seats, mouths gaping, holding their heads, covering their eyes, *screaming* "DUCK, DUCK!" "JERRY, LOOK OUT!" And then, at the last possible instant, Garcia steps forward and the first fiery ax whizzes past — *Whoosh!* — missing him by a whisker. As the next flaming hatchet hurtles toward his head, he bends over — in the nick of time! — to adjust his volume control. The audience is still howling "*Achtung!*" as the last axhead locks in on the Great Bearded One. Even the Karamazovs are miming helpless horror at the murderous metal fireball now spinning out of control and headed directly for Garcia's head!

JERRY GARCIA DECAPITATED ONSTAGE BY FLAMING HATCHET! Wow! But wait! Jerry spins around and — miraculously! — the last incendiary ax glides by him. A great cheer goes up, prayers to various local saints are heard. Slowly, however, it dawns on some folks that *three* near heart-stopping scrapes with death are too many, even for a sacred buffalo such as Jerry Garcia, and they burst into applause. It was a lovely hoax, and it wasn't even him! I had found a fat German hippie who looked enough like Garcia — the long hair, the beard — and put him in a big baggy black T-shirt and sent him out there. He sure could count.

The Dead have been touring continuously since their comeback in '76, averaging around seventy gigs a year. Except for Egypt, this spring tour of '81 is the band's first trip outside the U.S. since '74. They're playing dates in England, Denmark, Germany, France, and Spain. Back in San Francisco before we left we'd been asked if we would be interested in going to Amsterdam to participate in the One Word, One World Poetry Convention, being as the Dead are songwriters and therefore technically poets. We're flattered to be invited but I don't think about it until Bremen — the deadly zone.

The Stadthalle in Bremen is one of those excruciatingly lame German gigs. They're not riotously enthusiastic about the Grateful Dead in Northern Germany. We have a healthy following in the big cosmopolitan cities, Frankfurt, Munich, Hamburg. But we're not exactly the Beatles. In places like Düsseldorf, Essen, and Bremen everybody's like, *was ist los?* And tomorrow — the opening day of the One Word, One World thing in Amsterdam — it seems we have a day off.

"Hey, Jerry, want to go to Amsterdam, go meet William Burroughs, Jim Carroll?"

"Jim Carroll, the *Basketball Diaries* guy?"

"Yeah! And Simon Vinkenoop and a bunch of other hairy degenerate beatniks."

"Vinkenoop? You mean *the* Simon Vinkenoop? Who the hell is he?"

"Uh, a famous writer guy, the poet laureate or something, and his wife is like the national tennis champion. And they say he has the biggest library of psychedelia in the world" (I'm shameless). "But never mind about all that, it's sex and drugs and all the great living poets on the planet."

"Well . . ."

At this point it's just Jerry and me. I don't even ask Weir. I don't think he'll want to go, and I want to make this jaunt as simple as possible. Since I'm trying to be the road manager of this weird tour, I don't feel like carting a bunch of irate musicians along on my day off. But Garcia slips up and tells Weir that we're going to Amsterdam (hash, beatniks, etc.) and Weir wants to go. Weir is always up for escapades of whatever stripe.

There's adventure to be had! I think. Anyway, I'm going no matter what, because I want to see Jim Carroll, whom I met last year in New York. I figure it's a waste of time asking anybody else in the group;

we're leaving at 6:30 in the morning. I can't believe I'm doing it, myself. Garcia deals with it by coming at it from the other side — he just stays up all night. He loves adventures.

It's a matter of finding a taxi in this godforsaken place at the crack of dawn, catching a plane to Hamburg and on to Amsterdam. Simon Vinkenoop meets us at the airport and takes us into town, to this Gothic little hotel, two old buildings put together. Carroll and Burroughs are staying here, too. Burroughs, in porkpie hat and raincoat, looking like a ghost, is checking out as we arrive. He says the hotel is not seedy enough for him. It makes him nervous.

I introduce them — although they've met many times before, Burroughs doesn't have a great memory for rock stars. "Mr. Burroughs, do you remember Jerry Garcia from the Grateful Dead?"

"I've always liked the name of your band," says Burroughs. He repeats the words "the Grateful Dead" solemnly. ". . . wonderful occult ring to that. Never heard your music, though." Jerry offers him a tape, which he politely pockets, but you know he'll never play. In his esotero-pedantic strange Midwestern way, Burroughs wants to know does the name come from the old folk tale or is it from the Egyptian ship of the sun?

"Well we always thought of it more as, uh, the death of the ego than any specific legend," says Garcia.

"Good," says Burroughs like an indulgent tutor of occult sciences. "That is the way Jung would interpret it, too."

Garcia and Burroughs have a good old laugh about the name of the hotel — in Dutch "The Turtle" — the traditional name given to dealers. They always keep you waiting.

One of the appeals of coming to Amsterdam is dope, which is not all that hard to find here. We're with our Mr. Clean, Bobby Weir, so we have to be a little circumspect, but while he's checking out the cafés, Jerry and I pick up some opium and spend the afternoon high as kites at Vinkenoop's library of psychedelia. He's got the single biggest collection of books on psychedelic drugs in the world, and the Dutch, being who they are, have made his house into a national landmark on which he no longer has to pay rent. When he dies the house and the library go to the state and it becomes a museum, which it is already! *Everything* you'd ever want to know about psychedelics is here. Dr. Hoffman's bicycle may be in here somewhere for all I know.

The auditorium where the reading takes place is packed with

international literati. Garcia and Weir are applauded as they enter. They're treated like visiting dignitaries. More importantly they're treated like *poets*. It's flattering to rock stars to be welcomed so spontaneously into the immortal company of the bards. Kesey's here. "Great you came, man!" says Kesey. "Would Kerouac have missed this?"

The convention is moving over to the Melk Weg (Milky Way) for the musical part of the evening. Jim Carroll's a poet with a rock 'n' roll band and he's going to play over there. After the reading he talks Weir and Garcia into playing too. Garcia and Weir have brought their guitars with them — what troupers! — and are totally game.

They do a beautiful acoustic set, just the two of them. "Monkey and the Engineer," "All Around This World," "Cassidy," "Jack A Roe," "On the Road Again," "Bird Song," "It Ain't No Lie."

The next day we fly to Munich and hook up with the rest of the band. After the Olympia Halle in Munich we play Ruesselsheim, near Frankfurt. But a terrible storm is rolling across Europe and our next set of dates — bullfighting rings in the South of France — get rained out. Our next date is the Hippodrome in Paris.

Are we going to sit around a hotel outside Frankfurt until it stops raining? Hey, we just got back from Amsterdam, had a great time there, so . . . why not play the Milky Way for a couple of nights? What is our alternative? To just waste money in Paris? To sit around until the rains abide and then go to Paris?

No sooner have I mentioned the word "Amsterdam" than I am howled down by the predictably provincial gentlemen of the crew. Shouts of "Paris!" "Paree!" "Moulin Rouge!"

"No! It's gonna cost too much!" I insist. "Whereas in Amsterdam we can *make* money. The Milky Way only holds fifteen hundred people, but it's *something*. At least we're not getting rusty, and we're paying our expenses. Otherwise with the whole bunch of us in Paris, we're going to go under on this tour."

The crew are going "Aaaw, let's go to Paris." Typical Oregon tourist mentality. You know, "Let's go to France where the women wear no pants."

"Do you know what the rooms cost in Paris?" I tell them. "It's like two hundred dollars a night — per person. And if you guys have got time off in Paris, you're going to spend a fortune. Do you know what it's gonna cost you for a Bloody Mary? It's gonna cost you two to four bucks a drink, easily. We can't afford to do this! So we're either gonna sit here in the rain in Germany and watch our dates in France get rained out, or we're gonna go have fun in Amsterdam. What do ya want? Where's your spirit of adventure, dudes?"

Garcia and Weir are egging the band on: "Let's go play Amsterdam, man. We had so much fun there, you guys. It was far out!"

Presented with the horror of three days in Paris, France, with nothing to do but go souvenir shopping, I lurch into my role as shameless shill:

"Guys! Do you know what they have there? Hookers, man, sitting in plate-glass windows in their panties and teddies. And hash everywhere. In fact, in the club we're playing there's actually a hash blackboard with different varieties of hash from around the world listed. Weir, Garcia, back me up on this!"

The crew finally agree to go as long as we don't take any equipment.

"How, exactly, is the band going to play?" I want to know.

Garcia says, "We'll rent the gear!"

"Guitars? You don't rent a guitar! Why can't we take your guitars?"

The whole bunch of us go, band and crew, but with no equipment. Why the crew are coming along I don't know. I end up having to run all over town to guitar stores *begging*. Healy cobbles together a Heath-Robinson PA out of all the junk people lend us.

Our advertising is ad hoc, to say the least. In the Netherlands, you can buy the bottom banner in the daily newspaper. We have the banner printed in red and white: THE OOPS KONCERTEN, GRATEFUL DEAD FROM SAN FRANCISCO, CALIFORNIA, MELK WEG, TONIGHT AND TOMORROW NIGHT! *Auf Niederlandisch.* Give the times and all of that stuff. We call them the "Oops Concerts" as a joke on Vinkenoop's name. In Dutch there's all these loopy words with double o's and double a's, the woops and the koops and the doops. Thus the "Oops," since it's by accident we're here.

I get the Melk Weg to come up with handbills and we go around the town squares and to the university and poster and paper and put up cards everywhere.

We pack the place. The Milky Way is so jammed it soon turns into a steam bath. It's so hot even the blocks of hash are perspiring. You can only stand it for an hour or so and then you have to get out — or melt into a puddle on the floor. At which point we let somebody else in. So we have a fast turnover. We do that all night long and come out with about five thousand dollars each night. It pays for our hotel, it pays for our travel, and a bit more than that.

Fucking great shows they are, too! The second night — Weir's thirty-forth birthday — the Dead do an acoustic set of "On the Road Again," "Dire Wolf," "The Monkey and the Engineer," "Bird Song," "Cassidy," "Ain't No Lie," "The Race Is On" and "Ripple." And an electric set of "Playin' in the Band," "Hully Gully," "The Wheel," "Samson and Delilah," "Gloria," "Lovelight" "Goin' Down the Road Feelin' Bad," "Playin' in the Band" slight reprise, "Black Peter," and "Sugar Magnolia." The audiences are about half international students and the other half hippies, dopers, hash smokers, and midnight tokers.

It's a great jaunt, really spur of the moment. This is the last adventure I remember us going on, the last spontaneous thing we ever do. And the Dead used to be great at that. I could call Jerry and say, "We're going up to Columbia University" or "We're going to play on Haight Street" and in a split second Jerry would say, "Okay, what do we gotta do?"

Jerry is getting jittery about going to Paris, but I know the promoters in France have dope. It's heroin, not Persian, and it's a little harsher than we're used to but it'll get us through. One reason Jerry's never liked heroin is that it's a dodgy drug to use when you're performing. You can't control it. You never know at what point you're gonna nod off. With Persian you know pretty much where you're at. It puts you into a transcendental space where you can still function. With heroin, you're just as likely to nod off in the dressing room and never be able to get up and get out onstage. Or in your soup before you even get to the gig. Even if you manage to make it out onstage you're likely to nod off in the middle of a song. Garcia doesn't like the unpredictable quality of it. With white powder you never know what you're getting or what it's going to do to you. It could be the purest China White or smack that had been stepped on a dozen times. This is what happened to Janis. She got some very high quality dope and O.D.'d. Jerry doesn't like *that* aspect of it either.

Drugs not only dominate our lives by now, they dictate what we do, where we go, who we hang with. We hoard and scam and cadge, and hide the good shit from each other. The dope situation — who is holding and how to get it off them — gets to be fierce. On the road I constantly have Mickey and Billy hating me. They always know when I am holding. Otherwise how am I able to function? They can read the signs. How could I possibly get everybody on an airplane and off to Paris after the Milky Way unless I had scored something?

Dope is now our major concern on the road. Jerry is nervous about playing anywhere outside the United States. We no longer tour Canada. The last time we crossed the border (to play Seneca College outside Toronto in '77), Jerry had to submit to the indignity of being finger searched up his asshole with a rubber glove, which naturally soured him on playing in Canada for many years to come!

Jerry is an unpredictable animal. Often anxious about crossing borders carrying dope, just as often utterly reckless. This tour began in Edinburgh with an emissary from Pete Townshend meeting us at the airport with bindles of Persian.

We're no sooner through customs at the Edinburgh airport — which is tiny — than Jerry wants to do some dope. The Dead's advance man, Alan Trist, in his Brit manner is begging Jerry to wait till we get to the hotel. But sweet reasonableness — or basic caution — is having no effect at all on the impetuous and strung-out Garcia.

"Jesus, Jerry, we're like twenty feet from fucking customs, man. They could walk in here any minute!"

"Aw, nothin's gonna happen. Let's see the dope."

We retire to the gents. I lean on the door of the stall while Jerry gets high. It must be pretty good stuff because the beads of sweat are gone from his forehead, all the anxiety in his eyes has vanished. He is *way* gone. I want to be there myself.

We wouldn't even be high right now — we wouldn't even be touring Europe at all — if it hadn't been for Pete Townshend.

Back in January 1981, Pete Townshend called to ask if the Dead would be interested in replacing the Who on an already scheduled English and European tour. The Who were breaking up, at the end of their tether, too much cocaine and booze and bickering. Fights onstage.

Garcia's only reservation about doing it was the drug situation. He was totally strung out and loath to cross borders. Pete Townshend reassured him: "It's not a problem 'ere. We can get you anything your little heart desires. Gimme yer list. I'll put Percy on the case."

We played four nights at the Rainbow Theatre in London and took in the sights — visits to London junkiedom, the royal English strung-out lunch. We hung out with the redoubtable Percy, our source of Persian. Percy taught us new tricks, like how to shoot up Persian. You see, Persian isn't water soluble, which is why we smoke it. But these guys figured out that if you mix it with lemon juice it dissolves. After the second gig, Jerry and I figured we'd give it a try and Townshend joined us. He wasn't currently using, but no matter. . . . That's the thing about smack, almost any excuse will do. Pete was a mess, he'd separated from his family and was up to four pints of brandy a day. He was also a million dollars in debt, and the only way out was an even worse nightmare — another Who tour!

So instead of touring, the Who decided to do a live stereo broadcast from Germany over Westdeutsche Rundfunk. It was syndicated all over Europe; a live Eurovision feed from the Grugahalle in Essen, West Germany, that went to thirty countries, ran five hours and ended with the Dead and Pete Townshend jamming together on the last five numbers: "Not Fade Away," "Wharf Rat," "Around and Around," "Good Lovin'" and "One More Saturday Night."

Following the show we all went out and had a cheap dinner together, after which we returned to the hotel and a mad party going on in the bar. There is a noticeable difference in the type of fans the two groups attract. Grateful Dead groupies are in paisley and patchouli, Who groupies are all German blonde bombshells. It wasn't long before the Who crew began to get rowdy. The usual crew mayhem but with an edge of real menace. They knew that the band was breaking up; they were angry and frustrated and lost.

We were staying in a *faux* American hotel. This is a genuine school of architecture in Germany. It is almost a Holiday Inn, and it's eminently destroyable. The Who crew began demolishing the place piecemeal. It was a professional job. Partitions pulverized, walls collapsed. Toward morning they began manically dancing on top of the cocktail video machines and throwing those huge fucking beer mugs. The mugs would go clear across the room and — *SMASH!* — up against the wall. As the random devastation ground on its grim way, even the rowdy Dead got up and sneaked back to their rooms. Those guys were really fuckin' savages! (And we weren't about to stick around for the damages.)

At four in the morning, awakened by a guy screaming he was going to kill himself if his wife didn't let him in their room, I went downstairs and found a morose Garcia sitting by himself in the lobby. "Where are we?" he asked wearily.

We moseyed on outside. Down by the river we came across Pete Townshend with his face in his hands, a melancholy Mod Hamlet listening to nightingales. He is given to black fits of depression and suicidal thoughts, so we decided to join him — like maybe cheer him up, hah hah. And by and by inspiration came to us, to wit: why not do a little acid, like the old days.

A camaraderie had developed between Garcia and Townshend ever since Monterey. Parallel lives. Pete Townshend had once been called the "perfect rock star" because of his devotion to his fans, a title that might equally have been applied to Jerry. (After eleven fans were trampled to death in a stampede at a Who concert in Cincinnati the previous December and his subsequent salty remarks, Townshend had lost *that* title.)

Townshend and Garcia both seemed utterly exhausted, beset by problems with their bands, their personal lives, and drugs. But worst of all, the high hopes and best intentions of a little more than a decade earlier now seemed to taunt them mercilessly. They'd both believed in rock as a force for change, and the failure of that hope bewildered and confused them.

Garcia and Townshend both had serious, debilitating problems with drugs. They'd both become isolated from their bands, in part because of drugs and in part because each band's equilibrium had been upset by the loss of a key, charismatic member. The Dead lost Pigpen; the Who, Keith Moon. In the wake of Moon's death, Roger Daltrey, the lead singer, developed raging megalomania. Now, only *he* could sing Who songs, leaving Townshend to squeeze in a couple of new songs at the close of the set. So Townshend ranted on. And on.

"Fucking Roger fucking Daltrey and John Entwhistle and his bloody fucking bass. All they wanna do is to bash out the old hits night after night. I'd go out on me own 'cept the band has sucked every fuckin' song outta me!"

But as the dawn came up and the acid came on we sat and looked at the water and the birds and the early spring flowers. For the moment we forget all about our addictions and the host of worries they conceal.

"Fuck me," said Pete, brightening. "It's still out there, innit? Bloody Mother Nature, man!"

22

Chief Smoking Moccasin

I'VE BEEN LIVING up in Sonoma County for the past three years, but I don't spend all that much time there. For one thing, I don't usually feel like drumming all the way back up there after a day in the San Rafael office. Plus I've usually spent half the night getting ripped with Jerry and John Kahn, bass player from the Jerry Garcia Band. Things are so bad even *I'm* a wee bit paranoid about driving.

So I get an apartment in downtown San Rafael. It's a cool pad with a grape arbor in the backyard. Garcia and Kahn soon find out about it and the three of us begin hanging out there to do drugs. A cooler full of booze and dope, and not a soul to know we are there. Jerry loves hiding out.

I'm up to a gram of Persian a day, Garcia a gram and a half. So the Jerry Garcia Band now has another raison d'être: raising major drug money. And we are, unfortunately, cash rich from all those small club dates.

Garcia'd get back from a Dead tour, take two deep breaths, and be playing at the Keystone or at the Stone in San Francisco two nights later. As soon as his gear arrived, bang, he'd be in downtown San Francisco playing as the Jerry Garcia Band. Out to Santa Cruz, hit San Jose, Palo Alto, come back to the city, take another deep breath, and get back out on the road to the East Coast!

In the early eighties, when the Dead aren't on tour the Jerry Garcia Band plays almost every night. I go out with Jerry to most of these gigs, which are all over the Bay Area. When he decides to do an East Coast tour in June of '82, I help put it together. We figure the best way to do it is to get a bus. I am getting weary of hair-raising scenes in airports with Jerry and his little tins.

We're sick and tired of the commercial airlines. The situation is truly horrifying. We need . . . a new plan! Okay, we'll fly across the country and then pick up a tour bus. That way we can go right to the motel; nobody has to know who's checking in. The motel desk clerk never even *sees* the band. I just go get the keys, get back on the bus, and say, Just drive around to this wing; and here's your keys, gentlemen, take whatever you need out of the bus because we're locking it up for the night. Garcia takes *only* his briefcase, he never takes clothes with him. In the morning on our way to sound check I always have to say, Here's your bag.

Copping Persian on the East Coast is impossible. We have to have it sent. I enlist my brother, Dicken, to put it on the plane. Being strung out myself, I tell him, "I'm hiring you to look after me and look after the mail and look after the merchandise, so don't *you* go getting strung out." Then I proceed to go away on tour with the Jerry Garcia Band and when I return I find Dicken wide awake in the middle of the night doing cocaine and — that's right! — smoking Persian.

On one East Coast trip the Jerry Garcia Band has an unexpected windfall. We're staying at one of those big New York City hotels — one of the few that will still take us — and I call downstairs and ask for the accounting. Our bill has supposedly been put on the credit card already and they tell me that they owe *us* money. I know this is impossible — it's the first time it's ever happened to me in twenty years of road managing — but, hey, I'm not gonna argue with them. Anyway, we're frantic, we're late, and we've got to get checked out of this hotel and make it to Philadelphia in time for sound check. They're running around emptying cash registers in the lobby bar, then up to the mezzanine bar. Finally they present me with the twenty-one, twenty-three hundred dollars that they think they've overcharged me (maybe they haven't looked in the rooms yet).

I waltz onto the bus, which has been waiting outside for a half an hour while they resolve this difficulty. When Garcia hears about my *sack* of money, he goes, "Let me SEE it! We're gonna buy some STASH with this!" Needless to say, we almost miss the show in Philly.

Because of the huge money layouts for drugs, I know that I am under the gun at all times (and so does Garcia). We always deal very scrupulously with the take. We want to be fair to everybody and keep it as aboveboard as possible. We are making around $7,500 a night for the Jerry Garcia Band, $5,000 of which we give the band and crew. John Kahn gets $1,500; the other members of the band, say the gospel singers, $150 each; Parish, $500. Plus we have to pay for the schlepper, etc. Back in the car the bottom line is always: "How much do we have left over for *DRUGS?*"

"We've got a fat $2,678."

"Whooaaaa!!!" That lights him up! But inevitably the next question is, "Can we cop tonight?" No rest for the weary, I guess. Then, drug business taken care of, we move on to life as such.

The Keystone, Palo Alto, circa 1981. It's late. We leave way after all the waitresses have gone home. He's a very generous guy, Garcia, and the waitresses always get tipped by us because Garcia fans are notoriously bad tippers. They order water and figure it ought to be free and don't even *leave* a tip.

My head is ringing. Garcia plays his guitar in the Jerry Garcia Band way louder than in the Grateful Dead. We're using the Dead sound system, but we are working clubs that hold 750 people, 1,500 tops, and the open-backed amplifiers just shred your ears.

Whenever we play a long-distance gig, Garcia puts his seat back and *bang!* goes straight to sleep. Then he starts to snore. Operatic snoring complete with bassoons and whistles. Taking Highway 280 from Palo Alto into San Francisco, you go by San Francisco State, down 19th Avenue into Golden Gate Park. After a high-speed chase home, you start hitting stop lights at San Francisco State College. As soon as I stop for the first one, Garcia is wide awake and looking around for a place for me to pull over.

There's two places we usually stop: we either park by a pond one block inside Golden Gate Park or we go to the other side of the Golden Gate Bridge and pull into the view area on the Marin side — there're always tourists stopped there and we can get away with it. Golden Gate Park is a little trickier. The pond is the very spot where Jerry will get busted sitting in his BMW in 1985. They find twenty-three bindles with scrapings in them. He's nodded out with the foil pipe and his tin box. Supposed to be on his way to the hospital for a rehab session, he stopped for a little self-medication on the way.

Now he's awake he starts worrying about the supply.

"I'm gonna be out by the morning, Rock. What to do, what to do."

I've either got to stay up all night or sleep a little bit and then drive to these rug merchant/car dealers/drug dealers (the Persians) in the East Bay. It's a really long drive. I arrange to meet them in a parking lot at a Kmart but I'm so strung out I fall asleep in the car. They tell me later they were banging on the hood but I was out like a light. I wake up and look at my watch. God! It's a quarter to three in the fucking afternoon and nobody's showed up yet! It's hot as a pistol in the car. I call the Persians and they tell me they came but couldn't wake me up. Now I have to drive all the way over to their house in Walnut Creek and pick up the dope and then all the way back to Marin County over the Richmond–San Rafael Bridge.

I'm five hours late. Garcia is pissed. I'm pushing so hard to make time, I blow up my engine. I haven't got to the bridge yet and steam starts pouring out of the air-conditioning vents. I'm going, uh-oh, *smoke,* I'm in trouble, I'm in trouble! Garcia is doubly furious because they're expecting him at a band meeting on Front Street at three o'clock, and he doesn't want to go to the meeting until the stash gets to his house. I'm half an hour away with my car blown up and no way to get back there. I call Jerry and he immediately dispatches someone from the office to come and get me and bring me back to the house so he can get high before the meeting. It's now four thirty and the meeting is already an hour and a half late. The whole band is there plus the entire office. Everybody at Front Street around this big table, waiting for Garcia and me to show up. Meanwhile, Jerry's still up at the house waiting for the stash. Now, some might have gone to the meeting all raggedy and jonesing and got through it somehow or other, but Garcia refuses to budge until he is high. *Refuses.*

Everyone knows perfectly well what's going on at this point, but naturally I'm the one who has to take the fall. Often, admittedly, it is my fault! I try telling myself that doing this shit isn't in my job description, but these days doing this *is* my job. I have by now lost any face I ever had with the band and crew, along with any vestige of self-respect.

June 16, 1982. We're on the bus with the Jerry Garcia Band through the Jewish Alps of the Catskills on our way to an outdoor festival at Music Mountain in South Fallsburg, New York. Big old comfortable touring bus. Hidden safe with the goods in it. I get high, do the books. Jerry's plinking in the back. Somebody is telling Jack Ellis dirty jokes they just got from over the phone at the last stop. Jonestown Kool-Aid jokes, gay cancer jokes. Jack is part of that underground network that gets jokes across the United States in a matter of seconds. Jerry is addicted to these jokes.

We're doing a few East Coast dates with Bobby and the Midnites. Bobby's band closes one night and we close the next night. Garcia likes playing the opening set because he can leave early and get high. At this particular outdoor event in the Catskills, Garcia is happy to let Weir close because that way he can go back to the bus and relax and enjoy himself and smoke and do a few lines.

At the Concord, one of those places where Bill Graham used to work, Garcia gets almost mystical. He takes me into the main dining room and with great reverence says, "Take a good look at this dining room, Rock. Bill Graham actually *waited these tables!* Mickey Hart's grandparents, the Tessels, came here every summer and Bill Graham used to WAIT ON THEM!"

It's the middle of the night. Um, Jerry, can we go now? We check out the showroom, which is where all the famous comics play. It's all banquettes with a half-moon stage and beautiful lighting and velvet curtains and Garcia is swooning. "Oooo, I'd *love* to play in a place like this!" I mean, it *is* nice, it is. Not like our clubs in California with their black walls and cement floors and when the lights come on it's like we've been playing in a dungeon. The Keystone in Palo Alto used to be a supermarket, the Catalyst was a bowling alley. Just big ugly boxes.

◎

Back home in San Rafael, our hideaway has been exposed. Not by wives, band members, or the DEA, but by predatory fans. When Garcia plays at Palo Alto these weird girls, Gretchens and Loreleis, recognize his car and follow us all the way home. After a few weeks of these strange things sitting outside on the doorstep every night, I rent a new place. One advantage of this house is that there are several ways to get up to it.

We move into the *new* "secret" place together. Garcia takes the downstairs apartment and I take the one upstairs. Jerry's apartment is a sort of granny unit with a giant studio area when you walk in. It's an office where Garcia keeps his record collection and has his computer set up. The adjoining room runs the rest of the length of the house back to a countertop kitchen at the far end. Jerry's bed is just inside the wall of this room and mine is upstairs directly above it.

It's a great time, if *dark*. Light rarely enters through the heavy black curtain. The carpet is coal black felt. The place is like an efficiency *tomb*. Quite appropriate, too, because, although we aren't at first aware of it, we have entered the twilight world of the living dead — forget ship of the sun metaphors at this point — this *is* the afterlife, except that we are living it in suburban San Rafael.

Part of Jerry's withdrawal from the world has to do with his desire to separate himself from his image. Fame, fortune, drugs, and time have ripped holes in all the great ones of the sixties, but not Jerry. To his fans he continues to be the same amiable, cool, bumbling Furry Freak Brother he started out as. So flawlessly funky and rumpled. A (barely) animated R. Crumb cartoon: the scruffy, dope-smoking Buddha.

Lesh and Weir have always been envious of Garcia's Mr. Natural image, but Jerry's come to hate it. It's too much to live up to. Jerry can be just as cranky, crabby, and bloody-minded as anybody else and just as often. But Garcia's become almost a living trademark for the Grateful Dead. There's Cherry Garcia ice cream and Grateful Puffs snacks (complete with caricature of Garcia). With his beatnik disdain for self-promotion, this is an uncomfortable place to be.

But if *he* no longer wants to be "Jerry Garcia," there are plenty of people out there who do. There are more Grateful Dead imitators than you could ever imagine. There are professional Jerry Garcia impersonators buying cars and stereos and alligator boots. I get calls.

"Sorry to bother you, but we sold Mr. Garcia a Jaguar yesterday and he was meant to come back with it this morning to have it customized and . . ."

I run downstairs and ask Jerry if by any chance he'd gone over to Sausalito yesterday to pick up a Jaguar.

"Can't you see I'm reading? And what in the world are you talking about? Say, you're not holding out on me are you?"

There are new, alarming signs that things are beginning to go wrong. Jerry never takes a shower or changes his clothes, and becomes belligerent if anyone even mentions it to him.

"You don't like the way I smell? Spray *yourself* with cologne." It's someone's job to buy him T-shirts, get him clean clothes. At least I'm not doing *laundry* for him (yet). Nobody in the band will ride with him. He stinks to high heaven, he's filthy and crusty. His hair's all greasy and Rastafarian looking. Horrible! Plus, he now has great smudges of soot all over his face and hands. Smoking Persian, the bottom of the tinfoil gets all charcoaly from the Bic lighter and Garcia's so oblivious and stoned he'll rub his forehead and show up at the airport with all these big black smears all over his face like a chimney sweep. Horrifying! I'm walking around with baby wipes so he can clear the soot off once in a while.

The band are staring at him aghast because at this point they're all fashion plates. Weir smells like a lilac and has his Comme des Garçons sportcoat slung over one shoulder. Phil is immaculate. Kreutzmann looks like the cover of the L. L. Bean catalogue, the Northwoods guy with a plaid buffalo jacket and nouveau chaps. And here's Garcia as grungy as a bag lady with huge finger swipes of charcoal down his face and stuff caked around his mouth and burn spots in his beard. Ugh! But do they say anything? Does *anybody* say anything?

They know better. They know that Garcia doesn't give a fuck what he looks like and he especially doesn't care what *they* think about it. They know that even the mildest rebuke will elicit a snarly "Hey . . . you . . . get offa my cloud!" The band starts renting their own airplane for long-distance gigs.

In the early days Jerry and I had hilarious times, but eventually drugs kill any socializing. Conversation itself has basically disappeared. All we ever talk about these days is what's on television. Garcia'll call me in the middle of the night and say, "Put it on Channel 36!" He loves science fiction, horror, old classic movies. "It's BELA LUGOSI!"

Below me daily I hear Garcia plinking away, noodling on his guitar, and then all of a sudden, Ow-oooo-oooo-oooo! Thump-thump-thump! Garcia hopping around howling from a cigarette burn on his foot. It sounds like a fucking *tribe* of Indians down there.

I place smoke alarms on every wall. Right above his head, one on the side wall, one around the corner. They're going off constantly. Forever! Every time, he burns his fucking slippers. And he insists on wearing those sheepskin moccasins. They stink to high heaven. When he drops a cigarette he kicks them off because it's fallen into his slipper and burned his foot. But the slipper keeps smoldering, the cigarette burning the rancid, stinking sheepskin. Chief Smoking Moccasin goes through several pairs a month.

Everything burns. The carpet, the bedspread, the chairs. It becomes such a fire hazard down there that I start buying him fireproof everything. Fireproof bedspread, fireproof carpet. But under the incessant cigarette bombing even such a miracle as the inflammable rug begins to buckle. After countless burning cigarettes and joints, it looks like an undulating topographical map warped into little hills and gulleys. A boiling mass writhing from the relentless assault of various incendiary objects.

By 1983, Jerry's life is reduced to chord books, junk, junk food, Häagen Dazs, and cigarettes. Cocooning, he hides from the band. At the gigs he locks himself in his dressing room. Afterward, we crawl back in our caves. We are like creatures sinking deeper into a tar pit that we have no desire to crawl out of.

Drugs isolate you; you go off and do them by yourself. I wake up and find Garcia fumbling through my sock drawer looking for my stash! He finds it, too, the motherfucker! Of course, I do the same thing to him when he's holding. It's the beginning of the end.

The Persian obliterates everything from our lives. It eliminates girlfriends, eliminates even the *need* for them. After Mountain Girl left in 1975, Jerry had a few flings. With a New York copywriter, with various models, with Amy Moore, the mistress of Texas oil millionaire Roy Cullen, and for a while he went with Debbie Koons (his present wife). But there were long periods when he didn't have a steady girlfriend. For the most part, Jerry's relationships heat up during periods when he is trying, not too successfully, to wean himself from drugs (usually when he has run out). Once back into the drugs, he can't keep a girlfriend. He has no interest, and they can't handle the stench.

Now seriously strung out, we focus all our energy on scoring. An overwhelming inertia crushes every plan beyond the day. Jerry's increasing isolation is in direct proportion to his veneration and his role as leader, which he cannot abdicate. And because Jerry has no interest whatsoever in talking to the band, I become the go-between. Eventually people begin to think I am not allowing Jerry to speak to them. Kreutzmann is hitting on me to go see Jerry for him, Phil is asking me to talk to Jerry about this and that and could you arrange a meeting?

Jerry isn't even showing up at the office. Previously, Jerry had always been involved; he *lived* at the office for long periods. Now he won't leave the house for love nor money. Certainly not for photo sessions and band meetings. If the band wants to talk to him, they have to come to the house. Meetings are held in my living room. Even then there's no guarantee Garcia is going to appear. Often he'll just plain refuse to come upstairs. They twist my arm to go down and get him. He puts up a huge fight and then after agreeing, wants to get high (higher) before coming up. Meanwhile, the band members are upstairs twiddling their thumbs, knowing exactly what's going on.

Jerry's isolation threatens the end of the band, but the Grateful Dead is by now a multimillion-dollar corporation. A huge amount is at stake, although no longer the soul of the band. The Dead have become just what Jerry always dreaded — an endless party rolling down the road, but essentially an oldies band. Part of Jerry's descent into drugs comes from his horror at all this. The Dead are no longer innovating. They are basically just rehashing, and keeping the great corporate behemoth well fed. Jerry keeps suggesting the group disband for a year and try to reinvent itself rather than just grinding on like the other cash cows of rock — the Beach Boys, the Stones, the Who. But the band doesn't want to hear about it.

In desperation Kreutzmann delivers an ultimatum to Garcia from the band. "Either you gotta quit this Persian shit or you're fired."

Garcia laughs: "Promises, promises! Okay, after careful consideration, I'm afraid I have to go with the Persian."

"That's it, Jerry? That's all you've got to say to us?"

"Anyway, who you gonna hire? It's a lot easier to find a drummer than it is a lead guitar player."

Kreutzmann slinks out. He knows that without Jerry there is no Grateful Dead. Jerry *is* the Dead. His guitar, his personality. To most of the world, Jerry Garcia is an icon.

By the end of summer of '84, Garcia's condition is worsening daily. He never sleeps or lies down. He sits in a chair with the guitar cradled in his arm and plays night and day, frequently nodding off. He lives on a diet of ice cream, M&Ms, Persian, and cigarettes. Constantly dropping cigarettes, falling asleep upright smoking. Setting fire to carpet, bed, shoes.

He feels guilty. His self-loathing has reached hellish intensity and I'm walking on eggshells pretending to be completely oblivious to what's going on. I know I'm fucking up too, but I'm too far gone to stop. I just want to keep doing what I'm doing.

Part of the problem is Jerry's uncanny ability to convince himself that our addiction is a temporary state of affairs. We're just going through a phase — ha! This particular phase has been going on for almost ten years, pretty much nonstop. His sense of shame effectively precludes any discussion of the subject. I'm fully aware that one of the reasons Jerry and I remain tight is because I never bring the subject up. Jerry counts on this. But it's a double bind because as long as I turn a blind eye I only worsen the situation. With both of us using, it's become a mutual denial society from which there's no way out. (Unless both of us want to quit at the same time, but since we never discuss the subject, how would we ever know!)

The gloom that pervades our sepulchral existence is in stark contrast to our radiant beginnings. Everything seemed possible, the world might just change in the twinkling of an eye. Now it seems that instead of the incandescent future we envisaged we are — in the second term of Ronald Reagan — actually moving *backwards* in time. Any action on our part seems futile, the visions of the past mere pipe dreams. We fell out of paradise long ago. The Persian is just a convenient way of numbing ourselves to that fact.

This could be, I realize, just another junkie's rationalization for his worthless state. But at this point it's hard to tell, and too late to matter. We've gotten very good at finding excuses for our sorry asses. The mystic pursuit of the ourobouros has boiled down to chasing the dragon's tail.

Garcia's feet have become too swollen for him to walk. He can't tie his shoes, can't even get into his size 13 hightops (he normally wears a size 11). I am panicked. What if Jerry gets deathly ill on the road? Dr. Weisberg isn't going to be able to fly out and deal with it in time. Jerry is horribly bloated, he's got chronic swelling in the ankles, and he has absolutely no desire to look after himself. He's not eating right, he's pounding down piles of Häagen Dazs ice cream. I know it's only a matter of time before he gets seriously ill and collapses. I call Dr. Weisberg.

Dr. Weisberg is alarmed. Garcia's body is dangerously toxic. His cholesterol level is 900! He has critically high blood pressure and his kidney is close to failing. Jerry intensely resents my intrusion, even though Dr. Weisberg's prognosis is that Jerry is near death. He stares daggers at me. I know it's over. If we stick together we'll both be dead within a year.

Weisberg recommends that Jerry check himself into the hospital, but he doesn't. A year later, in January of 1985, he is busted for freebasing cocaine in Golden State Park. In his briefcase: twenty-three bindles containing traces of heroin and coke. In July of the following year he lapses into a diabetic coma for three days and almost dies.

So Kreutzmann takes me down to a rehab in L.A. I check into the Westwood Clinic, which is filled with quasi-celebrities withdrawing from one thing or another. I'm supposed to take six months off. After that, according to Jerry, I can come back. I'm only in detox for twenty-eight days, then I go home and get stoned. Just one more time, I tell myself, and strangely enough it turns out to be the truth. I never touch the stuff again.

I can feel a lot of resentment toward me after I get out of detox. I know there are many who want me out of the Grateful Dead family by hook or by crook. It's clear they want to protect Jerry, and see me as endangering him. Meanwhile, Jerry is out of the hospital but still using.

Steve Parish thinks I'm a bad influence (true) and calls me up on charges of thieving from Garcia and the band (false). He has only one specific allegation: that I stole money from the hotel that time in New York City when we were supposedly overcharged and they returned money to us.

I am hauled in front of the Court of Higher Nonsense, which is a full-on Grateful Dead meeting with all the secretaries and everything else and Parish accuses me of stealing from Garcia — the hotel money and all kinds of other money. I have no idea what he's talking about. Under other circumstances I might even find a farce like this amusing, but I quickly realize this is not the right tack to take. I try to summon up a serious (yet innocent) face.

"I've never taken *anything* from anyone," I mumble. I figure this is not the time to mention Jerry's and my raiding each other's stashes. "I dare you to come up with any evidence that I thieved from Garcia or the Grateful Dead," I say in a stupidly highhanded manner.

As I'm leaving the meeting, Kreutzmann gives me a "Good riddance, Scully!" which I take with a large grain of salt. I know he's on cocaine and boozed up nasty as a motherfucker.

I go off to Lake Tahoe and come back a month later, just in time for the next official Dead meeting. They haven't found anything and I —

not too brightly — demand an apology, in writing no less. I quickly realize that the only thing I might get in writing today are my walking papers.

Hunter comes to my defense. A wonderful, crazily impassioned speech. You know, sort of: "This man has devoted twenty years of his life, blah blah. How can you discard someone like this, blah blah?" What he's so shocked about I don't know. Just business as usual, baby.

They offer me six months with pay to get myself straightened out. Then I can get my old job back again. But six months come and go, and somehow I see no reason to return. The thrill is gone.

⊚

September 24, 1985. 2:15 A.M. I-5 Exit 19 (Lost Hills). I've driven all the way from San Francisco to L.A. and almost all the way back again. Twenty-two hours on the road. The muffler fell off somewhere back there and for the last 150 miles inexplicable wobbles and rattles, weird inner skull music from the unearthly didgeridoo hum of the three pairs of skis on the rack.

A fine drizzle of gravitational waves. What the hell is that? A small suitcase with yellow eyes hurtling toward the car. A-a-a-ayiiiii! . . . a Fire Troll! Fuck, I almost hit him. What's he doing out there? Poor misguided soul, no one's going to pick him up out here. Then a sickening thud. God, I really *did* hit something. I get out of the car. Oh no! It's a coyote. Now I really am doomed.

I've hit a coyote, dropped my muffler, had a fight with my girlfriend, lost my job with the Grateful Dead. . . .

Three A.M. I'm not more than twenty miles from home and I am *lost.* Jesus, I've only lived here for twelve years, where the hell am I?

God, and there's some poor bastard out in the middle of the road waving his arms. Shit, it's Jerry! What the hell is he doing all the way out here in the middle of the night? His car musta broke down. God, am I glad to see him!

I left under such strange circumstances — didn't even get to say goodbye properly — this is a perfect opportunity to say a few things that I didn't have a chance to say.

I'm not going to hit him with all my grievances — at least not right away. I'll break into it gently. Maybe a joke or two to start out.

"Hey, man, what's got twelve fuckin' arms and, you know, plays guitar or something, and died? Give up? Squid Vicious! Yeah, well. Look, I don't know how to say this but. . ."

"Hey, if it's about the Dead disco album, again, man. . . ."

"Look, it's not that I'm bitter about getting kicked out. . ."

"You're not with the band anymore? Since when?"

"Oh, c'mon, Jerry! Don't you remember the Court of Higher Nonsense and all that?"

"Well, man, see now, I thought when you called the doctor you *wanted* to get thrown out. I mean, why *else* would you call a doctor?"

Fuck, nobody there! The seat next to me is empty. Don't tell me I dreamt the whole thing. Well, it wouldn't be the first time. At least I got some stuff off my chest, y'know? Oh well, maybe these imaginary conversations all feed into the Akashíc Record somewhere out there in the cosmic ozone and — eventually — seep into the sleeping brain of the Great Barcia.

I'm somewhere over in the Chinatown hills, though how I got here I don't know. Must have blacked out back there somewhere. Hell, maybe I shouldn't have stopped at that redneck bar for a nightcap, but after that "Ghost Rider of Polonio Pass" business with Jerry I had a serious case of the shakes. I had to have something to steady my nerves.

Four A.M. I'm toasted to the max. Further action would be futile. This must be the place I'm meant to stop. I'll park here and catch a few winks and then I'll be in better shape to drive home.

I awake to the hustle and bustle of morning traffic. Infernal heavy metal orchestra tuning up. The slightest rustle of sound is picked up by a satanic goblin inside my head who takes a stack of pots and pans and throws them down an endless airshaft. And then I hear a ringing like the sound of Doomsday itself. The Great Bell of Beelzebub clanging for all the wrung-out souls in creation.

Ba-kriiiing!! Ta-drung!! Ba-daaang!! Ka-driiing!! Ta-klaaang!! The fiend! He's beating on his cable car bell, throwing himself into a Sun Ra hammer and kettle solo. I come awake with a start, roll down my window and look back. About ten feet away is a cable car, and I am sitting right in the middle of the track.

I take the emergency brake off and roll miraculously down the hill into the gas station on the corner. Well, at least I have *one* angel left.

My brains are scorched and my life a total disaster, plus my battery is dead. I am a miserable sinner, O Lord, I have squandered my days in riotous living, but I have learned my lesson. My life from now on will be one of abstinence and prayer. Right there on the corner of Jackson and Hyde I make a resolution to myself that the next ten years are going to be different. But I forget to say how.

Afterword: Adios, Black Jack

SHORTLY AFTER WE began writing this book in 1992, I ran into Jerry in San Rafael. When I told him I was working on a book about my life with the Dead he paused for a moment, made a quizzical face, and shrugged: "Hell, just tell the truth, man — and don't be too hard on me."

I'm sorry Jerry never got to read the book (it had just been finished at the time he died) because I thought of it as a long affectionate letter to him in the same way Robert Hunter's lyrics were often personal messages to Garcia, saying in all those poignant songs the things he could never say to his face.

⊚

The day Jerry died, Deadheads danced in Haight-Ashbury, Wall Street closed early, and people wept openly in the street. Newscasters, comparing his death to that of Lennon and Elvis, said his passing marked the end of an era for which he had become the last great symbol. Jerry would have been bewildered at being made a symbol for anything.

It was his fierce belief in the group spirit, the group mind even, that imbued the Dead with their aura of collective ecstasy. It was typical of Jerry's generosity of spirit to make it seem as if the whole band possessed qualities that were really his alone. But in the end he identified so absolutely with the Grateful Dead he ended up trapped inside it.

However much he would have protested, Jerry was the heart and soul and magic of the Grateful Dead and in the end that was too much of a burden for him to bear. It was already getting too much for him at the time I left the band in 1985. Ten years later, it killed him.

Jerry *was* the Grateful Dead not because he was the band's unofficial leader or its icon, but because of his noble spirit and stupefying resilience. However low we had sunk the night before, he would always come at the new day with an entirely unwarranted optimism.

Jerry had a nature so endlessly curious he could, at a moment's notice, take off down any new road, just to see what happened. His innate graciousness extended to practically anyone. So open and vulnerable was he that those who thought they were acting in his best interests began shielding him from new people and new experiences. It was a final irony that his boundless enthusiasms resulted in his being isolated from almost everyone. He hated the fame that had made him into a sacred monster.

When I stopped using heroin ten years ago I assumed it was only a matter of time before Jerry quit, and when I saw those mysterious pictures of him scuba diving surrounded by tropical fish I thought, He's in his own element at last. He had solved Kesey's riddle by finding a way to inhabit his own hallucinations without drugs. This was the new Jerry and all was well at last. But it was not to be. Jerry, it's true, did try a number of times to kick his habit. He died trying.

I think for Jerry drugs were a way of reconciling his contradictions. He was a nest of paradoxes: outgoing recluse, gullible hipster, ironic Utopian, self-effacing star. His attempt to hold any number of irreconcilable ideas in his head at once was reflected in the way he played guitar. His lightning fingering and chronic piling up of notes was an attempt to include everything. The flash of the spirit that unites was all that mattered to him, the moment-to-moment flow between the band and the audience, energy shifting through different forms in the twinkling of an eye.

He was an oddity in the narcissistic world of rock 'n' roll: a true beatnik who cared nothing for his image, a bashful lead singer, an introvert with such debilitating stage fright he was unable to eat anything before going on stage.

☺

Considering the dancing Day of the Dead skeletons and skulls that inevitably pursued the Grateful Dead, it's odd that Jerry was so superstitious about death. He would never say the word or allow himself to be photographed in front of a tombstone, and was always pained when promoters came up with graveyard scenes to advertise the band.

When Pigpen died, Jerry and I went to his funeral together. Lying in an open casket in his blue-jean jacket covered with his pins and buttons, Pig looked a lot better than he had in some time. But Jerry was appalled. "Don't ever let that happen to me," he said as we walked away from the coffin. "There are just two things I want you to promise me: Don't ever find me in the back of a record store signing records and don't bury me in an open casket."

✿

Whatever paradise he's transported to I hope it includes sunfish and coral reefs, and that in that liquid alchemy all the paradoxical elements in his nature transform themselves into something rich and strange. And, Jerry, if you're listening, I'll meet you at the Jubilee. I wish you'd held those cards, man — you had us all beat.

Index